Financial Time

We work with l<!-- -->

the strongest id<!-- -->

bringing cutting-edge thinking and best
practice to a global market.

We craft high quality books which help
readers to understand and apply their
content, whether studying or at work.

To find out more about Financial Times
Pitman Publishing books, visit our website:

www.ftmanagement.com

"The structure is very clever and allows the reader to dip into the areas of greatest interest ... the flowcharts act as an excellent route map, not only to tell people where they are and where they should go, but why they should go ... it really is quite a challenge to combine the scope of this magnum opus with its depth of technical treatment."

Lawrence Churchill, Managing Director, Life & Investment Services, NatWest Bank

"It is indeed very rare to find a book which can act as a standard work for the new entrant to our business, the experienced practitioner and also the consumer. Jack Oliver's book is not only that rarity. It is an exceptional book. Why? In taking seven stages in our lives, with which all the readers will identify, the recommendations for financial planning at each stage are, like the book itself, irresistible."

Leonard J. Warwick, CBE ALIA(dip), MIFP, Chairman, Personal Investment Authority Training Advisory Group; former Chairman, Securities and Investments Board Training and Competence Panel; Director of the Securities and Investments Board (SIB), 1989–96

"There is something for everyone in this book. Jack Oliver provides detailed and comprehensive advice and information to cover virtually every financial contingency – all of which is presented in a clear and accessible way."

Dr. Andrew Sentance, Chief Economist, British Airways; former member of the Treasury Panel of Independent Forecasters, the 'seven wise men'

"This is a superb book which deals with life from the cradle to the grave. Excellent case-studies and complex matters dealt with in a simple and readable way. I recommend all people involved in the sale of financial products to keep a copy of this publication very handy as a great reference help."

Frank Weisinger, FLIA, MLIA(dip), President of the Life Insurance Association, 1996–7

"It's a pity this excellent book was not available to me forty years ago, but I'm glad to say it's not too late for me to benefit from the last two chapters – on retirement and old age!"

Professor Patrick Dowling, FEng FRS, Vice-Chancellor and Chief Executive, University of Surrey

"A clear concise guide to a lifetime of financial planning, providing a perfect reference. A must for those who wish to conduct their own affairs. Highly recommended."

Colin M. Hart, MLIA(dip), National Chairman of Training and Competence, Life Insurance Association

THE
LIFETIME
FINANCIAL PLAN

The Seven Ages of Financial Health

DR JACK OLIVER

FINANCIAL TIMES
PITMAN PUBLISHING

FINANCIAL TIMES
MANAGEMENT

LONDON · SAN FRANCISCO
KUALA LUMPUR · JOHANNESBURG

*Financial Times Management delivers the knowledge,
skills and understanding that enable students,
managers and organisations to achieve their ambitions,
whatever their needs, wherever they are.*

London Office:
128 Long Acre, London WC2E 9AN
Tel: +44 (0)171 447 2000
Fax: +44(0)171 240 5771
Website: www.ftmanagement.con

A Division of Financial Times Professional Limited

First published in Great Britain in 1998

ISBN 0 273 63052 0

British Library Cataloguing in Publication Data
A CIP catalogue record for this book can be obtained from the British Library

10 9 8 7 6 5 4 3 2 1

Typeset by M Rules
Printed and bound in Great Britain by Redwood Books, Trowbridge, Wiltshire

The Publishers' policy is to use paper manufactured from sustainable forests.

This book represents Jack W. Oliver's understanding and interpretation
of the law, legislation and practice, Inland Revenue practice and general
information pertaining to all the subjects treated in the book as at 28
November 1997.

Every effort has been made to ensure the accuracy of this understanding
and interpretation but it will be appreciated that Jack W. Oliver cannot
accept responsibility for it.

In all tables the figures are typical. It will always be possible to find
higher and lower premiums on the market.

Photo: Mark Mallet

ABOUT THE AUTHOR

Dr. Jack W. Oliver
BSc., PhD., C.Math., FIMA, MLIA(dip), FPC,
Financial Planning Consultant.

Becoming a financial planning consultant after a university career lecturing in mathematics and the psychology of learning mathematics, Jack Oliver brought his own special expertise to his new profession. He combines an extensive technical knowledge with the ability to impart that knowledge to others.

Jack is consulted by professional colleagues who respect both his detailed analyses and his ease in keeping abreast of new developments. They are aware also of the thoroughness with which he addresses the needs of his clients.

This reflects Jack's personal approach. Proud of the financial planning help he gives, his clients range from the very young to those in retirement; from barristers and senior executives to nurses and teachers.

With this book, he is passing on his knowledge to you.

TO KIT, JOSE, KATE AND DEE
WITH MUCH LOVE

CONTENTS

6 THE AGE OF RETIREMENT   *391*

7 THE AGE OF OLD AGE   *431*

8 LIFETIME FINANCIAL PLANS IN ACTION   *449*

Appendix: Recent legislation affecting financial planning   *465*

Index   *473*

LIST OF FIGURES

LIST OF TABLES

ACKNOWLEDGEMENTS

Many people have been involved in the production of this book and my very sincere gratitude is due them.

Some have provided valuable information:

> Nigel Campbell, BA(Oxon), MSc(Oxon), MSc
> Simon Foster, MA, FIA
> Andy Heneghan
> Nick Wardrop
> Howard Maguire, BSc(Econ), MSIDip
> David Lloyd, FCA
> Philip Deardon, BA(Hons), ACA, ATII
> David Oakes
> Alan Tatershall
> Jeremy Fisher, BA(Hons)
> James Stewart.

Nigel Carter and Simon Lewer have been outstandingly helpful and I would like to thank them very much.

Some have made valuable comments on early drafts, including Barry McClean and Irvinder Bakshi, LLB(Hons), DipICArb, ACIArb, Barrister (NP). Here, my very especial thanks are due to Tony Stevens for the outstandingly high level and detail of his comments.

Phil Harris and especially David Sims, BA(Hons), helped me in the early days with their advice. My thanks to them.

The local branch of the Inland Revenue and the Pension Schemes Office have also been very helpful.

Richard Stagg, my publisher, has helped very much in the shaping and presentation of the book, for which I am grateful.

My especial thanks are due my secretary Kay Watts who typed draft after draft assiduously, always with good humour and who gave me many valuable comments and suggestions.

My thanks to my son, Joseph, and daughter, Kate, for their unfailing support, interest and suggestions.

To Dee who taught me a lot.

Lastly, my greatest and sincere gratitude to my wife, Kit, who supported me at all times, giving encouragement through the difficult times but, most importantly, sharing the good times with unstinted and genuine joy.

INTRODUCTION

All the world's a stage, and all the men and women
merely players: they have their exits and their entrances;
and one man in his time plays many parts,
his acts being seven ages.

(SHAKESPEARE, As You Like It, Act II, Scene VII)

William Shakespeare was, of course, right. In the seven ages of our lives we will all have our exits and entrances, and in our time play many parts. The only certainty is that the seven ages will span an uncertain future, bringing parts and pitfalls we don't yet know. When it comes to our futures, it isn't easy to predict what is going to happen in the years ahead.

Today, enjoying seven financially healthy and successful ages depends more than ever on planning for the future. With each new age comes new challenges and opportunities. For many it's simply a matter of wishful thinking – but financial prosperity is not that simple. It takes thought and planning, with a clear understanding of current needs and specific requirements.

How can you make financial plans to best suit your current situation? Which plans and investments will also meet your needs in the ages of your life to come? How can you evaluate your own requirements before consulting an adviser or selecting an investment?

As a financial planning consultant with 'all ages' of experience in helping clients to plan for a financially healthy future, I have written *The Lifetime Financial Plan* to help you answer these, and many other questions; to help you build a secure future with many rewarding ages of your own. Shakespeare's concept of the seven ages is as useful now as it was then, and so that is where we will begin. Our journey will guide us through the essential ages of birth and education, work, marriage, parenthood, career development, retirement and old age, pausing at each to assess needs and adjust plans. Our destination is a secure future with *The Lifetime Financial Plan*.

One chapter of the book is devoted to each age. The same pattern appears in each chapter. First, a general discussion of the age, the contingencies which may arise and the financial structures which need to be put in place in that age to give security in the future so that you know you and your dependants will be able to enjoy the financial life for which you wish. The second part of each chapter will give all the technical information needed to activate the plan. At the beginning of each chapter it will be clear what is included and at the end there is a summary. Flowcharts and exercises will make this a book to work with, pen in hand, rather than a book merely to read. The age relevant to each reader will be obvious and turning to the appropriate chapter the contents and flowcharts should immediately identify the particular topics most important to work through. However, if little or no financial planning has been done in the past, it may be wise to work through earlier ages to make sure of financial health in the age relevant now.

Life continues to be more and more demanding with the pace of change accelerating. So much so that many of my clients tell me they have little time to read and study anything which is not related to their work; they can only scan. This book is designed to cater for this problem and allow the reader quickly to identify the section of the book he or she needs with no real need to go further until the next age is reached. It is, of course, extremely important to review financial health at least every year even if there has been no movement to a new age.

The last chapter brings an additional or alternative way of using the book. It traces the total financial lives of several people in story form and follows them as, with the help of a professional financial planning consultant, they make their financial plans and modify them as they pass through the seven ages of financial health. The reader can get an overview of several lifetime financial plans in this final chapter, thus tasting the rich flavour of the process. Not only will he or she be able easily to place his or her own situation in the relevant age but also in the context of a lifetime plan.

Recent research has shown that to be in control of one's life reduces stress. To be in control of one's financial life is a crucial part of overall control. Of course you cannot control contingencies, the situations and events that life throws at you. In life we never know what is around the corner. However, a good financial plan will cater for the financial problems which *may* lie in the future and sleep will be easy in the knowledge that all possible potential disasters are catered for. To treat one's financial life haphazardly can lead to awful tragedies and misery. To go through life financially unplanned, meeting each financial upheaval only when it occurs, is to live a life of inestimable strain. It is often truly said that 'to fail to plan is to plan to fail'.

To make your own lifetime financial plan is a creative act which brings security, satisfaction and even a sense of your own value. Self-confidence increases because you are in control, as far as is possible, of your own destiny. One of the great joys of life is to know that you are financially dependent on no-one. If you work through my book with me, following the guidelines and acting upon them, you will have the best lifetime financial plan possible and the satisfaction of knowing you are in control of your financial life.

There was a time, when the welfare state conceived by William Beveridge was at its zenith, when the dream of the new Jerusalem appeared to be working and everyone had the inalienable right to free schooling, healthcare, social security, pensions and long-term care; when one might have said with some confidence, 'Ah, but the state will look after me, I have no need to take that responsibility on myself'. A lot has happened since the 1940s: social security expenditure has increased in absolute terms from £597 million in 1949/50 to the present total of £99.314 billion. Even adjusting these figures for the effect of inflation over those years and basing figures on 1995/96 prices, the result is £11.1 billion in 1949/50 to £90.7 billion in 1997/98.[1] Increasing unemployment has put a burden on the coffers of the state. The following figures illustrate this. In the 1980s unemployment was as high as 10 per cent, but although unemployment as a percentage of the labour force has decreased since then it is not likely to go below 5 per cent a year for the foreseeable future.[2]

Date	Unemployment (% of labour force)
October 1951	0.9
October 1965	1.4
June 1970	2.6
February 1974	1.9
May 1979	4.1
May 1997	6.1

Perhaps the biggest change, producing the heaviest financial burden, is the demographic timebomb of an ageing population, an ageing population which will need adequate income and long-term care for the duration of a much longer lifetime expectancy.

> When the welfare state began there were five working people contributing to support one pensioner. By the year 2030 for every five working people there will be three pensioners. The only way to ensure decent pensions without burdening future taxpayers is through saving and investing to pay for pensions.[3]

It is clear that taxes levied on a working population will increasingly be unable to support larger and larger numbers of pensioners. The real value of the basic state pension has already been severely eroded and because it is pegged to the Retail Prices Index (RPI) this trend will continue. In 1978/79 the basic state pension represented 21 per cent of the national average income. In 1995/96 this figure was just over 15 per cent. If real earnings grow by only a modest 1½ per cent per annum this pension will in the year 2030 represent only 9 per cent of those earnings.[4]

It is very clear that we will all have to be increasingly responsible for our own financial life, but what a satisfying challenge. Naisbitt says Asians 'do not have and will not have a social security system, or any of the other manifestations of the welfare state. . . . For Asians, the very idea of a central government being involved in family life is culturally unthinkable'.[5]

I have written this book because of the large number of people over the years who, at a first meeting, have clearly shown how confused they have been about financial planning. They did not understand the illustrations or explanations they had been given. They did not even understand the policies they had or the mortgages they were paying for. They often thought, for example, that a term life assurance designed to protect their dependants would pay out something to them at maturity. In the corporate sector the confusion was worse, where keyman arrangements were often mistaken for share protection and it was thought the only sort of pension from which the company could borrow was a small self-administered scheme. They had often gone from one adviser to another until eventually they had settled for the one they felt they could trust most, hoping they would end up with the policies most suited to their situation, but still not understanding.

Financial planning has its complexities but it is well within the grasp of the ordinary layman. My objective is that this workbook will make it easier to grasp, while making the grasp firmer. It is not meant to make those who read it into professional financial planning consultants, and I would suggest it will still be necessary to consult one. What it will do is to make it possible for the reader to create the first or second draft of his own lifetime financial plan. Thereafter a professional financial planning consultant will be able to help fill in the detail and bring the financial products into existence. You will be able to talk intelligently in the same language. No longer will you be confused. In addition, because you are talking the same language, it will be possible for you to choose a good consultant. You will be able to ask penetrating questions and if you do not get satisfactory answers then you can move on until you find the right professional.

> The practice of financial planning is the art of compromise, deciding what can be afforded in the present to pay for future eventualities which may be possible, probable or certain.

The book is also written for the professional: the financial planning consultant, the accountant, the solicitor, the banker and the university lecturer running courses such as the MBA. It should serve as an excellent reference book. Most professionals will be able to find something in it they were not quite sure about. It should serve as a template for financial planning analyses. In fact, for the professional, giving this book to his prospective clients and, after the relevant sections have been worked through, discussing in detail and in depth, can only enhance the final production of a satisfactory lifetime financial plan.

Through the course of the writing of this book I have employed the servo-mechanism of two reading panels: one professional, people whose profession is financial planning, and one lay whose members have encompassed lawyers, accountants, middle and top management in international companies and the owners and chief executives of their own close companies. They have read each chapter as it was written and offered comments, many of which have been extremely valuable, keeping me even more closely in contact with my intended readership.

You will find when you create your lifetime financial plan that it will necessarily be a compromise. The financial needs of the present will always be in conflict with those of the future. You may not always feel you can afford the perfect solution to a future potential problem. But, after all, is this not true of all life and human endeavour? The practice of financial planning is the art of compromise, deciding what can be afforded in the present to pay for future eventualities which may be possible, probable or certain.

I wish you luck with your financial plan. I am sure that if you work with my book you will produce the best lifetime financial plan possible and once you have done that you will know that your financial life is secure.

The environment in which financial planning takes place is always changing and often very quickly. Those changes which have occurred since the writing of *The Lifetime Financial Plan* began will be found in the appendix.

References

1 DSS (1993) *The Growth of Social Security*, HMSO. Social Security Department Report 1997/98 to 1999/2000.
Inflation and real spending figures correlated from two HM Treasury publications.
Public expenditure statistical analyses 1997/98, Her Majesty's Treasury, March 1997.
Financial Statement and Budget Report, Her Majesty's Treasury, July 1997.

2 The Centre for Economic Forecasting, London Business School, May 1997.

3 Peter Lilley, Department of Social Security, 5 March 1997.

4 *The Role of the Private and Public Sectors in the UK Pension System*, Budd and Campbell, Her Majesty's Treasury, 1997.

5 John Naisbitt (1996) *Megatrends Asia*, Nicholas Brealey Publishing Ltd.

THE LIFETIME FINANCIAL PLAN AT A GLANCE

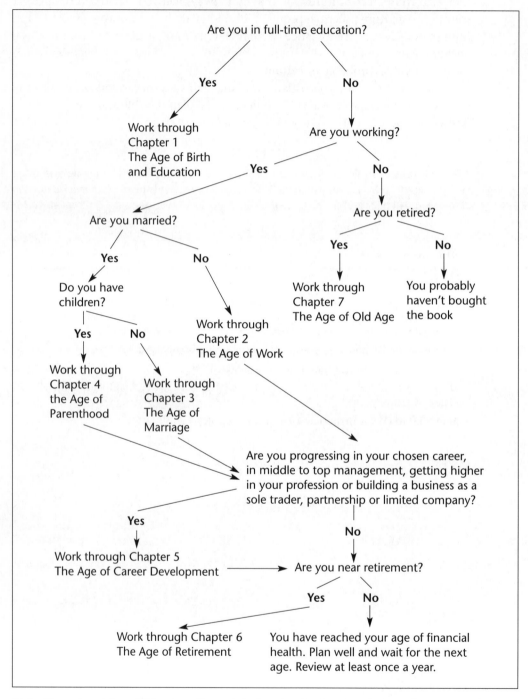

Note: If you have done little or no financial planning in the past you may have to work through several previous ages to achieve financial health in your own age. Chapter 8, Lifetime Financial Plans in Action, provides a valuable overview.

CHAPTER 1

THE AGE OF BIRTH AND EDUCATION

Birth and education	Work	Marriage	Parenthood	Career development	Retirement	Old age

FINANCIAL PLANNING AT A GLANCE –
THE AGE OF BIRTH AND EDUCATION

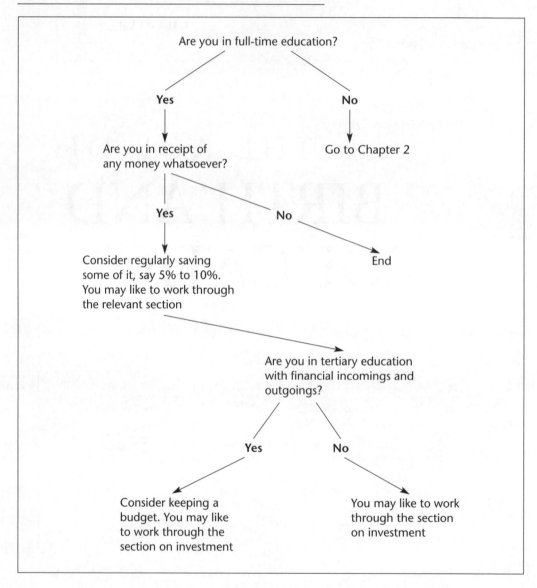

CONTENTS

In this age the following is discussed:

- saving any money you receive
- four investment considerations
- the concept of asset-backed investment
- investment vehicles
- non-asset-backed investments
- asset-backed investments
- tertiary education
- keeping a budget of incomings and outgoings
- local authority mortgage bonds
- tax exempt special savings accounts (TESSA)
- national savings
- British government stocks
- unit trusts
- investment trusts
- shares in the funds of an open ended investment company (OEIC)
- the personal equity plan (PEP)
- the corporate bond PEP
- investment bonds
- the taxation of investment bonds
- typical funds
- the with-profits fund
- the guaranteed equity bond
- comparing funds
- life assurance or life fund savings policy
- friendly society savings plan
- student loans

INTRODUCTION

In this age you are in full-time education. Even at an early age it is a good idea to start the habit of saving money. If you receive money either by way of gift, pocket money, or as the reward for doing part-time work either after studies or during the holidays, or even as a beneficiary of a trust, it is a good idea to spend less than you receive. The habit of saving money means you have already begun the process of planning your financial life. Trusts are treated in Chapter 4.

> The habit of saving money means you have already begun the process of planning your financial life.

It is wise to set yourself a figure, set yourself to save a given proportion of your income, say 5 to 10 per cent. Now you have refined your plan. You are not just saving haphazardly, as the fancy takes you, but you are following a plan.

FOUR INVESTMENT CONSIDERATIONS

Four considerations will dictate the vehicle used for saving:

1 **The term of saving**. Some investments have an initial charge of 6 to 7 per cent. They are clearly not suitable for short-term saving since it will take a while to make up for the charge before they show a growth. They could however be ideal for medium- to long-term investment which is anything from five years on.

2 **Accessibility**. A deposit account is immediately accessible with no penalty and is therefore ideal for use as a contingency fund where money may be needed at short notice. A TESSA is not so suited since if it is cashed in before the mandatory five years all the tax advantages are lost.

3 **Tax aspects**. Some investments carry tax advantages. The personal equity plan (PEP) for example can grow and receive income free of all UK taxes. This could be an enormous advantage especially to higher rate tax payers.

4 **Asset-backed or not**. The question of an investment being backed by an asset or not is extremely important. This means the investment produces a return in two ways: the asset will grow in value and, hopefully, not be eroded by inflation and, in addition, it will produce a yield. An example is investment property which increases in value and produces an income, the rental. Similarly, equities are assets since they represent a share of a particular company which could grow in capital value as well as producing dividends.

> Asset-backed investment increases your money both by capital growth and income.

It has to be said, however, that assets can go down in value as well as up so there is also a risk connected with these investments that does not exist with a deposit account. Figure 1.1 illustrates this and in particular the large drops in the 1970s and on 19 October 1987.

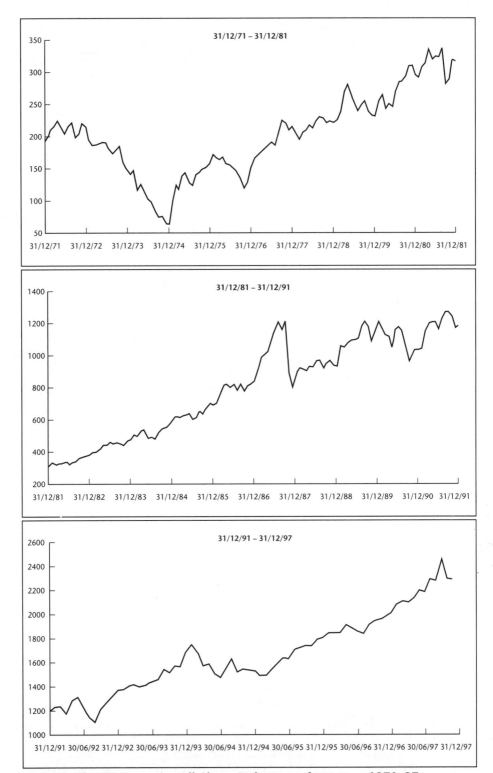

Fig. 1.1 The FT Actuaries All-Share Index – performance 1971–97
Source: Micropal

An investment which gives the best of both worlds is the guaranteed invest-ment or equity bond which invests in equities but can never go down in value. It has to be said, however, that it receives no income from dividends. This is treated later in the chapter. An example of an investment which is not backed by an asset is a deposit account. Here the money is literally lent to the bank or building soci-ety in return for an interest payment. The capital remains the same but in real terms is eroded by inflation. Consider a deposit of £1000 producing an average rate of interest over 10 years of 5 per cent per annum, with inflation also averag-ing 5 per cent per annum over the same period. At the end of 10 years the total interest received will be £500 but the buying power of the original £1000 will now be £613.91. For a discussion of inflation see Chapter 2. Clearly deposit accounts are not the best investment over the long term. Adams says, 'the riskiest place to leave your long term investments is in a deposit account'.[1]

Figures 1.2 and 1.3 compare investment over the medium- to long-term in deposit accounts over £25,000, with interest net of tax added, to that in UK equities measured by the FTSE 100 index.

> **Taking control of your own financial future can give you enormous satisfaction.**

Figure 1.4, for example, shows that from 1984 to 1998 an investment in such a deposit account would have grown by 168 per cent whereas the FTSE 100 index has increased by 445 per cent.

Whatever saving you are doing, to know that you are taking control of your own destiny, your own financial future, can give you enormous satisfaction and a feeling of your own value.

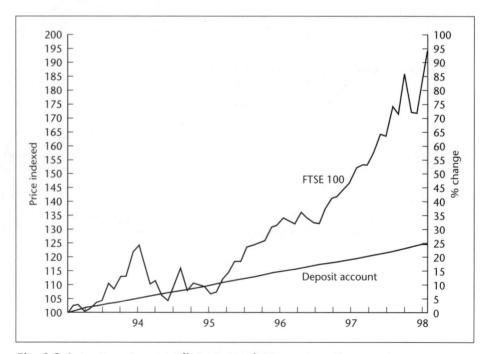

Fig. 1.2 Investments: a medium-term view
Source: Micropal

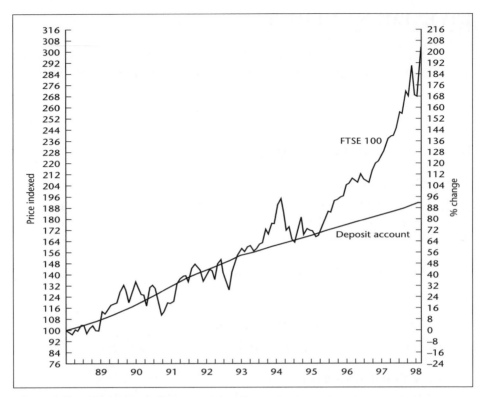

Fig. 1.3 Investments: a longer-term view
Source: Micropal

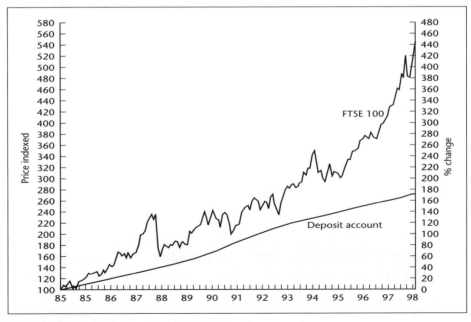

Fig. 1.4 Investments: a long-term view
Source: Micropal

INVESTMENT VEHICLES

I have included a wide range of investment vehicles, many of which will not be suitable for those in the age of birth and education. However, this is the age to develop the practice of saving and so to have some knowledge of the investments available can only be an advantage.

Non-asset-backed investments

Deposit accounts

These would be either instant access or deferred access from one month to two years. They would be ideal for short-term investment and the type of deposit would depend on the accessibility required.

Local authority mortgage bonds

These are a form of deposit account.

Tax exempt special savings accounts (TESSA)

These are virtually deposit accounts with tax advantages.

National Savings

There are ten different savings products under this heading. They can be found listed with all their details later in the chapter. It will be possible to judge at a glance suitability of term, accessibility and tax aspects. The whole list has been included, but clearly some products such as Premium Bonds Series 3 will not be applicable to the age of birth and education but will be very relevant in the age of retirement and the age of old age.

British government stocks

These are also called British funds, gilt edged securities or simply gilts. Although these are non-asset-backed investments they can make a capital growth as well as producing an income.

Asset-backed investments

Equities

These are shares in public companies which produce a dividend, usually twice yearly, declared by the company. Risk is reduced if this sort of investment is made through a pooled fund such as those listed under 'Pooled fund investments'.

Pooled fund investments

- unit trusts
- investment trusts
- shares in the funds of an open ended investment company (OEIC) (pronounced *oik*)
- the personal equity plan (PEP)
- investment bonds
- the guaranteed equity bond
- life assurance or life fund savings policies
- friendly societies
- offshore investment funds and investment bonds (treated in Chapter 5).

TERTIARY EDUCATION

In the case of tertiary education there may be a student grant, parents may be helping to fund the education, there may be a student loan. Now money is coming and going in a much more complicated manner. Clearly a budget is advisable in order to manage these financial affairs. It is important to ensure that income is greater than outgoings and to predict the future effect of any money borrowed. In the case of a student loan it is not, currently, necessary to pay interest, or to pay back capital while still in full-time education. However, the time will come when this has to be done.

It is a good idea to have a budget written down. What is the itemised weekly, monthly, annual income? What are the weekly, monthly, annual outgoings? What are the assets, e.g. money in building society, PEP, etc? What are the liabilities, e.g. student loan, loan from parents, etc? Parents may divulge, for example, that in year two of studentship a savings plan set up by grandparents will mature. This eventuality will need to be written into the financial plan.

It is never too early to start finding out about the wider financial implications which will occur when full-time education is over and work has started, such as contracts of employment and contingencies which would cause severe financial problems. It might therefore be a good idea to look at Chapter 2 as well. Your parents may even have asked you to be a trustee of a trust fund they have set up, say to ameliorate inheritance tax (IHT). You may be a beneficiary of such a trust. It would be a good idea to find out as much about such things now as you can. You can find information in Chapter 5.

■ Case Study 1.1

John Jones is 20. He is reading history at university and has a grant of £2000 p.a. and a student loan of £5000 of which £2500 remains. This is invested in a building society and receiving annual interest of 6% with instant access. He receives this interest gross having completed form R85. This form simply requires the depositor's full name, address, date of birth and national insurance number. It also includes a declaration that the depositor is unlikely to be liable for income tax. His fees are paid. His parents allow him £500 p.a. He works in the holidays and earns a further £1900 p.a.

There will be no tax to pay on his earnings or his building society interest since currently in tax year 1997/98 the amount of income receivable before tax is levied, i.e. the personal allowance, is £4045 p.a. The allowance from his parents is a gift. There will be no transfer tax on this as they are allowed to gift up to £3000 p.a. free of tax. (See Chapter 6.) His student grant is totally free of tax. He currently pays no interest on his loan. He keeps careful control of his finances. He spends his holidays, four months in total, at home where his board and lodgings are financed by his parents. His budget is shown in Form 1.1.

■ Form 1.1 BUDGET ANALYSIS

Name John Jones		*Year* 1997/98	
Income		Capital	Capital
Source	*Amount £ p.a.*	*Assets £*	*Liabilities £*
Grant	2000	Remaining	Original
Allowance	500	in building	student
Work	1900	society	loan
Total p.a. gross	4400	2500	5000
Total p.a. net of tax and NIC	4400		

Expenditure (averaged over a full year although some is only paid for 8 months of the year)		
	£ p.w.	*Net income £*
Food, drink and toiletries	35.00 (Average. He lives at home during holidays)	
Rental/mortgage payments	55.00 (Average. He lives at home during holidays)	
Heating, lighting and cooking	4.00	
Transport	15.00	
Clothes	4.00 (Average)	
Entertainment	10.00	
Books and journals	6.00 (Average)	
Telephone	3.00	
Other outgoings		
Total p.w.	132.00	84.61
p.a.	6864.00	4400.00
Surplus p.w.	Deficiency p.w.	[47.39]
p.a.	p.a.	[2464.28]

His outgoings are greater than his income. He cannot at this juncture of his life make any savings. His main objective is to support himself while studying for his degree.

He sees he will have to call on his capital and withdraw £47.39 per week. Thus at the end of the year he will be left with £113.21 because the money left in the building society over the year, a reducing amount, will have been credited with annual interest at 6%.

John decides to stay on another year to take a masters degree. His grant goes up to £3000 p.a., his annual income from work increases to £2100 and a savings plan funded by his grandparents for him matures at a value of £3000. He invests the £3000 in the same building society account receiving a gross annual interest of 6%.

His budget for his masters year is shown in Form 1.2.

■ **Form 1.2 BUDGET ANALYSIS**

Name John Jones		*Year* 1998/99	
Income		Capital	Capital
Source	*Amount £ p.a.*	*Assets £*	*Liabilities £*
Grant	3000	Remaining	Original
Allowance	500	in building	student
Work	2100	society	loan
Total p.a. gross	5600	3113.21	5000
Total p.a. net of tax and NIC	5600		

Expenditure
(averaged over a full year although some is only paid for 8 months of the year)

	£ p.w.	*Net income £*
Food, drink and toiletries	37.90 (Average. He lives at home during holidays)	
Rental/mortgage payments	56.20 (Average. He lives at home during holidays)	
Heating, lighting and cooking	4.00	
Transport	15.20	
Clothes	5.00 (Average)	
Entertainment	15.00	
Books and journals	6.80 (Average)	
Telephone	3.00	
Other outgoings		
Total p.w.	143.10	107.69
p.a.	7441.20	5600.00
Surplus p.w. Deficiency p.w.		[35.41]
p.a. p.a.		[1841.20]

This year he has to draw £35.41 per week from his capital. At the end of his year his position is:

Capital assets £	Liabilities £
Remaining in building society 1401.50	5000
(because once again the reducing cash remaining in	
the building society has made interest at 6% gross)	

He now starts work at £15,000 p.a. which, of course, will be taxed. He decides to maintain the habit of keeping a budget so that he remains in control of his finances. He has moved into the age of work.

■ Exercise 1.1

You may decide to keep a budget using Form 1.3.

■ Form 1.3 BUDGET ANALYSIS

Name		Year	
Income		Capital	Capital
Source	*Amount £ p.a.*	*Assets £*	*Liabilities £*
Total p.a. gross			
Total p.a. net of tax and NIC			
Expenditure	*£ p.w.*		*Net income £*
Food, drink and toiletries			
Rental/mortgage payments			
Heating, lighting and cooking			
Transport			
Clothes			
Entertainment			
Books and journals			
Telephone			
Other outgoings			
Total p.w.			
p.a.			
Surplus p.w.	Deficiency p.w.	[ ]	
p.a.	p.a.	[ ]	

DETAILED INFORMATION AND ANALYSIS

INVESTMENTS

Local authority mortgage bonds

These are issued for a fixed term, usually between two and seven years. Interest is taxable and is paid net of basic rate tax. Non-tax payers can claim back the tax. Rates of interest can be competitive. These bonds are advertised in the national press.

Tax exempt special savings accounts (TESSAs)

Introduced on 1 January 1991 TESSAs provide medium-term saving producing interest which is tax free as long as they are maintained for five years, at which point a new TESSA could be opened under the regulations then in force. A total of up to £9000 can be placed in a TESSA either as payments of up to £150 per month or as a lump sum of up to £3000 at the start of the first year followed by annual payments of up to £1800 in the three succeeding years, and up to £600 in the final year. Interest is credited net of basic rate tax over the five years and at the end of that period the basic rate tax paid is credited back to the account. The net interest can be withdrawn during the five years without prejudicing the tax exemption. Each individual over 18 years old is allowed one TESSA.

National savings

The position with regard to the various national savings options is laid out fully in Table 1.1.

British government stock or British funds or gilt edged securities or gilts

These investments represent borrowings by the government which will pay a fixed interest (the coupon) in return. Thus the owner of £100 nominal of Treasury $8\frac{1}{2}$ per cent 2007 will receive £8.50 per annum until that date.

Gilts are listed and traded on the stock market and their capital value can vary. Thus, although they are not truly asset backed they can potentially make a capital growth. For example, in times of low interest rates it could be worth paying more than £100 for £100 nominal of the gilt just described. Let us say that interest rates on deposits are currently 5 per cent per annum then paying £115, for example, for £100 nominal of this stock producing £8.50 per annum would mean the yield would still be,

Table 1.1 National Savings

	11th INDEX-LINKED SAVINGS CERTIFICATES	44th ISSUE SAVINGS CERTIFICATES	CHILDREN'S BONUS BONDS ISSUE H	FIRST OPTION BONDS	INCOME BONDS
Rate of return	Index linking plus guaranteed extra interest of 2.75% compound when held for 5 years	5.35% compound guaranteed when held for 5 years General extension rate for matured certificates = 3.51%	6.75% compound guaranteed when held for 5 years. Further guaranteed returns notified before each following fifth anniversary. (No more returns after holder 21)	6.75% gross guaranteed to first anniversary (=5.4% net). £20,000+ earns bonus of 0.25% gross (0.2% net). Further guaranteed rates notified annually. (Tax paid rates assume tax at 20%)	(From 12 December 1997) Under £25,000 6.75% gross £25,000+ 7.% gross Rates variable
Tax position	Free of UK income tax at all rates and capital gains tax			Tax (at 20%) deducted at source. No further liability for basic or lower rate taxpayers	Taxable
Special features	A guaranteed real return in additio to inflation proofing, fixed for 5 years	Fixed return for 5 years	No tax liability on parents' gifts	Rates guaranteed 12 months at a time. Bonds can be held indefinitely	Regular monthly income All holders get gross interest automatically – no Inland Revenue registration form for non-tax payers to fill in
Minimum	£100. Larger purchases can be for any amount within holding limit	£100. Larger purchases can be for any amount within holding limit	£25. Then in units of £25	£1000. Larger purchases can be for any amounts within holding limit	£2000 (£1000 for further purchases). Larger purchases can be for any amount within holding limit
Maximum	£10,000. No limit on reinvesting matured certificates and Ulster Savings Certificates	£10,000. No limit on reinvesting matured certificates and Ulster Savings Certificates	£1000 per issue	£250,000 sole or joint	£250,000 sole or joint
Who may invest	Individuals (also jointly), trustees, charities, some clubs and voluntary bodies		Anyone over 16 for individuals under 16. (No trust holdings)	Individuals over 16; two jointly; trustees for not more than two individuals	Individuals; two jointly; trustees for not more than two individuals
Repayment terms	Allow at least 8 working days No interest if repaid in first year (except reinvestment certificates). If held less than 5 years, see prospectus		Allow at least 8 working days for repayment at 5 year anniversary points or 21st birthday No interest if repaid in first year. Otherwise 5% if repaid before 5th anniversary	Allow a few days. No penalty for repayments at anniversary dates. Otherwise half interest since last anniversary. No interest if repaid in first year	3 months' notice without penalty. Or without notice but with penalty equal to 90 days' interest. Repayment by crossed warrant

Source: The Department of National Savings [correct at 31 October 1997]

PENSIONERS' BONDS SERIES 3	CAPITAL BONDS SERIES J	INVESTMENT ACCOUNT	ORDINARY ACCOUNT	PREMIUM BONDS	TREASURER'S ACCOUNT
7.0% gross fixed for first 5 years. Paid monthly	6.65% compound guaranteed when held for 5 years. Gross	Under £500 4.75% gross £500+ 5.25% £2500+ 5.5% £10,000+ 5.75% £25,000+ 6.0% Rates variable	Standard rate 1.5% Higher rate 2.5%	Prize fund 5.0%	£10,000–£24,999 5.75% gross £25,000–£99,999 6.0% £100,000+ 6.25% Note: Balances under £10,000 2.85% Rates variable
but credited in full without deduction of tax at source			No UK income tax on first £70 (£140 joint) annual interest	Prizes tax free	Taxable but credited in full without deduction of tax at source
Regular monthly income All holders get gross interest automatically – no Inland Revenue registration form for non-taxpayers to fill in	Fixed return for 5 years All holders get gross interest automatically – no Inland Revenue registration form for non-taxpayers to fill in	All holders get gross interest automatically – no Inland Revenue registration form for non-taxpayers to fill in Bank book records all transactions	Interest earned for whole calendar months. Interest credited every 31 December	Odds fixed at 19,000 to 1 per £1 bond Over 440,000 prizes per month. Top monthly prize of £1 million. Bonds elligible for prize draws one clear month after purchase	Postal notification of interest rate changes. Transactions by telephone. Annual tax statements. Monthly statements following transactions.
£500. Larger purchases can be for any amount within holding limit	£100. Larger purchases can be for any amount within holding limit	£20	£10	£100	£10,000 opening deposit
£50,000. (£100,000 joint – in addition to holdings of any earlier series)	£250,000 – applies to total holdings from Series B onwards	£100,000 sole or joint	£10,000	£20,000	£2 million per organisation
Individuals (or two jointly) over 60, trustees for not more than two individuals over 60	Individuals; two individuals jointly; trustees for not more than two individuals	Individuals; two individuals jointly; not more than two trustees for not more than two individuals	Individuals; two individuals jointly; not more than two trustees for not more than two individuals	Individuals over 16. Under 16, by parents, guardians, grandparents and great-grandparents	Non-profit-making organisations
60 days' notice with no interest during notice period – except at 5 year anniversaries. Or without notice but with penalty equal to 90 days' interest. Repayment by crossed warrant direct to account	Allow two weeks No interest if repaid in first year. If held less than 5 years, see prospectus	One month's notice. Or without notice but with penalty equal to 30 days' interest	Up to £100 on demand. (Regular customer accounts: up to £250 at chosen post office.) For larger amounts allow a few days	Allow at least 8 working days	30 days' notice. Or without notice but with penalty equal to 30 days' interest.

$$\frac{8.5}{115} \times 100 = 7.7\%$$

The nominal value only will be repaid by the government at the end of the term. It is clear that knowing when to buy and when to sell needs considerable expertise. Hence a stockbroker would be needed, or the risk could be reduced by investing in a pooled fund such as those listed under asset-backed investments. In March 1991 the first issue of index-linked gilt edged securities was launched with both capital growth and interest linked to the Retail Prices Index (RPI). Interest on all gilts is paid net of basic rate tax unless they are bought through branches of the Post Office or by direct application to the National Savings Stocks and Bonds Office in Blackpool, when it is paid gross. Newly issued stock can be bought directly through the Bank of England.

Unit trusts

A unit trust is a pooled investment. It will be invested, for example, in stocks and shares of a number of companies, often as many as 200 to 300 (see Fig. 1.5). The fund will be unitised, i.e. divided into units. Each unit will represent a small part of the total investment. An investor will purchase units at the prevailing unit price and will therefore have a share of the pooled investment. Usually the particular unit trust is valued each day and this will result in a daily unit price. As the unit price varies so will the value of the person's particular investment. Thus the unit trust allows investors to participate in a large and professionally managed portfolio. Unless the investor has a considerable amount of money he would never acquire such a spread by investing directly in the stock markets of the world. Because the risk is spread in this way the unit trust is relatively safe. A small personal share portfolio might contain 20 or so shares whereas the same amount of money invested in unit trusts could purchase 20 unit trusts and therefore a very large number of different companies.

> Saving money in unit trusts allows you to invest on the stock markets of the world at a much lower risk.

One company in a small share portfolio losing value badly would represent a large proportion of the total investment, whereas the same situation in the unit trust portfolio would represent a very small part of the total investment. Thus a small share portfolio investment is relatively more risky. Also, good investment results will not simply depend on choosing the right shares at outset but deciding when to change them. This is difficult enough for the professional fund manager, but far more so for the private investor struggling to keep abreast of business, economic and political developments worldwide. In addition to this, the costs of changing shares and increasing paperwork can make the small investment portfolio difficult to run.

Just as any investment on the stock market will have an initial cost, called the bid offer spread including stockbroker fees, VAT and stamp duty, so too does the unit trust. The insurance company will also make an initial charge, included in

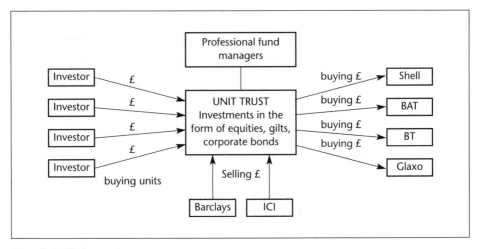

Fig. 1.5 Unit trusts

the bid offer spread which is typically in the region of 5 to 7 per cent. There will also be an annual management charge for the expertise of the fund managers and administration. Typically this could be in the region of 1 to 1½ per cent. Thus it will take a while for the initial charge to be made up and a real growth begin to accrue. For these reasons a unit trust investment should be considered to be medium to long term and the intention should be to keep it for at least five years. A unit trust will vary in value with, hopefully, an overall upward trend. It will also produce an income. This income will be distributed to the investor. The income will be paid net of a tax of 20 per cent, representing the advanced corporation tax paid by the individual companies on the dividend. If the unit trust holder is a basic rate tax payer, no further tax will be due but a higher rate tax payer will pay additionally the difference between the higher rate tax and 20 per cent. Non-tax payers will be able to reclaim the 20 per cent tax paid on the income from their unit trusts. This would also be possible in the case of children, up to the value of their personal allowance, currently, in the tax year 1997/98, £4045 (see Chapter 2) if the unit trusts have been given to the child by persons other than their parents. In the case of gifts from their parents tax can be reclaimed up to a limit of an equivalent gross annual income of £100. Within the trust no capital gains tax will be paid on the sale of industrial shares. However, the investor will be liable to pay capital gains tax on any disposal of his unit trusts. (For capital gains tax see Chapter 5.) Most unit trusts will allow the reinvestment of income and some which are called accumulation unit trusts do not actually distribute income – its receipt by the unit trust is reflected in an increase in the value of the unit trust. Although the income is not distributed it is still liable for income tax.

Many companies provide a monthly investment facility so that a regular amount can be paid each month to purchase unit trusts thus building a substantial investment over the years. This facility can make the investment a suitable vehicle for the repayment of a mortgage. It is possible to get a projection from the insurance company of the amount which such an investment would grow to over a number of years at a particular assumed rate of growth. Using these assumptions a monthly investment can be designed to produce the amount needed to pay off the mortgage over a given number of years. It should be noted that, unlike the endowment, there is no life assurance element in this investment. Furthermore it will be the investor's responsibility to see that the investment remains on track to pay off the mortgage.

Typical areas of investment covered by unit trusts are:

- **growth**. The prime objective is to achieve capital growth.
- **income**. Designed to provide a high and growing income without sacrificing potential for capital growth. These would include government securities.
- **balanced or general**. Providing a mix of growth and income.
- **international**. Invested in overseas economies.
- **specialist**. Invested in specific sectors such as technology, commodities, asset value, smaller companies, recovery aspects or companies making most of their profit overseas.
- **deposit fund**. Invested in deposit accounts.
- **corporate bonds**. These will usually contain UK corporate bonds which represent a loan to a company and as such not only are they a means for the company to raise capital but they pay a fixed interest which is usually higher than that obtainable from deposit accounts.

This last type of unit trust will usually also include gilt edged securities and convertibles of UK companies which again represent a loan to the company but carry the right of conversion into the company's ordinary shares. Most companies will allow switching between the various unit trusts they manage at a discount of usually 2 per cent. This means that instead of paying another full bid offer spread of 5 to 7 per cent it would be reduced to 3 to 5 per cent. Switching between unit trusts is seen by the Inland Revenue as a disposal and is therefore liable to capital gains tax.

Investment trusts

The investment trust is another type of collective investment which enables investors to pool their resources to create a common fund for investment by professional investment managers. Unlike unit trusts it is a limited company investing in equities, government securities, or property usually by way of shares in property companies and other more sophisticated investments such as warrants (see Fig. 1.6). The investment trust is also allowed to borrow money. The shares of an investment trust will be quoted on the stock market and their value will be influenced by supply and demand. The individual invests in the shares of the

Putting money into an investment trust purchases shares in the company which manages the underlying investments. It is not a direct purchase of a share in these investments.

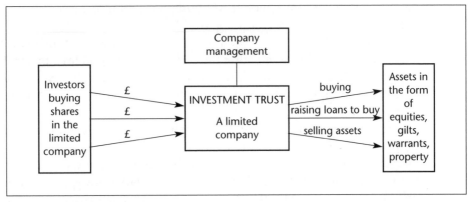

Fig. 1.6 Investment trusts

investment trust which manages the underlying investments – he or she does not, however, make a direct investment into those underlying investments. The value of his or her shares will not usually reflect the underlying value of the assets of the investment trust and will often be at a discount of 15 to 25 per cent. The shares will only usually reflect the true value of the underlying assets when the whole investment trust is sold or wound up.

While the collective investment spreads the risks the other factors mentioned make the investment trust more sensitive to movements in the market. An investment trust will usually have a more flexible investment policy than a unit trust and like most trusts it does not pay capital gains tax on the sale of the investments within the trust. The investor will have a liability to capital gains tax on the sale of his or her shares. Income from the investment trust in the form of dividends is taxed in exactly the same way as that described under unit trusts. Regular savings plans are sometimes offered by the managers of investment trusts and these could be used as the vehicle for repaying a mortgage. However, because of the greater sensitivity to fluctuations in the stock market this could represent a greater risk.

Shares in the funds of an open ended investment company (OEIC)

To date only very few unit trust and life funds have changed to the investment funds of an open ended investment company (OEIC). However, it is a trend which will rapidly gain favour. The main differences with such funds are that they will have a single price, their management will be simpler and it will therefore cost less to invest in them. Upfront charges will probably range from $3\frac{1}{2}$ to $4\frac{1}{2}$ per cent, management charges probably from 1 to $1\frac{1}{2}$ per cent per annum. Where a company changes to this form unit trusts will become shares in the investment funds. Investment bonds, using life funds, will consist of a choice of these investment funds with a life assurance aspect added.

The new form will also allow investments designated in other world currencies besides sterling and in general it will bring this part of the investment sector in the UK into line with the rest of the world.

Currently, if there is a big exodus of funds from a unit trust the managers will widen the bid offer spread to offset the cost, thus causing all investors at that time to pay more. This is called a 'dilution levy'. With the new structure the fund managers will levy an extra charge only on those causing the exodus, so the general investor will not suffer.

Switching between funds and life funds will again be a feature but in the case of the OEIC the charges for this are likely to be vastly reduced to the region of a quarter of 1 per cent. Although switching between life funds will not attract a liability to capital gains taxes, those between ordinary funds will unless held in a discretionary portfolio for the client by the fund managers.

The personal equity plan (PEP)

The personal equity plan introduced in the 1986 budget is a tax-efficient container for other investments. These investments are meant particularly to be equities but can be in the form of unit trusts, OEIC funds or investment trusts and will thefore contain the additional investments open to an investment trust. Income and capital gains are totally free of UK taxes, regardless of how long the PEP is maintained. The PEP investor does not even have to enter income, or any capital gain from the PEP, on his or her tax returns.

Putting investments inside a PEP shields them from UK tax.

There is no mandatory period during which the PEP has to be held so that it could be redeemed one second after it is invested in if so desired. However this would be very unwise since there will always be charges involved – either an upfront charge, usually 5 to 7 per cent, an annual management charge, typically 1 to $1\frac{1}{2}$ per cent, and sometimes an exit charge which is administered on redemption. Clearly, because of the form of investment it is best considered to be medium to long term, in other words five years or more.

The income from the PEP can either be received free of UK tax or can be reinvested in the PEP free of UK tax.

There are two types of PEPs, the general PEP as described and the single company PEP introduced on 1 January 1992 which is an investment in the shares of one single company and receives exactly the same tax advantages as does the general PEP. The single company PEP is clearly a higher risk investment since there is no spread.

Each individual is limited with respect to the amount he or she can invest in PEPs and in the fiscal year 1997/98 this stood at,

General PEP	£6000	(75 per cent of which must be in shares of UK or European companies directly or through pooled investments)
Single company PEP	£3000	

Eligibility to make these investments carries certain constraints,

- The investor must be 18 years or over, and must be resident and ordinarily resident in the UK, or be a Crown employee working overseas, whose duties are treated as performed in the UK.
- He or she must not have subscribed to another PEP of the same type with another provider during the tax year in which the application is made.
- If he or she is found to have made an ineligible application for a PEP, the Inland Revenue will deem the PEP to be void and all PEPs of that type for that year will be disqualified. Any tax refunds received will have to be repaid to the Inland Revenue.
- PEPs are only available to individuals.
- The Inland Revenue rules permit payment into a PEP only from an individual's own personal or joint bank account, or personal or joint building society account.
- In order to maintain its tax-free status the PEP must remain in the beneficial ownership of the individual who took it out.
- An assignment of a PEP, whether into a trust for collateral purposes, or even as a straightforward gift, will remove its tax-free status thereafter and it will no longer be a PEP.

A PEP cannot be assigned to a lender.

Many companies run a monthly investment facility into a PEP. This again makes this form of investment suitable as a vehicle of repayment for a mortgage. And this time it is much more tax efficient.

■ The corporate bond PEP

On 6 July 1995 it became possible for a PEP to contain certain corporate bonds and convertibles of UK companies, discussed on p. 18. The crucial point is the relatively high rate of interest payable and hence this particular PEP will produce a high income and since this income is paid free of all UK taxes the corporate bond PEP can be extremely valuable to certain types of investor, in particular retirees paying higher rate tax.

Investment bonds

The investment bond in simple terms is a single premium life assurance. It will therefore be invested in pooled funds usually called life funds which is exactly where life savings plans, endowments and whole of life policies invest (see Chapter 3). The bond will carry some life assurance which will take the form of guaranteeing that on death the value of the bond will never be less than the original investment even though the true value of the bond may have fallen below this. Life funds will, in general, be invested in the stock markets of the world, although some will include other sectors of investment such as commercial property, gilts and deposits.

Life funds pay tax at 24 per cent on capital gains and 20 per cent on income but actual tax is less because capital gains can usually be deferred into the future and certain expenses incurred through the running of the fund can be offset against tax on income.

Because this investment is a life assurance there will be not only an owner but also a life assured. This is usually one and the same person but, in fact, there are several ways in which the bond can be written:

1 Single life – single ownership
2 Joint life second death – single ownership
3 Joint life second death – joint ownership
4 Children's investments.

Life assurance companies will usually allow a person over the age of 12 to invest in a bond – this would be single life single ownership. Investments for those under 12 can be made but they are usually initiated by a benefactor and involve various trusts. This aspect will be treated in Chapter 7.

Because the investment is basically in equities there will be, as with unit trusts, a bid offer spread. This will usually be between 5 and 7 per cent and will constitute the upfront charge, which makes this a medium- to long-term investment. There will also usually be an annual management charge of anything between $\frac{3}{4}$ and $1\frac{1}{2}$ per cent.

■ The taxation of investment bonds

The proceeds of an investment bond in the hands of an investor are taxed as income. As a result of the Finance Act 1975 and since 13 March 1975 a policyholder may withdraw up to 5 per cent of the initial investment in any policy year without tax liability. This 5 per cent is cumulative, hence if in years one and two only 3 per cent is withdrawn each year the policy holder could, if he or she wished, withdraw 9 per cent in year three. The total amount that can be withdrawn with no tax liability is 100 per cent of the initial investment spread over 20 years at 5 per cent per annum.

There will be a potential tax liability when a chargeable event occurs. This occurs,

1 when a bond is cashed in
2 on the death of the life assured or, in the case of a joint life second death bond, on the death of the second life assured
3 if a bond holder makes a withdrawal in a policy year in excess of the cumulative allowance of 5 per cent per annum
4 on withdrawals after 20 years' worth of 5 per cent allowances have been taken.

The insurance company is obliged by statute to send details of all chargeable events to the Inland Revenue.

On any one of these occurrences someone who is already a higher rate taxpayer pays the difference between higher rate and basic rate tax, which, in the fiscal year

1997/98, stood at 40 per cent and 23 per cent respectively, on the total gain. Tax is payable in the tax year in which the policy year ends.

For basic rate tax payers the mechanism of 'top slicing' is used and this is best illustrated by an example.

■ Example 1.1

Marion Walters purchased her investment bond on 23 March 1993 for £10,000. She cashes in the bond on 11 April 1997 for £14,640, total gain £4640. She has owned the bond for four years, therefore she divides the gain by four to get her 'slice'. This is £1160. She adds this to her income in the current tax year which is £25,400 after reliefs to get £26,560. The excess over basic rate, which in the tax year 1997/98 stood at £26,100, is £460. This amount on each of her four slices is therefore taxed at the difference between higher rate tax and basic rate tax.

Hence tax on the gain in the bond is,

$$4 \times (40\% - 23\%) \text{ of } £460$$
$$= 4 \times £78.20 = £312.80$$
$$[17\% \text{ of } £460 = \frac{17}{100} \times £460 = 0.17 \times £460 = £78.20]$$

■ Example 1.2

David Jones buys an investment bond on 31 January 1989 for £5000, and on 3 February 1993 he withdraws £1500.

Cumulative allowance = £5 × 5% of £5000 (since he is in the fifth fiscal year)
= £1250
Excess = £250 (5% of £5000)
Slice = £250 divided by 4 (4 complete years) = £62.50
Income after reliefs + slice = £23,000 + £62.50 = £23,062.50

In tax year 1992/93 the higher rate tax threshold occurred at £23,700 p.a., hence he pays no tax.

On 29 July 1995 he withdrew £3000. There have been a further two complete policy years since last chargeable event.

Allowance 2 × £250 = £500
Hence gain £2,500
Slice = £2500 divided by 2 = £1250
Income + slice = £23,500 + £1250 = £24,750
Higher rate threshold in 1995/96 was £24,300 after reliefs
Excess is £450
Hence tax is 2 × (40% – 25%) of £450 = 2 × 15% of £450
$$(15\% \text{ of } £450 = \frac{15}{100} \times £450 = £67.50) = £135$$

Higher rate and basic rate tax in 1995/96 are 40% and 25% respectively.
On 14 December 1997 he cashed in the whole bond for £5130.

Gain = (surrender value + previous withdrawals) less (purchase price + previous gains)

= (£5130 + £4500) – (£5000 + £2750)

= £9630 – £7750

= £1180

There have been two further complete policy years, hence slice = £590.

Income (after reliefs) + slice = £24,000 + £590 = £24,590

Higher rate threshold in 1997/98 is £26,100, hence no further tax to pay.

Most insurance companies will offer a choice of funds and switching between them can usually be done at a discounted price paying perhaps 2 per cent less than the usual bid offer spread. Switching between life funds attracts no liability to capital gains tax. Most funds will be unit linked. In other words the fund is divided into units whose price at any time will reflect the overall value of the fund. Investment is by purchase of units. With-profits funds are rather more complicated and will be treated fully in Chapter 3.

Most life funds are now divided into units in exactly the same way as unit trusts and are, therefore, called unit-linked funds. The number of units owned by an investor will represent a proportion of the actual fund and so its value will reflect that of the fund, after charges, exactly. The with-profits fund is different from this as is the guaranteed equity fund and these will be described later.

Typical funds

Typical funds include the following:

- equity – predominantly UK
- UK property
- deposit fund – invested in deposit accounts and besides being a straight investment medium can also be used as a consolidation instrument allowing a switch to this fund if the intention is to cash in within the next four years or so. This can be a protection against a sudden drop in the stock market such as occurred in the 1970s and on 19 October 1987, when the market dropped 30 per cent (see Fig. 1.1).
- gilt edged
- overseas earnings
- American equity
- American property
- Far East equity
- European equity
- international equity

- high income – invested in high yield UK equities
- with profits
- managed or mixed – currently typically
  - UK equities (50 per cent)
  - American equities (4 per cent)
  - European equities (9 per cent)
  - Far Eastern – Pacific equities (15 per cent)
  - property (5 per cent)
  - gilts (10 per cent)
  - deposits and cash (7 per cent) (Total 100 per cent)
- American managed.

The with-profits fund

There is an investment fund underlying the policies which it serves. The funds of these policies are in reality non-existent, although they have a value which is governed by the underlying fund.

Each year a reversionary bonus is declared which will be based on the existing fund at the time or, in the case of life policies, the sum assured. This bonus, although declared will not actually be added until maturity of the policy or prior death. There is also a terminal bonus which will be, depending on the contract, both declared and added at maturity or death.

Bonuses once declared cannot be removed. Therefore the with-profits fund can *never go down in value*. This makes it fundamentally different from the unit-linked fund which can go down as well as up. These bonuses then constitute guarantees and sometimes other initial guarantees are given with pension policies and endowment policies.

It is because of these guarantees that premiums go into this underlying fund which must always maintain an adequate solvency margin. The solvency margin is the difference between the liabilities on the fund, i.e. all the guaranteed amounts which will eventually have to be paid out and the value of the fund. Insurance companies must maintain adequate margins and this is currently monitored by the Department of Trade and Industry, which will also ensure that fairness is maintained between the profits retained by the company and the bonuses paid to the clients.

The company actuary then, has to maintain a delicate balance between these variables which also includes his or her prognosis for the future investment climate. An eye has, also, to be kept on the surplus with respect to future terminal bonuses which may be declared.

There is always an element of smoothing in this sort of investment, which will go steadily up, since the actuary will be unlikely to react immediately to sudden fluctuations in investment values either up or down.

Charges on this type of policy are not quoted and are simply taken from the fund.

It is extremely important to realise that reversionary bonuses are not actually added to the policy at declaration so that if it is cashed in its value will not be that indicated by the bonus and, of course, any terminal bonus will be lost.

The process is relatively straightforward to describe when we are considering the funds being used in pension policies and endowment policies, which we will treat in more detail later, because they have a set time and it is known when they will mature.

In the case of the fund being used in the structure of an investment bond this is more difficult because the time is not known. Such devices as assuming a time have been used and, if cashed in before that, to ensure fairness between those policies continuing in the fund and those being removed a 'market level adjuster' is used which will mean a reduction in the notional value of the bond being encashed.

Reversionary bonuses are of two types: simple, which is a bonus on the value of the fund or sum assured, and compound, which in addition declares bonuses on those bonuses already declared. Occasionally, special reversionary bonuses will be declared for certain generations of business in order to maintain equity between all the generations.

In recent years an innovation has been introduced which is the unitised with-profits fund. It is the same as the funds described earlier in all respects except that premiums buy units and charges are made explicit at outset. Bonuses are declared on the units and result in an increase in the actual value of these units or additional units being added. The bonuses are declared, as before, by the company actuary based on exactly the same criteria as before. These funds have become increasingly popular and probably represent the greater part of with-profits business today (see Fig. 1.7).

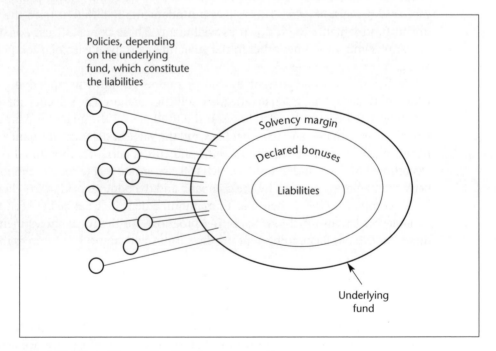

Policies, depending on the underlying fund, which constitute the liabilities

Solvency margin

Declared bonuses

Liabilities

Underlying fund

Fig. 1.7 The with-profits fund

Clearly, because with-profits policies cannot go down in value, dictating the different kinds of guarantees, the underlying fund must be cautious rather than adventurous and will, therefore, be not dissimilar from the unit-linked managed fund.

A typical with-profits fund could be:

Fixed interest	14%
Property	19%
UK equities	54%
Non-UK equities	11%
Other investments	2%

The guaranteed equity bond (GEB)

The fund in this bond is a recent innovation which enables less speculative investors to invest on the stock market without the fear of suffering the sort of sudden large drop in value just described. Using such financial instruments as derivatives these funds can guarantee a minimum return of capital such as 95 to 100 per cent together with a proportion of the growth in the Financial Times Stock Exchange 100 Index, FTSE 100 or 'Footsie' over a specified period. (The FTSE 100 Index reflects the changing value in the top 100 companies on the UK Stock Market. It takes no account of dividend income.)

The growth in the FTSE 100 Index is monitored over a period, for example, three months. At the end of the period if the FTSE 100 Index has gone up then a given proportion of this is added to the value of the fund; if it has gone down then the decrease in the value of the fund is limited by the guarantee. For example, if the guarantee of return of capital is 95 per cent then the decrease in value is limited to 5 per cent and so on. This is achieved by putting enough money in flat rate deposit at the beginning of each period to grow back to the guaranteed sum by the end of the quarter.

It is the leftover money which is invested in derivatives such as options which produces the proportion of the Footsie growth required. It is clear that the lower the guarantee the more money available and hence the higher the proportion can be.

Hence proportion of growth added is indirectly proportional to the guarantee. Thus the higher the guarantee the smaller the proportion and vice versa. These additions to the fund are locked in. If an investor switches out of this fund other than at the end of the period that particular increment of growth is lost. It can be seen that there is not the potential for growth that a straight equity fund has, but neither can there be large sudden drops in value. In the case of 100 per cent guarantee, for example, the proportion of growth to be added can be expected, usually over the medium to long term, to be between 20 and 40 per cent. Each interval of time will begin with a set date, for example, the 1st of every December, March, June and September. The proportion of growth will be added at the end of the interval. The charges will be similar to those of other investment bonds and there will be the same element of life insurance.

The value of a guaranteed equity fund can never drop below the guaranteed value.

■ Example 1.3

Brian Carter has a 100% guaranteed equity bond worth £5500 on the December set date. The starting level of the FTSE 100 Index is 2400. The proportion of growth declared for the next quarter is 30% net of taxes and charges.

1 At the end of the quarter the Footsie has risen to 2610, a rise of 8.75%. Hence at the end of the quarter 30% of 8.75% = 2.63% will be added to Brian's bond, i.e. 2.63% of £5500 = £144.65. So its value will increase to £5644.65. This growth is now locked in and is the new guaranteed sum entered for the next quarter.

2 The declared proportion of growth for this quarter is again declared at 30%. At the end of the quarter the Footsie has risen to 2675, a rise of 2.5%. For this quarter then 30% of 2.5% = 0.75% is added. 0.75% of £5644.65 is £42.33 and the value of Brian's bond increases to £5686.98. This growth is now locked in and the new guaranteed sum entered for the next quarter is £5686.98.

3 The declared proportion of growth for the next quarter is declared as 32%. At the end of the quarter the Footsie has fallen to 2300, a drop of 14.0%. The value of Brian's bond is unaffected and remains at £5686.98.

4 The proportion of growth for this quarter is declared as 33%. The Footsie has risen by 8.3% by the end of the quarter. NB: the starting point for this quarter is the end of the previous quarter. Doing the same calculation we now see that the value of Brian's bond becomes £5844.50. Hence over the full year the value of Brian's bond has increased by 6.3% while the Footsie itself has risen by only 3.8%.

Note: see Fig. 1.8.

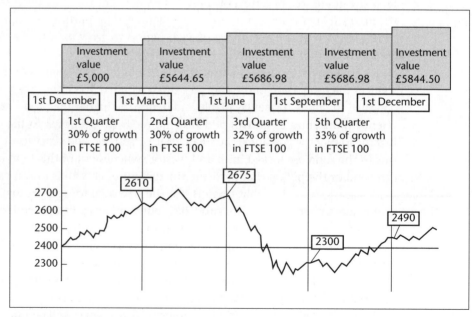

Fig. 1.8 How the GEB works

Just as the amount of guarantee can vary so too can the gearing mechanism or method of adding the proportion of Footsie growth. There are usually two mechanisms used. One method which we have already seen where the growth in the Footsie used is the difference between the end of the set period and the beginning. The other method measures the difference between the average value of the Footsie during the set period and that at the beginning. The gearing is based on market conditions at the time and hence the numbers will usually change every quarter. As an illustration only, had this been based on market conditions in March 1997 typical numbers would have been as shown in Table 1.2.

Table 1.2 An example of Footsie gearing

	Gearing	
Level of guarantee	Beginning and end of period	Average
100%	40%	75%
97.5%	117%	217%

In the case of the 'average' mechanism the higher gearing will typically be applied to a lower level of Footsie increase.

In the case of the 97.5 per cent guarantee any growth achieved will be added to 97.5 per cent of the value at the beginning of the period. However, in this case there will be a higher gearing.

Comparing funds

It is extremely difficult to assess the relative potential for growth of the various funds but there are certain guidelines it is possible to follow. There are a number of magazines that publish past investment performance of all the funds together with the date of launch of the fund and its size. These factors would be the starting point for a comparison although they must be used with care. By far the most important factor in investment performance is consistency. It would be very unwise to invest in a fund which had been at the top of the league table measured over a short period and then at the bottom in the next. New funds will have very little track record so that it would not be possible to judge them on consistency.

New funds can do extremely well in the early years because they will be investing new money and the investment climate can be reacted to quickly. It is much more expensive for fund

The most important factor in investment performance is consistency.

managers to change existing investments. This brings us to the question of cashflow, the flow of money into the fund. If this is large then considerable flexibility is given to the fund managers because it is the new money which they can use to react to the changes in investment climate.

Some large funds every week take in premiums equal to the total value of some of the smaller funds.

Fund managers will have a more difficult task with established funds which have remained small meaning that flow of money into the funds is small. Another problem hitting the fund with small cashflow is a possible sudden outflow of funds with investors wanting to change their investment or transfer to another company. If cashflow is small then investments have to be cashed in, which can be expensive. Large cashflow will accommodate this problem from new premiums.

> **Large cashflow into large funds gives greater investment flexibility.**

A large cashflow into a property fund can also be extremely valuable as it gives the fund managers the chance to buy a property at very short notice. Another benefit of large funds is that fund manager expertise is attracted to them. There is greater kudos, and probably salary, attached to managing very large funds so that the companies running these large funds can cherry pick when recruiting additional fund managers.

Length of time since establishment of the fund will be very important because the track record will be much longer encompassing both very bad investment times and very good, for example, how the fund has coped with the disastrous drops in stock market value which occurred in the 1970s and on 19 October 1987.

To summarise so far: good long-term consistent performance is paramount which will almost certainly mean the fund is not at the top of the league table but neither has it ever been near the bottom. It has consistently given a good solid return. Long establishment and large size will be important factors in this. A good broad spread of investment will enhance this requirement of consistent performance. Very specialist funds may rocket to the top at times but are open to sudden disastrous drops.

It would be important when choosing a fund to look not only at that particular fund but also to look at the performance of all the other funds offered by that particular insurance company. This is important for two reasons:

1 It gives a measure of the performance of the total team of fund managers and means that not all the expertise is concentrated in pushing a particular fund to the top of the league tables.
2 At some point, other good funds may be needed for switching into.

> **Continuity of fund management is crucially important.**

Continuity of management is crucially important. A change could alter performance in a very short time. Connected with this is again size. A small company is much more likely to be bought and very quickly suffer a change of investment management. As in the commercial world in general, the tendency in the financial services sector is towards large conglomerates. The smaller companies are beginning to be taken over and there is little doubt that this trend will continue.

The financial standing and size of the company together with the reputation of its management will, in the end, play a large part in the choice of fund.

Life assurance or life fund savings policy

Just as the bond is a particular wrap or envelope which contains the life funds (an envelope which gives the product a certain structure which will dictate its tax treatment) so too is the savings plan – often called a maximum investment policy. The bond introduces a minimal amount of life assurance which makes it a single premium non-qualifying life assurance.

If the life assurance savings plan is wrapped around these life funds, once again life assurance is added and it becomes a regular premium, qualifying term life assurance.

The crucial point is the tax treatment. In the hands of the policy holder the proceeds of a qualifying life assurance policy are free of all UK taxes, both at maturity and on death. It is clear that this is a more favourable treatment than that of the investment bond but, since life funds are used again, they will have been already taxed as described earlier. The premiums for these policies will, of course, include the cost of the life assurance which will increase with age.

For a policy to be qualifying,

- premium paying period is 10 years or more
- the premiums payable in any one year do not exceed more than twice the premium payable in any other year or $\frac{1}{8}$th of the premiums payable over 10 years
- the sum assured payable on death must not be less than 75 per cent of the premiums payable during the term of the policy.

These rules dictate the level of life assurance in the savings policy which will be set at the minimum possible to comply with the rules, since it is primarily meant as an investment vehicle.

In the case of early encashment there will still be no liability to tax if premiums have been paid for at least 75 per cent of the term or 10 years, whichever is less.

If the policy becomes non-qualifying because of early encashment then the proceeds are treated for tax purposes in the same way as investment bonds.

Before 25 February 1988 these policies had an even greater advantage since after the 10 year term they could be maintained by paying an annual premium as low as £1 and an income could be taken from them totally free of tax in the policy holder's hands. This was an enormous advantage for the higher rate tax payer. However, it was an advantage challenged by the Inland Revenue, and withdrawn from qualifying policies from 25 February 1988 on. Currently, after a policy has been running for 10 years, as long as the reduction in premium has not been as drastic as that just mentioned, the income withdrawal benefit can still be obtained. Most such policies now work on a 50 per cent reduction. The maximum investment plan, since it is a qualifying life assurance policy, will have all the automatic and optional benefits associated with other life assurance policies. These are described fully in Chapter 3.

Charges for these maximum investment policies will usually include those for the life funds plus a monthly administration charge of £2 to £3. There will also be a charge to cover the cost of the small amount of life assurance. Switches between funds will be possible and these will usually carry a fixed charge for each switch of £25 or so.

The life assurance aspect will be reducing term (see Chapter 3) and designed in such a way that, while the investment is growing, its value plus that of the life assurance would equal the guaranteed sum assured. Once the investment value overtakes this the life assurance will drop away.

These policies are usually available for anyone aged three months or more, but under twelve years of age most insurance companies will want to involve a trust situation. This aspect will be dealt with in Chapter 7. From 12 years on it is usually possible to have the policy in one's own right. It could therefore form part of valuable long-term saving.

Life assurance policies will always have a sum assured which would pay out on death whether the policy were qualifying or not. However, the tax advantages of the investment aspect of such policies will be at a maximum when the policy is qualifying. Life assurance policies will range from those with no investment aspect whatsoever, the term policy, to those with a great deal, the maximum investment policy.

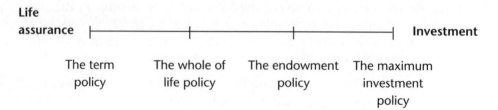

For details of other life assurance policies see Chapter 3.

Friendly Society savings plan

The Friendly Society savings plans have the same tax advantages as the PEP in that all income and capital gains inside the fund are totally free of all UK taxes. There is a limit on what can be invested which is currently in the fiscal year 1997/98 £270 per annum. Savings plans are only 10 year term and can be unit linked or with profits. They are available to people of 18 years or older. Clearly these could also be used as repayment vehicles for a mortgage at least in part.

STUDENT LOANS

Student loans are available for those in higher education leading to qualification such as a first degree or its equivalent, or for those attending any other higher education course for which a mandatory award or its equivalent is available.

The maximum loans available in the attendance year 1997/98 are contained in Table 1.3.

Table 1.3 Maximum student loans, 1997/98

	Full year	Final year
Students living away from their parents' home and studying:		
In London	£2085	£1520
Elsewhere	£1685	£1230
Students living at their parents' home	£1290	£945

It is necessary to meet the requirements for residence and to have started the course before reaching the age of 50.

In granting a loan the following will be ignored:

■ the amount of grant or award already obtained or any other income
■ any earlier loan which may have been allowed
■ income of parents, husband or wife, partner or other relatives
■ financial record.

Loans can be paid in up to three instalments. Repayments of the loan start in the April after the course is finished or left. It is normally paid back over five years, but for a student borrowing over five years it is paid back over seven.

What is paid back is the real value of the loan, in other words the original loan is adjusted for inflation. This will mean there is a notional interest included in the monthly payments which is adjusted each year.

Various factors are involved in repayment or cancellation of the loan:

■ In the event of death the loan is cancelled.
■ Repayments may be delayed if gross income is below 85 per cent of the national average earnings.
■ If a loan has not been repaid within 25 years and payments are not behind any remaining amount is cancelled. The same will be true at age 50 if earlier.
■ If the last loan was taken at age 40 or over then cancellation could occur at age 60.

SUMMARY

In this age we have worked through the following:

1 The importance of saving 5 to 10 per cent of money received.

2 Four investment considerations.

3 Asset-backed investment increases in value both by capital growth and income.

4 Keeping a budget gives control of personal financial future.

5 A wide range of investments.

You have now achieved financial health in the age of birth and education and started your lifetime financial plan.

References

1. D.W. Adams (1996) *Investment and Savings Handbook*, ed. David Ballance, Pitman Publishing: London.

CHAPTER 2

THE AGE OF
WORK

Birth and education	Work	Marriage	Parenthood	Career development	Retirement	Old age

FINANCIAL PLANNING AT A GLANCE – THE AGE OF WORK

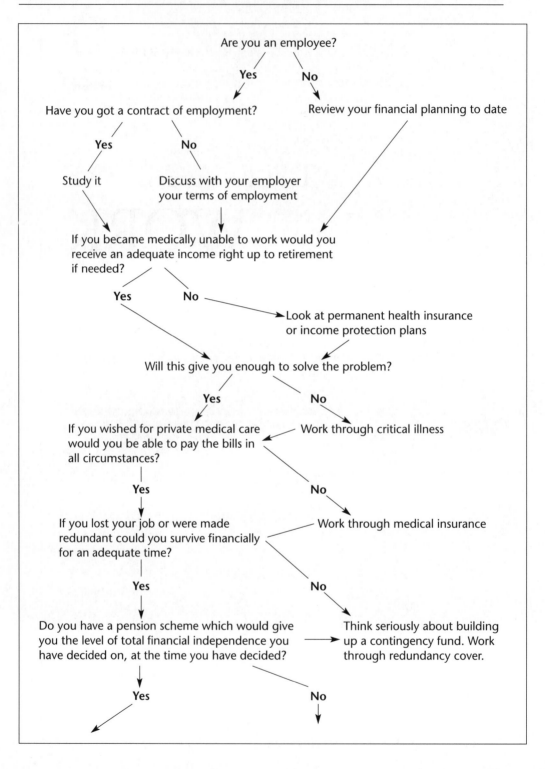

Are you an employee?

Yes → Have you got a contract of employment?

No → Review your financial planning to date

Have you got a contract of employment?

Yes → Study it

No → Discuss with your employer your terms of employment

If you became medically unable to work would you receive an adequate income right up to retirement if needed?

Yes

No → Look at permanent health insurance or income protection plans

Will this give you enough to solve the problem?

Yes → If you wished for private medical care would you be able to pay the bills in all circumstances?

No → Work through critical illness

If you wished for private medical care would you be able to pay the bills in all circumstances?

Yes

No → Work through medical insurance

If you lost your job or were made redundant could you survive financially for an adequate time?

Yes

No → Think seriously about building up a contingency fund. Work through redundancy cover.

Do you have a pension scheme which would give you the level of total financial independence you have decided on, at the time you have decided?

Yes

No

FINANCIAL PLANNING AT A GLANCE (continued)

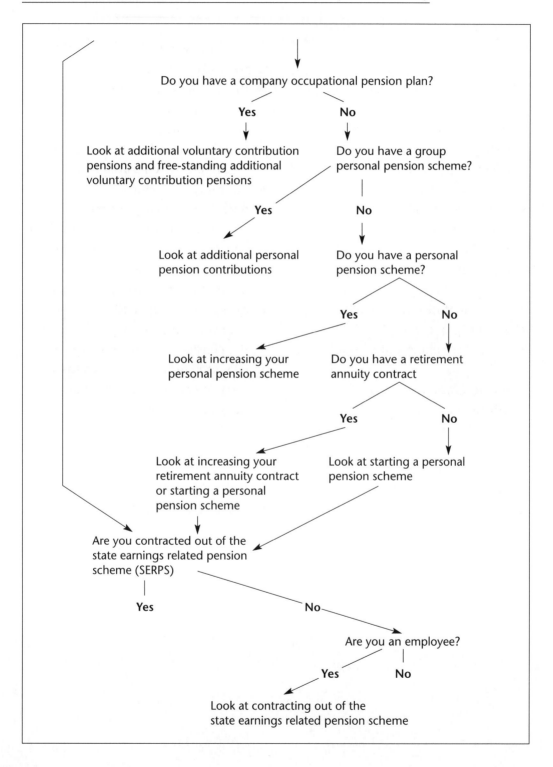

CONTENTS

In this age the following is discussed:

- three core questions
- contract of employment
- what happens if I become medically unable to work?
- state benefits:
  - statutory sick pay
  - incapacity benefit
  - additional payments
- policies available
- loss of job or redundancy
- what happens if I live too long?
- inflation
- the Rule of 70
- permanent health insurance (PHI)
- income protection plan (IPP)
- accident sickness and unemployment (ASU) policy
- medical insurance
- critical illness policy
- critical illness policy including life cover
- state pension benefits
- pensions in general
- the company pension scheme
- the defined benefit scheme (DBS) or final salary pension scheme
- the money purchase scheme (MPS)
- the with-profits scheme
- the unit-linked scheme
- additional voluntary contribution pension scheme
- free-standing additional voluntary contribution pension scheme
- typical types of annuity
- retirement annuity contracts (RAC) and personal pension schemes (PPS)
- benefits in kind or P11D benefits
- what happens to your pension fund if you die before maturity?
- medical disability and waiver of contribution (WOC)
- the pension guarantee policy
- GPs and dentists – special situation
- carry forward of unused relief
- carry back provisions
- the self-invested personal pension (SIPP)
- the deferred annuity purchase
- income withdrawal facility
- contracting out of SERPS

INTRODUCTION

In this age, you have left full-time education and started your working career. You have entered the age of work. You may have done this very recently or some years ago. Unlike the previous age when you had to depend on others partially or totally for financial support you are now financially independent. Now your financial life truly begins. Just as you may have mapped out a plan for your future career now is the time to seriously plan your financial life.

THE CORE QUESTIONS

There are three questions which are at the core of financial planning, three questions which have to be continually asked, and which occur in every age of life.

- What happens if I become medically unable to work before financial independence has been achieved?
- What happens if I die too soon, before financial independence has been achieved, leaving dependants unprovided for?
- What happens if I live too long – when work days are over, there is no earned income and financial independence has not been achieved?

Three questions run throughout financial life: What happens if I become medically unable to work? What happens if I die too soon? What happens if I live too long?

If these questions are answered satisfactorily in all the ages of life then there will be financial health.

The only satisfactory answer to all three questions is, 'I and my dependants will be totally financially independent and will be able to deal with whatever financial contingencies might arise.'

Even before attempting to answer these core questions it is necessary to know in detail one's exact financial situation and the place to start is with the job. What is the salary, annual holiday entitlement, basic hours, notice necessary on both sides, bonus situation, prospects, company pension, car, medical insurance? How long would salary continue in the event of medical inability to work?

A contract of employment should answer all these questions. If there is no contract, then initiate a discussion with the employer. In the case of the self-employed the basic questions can be answered from the accounts, the rest are a matter of personal decision and affordability.

You may wish at this point to study your contract of employment.

Now we are ready to start on the first core question.

WHAT HAPPENS IF I BECOME MEDICALLY UNABLE TO WORK?

What happens if I become medically unable to work, perhaps for a very long time, perhaps permanently?

One in sixteen working people will be off work at any one time.

Over 1.65 million people of working age will be off work at any one time through sickness or disability and will have been off work for at least six months.[1] The total working population is 26,147,000.[2] This means that at least 6.3 per cent, i.e. approximately one in sixteen working people will be off work at any one time.

Imagine visiting a car manufacturing factory and glancing down the assembly line, seeing that every 16th working space is empty, or visiting a large office and finding every 16th desk empty.

Twenty per cent of all people who consulted their GP were diagnosed as having a long-standing illness, i.e. one which limits the patient's activities in any way.[3]

While work continues, income continues. It pays for all necessary financial requirements. It produces financial independence which can only be maintained while work continues. If work stops, money stops and this could be a disaster.

When applying for a job the whole package should be studied, not just the salary.

Hopefully the previous exercise has been completed and the exact financial situation is known if medical inability to work occurred. In some cases a company may offer support right up to retirement age, even continuing with pension contributions, but these situations are rare and this is one reason why, when applying for a new job, the whole package should be carefully studied.

What would the state provide?

State benefits

These benefits are payable to people under state pension age, currently men aged 65 and women aged 60, who have made sufficient national insurance contributions.

If you are single your long-term state incapacity benefit is £3247.40 per annum.

We can see that annual state long-term benefit for a single person is £3247.40. In Chapter 1, the student's annual outgoings were £6864.

The benefit is increased only to £6286.80 per annum with a spouse and two children to support (see Fig. 2.1).

Table 2.1 State benefits

State benefits	Payment per annum	Payment terms
Statutory sick pay Only for employees earning £3224.00 p.a. or more	£2896.00	Payable for up to 28 weeks
Incapacity benefit Short-term lower rate	£2449.20	Payable from 4th day to 28th week of incapacity. Taxable
Short-term higher rate	£2896.40	Payable from 28th wek to 52nd week of incapacity. Taxable
Long-term rate	£3247.40	Payable from 52nd week of incapacity. Taxable

Table 2.2 Additional state payments

Additional payments	Payment per annum	Payment terms
Adult dependant allowance First 52 weeks	£1515.80	Taxable. Not payable if a dependant earns more than £1515.80 p.a.
53rd week on	£1942.20	Not payable if a dependant earns more than £1942.20 p.a.
Child dependant allowance		Payable from 29th week. Taxable.
First child	£514.80	Not payable if dependant earns more than £7020.00 p.a.
Each subsequent child	£582.40	Allowable earnings increase by £884 p.a. for each child
Age allowance Under 35	£683.80	Related to age at the start of incapacity. Taxable. Payable from 53rd week
35 to 44	£343.20	
44 and over	nil	

Policies available to solve the problem

These policies provide an income in the event of medical inability to work and are called permanent health insurance or income protection policies. They will start to pay out after a period of time has elapsed since the onset of the situation and continue to do so until return to work or termination age.

Accident and sickness policies which provide an income over a short period are another possibility.

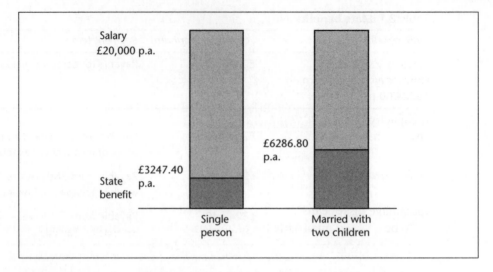

Fig. 2.1 State benefit for someone on a salary of £20,000 p.a. who becomes medically unable to work

Some people suffering a serious illness may prefer private medical treatment rather than that provided by the National Health Service. There are arguments for and against. Details of medical insurance which would provide private medical treatment are discussed later in this chapter.

There are also policies which pay out a tax-free lump sum on diagnosis of one of a number of critical illnesses such as stroke, cancer or heart attack. Medical science has progressed so far that death is no longer an inevitable consequence of these illnesses but very often one's earning power is seriously impaired. These policies are treated in detail later in the chapter.

One in three people develops cancer at some time in his or her life. One in four dies of it. Approximately one in fourteen men develops cancer before the age of 60, and one in eleven women.[4]

LOSS OF JOB OR REDUNDANCY

The work situation has changed vastly over the last twenty years. There is no longer the job security that once existed. Many feel that jobs are easily lost or redundancy occurs. We discussed in Chapter 1 the habit of saving money and it was suggested that 5 to 10 per cent of net income could be something to aim for; the building up of a contingency fund, say equal to three to six months of net salary, of easily accessible money, possibly in a deposit account. Then in the event of unemployment there is the knowledge of certain financial security, at least for a number of months.

In addition to this, unemployment benefit, which was replaced by job seeker's allowance (JSA) in October 1996, may be available. To qualify enough national insurance contributions must have been paid. The benefit for those aged 18 to 24 years is £2022.80 per annum, and for those aged 25 years and over is £2555.80. This will be paid for up to 182 days.

What about redundancy? The current situation results from the Employment Protection (Consolidation) Act 1978. If the reason for dismissal from work is redundancy there is an entitlement to a redundancy payment. Such dismissals would be caused by the employer's need to reduce his or her workforce. This might arise because a workplace is closing down or fewer employees of a particular kind are, or are expected to be, needed. In other words the employee's work must have disappeared.

To be deemed qualifying for redundancy three conditions must be satisfied:

1 At least two years' continuous service with the employer must have been completed.
2 Age must be 20 years or more, since service before the age of 18 does not count for redundancy purposes.
3 The applicant must be an employee.

You may not be entitled to a payment if new work is offered with the same employer, or an associated employer, or a successive employer who takes over the business. The new work must be offered before the old work contract expires, and should start within four weeks. A final decision to accept or reject the offer of new work need not be made until the end of a four week trial period in the new job. If the new work is then rejected because it is not a suitable alternative judged on good personal reasons, you will be considered to be redundant. If a suitable offer of alternative employment is unreasonably refused no redundancy payment will be due.

The redundancy payment is calculated by multiplying one week's gross pay by the total number of years worked, and then multipying by factors according to age:

■ For every year worked while the employee is aged 41 or over the factor is $1\frac{1}{2}$.
■ For every year worked while the employee is aged 22 to 40 the factor is 1.
■ For every year worked while the employee is aged 18 to 21 the factor is $\frac{1}{2}$.

Years before 18 do not count. The statutory maximum of years worked which can qualify is 20. There is a statutory maximum for the one week's gross pay which is reviewed each year and has not changed (tax year 1997/98) since it was set at £210 with effect from 27 September 1995. An employee's 'one week's gross pay' is the amount payable for a week's work under the contract of employment in force on the calculation date. The calculation date is the date on which the minimum notice of redundancy required by statute was given, usually one week for every year worked up to a maximum of twelve years.

Table 2.3 Ready reckoner for redundancy payments

Service (years)

Age (years)	2	3	4	5	6	7	8	9	10	11	12	13	14	15	16	17	18	19	20
20	1	1	1	1	—														
21	1	1½	1½	1½	1½	—													
22	1	1½	2	2	2	2	—												
23	1½	2	2½	3	3	3	3	—											
24	2	2½	3	3½	4	4	4	4	—										
25	2	3	3½	4	4½	5	5	5	5	—									
26	2	3	4	4½	5	5½	6	6	6	6	—								
27	2	3	4	5	5½	6	6½	7	7	7	7	—							
28	2	3	4	5	6	6½	7	7½	8	8	8	8	—						
29	2	3	4	5	6	7	7½	8	8½	9	9	9	9	—					
30	2	3	4	5	6	7	8	8½	9	9½	10	10	10	10	—				
31	2	3	4	5	6	7	8	9	9½	10	10½	11	11	11	11	—			
32	2	3	4	5	6	7	8	9	10	10½	11	11½	12	12	12	12	—		
33	2	3	4	5	6	7	8	9	10	11	11½	12	12½	13	13	13	13	—	
34	2	3	4	5	6	7	8	9	10	11	12	12½	13	13½	14	14	14	14	—
35	2	3	4	5	6	7	8	9	10	11	12	13	13½	14	14½	15	15	15	15
36	2	3	4	5	6	7	8	9	10	11	12	13	14	14½	15	15½	16	16	16
37	2	3	4	5	6	7	8	9	10	11	12	13	14	15	15½	16	16½	17	17
38	2	3	4	5	6	7	8	9	10	11	12	13	14	15	16	16½	17	17½	18
39	2	3	4	5	6	7	8	9	10	11	12	13	14	15	16	17	17½	18	18½
40	2	3	4	5	6	7	8	9	10	11	12	13	14	15	16	17	18	18½	19
41	2	3	4	5	6	7	8	9	10	11	12	13	14	15	16	17	18	19	19½
42	2½	3½	4½	5½	6½	7½	8½	9½	10½	11½	12½	13½	14½	15½	16½	17½	18½	19½	20½
43	3	4	5	6	7	8	9	10	11	12	13	14	15	16	17	18	19	20	21
44	3	4½	5½	6½	7½	8½	9½	10½	11½	12½	13½	14½	15½	16½	17½	18½	19½	20½	21½
45	3	4½	6	7	8	9	10	11	12	13	14	15	16	17	18	19	20	21	22
46	3	4½	6	7½	8½	9½	10½	11½	12½	13½	14½	15½	16½	17½	18½	19½	20½	21½	22½
47	3	4½	6	7½	9	10	11	12	13	14	15	16	17	18	19	20	21	22	23
48	3	4½	6	7½	9	10½	11½	12½	13½	14½	15½	16½	17½	18½	19½	20½	21½	22½	23½
49	3	4½	6	7½	9	10½	12	13	14	15	16	17	18	19	20	21	22	23	24
50	3	4½	6	7½	9	10½	12	13½	14½	15½	16½	17½	18½	19½	20½	21½	22½	23½	24½
51	3	4½	6	7½	9	10½	12	13½	15	16	17	18	19	20	21	22	23	24	25
52	3	4½	6	7½	9	10½	12	13½	15	16½	17½	18½	19½	20½	21½	22½	23½	24½	25½
53	3	4½	6	7½	9	10½	12	13½	15	16½	18	19	20	21	22	23	24	25	26
54	3	4½	6	7½	9	10½	12	13½	15	16½	18	19½	20½	21½	22½	23½	24½	25½	26½
55	3	4½	6	7½	9	10½	12	13½	15	16½	18	19½	21	22	23	24	25	26	27
56	3	4½	6	7½	9	10½	12	13½	15	16½	18	19½	21	22½	23½	24½	25½	26½	27½
57	3	4½	6	7½	9	10½	12	13½	15	16½	18	19½	21	22½	24	25	26	27	28
58	3	4½	6	7½	9	10½	12	13½	15	16½	18	19½	21	22½	24	25½	26½	27½	28½
59	3	4½	6	7½	9	10½	12	13½	15	16½	18	19½	21	22½	24	25½	27	28	29
60	3	4½	6	7½	9	10½	12	13½	15	16½	18	19½	21	22½	24	25½	27	28½	29½
61	3	4½	6	7½	9	10½	12	13½	15	16½	18	19½	21	22½	24	25½	27	28½	30
62	3	4½	6	7½	9	10½	12	13½	15	16½	18	19½	21	22½	24	25½	27	28½	30
63	3	4½	6	7½	9	10½	12	13½	15	16½	18	19½	21	22½	24	25½	27	28½	30
64	3	4½	6	7½	9	10½	12	13½	15	16½	18	19½	21	22½	24	25½	27	28½	30

∎ Example 2.1

John Lord has worked for Bookforce Ltd since his 36th birthday, 11 years ago. He received notice of redundancy today. Under his contract of employment he is earning £200 per week, and his work will terminate 11 weeks from now.

Years worked while 41 or more = 6; years worked while his age was 22 to 40 = 5. His redundancy payment will be,

$$(6 \times 1\frac{1}{2} + 5 \times 1) \times £200 = 14 \times £200 = £2800$$

∎ Example 2.2

Grace Wentworth has worked for her company since she was 16. She is now 45 and has been given notice of redundancy. Under her contract of employment her annual salary is £17,000.

Her work will terminate in 12 weeks' time (maximum number of weeks notice).

Years worked while 41 or more = 4; years worked while her age was 22 to 40 = 19. However, maximum number of years which can be counted is 20, so we can only count 16 in this section.

One week's gross pay = £326.92, however the maximum amount which can be counted is £210. Hence redundancy payment will be,

$$(4 \times 1\frac{1}{2} + 16 \times 1) \times £210 = 22 \times £210 = £4620$$

∎ Exercise 2.1

Peter Street has worked for Petersfield Mints Ltd for 16 years since he was 38. He is earning £21,000 p.a. He has received notice of redundancy today. What statutory minimum notice must he receive? What is his redundancy payment? Use the ready reckoner in Table 2.3.

Read off the employee's age and number of complete years' service. The table then shows how many weeks' pay the employee is entitled to.

Policies are available which offer protection from the contingency of unemployment. These do not usually pay out over a long period but offer support for a while. There are more details on these policies later in the chapter.

When you have worked through the detail relating to the discussion so far you will be in a position to answer the first core question satisfactorily and that part of your lifetime financial plan will have been completed.

WHAT HAPPENS IF I DIE TOO SOON?

The second question applies only to those with dependants and will be dealt with in Chapter 3 and Chapter 4.

WHAT HAPPENS IF I LIVE TOO LONG?

Now we come to the third question, 'What happens if I live too long?'

There comes a time in life when it is extremely important to know that there is no longer a necessity to earn a living; there is enough money whether one works or not; there is choice. A time when one knows that one's choice of lifestyle and that of dependants is completely free of the necessity to work. This is total financial independence, a cherished state.

> There comes a time when it is extremely important to be totally financially independent whether you work or not.

This does not necessarily mean retirement, although retirement is eminently possible if desired. When this is achieved protection policies are no longer needed, not permanent health insurance, not critical illness cover, not life assurance. Total and utter financial independence has been reached. Few people achieve it and if it is to be achieved an early start is crucial, an early start along the right lines because thinking is clear. It is not enough to say, 'I have a company pension, I'm fine!'

If you work through this section on pensions, do the calculations and apply them to your own situation you will be able to answer this question satisfactorily. You will have total financial independence at the time that you decide you want it.

For financial health in this respect subsidiary questions have to be answered:

- When do I want to be totally financially independent? At 55, at 60 or when?
- Thinking in today's terms, what is total financial independence for me?
- How much income does this represent?

Inflation

Let us say you want to be financially independent in 32 years' time and total financial independence for you in today's terms is £20,000 per annum. However, inflation is with us and likely to stay, and therefore in 32 years' time £20,000 per annum will buy only a fraction of what it would buy today. Your figure has, therefore, to be adjusted for inflation and here we will have to make an assumption of what inflation will average over the long term and each person will have his or her own view of this. Let us say the figure is 4 per cent per annum then in 32 years' time, the cost of living will be 3½ times more than it is today, or your £20,000 will buy 3½ times less than it will buy today. Therefore in 32 years' time financial independence for you will have to be £70,000 per annum.

The Rule of 70

The Rule of 70 provides an approximate answer for the effect of inflation on the cost of living. Simply take the average inflation, divide it into 70 and the result gives the number of years for costs to double, thus if the estimate is inflation of

---

The Rule of 70 will calculate approximately the effects of inflation.

---

4 per cent then 70 divided by 4 gives 17½ meaning that costs will double in 17½ years, and therefore quadruple in 35 years, which agrees with the more accurately calculated figure just quoted. Costs would double again in 17½ years and therefore costs will be eight times greater after a period of 52½ years.

■ **Exercise 2.2**

If inflation is 7% p.a. how many years would it take for costs to have multiplied by 8?

By asking these two subsidiary questions seriously, and getting accurate answers as early in a career as possible, there is more chance of successfully achieving total financial independence at the desired age. What do you do next? You have seen earlier where you are financially, and you will know what pension provision you have, if any. If you are provided with a company pension scheme then it would be important to study it carefully. See what you would receive at your chosen age for financial independence. See how it relates to your figure for what financial independence is for you and you will know whether you have a shortfall or not. If you have a shortfall the answer is to make some additional provision.

If you already have a company pension scheme then the way to supplement it will be through additional voluntary contribution schemes run by your company or free-standing additional voluntary contribution schemes run by life assurance companies. The company scheme may not be designated occupational. It may be what is known as a group personal pension scheme and in this case it is possible to make additional personal contributions directly to the scheme.

In the case of the self-employed it could be a case of simply increasing what is already there.

If no provision whatsoever is being made then it is a case for the personal pension scheme.

In the section on pensions you will find tables and examples to help you achieve your plan for financial independence. If you work through these and apply them to your situation you will have financial health in this age.

What about the state? This must play a part in the calculations. Currently an employed person paying national insurance contributions can expect to receive the basic state pension, and, in addition, the state earnings related pension (SERPS). The self-employed paying national insurance contributions can expect to receive the basic state pension but nothing more. They are not eligible for SERPS.

All these pension schemes are treated in detail later in the chapter.

DETAILED INFORMATION AND ANALYSIS

PERMANENT HEALTH INSURANCE (PHI) OR INCOME PROTECTION PLAN (IPP)

A permanent health insurance or income protection plan provides an income in the event of medical inability to work. It will be a proportion of the income before becoming ill. Most insurance companies will look back over the twelve previous months and will require documentary evidence of income. If there have been any serious short-term fluctuations they will usually look back a further two years and take a view on the true level of benefit. The objective will be to give the right level of benefit for a bona fide claim.

> A permanent health insurance policy pays an income in the event of becoming medically unable to work.

Only a proportion of total income is insurable, thus retaining the motivation to return to work. Up until 1996 this was usually 75 per cent of income less the state long-term benefit. After a short tax holiday, the payments were taxed.

The Budget of November 1995 announced that from 6 April 1996 the benefit from personal policies would be free of all taxes. This inevitably increased its value since it would now represent a much higher proportion of after taxed income. Insurance companies reacted to this by redrafting the formulae by which they calculated benefits for all future policies as they felt otherwise the benefit would be too high.

A typical formula for calculating this proportion would now be 65 per cent of gross income minus the state long-term incapacity benefit, which, in the fiscal year 1997/98 was £3247.40, up to say a maximum benefit of £60,000. Other companies may not have this sort of cap but work on a basis of 65 per cent of gross income up to £45,000 and thereafter 1/3rd of all further gross income minus the state long-term incapacity benefit. However there is usually an overall cap imposed by the reinsurers who take on some of the risk for larger policies and this would be around the benefit level of £100,000, although it is sometimes possible to get special dispensations for higher levels.

Company permanent health schemes pay the benefit to the company, which is then paid out to the employee in salary and this is taxable. Sometimes part of the benefit is used for pension contributions and because of this it is possible to insure higher proportions of salary.

■ Example 2.3

John Jones is on an annual income of £30,000. Since this is below £45,000, calculations on either method will give,

> 65% of £30,000 = £19,500 p.a.
> Maximum benefit = £19,500 − £3,247.40 p.a. = £16,252.60 p.a.

■ Example 2.4

Peter Street is earning £261,000 p.a.

Using formula one:

> 65% of £261,000 = £169,650 p.a.
> Potential maximum benefit = £169,650 – £3247.40 p.a. = £166,402.60 p.a.
> However, there is a cap of £60,000 p.a., hence maximum benefit is £60,000.

Using formula two:

> 65% of £45,000 = £29,250 p.a.
> ⅓rd of (£261,000 – £45,000) = ⅓rd of £216,000 = £72,000 p.a.

> Hence potential maximum benefit = (£29,250 + £72,000) – £3247.40
> $$= £101,250 – £3247.40$$
> $$= £98,002.60 \text{ p.a.}$$

Since there is no cap on benefit this time

> maximum benefit = £98,002.60 p.a. tax free

It is possible to index this benefit and some companies will use the Retail Price Index (RPI), others will use the Average Earnings Index (AEI), yet others will use a formula which is indexed at say 4 per cent per annum or in line with the RPI, whichever is the lower. Termination age for the policy would be chosen at outset and would usually be anywhere from age 50 to 65. There would also be a deferment period during which no payment would be made, usually one month after first becoming medically unable to work, three months, six months or twelve months. Obviously the longer the deferment period the less expensive the cover.

The new legislation making the benefit tax free has given a considerable boost to the real value of what might be received, especially for those people who had these plans prior to the change who will have a benefit calculated on a more generous formula, e.g. 75 instead of 65 per cent of gross income. If your company provides a scheme for you the benefit would not in this case, in general, be paid tax free but would be taxed.

Another factor which has operated throughout the 1990s is an escalation in claims costing the insurance companies enormous amounts of money. As a result of this there has been a general trend to increase premiums. In particular, claims have increased in the areas of stress and musculo-skeletal problems. As well as a rise in premiums, underwriting has become more strict because of this so that if for example there is an existing back problem this would usually be excluded from the cover.

The number of permanent health claims in the areas of stress and musculo-skeletal problems have increased.

The following tables will give some idea of the sort of premiums payable for this protection. There is usually a gradation of cost depending on the statistical likelihood of someone in a particular profession becoming medically unable to work. Thus in general an office worker would pay less than a builder. Table 2.4 shows typical premiums payable by the 'safer' professions.

Table 2.4 Typical premiums for permanent health insurance (PHI) or income protection plan (IPP)

Men: Fully indexed in line with the Average Earnings Index, to age 60 with a deferment period of 6 months

Benefit										
£	10,000	20,000	30,000	40,000	50,000	60,000	70,000	80,000	90,000	100,000
Age										
20	9.08	15.18	21.28	27.38	33.48	39.58	45.68	51.78	57.88	63.98
25	9.48	15.98	22.48	28.98	35.48	41.98	48.48	54.98	61.48	67.98
30	11.08	19.18	27.28	35.38	43.48	51.58	59.68	67.78	75.88	83.98
35	13.50	24.18	34.78	45.38	55.98	66.58	77.18	87.78	98.38	108.98
40	18.38	33.78	49.18	64.58	79.98	95.38	110.78	126.18	141.58	156.98
45	24.08	45.18	66.28	87.38	108.48	129.58	150.68	171.78	192.88	213.98
50	28.38	53.78	79.18	104.58	129.98	155.38	180.78	206.18	231.58	256.98

Men: Fully indexed in line with the Average Earnings Index, to age 60 with a deferment period of 3 months

Benefit										
£	10,000	20,000	30,000	40,000	50,000	60,000	70,000	80,000	90,000	100,000
Age										
20	13.08	23.18	33.28	43.38	53.48	63.58	73.68	83.78	93.88	103.98
25	13.68	24.38	35.08	45.78	56.48	67.18	77.88	88.58	99.28	109.98
30	18.58	34.18	49.78	65.38	80.98	96.58	112.18	127.78	143.38	158.98
35	24.38	45.78	67.18	88.58	109.98	131.38	152.78	174.18	195.58	216.98
40	32.38	61.78	91.18	120.58	149.98	179.38	208.78	238.18	267.58	296.98
45	41.38	79.78	118.18	156.58	194.98	233.38	271.78	310.18	348.58	386.98
50	48.18	93.38	138.58	183.78	228.98	274.18	319.38	364.58	409.78	454.98

Women: Fully indexed in line with the Average Earnings Index, to age 60 with a deferment period of 6 months

Benefit										
£	10,000	20,000	30,000	40,000	50,000	60,000	70,000	80,000	90,000	100,000
Age										
20	16.98	30.98	44.98	58.98	72.98	86.98	100.98	114.98	128.98	142.98
25	17.78	32.58	47.38	62.18	76.98	91.78	106.58	121.38	136.18	150.98
30	22.28	41.58	60.88	80.18	99.48	118.78	138.08	157.38	176.68	195.98
35	28.48	53.98	79.48	104.98	130.48	155.98	181.48	206.98	232.48	257.98
40	37.28	71.58	105.88	140.18	174.48	208.78	243.08	277.38	311.68	345.98
45	46.38	89.78	133.18	176.58	219.98	263.38	306.78	350.18	393.58	436.98
50	48.88	94.78	140.68	186.58	232.48	278.38	324.28	370.18	416.08	461.98

Table 2.4 (continued)

Women: Fully indexed in line with the Average Earnings Index, to age 60 with a deferment period of 3 months

Benefit

£	10,000	20,000	30,000	40,000	50,000	60,000	70,000	80,000	90,000	100,000
Age										
20	22.08	41.18	60.28	79.38	98.48	117.58	136.68	155.78	174.88	193.98
25	24.48	45.98	67.48	88.98	110.48	131.98	153.48	174.98	196.48	217.98
30	34.48	65.98	97.48	128.98	160.48	191.98	223.48	254.98	286.48	317.98
35	49.58	96.18	142.78	189.38	235.98	282.58	329.18	375.78	422.38	468.98
40	61.88	120.78	179.68	238.58	297.48	356.38	415.28	474.18	533.08	591.98
45	72.58	142.18	211.78	281.38	350.98	420.58	490.18	559.78	629.38	698.98
50	72.58	142.18	211.78	281.38	350.98	420.58	490.18	559.78	629.38	698.98

To get an accurate picture of the real value of this benefit it is useful to calculate its proportion to the income it is based on net of tax (see Table 2.5) and national insurance contributions (NIC) (see Table 2.6).

Table 2.5 Tax rates and allowances (fiscal year 1997/98)

Income tax rates

£0 – £4100	20%
£4101 – £26,100	23%
Over £26,100	40%
Personal allowance (basic)	£4045
Personal allowance (age 65–74)	£5220
Personal allowance (age 75 and over)	£5400

Allowances restricted to 15%

Married couple's allowance (basic)	£1830
Married couple's allowance (age 65–74) (only has to apply to one spouse)	£3185
Married couple's allowance (age 75 and over) (only has to apply to one spouse)	£3225

Notes
1. The higher personal allowance for those over 65 is only applicable, in total, to incomes of £15,600 p.a. or below. Any income over this reduces the 'age allowance' by an amount equal to 50% of the excess. Thus someone in receipt of income, for example, of £16,100 is £500 over and hence the allowance of, say, £5220, would be reduced by (½ × 500 = £250) to £4970.
2. A husband whose legally married wife is living with him can claim the married couple's allowance. A wife can claim 50% of it. Husband and wife together can elect for the whole allowance to apply to wife's income. If neither has income to use his or her share of it the unused part can be transferred to the other.
3. Only husband's income affects the age-related married couple's allowance and once he has lost the additional age-related personal allowance with an income of £17,950 p.a. any income above this affects the married couple's allowance in the same way.

Consider £100 of income above £15,600: this would be liable to £23 tax. However, it would result in £50 being removed from the allowance and that paying tax of £11.50. Hence the total tax on that £100 is £34.50, which is a tax rate of 34.5 per cent. Hence for those 65–74 years old, for example, any income over £15,600 up to £17,950 per annum is being taxed at 34.5 per cent. After that it will revert to basic rate of 23 per cent until it goes into higher rate at £30,145 per annum. Any loss of married couple's allowance results only in removing relief of 15 per cent on it.

Table 2.6 National insurance contributions (NIC) (fiscal year 1997/98)

Class 1 (Employees)

Weekly earnings (£)	Employee	Contracted in rates Employer	Annual earnings (£)
0–62	nil	nil	0–3224
62–110	2% of £62	3%	3224–5720
110–155	plus	5%	5720–8060
155–210	10% of	7%	8060–10,920
210–465	£62–£465	10%	10,920–24,180
465+	—	10%	24,180+

	Weekly	Monthly	Annual	
Lower earnings limit (LEL):	£62.00	£268.66	£3224.00	(below which no NIC is paid)
Upper earnings limit (UEL):	£465.00	£2015.00	£24,180.00	(above which no NIC is paid by employee)

Class 2 (self-employed)	flat rate:	£6.15 per week
	where earnings are over	£3480 per annum
Class 4 (self-employed)	on profits £7010–£24,180	6%

■ Example 2.5

Jane Smith, personnel officer, is 29. Her annual income is £20,105. She could be insured, with a personal PHI policy, to receive a tax-free benefit of £9821 p.a. totally indexed to age 60, deferment period six months, premium £21.13 per month. She would also receive £3247.40 p.a. (taxable) long-term state benefit. Since her personal allowance is £4045 however, she will pay no tax on this.
So total benefit is £13,866 p.a.

The nearest age we can get on Table 2.4 is 30, so using this age to get an approximate cost for her premium we see that £10,000 p.a. benefit would cost £22.28 per month. Hence £9821 p.a. benefit would cost,

$$\frac{9821}{10,000} \times 22.28 = £21.88 \text{ per month}$$

As there are typical costs in Table 2.4 this figure is close enough to get a good approximation to the sort of cost involved.

It would be interesting to see what proportion the total benefit is of her present income net of taxes and NIC contribution. This is worked out in Form 2.1.

■ Form 2.1 INCOME TAX AND NIC ANALYSIS

INCOME TAX			
Name Jane Smith	*Year*	1997/98	
	£	*Remaining income £*	*Tax £*
Gross income	20,105		
Gross contribution to pension paid personally*			
Personal allowance	4045	16,060	None
Income taxed at 20%	4100	11,960	820.00
Income taxed at basic rate 23%	11,960	None	2750.80
Income taxed at higher rate 40%			
Total	20,105		3570.80
Less married couple's allowance			
Total tax payable			

* Some pension contributions paid personally are net of basic rate tax. For the purposes of this form this would need to be grossed up.

NATIONAL INSURANCE CONTRIBUTION (NIC) (Employed)			
	£	*Remaining income £*	*NIC £*
Gross income	20,105		
Income up to LEL £3224 p.a. NIC at 2%	3224	16,881	64.48
Income up to UEL £24,180 p.a. minus £3224 p.a., the LEL NIC at 10%	16,881	None	1688.10
Total	20,105		1752.58

NATIONAL INSURANCE CONTRIBUTION (NIC) (Self-employed)
Flat rate paid if income over £3480 p.a. £6.15 p.w.
On profits between £7010 and £24,180 p.a. 6.0%
Total
Income after tax and NIC deductions   20,105−3570.80−1752.58 = 14,781.62

To find the proportion we do a simple calculation:

$$\frac{13,866}{14,782} \times 100 = 93.80\%$$

The benefit from a personal permanent health policy is now totally tax free. This means the real value of the benefit is considerably increased.

Hence in real terms her total benefit is 93.80% of her income. Do not forget that £9821 p.a. of this is indexed in line with the National Average Earnings Index right up to age 60. Hopefully the long-term state benefit would also attract some indexation.

It seems certain that Jane would have been enormously thankful she had done her financial planning and taken out a permanent health insurance at a cost of £21.88 representing only 1.8% of her net income. This is calculated as follows,

$$\frac{21.88 \times 12}{14,782} \times 100 = 1.8\%$$

■ Example 2.6

Steve Turner is 47, he is a barrister and therefore self-employed. His before tax profit is £200,000 p.a He could have a benefit of £77,669 p.a. fully indexed covering him right up to age 60 with a deferment period of six months. He has a severe heart attack and finally his specialist tells him he can never work again. Together with the £3247.40 from the state, his total benefit would be £80,916.40 p.a. Steve is nearer to 45 than he is to 50 so in Table 2.4 we will use age 45 to get an approximate cost for his cover. £77,669 is nearest to £80,000 benefit which would cost £171.78.

Hence cost of Steve's cover is,

$$\frac{77,669}{80,000} \times 171.78 = £166.77 \text{ per month}$$

His situation is worked out in Form 2.2 on p. 55.

Hence his total benefit of £80,916.40 p.a. is 64.8% of his net income. This has cost him £166.77 per month, i.e.

$$\frac{166.77 \times 12}{124,828} \times 100\% = 1.6\% \text{ of his net income}$$

Steve may wish to supplement this benefit with critical illness cover.

Looking at the enormous amount of tax he pays he would certainly be wise to be paying pension contributions to reduce this.

■ Example 2.7

Gillian Forbes is a personnel officer with a merchant bank. She is 30. Her annual salary is £25,000. She has an excellent package which includes payment of 65% of salary in the event of her becoming medically unable to work.

She would therefore be paid £19,500 p.a.

However, this would be paid as continuing salary and therefore subject to tax and NIC payments.

■ Form 2.2 INCOME TAX AND NIC ANALYSIS

INCOME TAX

Name	Steve Turner		Year	1997/98	
		£		Remaining income £	Tax £
Gross income		200,000			
Gross contribution to pension paid personally*					
Personal allowance		4045		195,955	None
Income taxed at 20%		4100		191,855	820
Income taxed at basic rate 23%		22,000		169,855	5060
Income taxed at higher rate 40%		169,855		None	67,942
Total		200,000			73,822
Less married couple's allowance					
Total tax payable					

* Some pension contributions paid personally are net of basic rate tax. For the purposes of this form this would need to be grossed up.

NATIONAL INSURANCE CONTRIBUTION (NIC) (Employed)

	£	Remaining income £	NIC £
Gross income			
Income up to LEL £3224 p.a. NIC at 2%			
Income up to UEL £24,180 p.a. minus £3224 p.a., the LEL NIC at 10%			
Total			

NATIONAL INSURANCE CONTRIBUTION (NIC) (Self-employed)

Flat rate paid if income over £3480 p.a. £6.15 p.w.	319.80
On profits between £7010 and £24,180 p.a. 6.0% 6% × (24,180-£7010) =	1030.20
Total	1350.00
Income after tax and NIC deductions 200,000−73,822−1350 = 124,828.00	

■ **Permanent health insurance (PHI) or income protection plan (IPP)**

■ Example 2.8

Morgan Davies is 42 and works in a large department store. His income is £18,000 p.a. He makes personal contributions to his company pension scheme of £75 monthly. He could be insured with a personal PHI policy to receive a tax-free benefit of £8,452.60 p.a. totally indexed to age 60, deferment period of six months.

Morgan's age is nearest to 40 on Table 2.4 and the benefit he can have is nearest to £10,000 p.a. The figure for a benefit of £10,000 p.a. at age 40 from the table is £18.38 monthly. Hence annual benefit of £8452.60 will cost,

$$\frac{8452.60}{10,000} \times 18.38 = £15.54 \text{ per month}$$

Morgan's situation is worked out in Form 2.3 on p. 57.

If Morgan had been paying to a personal pension scheme he would have been paying net of basic rate tax £57.75. To gross this up to Table 2.4 the calculation is,

$$\text{gross pension } 57.75 \times \frac{100}{77} \text{ since basic rate tax is 23\%} = £75 \text{ per month}$$

His total annual benefit is £8452.60 + £3247.40 = £11,700

$$\frac{11,700}{12,885} \times 100\% = 90.8\% \text{ of net income}$$

$$\text{for a cost of } \frac{15.54 \times 12}{12,885} \times 100\% = 1.4\% \text{ of net income}$$

■ Exercise 2.3

Joan Tucker, 38 years old, earns £35,000 annually. She suffers a serious car accident and can never work again. Luckily she had taken out permanent health insurance at the maximum level possible, and six months' deferment.

Using Form 2.4 on p. 58 calculate:

1 The tax-free benefit from her policy.
2 Her income net of taxes and NIC before the accident.
3 Her total benefit including long-term state benefit.
4 The percentage that total benefit represents of her previous income net of tax and NIC.
5 The percentage of her net income represented by her premiums.

■ Exercise 2.4

Perhaps you would like to use the PHI Table 2.4 (p. 50) and Form 2.4 (p. 58) to calculate your own situation.

■ **Form 2.3 INCOME TAX AND NIC ANALYSIS**

INCOME TAX			
Name Morgan Davies	*Year*	1997/98	
	£	*Remaining income £*	*Tax £*
Gross income	17,100		
Gross contribution to pension paid personally*	900	16,200	None
Personal allowance	4045	12,155	None
Income taxed at 20%	4100	8055	820.00
Income taxed at basic rate 23%	8055	None	1852.65
Income taxed at higher rate 40%			
Total	17,100		2672.65
Less married couple's allowance			
Total tax payable			

* Some pension contributions paid personally are net of basic rate tax. For the purposes of this form this would need to be grossed up.

NATIONAL INSURANCE CONTRIBUTION (NIC) (Employed)			
	£	*Remaining income £*	*NIC £*
Gross income	17,100		
Income up to LEL £3224 p.a. NIC at 2%	3224	13,876	64.48
Income up to UEL £24,180 p.a. minus £3224 p.a., the LEL NIC at 10%	13,876	None	1387.60
Total	17,100		1452.08

NATIONAL INSURANCE CONTRIBUTION (NIC) (Self-employed)		
Flat rate paid if income over £3480 p.a. £6.15 p.w.		
On profits between £7010 and £24,180 p.a. 6.0%		
Total		
Income after tax and NIC deductions	17,100 – 2672.65 – 1452.08 = 12,975.27	

■ Permanent health insurance (PHI) or income protection plan (IPP)

■ **Form 2.4 INCOME TAX AND NIC ANALYSIS**

INCOME TAX			
Name		*Year*	
	£	*Remaining income £*	*Tax £*
Gross income			
Gross contribution to pension paid personally*			
Personal allowance			
Income taxed at 20% Income taxed at basic rate 23% Income taxed at higher rate 40%			
Total			
Less married couple's allowance			
Total tax payable			
* Some pension contributions paid personally are net of basic rate tax. For the purposes of this form this would need to be grossed up.			
NATIONAL INSURANCE CONTRIBUTION (NIC) (Employed)			
	£	*Remaining income £*	*NIC £*
Gross income			
Income up to LEL £3224 p.a. NIC at 2%			
Income up to UEL £24,180 p.a. minus £3224 p.a., the LEL NIC at 10%			
Total			
NATIONAL INSURANCE CONTRIBUTION (NIC) (Self-employed)			
Flat rate paid if income over £3480 p.a. £6.15 p.w.			
On profits between £7010 and £24,180 p.a. 6.0%			
Total			
Income after tax and NIC deductions			

ACCIDENT SICKNESS AND UNEMPLOYMENT (ASU) POLICIES

These policies are often known as mortgage payment protection policies (MPP) because most of them are related to mortgage payments. Most are offered in composite form covering all three of the contingencies mentioned earlier in the same contract. There are also stand-alone sickness and accident policies and stand-alone unemployment cover policies. Unemployment cover can also be added to some permanent health insurance policies.

Cover is usually restricted to a 12 month term but can be as short as 9 months or as long as 24 months. There will be a deferment period of anything from 30 days to 90 days after the onset of the contingency when no claim can be made. Once the claim has been accepted payment will be made from the end of the deferment period in most cases, but some policies will then pay benefit from day one of the onset of the contingency. There will almost certainly be an exclusion period for the unemployment part of the cover and often for the sickness and accident. This can vary between 30 days and 120 days. An exclusion period is the time from commencement of the policy during which no claim would be accepted. This protects the provider from the purchaser who has a fair idea that he is about to lose his work. Age eligibility is usually from 18 years to 60 years, but some will only go to 55 where others will extend to 65.

> Accident, sickness and unemployment policies are usually related to mortgage payments.

The vast majority of providers will restrict the benefit to cover mortgage payments, sometimes including the payment of mortgage-related insurance premiums and sometimes adding up to an additional 25 per cent to cover possible future increases in interest rates and therefore mortgage payments. It is also usual to impose a ceiling on the benefit of £1000 per month, sometimes as high as £2000, but this will still have to be related to the mortgage payments. There are a few providers who offer greater freedom and will relate the cover to income requiring no connection with mortgage payments whatsoever. This will usually be limited to 65 per cent of income minus the state long-term incapacity benefit. Since 6 April 1996 the benefit has been totally tax free as in the case of permanent health insurance.

Providers of mortgage-related policies will often protect themselves from purchasers taking out a policy knowing unemployment is imminent by making more restrictive terms for existing borrowers such as higher premiums and longer exclusion periods. This is because new borrowers have recently been underwritten from the point of view of work and are hardly likely to be embarking on the responsibility of a mortgage if they know redundancy is looming.

Another requirement is work history. The standard length is six months, although once again this can vary from nil to 12 months. To prove unemployment most providers will require that the claimant is registered with the Benefits Agency, an executive agency of the Department of Social Security (DSS). Some require the claimant actually to be in receipt of state benefits. The self-employed would usually need to show that their business had terminated, while shareholding directors could usually only claim if their company had gone into liquidation. Contract workers would need to show that their contract was normally renewable. With sickness and accident cover pre-existing conditions, which could recur and cause a claim, will be excluded for a period from commencement of policy. This could be 12 months but in many cases is for the duration of the policy.

Typical premiums are,

- for accident, sickness and unemployment premiums will range from £4.75 per month for cover of £100 per month to £7.00 for cover of £100
- for accident and sickness alone premiums could range from £2.60 per month for cover of £100 per month to £3.85 for cover of £100
- for unemployment cover alone premiums could range from £2.80 per month for cover of £100 per month to £6.00 for cover of £100.

In general there is a balance between the benefits and the price paid. Thus the more expensive policy will usually give a longer term of benefit and/or a shorter deferment period and/or a shorter exclusion period. For those policies including unemployment benefit a differential will often be applied for existing borrowers making the same policy more expensive or with longer deferred period and/or exclusion period. As explained earlier this is a means of protection against higher risk applicants.

■ Example 2.9

David Porter has just taken a mortgage involving monthly payments of £604 with associated monthly insurance premiums of £135. He selects a mortgage payment protection (MPP) policy which allows him to add 25% for possible increases in interest rate. The monthly premiums will be £4.37 for £100 per month of cover.

Mortgage payment	= £604 per month
25% of this	= £151 per month
Insurance premium	= £135 per month
Total	= £890 per month

To find the cost of the MPP premium the calculation is:

$$\frac{890}{100} \times 4.37 = 38.89 \text{ per month}$$

■ Exercise 2.5

Veronica Platt makes mortgage payments of £493, plus insurance premiums of £104, monthly. What is the maximum ASU cover she could have? If this costs £5.90 per month for £100 of cover monthly, what will her premiums be?

MEDICAL INSURANCE

Quite a number of companies offer this form of insurance. In return for premiums, fees for medical treatment and accommodation in hospital will be paid by the insurance company. There is usually a number of levels of payment from which one can choose. Higher payments will usually secure enhanced benefits or better accommodation or treatment in the bigger hospitals such as the large London teaching hospitals (see Table 2.7).

Table 2.7 Typical costs of medical insurance (per month, £)

	Single	Married	Family	One parent family
Up to 25	32.43	61.45	87.20	56.23
26–30	34.50	63.00	90.20	58.10
31–35	40.21	79.10	98.14	61.80
36–40	40.93	77.23	99.14	60.32
41–45	41.32	80.72	102.14	63.14
46–50	43.24	83.14	105.30	64.92
51–55	52.83	98.92	128.10	78.72
56–60	60.14	116.18	146.93	92.10
61–65	70.78	133.47	171.43	106.74

[Age will be taken as that of the older person.]

Typical schedule of benefits

1 Hospital charges
  Nursing and accommodation
  In patient and daycare
  Operating theatre and recovery room   full payment
  Drugs dressings and other ancillary charges
  Pathology, physiotherapy and diagnostic
  procedures

  Prosthesis and artificial parts when implanted as an   up to £2500
  integral part of surgical procedure

2 Surgeons' and anaesthetists' fees for each operation   full payment

3 Specialist physicians' fees   each day up to £40

4 Home nursing   each year up to £280

5 Radiotherapy/Chemotherapy   each year up to £2500

6 Alternative medicine, acupuncture, homeopathy
  chiropractice and osteopathy following referral   each year up to £400
  by GP

7 Private ambulance   each year up to £150

Clearly different insurance companies will offer different benefits and different levels of payment. As with everything the quality of benefit will be determined by the amount paid. Often discounts are available by virtue of belonging to associations such as AA, the National Trust, etc. Additional discounts are usually available for members of professional bodies such as the Law Society, Institute of British Architects etc.

Costs for medical insurance have increased considerably in recent years which has caused a noticeable decrease in the numbers using policies.

A new type of policy is starting to appear to cater for this trend in which the first £1000, £2000 or whatever of any claim is paid by the policy holder. This considerably reduces premiums.

CRITICAL ILLNESS POLICY

The enormous advance of medical science over recent years has meant that very serious illnesses such as heart attack, cancer and stroke no longer necessarily result in death. The sufferer survives and often leads a rewarding life. However, in a majority of cases the ability to generate an income has been severely affected. For example after heart attack the sufferer will often be told by his specialist to take things a lot easier, to work fewer hours, to work at a much reduced rate and to avoid the stress that work previously caused, or, indeed, to stop work completely. All of this will seriously affect earning capacity. Thus although what was a devastating medical problem has been considerably eased it has been replaced by a severe financial problem. It must be clearly understood that in these circumstances a life assurance policy would not pay out.

Had the sufferer been well financially prepared then he or she would have had the benefit of an income protection policy and would be in receipt of an income, albeit a reduced one. However, in these circumstances an injection of capital could be invaluable. It could, for example, pay off the mortgage and remove what could be, for a physically impaired person, an enormous burden; it could pay for a long recuperative period of convalescence; it could pay for necessary alterations to a home.

If you have a critical illness and recover your life assurance will not pay out.

It was because of these developments that the critical illness or serious illness policy was produced. This policy will carry a sum assured which would become payable on the diagnosis of a long list of serious illnesses, or upon undergoing an operation to ameliorate such a serious illness or on being placed upon the waiting list for such an operation. Before the policy pays out there would be a deferment period after the incidence of one of the above during which the policy holder would have to survive. This is usually of the order of 28 days.

Typical critical illnesses and operations covered are:

- aorta graft surgery (the surgical removal and replacement of the aorta or a segment of it)
- benign brain tumour
- blindness
- cancer
- coma (usually unconsciousness, with no reaction to stimuli, which continues for at least 96 hours. Life support systems must be required throughout the period of unconsciousness)
- coronary artery surgery
- heart attack
- heart valve replacement
- kidney failure
- loss of limbs
- loss of speech
- major organ transplant (some insurance will pay out on joining the waiting list for a major organ transplant)
- motor neurone disease
- multiple sclerosis
- paralysis (usually the total and irreversible loss of the use of two or more limbs)
- permanent total disability from performing any occupation
- severe burns (usually third degree burns covering 20 per cent or more of the body's surface area)
- stroke
- terminal illness (usually described as a worsening, incurable disease which has reduced the expectancy of life to less than 12 months).

Some policies include children's critical illness. Typically this covers children between 3 and 18 and will pay a sum of £12,000 to £18,000 in the event of the following critical illnesses or operations:

- most serious cancers
- coronary artery bypass surgery
- balloon agioplasty (in certain serious cases)
- heart attack
- heart valve replacement
- kidney failure
- major organ transplant (or joining the waiting list for a major organ transplant)
- motor neurone disease
- multiple sclerosis
- paralysis
- permanent total disability
- stroke
- terminal illness.

Usually a claim for a child will not bring the policy to an end.

Sometimes policies will offer additional critical conditions which can be added to the policy for increased premiums. Typically such additions are:

- Alzheimer's disease
- loss of hearing
- loss of independent existence
- Parkinson's disease
- permanent total disability to perform one's own occupation (usually meaning to become totally and irreversibly unable to carry out all the tasks involved in the gainful occupation of the policy holder).

An example of this could be a dentist who develops rheumatism in his hands. Although he is not permanently totally disabled, he is permanently totally disabled from his profession as a dentist.

If the policy holder dies within the deferred period then these policies would pay out either nothing or at most something like one year's premiums.

Versions of the policy

There are two versions of the policy:

- Single life which would pay out on the valid claim of the insured.
- Joint life which would be written on two people and would pay out on the first valid claim to be made by either.

The policy would then come to an end. It is very important to note that in most cases of this sort of joint life policy, if one of the assured were to die the policy would pay out, at most, something like twelve months' premiums and would then come to an end. When deciding whether to have two separate policies or one joint life policy this consideration becomes crucially important, since if one policy holder dies only a minimal amount, if anything, is paid out and the survivor is left with no continuing protection. It is important to balance what little is usually saved in premium costs with a joint life policy against the possible consequences. These sorts of points are often not clearly understood.

Options which can be included

There are often additional options which can be included or are sometimes included automatically.

■ Indexation benefit

At the commencement of the policy the applicant can choose to have the benefit level or indexed. Indexation could be in line with the Retail Prices Index (RPI) or the National Average Earnings Index (AEI) or at a fixed percentage. On increasing the cover at each anniversary no further medical evidence would be required.

The increase in premium would be that related to the age of the policy holder at the time.

■ Mortgage increase option

Since these policies are often used in connection with a mortgage it is often possible to include a mortgage increase option. This means that in the event of the policy holder increasing his or her mortgage the critical illness policy can be increased by the same amount with no further medical evidence required. The increase in premiums would, of course, be that relating to the age of the policy holder at the time. This option would usually allow the term of the policy to be increased if necessary.

■ Waiver of contribution option (WOC)

For a small increase in premium this option would guarantee that should the policy holder become medically unable to work all premiums would be waived. There would usually be a deferred period, perhaps three months from the incidence of the disability, before premiums were waived but then, in the case of some insurers, premiums paid during the deferment period would be refunded. The premiums would usually be waived while the disability persisted and if necessary to the end of the term of the policy but not later than the 65th birthday. It is important to note that this facility would only operate if the medical inability to work took place while the policy holder was in gainful employment. This is another of those points which is sometimes not clearly understood.

In the case of joint life policies the policy holders would have the choice of to whose life the waiver of contribution option should apply. This choice would be made at the commencement of the policy. It is also an important point to make that should the waiver of contribution option and indexation option both be included and if the policy holder became medically unable to work, not only would the premiums be waived but the cover would continue to be indexed at each anniversary and no premiums would be required.

■ Normal increases

Apart from the options which allow the sum assured to be increased with no further medical evidence, most policies will allow the holder to increase the sum assured in the usual way submitting to the usual medical requirements rather than needing to take out an additional policy.

Types of policy

The critical illness policy comes in two basic types.

■ The term policy

This policy will run for a given term. It will have no investment aspect and when the term comes to an end, if no claim has been made, there will be nothing to come back to the policy holder. Again this is a point which needs to be clearly understood at outset (see Table 2.8).

Table 2.8 Typical premiums for critical illness policy (sum assured £100,000, term 25 years)

Men	Monthly cost (£)		
Age	Non-smoker	Percentage increase for smoker	Percentage increase for waiver of contribution
20	18.56	23.7	2.0
25	25.70	26.9	2.0
30	35.38	39.6	2.0
35	52.16	54.2	2.0
40 (20 years)	75.90	61.1	3.0
45 (15 years)	108.28	68.8	3.0

Women	Monthly cost (£)		
Age	Non-smoker	Percentage increase for smoker	Percentage increase for waiver of contribution
20	20.26	4.4	2.5
25	27.40	8.4	2.5
30	37.40	17.1	2.5
35	50.96	24.9	2.5
40 (20 years)	67.86	28.6	4.0
45 (15 years)	89.08	33.8	4.0

Joint life first death, woman 3 years younger than man				
	Monthly cost (£)			
Man's age	Non-smoker	Percentage increase for smoker	Percentage increase for waiver of contribution	
			Men	Women
20	31.76	16.0	2.0	2.5
25	44.80	18.3	2.0	2.5
30	62.76	28.0	2.0	2.5
35	90.70	40.7	2.0	2.5
40 (20 years)	128.00	46.6	3.0	4.0
45 (15 years)	176.96	53.8	3.0	4.0

■ Example 2.10

Steve Turner from Example 2.6 only managed to insure himself for 64.8% of his net income. He decides to take £200,000 of critical illness cover to age 60, indexed. He is 47 so nearest age is 45 with term 15 years. This would cost with waiver of contribution, as he is a non-smoker,

£108.28 + 3% of £108.28 per month

This is

$$£108.28 + \frac{3}{100} \times 108.28 = £108.28 + £3.25 = £111.53 \text{ per month}$$

which gives us an approximate cost.

The sum assured of £200,000 being indexed would keep pace with inflation, thus if it were called upon before Steve was 60 it would relate to values at that time. Invested on the stock market in higher yielding shares through the funds of an OEIC, say, it could be expected to yield approximately 5% p.a. gross. Historically the yield from these investments has steadily increased, keeping pace well with inflation. The interesting thing is that although the capital value of shares can fluctuate rapidly at times, the income from them steadily increases, smoothing out violent changes (see Fig 2.2).

■ Example 2.11

Gillian Forbes from Example 2.7 was also underinsured from the point of view of PHI. £100,000 sum assured critical illness over 25 years, indexed, would cost her, as she is a smoker,

£37.40 per month + 17.1% of £37.40

$$= £37.40 + \frac{17.1}{100} \times £37.40 = £37.40 + £6.40 = £43.80 \text{ per month}$$

She decides to add waiver of contribution which increases the cost,

$$2.5\% \text{ of } £43.80 = \frac{2.5}{100} \times £43.80 = £1.10$$

to a total cost of £44.90 per month.

Of course she would really need a policy taking her to age 60, her retirement age, and this would be a little more expensive, but our figure gives a reasonable approximation. As in Example 2.10 the proceeds of the policy could be invested to give, in today's terms, an annual yield of 5% gross, increasing in line with inflation.

Renewability option

The term policy will often carry a renewability option which will either be automatically included or possible to be added for an extra cost. This option would

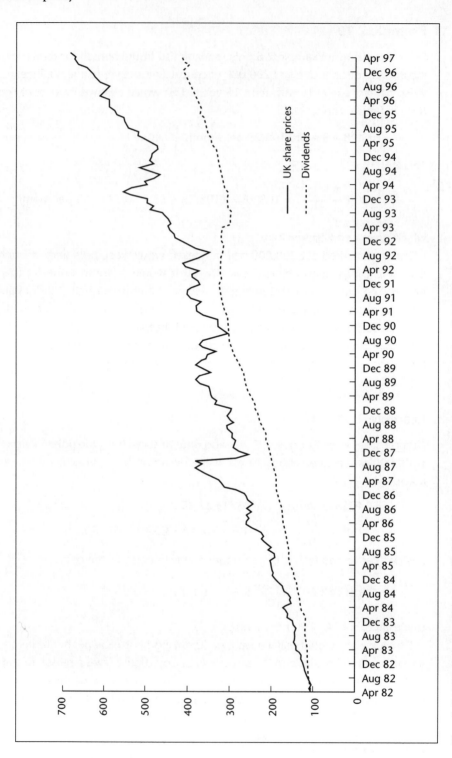

Fig. 2.2 UK share price and dividend growth – 15 years to end April 1997
Source: Datastream

Table 2.9 Typical premiums for whole of life critical illness policy (sum assured £100,000)

Men	Monthly cost (£)		
Age	Non-smoker	Percentage increase for smoker	Percentage increase for waiver of contribution
20	24.40	58.2	2.0
25	32.88	65.7	2.0
30	45.16	74.1	2.0
35	63.52	84.0	2.0
40	89.08	92.8	3.0
45	120.16	92.2	3.0

Women	Monthly cost (£)		
Age	Non-smoker	Percentage increase for smoker	Percentage increase for waiver of contribution
20	23.76	36.6	2.5
25	31.28	41.2	2.5
30	40.90	48.4	2.5
35	53.32	58.0	2.5
40	72.36	62.2	4.0
45	102.80	58.0	4.0

Joint life first death, woman 3 years younger than man

Man's age	Monthly cost (£)			
	Non-smoker	Percentage increase for smoker	Percentage increase for waiver of contribution	
			Men	Women
20	37.00	51.6	2.0	2.5
25	50.30	57.1	2.0	2.5
30	68.76	64.0	2.0	2.5
35	95.32	73.2	2.0	2.5
40	132.16	81.9	3.0	4.0
45	186.64	82.9	3.0	4.0

> **To be able to renew your critical illness policy with no further medical evidence could be invaluable.**

guarantee that the policy could be renewed at the end of the term for a further term with no further medical evidence required, which could be invaluable. Clearly the premiums for the renewed policy would be calculated according to the age of the policy holder at the time of renewal.

■ The whole of life policy

This policy is what it says it is. It will continue for the whole of the life of the policy holder, unless a valid claim is made or it is discontinued. There will usually be a small investment aspect included in the whole of life policy (see Table 2.9).

Cash value

Because of the investment aspect the whole of life policy will acquire a cash in value. Thus after a time, if it is discontinued there could be a cash value to come back to the policy holder.

Partial cash withdrawal

Some policies will allow a partial encashment of the policy without bringing it to an end, so that after the partial encashment, premiums and therefore cover can continue. A partial encashment will often decrease the cover or make it necessary to increase the premium.

Continuation of critical illness cover

With many policies, because they have an investment aspect, the sum assured cover can continue even though premiums stop. The cash value of the policy will be used to fund the cover and eventually this cash value is likely to be exhausted. It is important to be clear that if a policy is discontinued and not cashed in, then this may happen automatically and eventually the policy would have no value. The insurance company would of course alert the client to this possibility but in the course of a busy life it is often possible to miss these things.

■ The low start or enhanced cover whole of life policy

This policy offers a way of achieving the level of cover required but with a premium which is initially lower than the true whole of life form. The policy will have a lower underlying level of whole of life cover which will be supplemented in the first ten years to the higher level required. At the end of the ten years the sum assured will revert to the lower underlying level of sum assured. The premiums will remain the same throughout. At the end of ten years the policy holder will have various choices. The policy can be left where it is with its underlying level of whole of life sum assured (See Fig. 2.3 and Table 2.10).

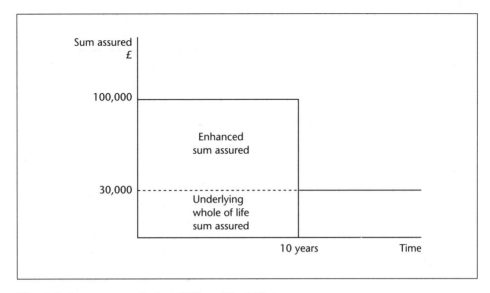

Fig. 2.3 Low start whole of life critical illness

By paying increased premiums the underlying level can be increased by any amount up to the full initial level of sum assured. The policy would then continue for the whole of life at this level (see Fig. 2.4).

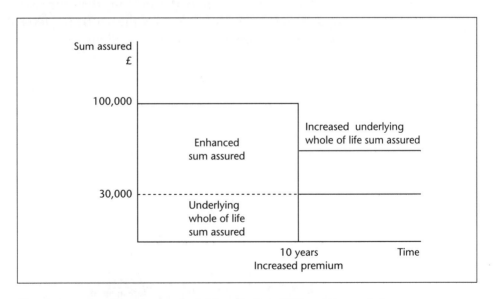

Fig. 2.4 Increasing the underlying whole of life sum assured

The level of enhanced sum assured applicable during the first ten years can be maintained for a further ten years. At the end of the second ten years the same choices would be available (see Fig. 2.5).

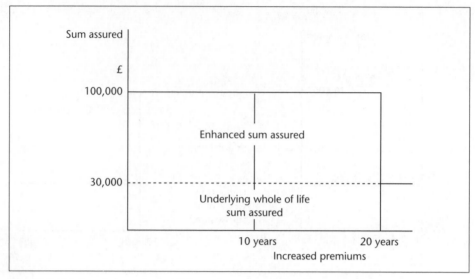

Fig. 2.5 Maintaining the enhanced sum assured for a further 10 years

At any time during the initial or subsequent ten years of enhanced cover the underlying level of whole of life cover could be increased by increasing the premiums. In which case the new underlying level of whole of life cover would come into effect at the end of the ten years. Since the increased premiums will relate to the age of the policy holder at the time, the earlier the underlying level of whole of life cover is increased the cheaper it will be (see Fig. 2.6).

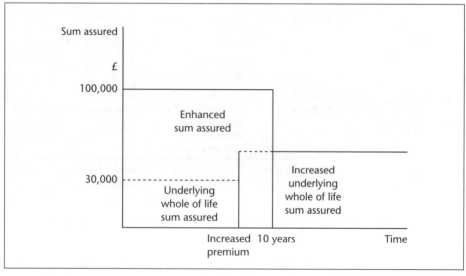

Fig. 2.6 Increasing the underlying whole of life sum assured at any time during the first 10 years, or subsequent 10 years

Table 2.10 Typical premiums for low start whole of life critical illness policy (sum assured £55,000 enhanced to £100,000 for the first 10 years)

Men		Monthly cost (£)		
Age	*Non-smoker*	*Percentage increase for smoker*	*Percentage increase for waiver of contribution*	
20	15.50	61.3	2.0	
25	21.20	66.7	2.0	
30	29.62	78.6	2.0	
35	41.80	87.5	2.0	
40	58.78	98.3	3.0	
45	87.46	92.0	3.0	
Women		*Monthly cost (£)*		
Age	*Non-smoker*	*Percentage increase for smoker*	*Percentage increase for waiver of contribution*	
20	14.80	33.0	2.5	
25	18.26	36.2	2.5	
30	24.86	42.3	2.5	
35	34.24	51.2	2.5	
40	46.36	56.5	4.0	
45	54.20	90.1	4.0	

Joint life first death, woman 3 years younger than man

Man's age	Non-smoker	Percentage increase for smoker	Percentage increase for waiver of contribution	
			Men	*Women*
20	23.80	47.8	2.0	2.5
25	31.48	54.8	2.0	2.5
30	41.64	65.9	2.0	2.5
35	59.38	72.9	2.0	2.5
40	84.78	83.8	3.0	4.0
45	123.18	84.6	3.0	4.0

Table 2.11 Typical premiums for whole of life critical illness plus whole of life life assurance (sum assured £100,000)

Men	Monthly cost (£)		
Age	Non-smoker	Percentage increase for smoker	Percentage increase for waiver of contribution
20	32.06	63.6	2.0
25	42.00	72.4	2.0
30	57.40	78.9	2.0
35	81.66	81.9	2.0
40	116.96	83.1	3.0
45	168.10	77.2	3.0

Women	Monthly cost (£)		
Age	Non-smoker	Percentage increase for smoker	Percentage increase for waiver of contribution
20	27.40	46.4	2.5
25	35.74	52.5	2.5
30	46.92	60.4	2.5
35	61.96	67.6	2.5
40	85.96	67.8	4.0
45	125.32	59.0	4.0

Joint life first death, woman 3 years younger than man

Man's age	Non-smoker	Monthly cost (£) Percentage increase for smoker	Percentage increase for waiver of contribution Men	Women
20	46.46	59.8	2.0	2.5
25	60.80	67.6	2.0	2.5
30	82.36	74.5	2.0	2.5
35	115.14	79.1	2.0	2.5
40	162.70	81.5	3.0	4.0
45	232.76	77.7	3.0	4.0

Critical illness policy including life cover

Some critical illness policies will allow the inclusion of life cover up to the value of the critical illness sum assured. In this case the policy would pay out on the first event to occur be it death or a valid critical illness claim. It is very important to realise that the policy will then terminate even though the policy holder may still be alive. It cannot be kept running in the hope of making a second claim should the policy holder die. This may seem perfectly obvious but it is so often an area of real confusion. In other words a combined critical illness, life assurance policy is not actually two policies, it is one or the other (see Table 2.11).

> A combined critical illness, life assurance policy is not actually two policies for the price of one. It is one or the other.

The policy holder comparing prices often makes the wrong comparison between a composite policy of this sort and the taking of two separate policies, one for critical illness and one for life assurance. It is often misguidedly thought that two policies for little more than the price of one have been acquired. But two policies have not been obtained. What the policy holder has is one or the other and not both.

■ Example 2.12

Gordon Truscott is 34 and decides to take out whole of life critical illness cover with waiver of contribution option for a sum assured of £120,000. He is a non-smoker. The nearest age in Table 2.6 (p. 52) is 35. His policy will cost,

$$\frac{120,000}{100,000} \times (63.52 + 2\% \text{ of } 63.52) = 1.2 \times 64.79 = £77.73 \text{ per month} \\ \text{approximately}$$

STATE PENSION BENEFITS

Everyone who qualifies receives the basic old age pension, which stood at £3242.40 per annum in fiscal year 1997/98 for a single person and £5189.60 per annum for a married couple. Qualification rules are that women must have reached the age of 60 and men 65 and have paid national insurance contributions (NIC). A full pension will be received if national insurance contributions at the full rate have been paid or credited for most of a working life. This means contributions have been paid for three out of every four years of working life. Those not entitled to the full pension may get a reduced one if contributions have been paid for at least 25 per cent of the years needed for a full pension. Employees paying tax on a pay as you earn (PAYE) basis will also be eligible to receive in addition the state earnings related pension scheme (SERPS). Qualification rules are that women must have reached the age of 60 and men 65 and have paid Class 1 national insurance contributions for at least one year. SERPS is paid for from NIC contributions of both the employer and employee. The self-employed will not receive it.

NIC contributions also pay for other benefits such as short-term sickness, the National Health Service and redundancy payments. SERPS came into being in April 1978 as a result of the Social Security Pensions Act 1975. The single person's old age pension at that time was approximately 21 per cent of the national average earnings. The objective of SERPS was to increase that by a further 25 per cent. We will see later that this objective was never achieved. SERPS is paid out at age 65 (men) and currently 60 (women). The November 1993 Budget announced the change in retirement age for women from 60 to 65. This will be phased in over a ten year period commencing April 2010. Thus women born before April 1950 will retire at 60, up to April 2010. Those born after March 1955 will retire at 65 after March 2020. Those born between these two dates will retire at an age greater than 60, but less than 65, between April 2010 and March 2020. This will happen on a sliding scale so that for example, a woman born 7 April 1953 will retire at age 63 years 1 month, on 7 May 2013 (see Table 2.12).

> **The self-employed will receive the state basic pension but not the state earnings related pension.**

The qualifying conditions for receiving SERPS are that,

- pensionable age has been reached, currently 65 men and 60 women
- retirement from regular employment has taken place
- Class 1 national insurance contributions have been paid for at least one year since 6 April 1978.

The amount of SERPS receivable was originally calculated as follows:

1 Earnings on which Class 1 national insurance contributions (NIC) have been paid in each tax year since 1978/79 are taken.
   NB: This will be earnings up to the upper earnings level (UEL), currently in tax year 1997/98 £24,180 per annum. The individual does not pay NIC for earnings above this. See Table 2.6.
2 The earnings in each of these years is then indexed by the National Average Earnings Index (i.e. increase in national average earnings) since the tax year concerned.
3 Each annual figure is then decreased by the lower earnings level (LEL) applicable to the tax year in which men reach the age of 64 and women reach the age of 59.

> **Women born after March 1955 will not be able to take their state earnings related pension scheme (SERPS) before the age of 65.**

The LEL is the earnings level up to which no Class 1 national insurance contribution is paid. This was £3224 per annum in the tax year 1997/98.

The Pensions Act 1995 has changed number 3 in this list by reducing each annual figure by the LEL for that particular tax year, which will result in a smaller eventual figure since the LEL and UEL have usually increased in line with the Retail Prices Index.

Table 2.12 Ready reckoner for new retirement ages for women

Date of birth	Pension age	Pension date
6.4.50 – 5.5.50	60.1 – 60.0	6.5.2010
6.5.50 – 5.6.50	60.2 – 60.1	6.7.2010
6.5.50 – 5.7.50	60.3 – 60.2	6.9.2010
6.7.50 – 5.8.50	60.4 – 60.3	6.11.2010
6.8.50 – 5.9.50	60.5 – 60.4	6.1.2011
6.9.50 – 5.10.50	60.6 – 60.5	6.3.2011
6.10.50 – 5.11.50	60.7 – 60.6	6.5.2011
6.11.50 – 5.12.50	60.8 – 60.7	6.7.2011
6.12.50 – 5.1.51	60.9 – 60.8	6.9.2011
6.1.51 – 5.2.51	60.10 – 60.9	6.11.2011
6.2.51 – 5.3.51	60.11 – 60.10	6.1.2012
6.3.51 – 5.4.51	61.0 – 60.11	6.3.2012
6.4.51 – 5.5.51	61.1 – 60.0	6.5.2012
6.5.51 – 5.6.51	61.2 – 61.1	6.7.2012
6.6.51 – 5.7.51	61.3 – 61.2	6.9.2012
6.7.51 – 5.8.51	61.4 – 61.3	6.11.2012
6.8.51 – 5.9.51	61.5 – 61.4	6.1.2013
6.9.51 – 5.10.51	61.6 – 61.5	6.3.2013
6.10.51 – 5.11.51	61.7 – 61.6	6.5.2013
6.11.51 – 5.12.51	61.8 – 61.7	6.7.2013
6.12.51 – 5.1.52	61.9 – 61.8	6.9.2013
6.1.52 – 5.2.52	61.10 – 61.9	6.11.2013
6.2.52 – 5.3.52	61.11 – 61.10	6.1.2014
6.3.52 – 5.4.52	62.0 – 61.11	6.3.2014
6.4.52 – 5.5.52	62.1 – 62.0	6.5.2014
6.5.52 – 5.6.52	62.2 – 62.1	6.7.2014
6.6.52 – 5.7.52	62.3 – 62.2	6.9.2014
6.7.52 – 5.8.52	62.4 – 62.3	6.11.2014
6.8.52 – 5.9.52	62.5 – 62.4	6.1.2015
6.9.52 – 5.10.52	62.6 – 62.5	6.3.2015
6.10.52 – 5.11.52	62.7 – 62.6	6.5.2015
6.11.52 – 5.12.52	62.8 – 62.7	6.7.2015
6.12.52 – 5.1.53	62.9 – 62.8	6.9.2015
6.1.53 – 5.2.53	62.10 – 62.9	6.11.2015
6.2.53 – 5.3.53	62.11 – 62.10	6.1.2016
6.3.53 – 5.4.53	63.0 – 62.11	6.3.2016
6.4.53 – 5.5.53	63.1 – 63.0	6.5.2016
6.5.53 – 5.6. 53	63.2 – 63.1	6.7.2016
6.6.53 – 5.7.53	63.3 – 63.2	6.9.2016
6.7.53 – 5.8.53	63.4 – 63.3	6.11.2016
6.8.53 – 5.9.53	63.5 – 63.4	6.1.2017
6.9.53 – 5.10.53	63.6 – 63.5	6.3.2017
6.10.53 – 5.11.53	63.7 – 63.6	6.5.2017
6.11.53 – 5.12.53	63.8 – 63.7	6.7.2017
6.12.53 – 5.1.54	63.9 – 63.8	6.9.2017
6.1.54 – 5.2.54	63.10 – 63.9	6.11.2017
6.2.54 – 5.3.54	63.11 – 63.10	6.1.2018
6.3.54 – 5.4.54	64.0 – 63.11	6.3.2018
6.4.54 – 5.5.54	64.1 – 64.0	6.5.2018
6.5.54 – 5.6.54	64.2 – 64.1	6.7.2018
6.6.54 – 5.7.54	64.3 – 64.2	6.9.2018
6.7.54 – 5.8.54	64.4 – 64.3	6.11.2018
6.8.54 – 5.9.54	64.5 – 64.4	6.1.2019
6.9.54 – 5.10.54	64.6 – 64.5	6.3.2019
6.10.54 – 5.11.54	64.7 – 64.6	6.5.2019
6.11.54 – 5.12.54	64.8 – 64.7	6.7.2019
6.12.54 – 5.1.55	64.9 – 64.8	6.9.2019
6.1.55 – 5.2.55	64.10 – 64.9	6.11.2019
6.2.55 – 5.3.55	64.11 – 64.10	6.1.2020
6.3.55 – 5.4.55	65.0 – 64.11	6.3.2020
6.4.55	65.0	6.4.2020

4 The resulting amounts are called the 'surpluses' for these years. These surpluses are used to calculate the amount of pension received.

The original basis of this calculation was as follows:

- ■ Retirement in 1998/99 or earlier. The total of 1/80th of each of the surpluses or in other words 25 per cent of the average surplus of these 20 years.
- ■ Retirement in 1999/2000 or later. 1/80th of the surpluses on each of the best 20 years or in other words 25 per cent of the average surplus of the best 20 years.
- ■ The system is known as a 'pay as you go' system. Thus there is no investment fund as such.
- ■ It is the contributions of those in employment that pay for the pensions of those who have already retired.
- ■ In only two years since 6 April 1978 have the contributions been sufficient to pay the pensions and the scheme has had to be supplemented from other funds.

Peter Lilley stated in March 1997,

> When the welfare state began there were five working people contributing to support one pensioner. By the year 2030 for every five working people there will be three pensioners. The only way to ensure decent pensions without burdening future tax payers is through saving and investing to pay for pensions.

This is not a problem unique to the UK. Populations worldwide are becoming more elderly – probably because of better medicines, better hygiene, better food and better lifestyles. The proportion of retired to working is growing. Thus SERPS is becoming more and more difficult to sustain. Either much more money will have to be collected in taxes to pay for these pensions or the benefits will have to be decreased. The latter has already begun with the Social Security Act 1986 and since 6 April 1988 the calculation of SERPS benefits has been changed. These benefits will no longer be based on the average of the best 20 years of a working life but on the average of the total number of working years. They will also no longer be based on 25 but on 20 per cent.

Since 1978/79 state earnings related pension scheme benefits have been reduced.

This will, as usual, be phased in over a period as follows:

1 Retirement in 1998/99 or earlier: the total of 1/80th of each surplus.

2 Retirement in 1999/2000 – 2008/09: 25%/N of the surpluses for the tax years 1978/79 to 1987/88 inclusive plus (20 + X%)/N of the surpluses for the tax years 1988/89 onwards.

3 Retirement in 2009/10 onwards: 25%/N of the surpluses for the tax years 1978/79 to 1987/88 inclusive plus 20%/N of the surpluses for the tax years 1988/89 onwards.

Where: N = the number of tax years in the pensioner's working life after 5 April 1978
X = 0.5 for each tax year by which retirement precedes the tax year 2009/10.

It can be seen that this was already a considerable decrease in benefit. The change in retirement age for women is a further reduction, shortening the time the pensions will need to be paid and so too is the method of calculating the surpluses brought about by the Pensions Act 1995. As mentioned in the introduction the whole question of supporting the cost of the welfare state is in very serious debate. At least the UK has started to address this problem – many of the other European states have not.

It is impossible to predict SERPS benefits with any degree of accuracy since although historically they have kept roughly in line with the Retail Prices Index this is not the official stated objective. However, the basic state pension is pegged in this way so that in terms of prices, its value in 20 years' time will be the same as it is now. However, its true value will be represented by its proportion to real earnings and we have seen in the introduction how seriously this has been, and continues to be, eroded. This is a result of the Average Earnings Index (AEI) outstripping the Retail Prices Index (RPI), illustrated in Fig. 2.7.

> The old age pension is pegged to the Retail Prices Index and so in real terms it remains static in value.

In addition to this it is impossible to predict increases in one's personal salary and as this increases over the upper earnings level (UEL) the proportion of basic state pension and SERPS income becomes less and less.

However, if we assume salary increases in line with inflation, as does the basic old age pension, then this makes the value of this pension in today's terms stand at what it is today. Similarly if we assume the LEL and UEL also increase at exactly the same rate this makes the value of each future surplus in today's terms remain at what it is today. Hence, the concept of pegging everything to the RPI will help us get some idea in today's terms of future values of basic state pension and SERPS which will, of course, be necessary for the calculations needed for our lifetime financial plan.

■ Example 2.13

Sinclair Simms retires on 6 April 1998, completing 20 years' work after 1978. He is 65 and has a final annual salary of £18,000.

His state pensions benefits in today's terms would be,

> SERPS = $\frac{1}{80}$th of each surplus from 6 April 1978 to 5 April 1998
> = $\frac{1}{80}$th $\times 20 \times (18,000 - 3274)$
> = $\frac{1}{4} \times 14,726$
> = 3681.50 which is 20.45% of final income
> Old age pension= 3274.40
> Total = £6955.90 which is 38.6% of final income

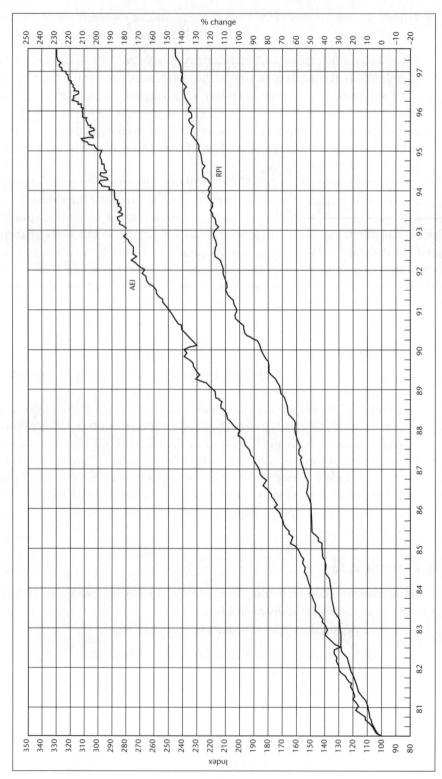

Fig. 2.7 Comparison of National Average Earnings Index (AEI) with Retail Prices Index (RPI)
Source: Micropal

■ **Example 2.14**

Peter Tripp retires in the year 2018 at 65 after 40 years' work on an annual income (in today's terms) of £18,000. His state pension benefits would be,

$$\text{SERPS} = \frac{25\%}{40} \times \text{surpluses for tax years 1978/79 to 1987/88 inclusive}$$

$$\text{plus } \frac{25\%}{40} \times \text{surpluses for the tax years 1988/89 on}$$

$$= \frac{25\%}{40} \times 10 \times (18,000 - 3274) + \frac{20\%}{40} \times 30 \times (18,000 - 3274)$$

$$= \frac{25\%}{4} \times 14,726 + \frac{20\%}{4} \times 3 \times 14,726$$

$$= 920.38 + 2208.90$$

$$= 3129.28, \text{ which is 17.38\% of final income}$$

$$+ \text{ old age pension} = 3247.20$$

$$\text{Total} = £6376.48, \text{ which is 35.4\% of final salary}$$

■ **Example 2.15**

Lorna Downs retires at 65 in the year 2035 after 45 years' work on an annual income of £18,000 (in today's terms). Her state pension benefits would be,

$$\text{SERPS} = \frac{20\%}{45} \times \text{surpluses for tax years 1990/91 to 2035/36}$$

$$= \frac{20\%}{45} \times 45 (18,000 - 3274) = 20\% \text{ of } 14,726 = 2945.20$$

which is 16.36% of final salary
Old age pension = 3247.40
Total = £6192.60, which is 34.4% of final salary

These examples demonstrate the reduction in state pension benefits. Taking only the SERPS figures, we see that these as a percentage of final income have reduced from 20.45 through 17.34 to 16.36 per cent. The reality is that income is much more likely to increase at a faster rate than inflation since if it were not to salaries, in real terms, would just stand still. In real terms, this decreases the percentages even further. In fact even in 1978/79 SERPS never was 25 per cent of national average earnings, since the lower earnings level (LEL) was always deducted before the percentage calculation was applied. The situation in the tax year 1997/98 is shown in Table 2.13.

In reality state pension provision is a reducing benefit.

Table 2.13 Basic state pension as percentage of final salary, 1997/98

Final salary in £000s	10	20	30	40	50	60	70	80	90	100
OAP as percentage	32.7	16.4	10.9	8.2	6.5	5.5	4.7	4.1	3.6	3.3

These figures are particularly important for the self-employed who are not eligible for SERPS and who will have only the old age pension.

There is also an upper limit on the actual SERPS benefit dictated by band earnings, i.e. the upper earnings level minus the lower earnings level. Once income reaches the upper earnings level SERPS becomes fixed and as income increases beyond that SERPS is an ever decreasing percentage of that income (see Table 2.14). In order to get some numerical idea of this decreasing percentage let us look at increasing salaries making the same assumptions as before and taking 20 per cent of the average surplus which will be the case for those whose workspan does not include the years 1978/79 to 1987/88 and who reach retirement age after the year 2010.

Table 2.14 SERPS as percentage of final salary

Final salary in £000s	10	20	24,180	30	40	50	60	70	80	90	100
SERPS	1345	3345	4181	4181	4181	4181	4181	4181	4181	4181	4181
SERPs as percentage	13.5	16.7	17.3	13.9	10.5	8.4	7.0	6.0	5.2	4.6	4.2

For higher salary earners state pension provision is a drastically reducing benefit.

It is interesting to see that the maximum percentage occurs at an annual income of £24,180, the UEL, whereas national average earnings in the fiscal year 1997/98 were approximately £21,491.

This clearly illustrates the decreasing proportions of income that SERPS and OAP represent as income increases. All of this strongly reinforces the need to create a financial plan in respect of eventual total financial independence.

Clearly there is a great need to create a financial plan in respect of eventual total financial independence.

On the death of a husband his widow would inherit 100 per cent of the SERPS earned up to the date of the husband's death. This will be reduced to 50 per cent if husband dies after 5 April 2000. It can be seen that this conforms to the inevitable reduction in these benefits.

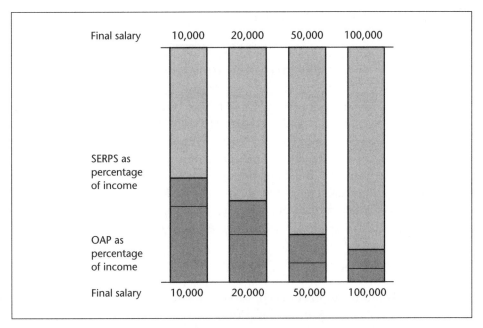

Fig. 2.8 SERPS and basic state pension as a percentage of income

■ **Exercise 2.6**

Anna Porter started employment in the fiscal year 1982/83 at 16 years old. She will retire in the fiscal year 2027/28 on an income (in today's terms) of £15,000 p.a. Make the same assumptions as made earlier, i.e. lower earnings limit, upper earnings limit, old age pension and her income all increase at exactly the same rate over her working life, which is tantamount to saying everything remains as it is in today's terms. Calculate her total state pension benefit and express it as a percentage of her final salary.

■ **Exercise 2.7**

Francis Perks retired in the fiscal year 2015/16 after completing 40 years working for himself as an interior decorator. His final income was £27,000 p.a. Calculate his total state pension benefit and express this as a percentage of his final income.

■ **Exercise 2.8**

Gillian Smith retired on 5 April 2004 after completing 22 years of paid employment after 6 April 1978. Her final income, in today's terms, was £55,000 p.a. Calculate the percentage of her final income represented by her total state pension benefit.

PENSIONS IN GENERAL

The contributions made to pensions either by a company or an individual attract tax relief at the highest rates paid, either as corporation tax or income tax. The growth of the funds inside the pensions are free of all UK taxes. A pension must be taken by the policy holder's 75th birthday. There is no minimum age for entry to a pension, the individual needs only to be in receipt of net relevant earnings (see later). A pension in payment is taxed as earned income which was an important consideration when investment income surcharge was applied to investment income. Some of the pension may be commuted for a tax-free cash sum. Considerable detail on different types of pension follows, suitable for the purposes of this chapter. In Chapter 5, when an individual may have more control over pension decisions and in Chapter 6, more detail relevant to these ages will be given.

The company pension scheme

This could be an exempt approved scheme which is approved by the Pension Schemes Office (PSO) and therefore receives certain tax advantages, i.e. 1. contributions made by the employer or the employee receive tax relief at the highest rate paid; 2. any growth or income in the underlying investment is totally free of UK taxes. These schemes are known variously as occupational pension schemes, executive pension schemes, company pension schemes, superannuation funds, or variations on these themes.

If not paying into an exempt approved scheme, the employer could be paying contributions into a personal pension scheme in the form of a group personal pension scheme (GPPS). This has only been possible since the 1 July 1988 when personal pension schemes started. They were introduced by Finance (No.2) Act 1987 and are now incorporated in the Income and Corporation Taxes Act 1988.

The exempt approved scheme could be one of two types, either a defined benefit or final salary scheme, or a money purchase or defined contribution scheme. A defined benefit scheme guarantees the pension from the outset, making it independent of fluctuations in the investment climate. All pensions in payment are taxed as earned income.

■ The defined benefit (DBS) or final salary pension scheme

A typical pension of this sort could give an income equal to 1/60th of final salary for every year of employment with the company, with the option to commute part of this pension for a tax-free lump sum usually equal to 3/80ths of final salary for every year of service with the company. Most schemes work on the basis that for a normal retirement age (NRA) of 65 then £9 to £9.80 of tax-free cash is obtained by commuting £1 of pension annually. For the few defined benefit schemes with an NRA of 60 the figures could be £10.20 to £11 for each £1 annually. These figures relate to the level of annuity which is currently in operation (see later in the chapter).

Typical retirement age for this sort of scheme was 65 for men and 60 for women but as a result of the case of *Barber* v. *GRE* a directive from the European Court on 17 May 1990 decreed that retirement age must be equalised. It is usually felt that to equalise down is too expensive so most schemes have equalised up, making retirement age 65 for both men and women.

There would normally also be benefits for dependants in the event of death before retirement, i.e. death in service (DIS) or after retirement, i.e. death in retirement (DIR). Typical DIS benefits would be a lump sum equal to up to four times salary at death and a pension for spouse equal to half the pension which would have been achieved if work had continued right up to retirement and based on salary at death. Typical DIR benefits would be a guarantee of five years so that if death occurred within the first five years of retiring the remainder of the pension which would have been paid in those five years is paid to spouse tax free, also a pension is provided for spouse of 50 per cent of the pension being paid at death.

Additional pensions are also sometimes paid for children on DIS or DIR up to the age of 18, or further if they are still in full-time education, 50 per cent of spouse's pension for each child but not more than a total of 100 per cent however many children. Employee pensions and dependants' pensions can also be indexed.

> **If you are contracted out of SERPS in a defined benefit pension scheme you will not receive SERPS in addition to your pension.**

It should be noted that there is usually no choice in these schemes, every member will have the same benefit structure, although for a single person with no dependants DIS and DIR benefits are of little use. These schemes are usually contracted out of the state earnings-related pension scheme (SERPS). In return for this the government will allow a reduction in national insurance contributions of both the employer and the employee. (Contracting out is dealt with later in the chapter.)

The contracted out employee will not receive SERPS, and in return for the lower NIC rates the employer takes over the responsibility for paying a pension at least equivalent to SERPS. It is important to realise, when studying a company pension and basing financial independence calculations upon it, that if contracted out, SERPS will not be received on top of the company pension, but its equivalent will be included in it and will be paid as part of the company pension at the normal retirement age of that pension.

Most of these company pension schemes require the employee to make a contribution to them but some are non-contributory, i.e. the employer guarantees the defined benefits and takes on the responsibility of investing sufficient money to ensure that they will be provided. However, it is vital to realise when doing financial independence calculations that the salary being used is usually less than actual salary.

It is described as pensionable salary and usually means actual salary minus the lower earnings level (LEL). In the fiscal year 1997/98 this was £3224. Also it is

| Salary used to calculate pensions in a defined benefits scheme is rarely actual full salary. |

unusual for bonuses to be considered as pensionable salary. Company schemes will therefore vary enormously from the excellent, offering very good guaranteed benefits to those that, although they too are guaranteed, will produce little more than SERPS would have done. The contributions to these pension schemes will be invested and managed either in house by the company probably using an actuary, or by an insurance company on behalf of the company.

If the employee leaves the company he is working for he leaves the company pension scheme. It is mandatory since the Pensions Act 1995 that his pension must grow by at least 5 per cent per annum until normal retirement age.

■ Example 2.16

John Jennings has just started work with Potter and Prince Ltd and has been given a pension booklet describing the company pension scheme he has joined. It gives the following information:

- It is a defined benefit or final salary scheme, contracted out of SERPS.
- Normal retirement age 65 years.
- Employee contributions will be 3% p.a. of pensionable salary, which is full salary minus the lower earnings level (LEL).
- Pension at retirement = 1/60th × number of years service with the company × pensionable salary. Pension will be indexed at the level of the Retail Prices Index (RPI) or 3% p.a. whichever is lower.

NB: Pensionable salary is usually defined as basic salary not including bonuses or the equivalent notional salary generated by such benefits as a company car, free accommodation or medical insurance, minus the NIC lower earnings level. The thinking here is that the member will be getting the basic state pension anyway which is approximately equal to the LEL. Contracting out of SERPS is dealt with later in the chapter.

Some of the pension may be commuted for a tax-free cash sum up to an amount equal to 3/80ths × number of years service with the company × pensionable salary. This will be based on £9 of cash for every £1 of pension commuted.

If death in service were to occur the spouse would receive,

1 A tax-free sum of money equal to three times pensionable salary at death.
2 A pension equal to 50% of the pension receivable had work continued till normal retirement age and achieved a pensionable salary equal to that at the time of death.

In the case of the DBS it is very easy to calculate the final pension in today's terms since it is always given as a proportion of final salary whatever the effects of inflation have been. In fact the calculations are likely to be pessimistic since AEI is almost certain to increase faster than RPI. It is better to be pessimistic with these calculations as the figures are therefore safer.

John is 35 so at 65 he will have completed 30 years' service. His annual salary is £25,000. Hence in today's terms, at age 65 he would receive a pension of $\frac{1}{60}$th $\times$ 30 $\times$ (25,000−3224) = $\frac{1}{2}$ $\times$ 21,776 = £10,888 p.a. indexed. Do not forget, this includes the equivalent of SERPS.

> **In the case of the defined benefit pension scheme it is possible to calculate final pension in today's terms relatively accurately.**

If he decided to commute for tax-free cash the maximum possible he would receive in today's terms 3/80th $\times$ 30 $\times$ 21,776 = £24,498. This, of course, would reduce his pension by 24,498/9 = £2722 p.a. to a figure of £8166 p.a.

Suppose in ten years' time with a pensionable salary in today's terms of £26,000 he became seriously ill. If he died his wife would receive,

1 Tax-free cash of 3 $\times$ 26,000 = £78,000 in today's terms.
2 A pension of $\frac{1}{2}$ $\times$ $\frac{1}{60}$th $\times$ 30 $\times$ 26,000 = £6500 p.a. indexed, in today's terms.

On death while in retirement the pension is guaranteed for five years. This means that death within five years would entitle the spouse to receive the remainder of the pension payable to the end of the five years. She would receive this in one lump and it would be tax free.

She will also receive immediately half the pension paid just before death and usually indexation will be taken into account.

Let us say John dies just over three years after retirement. He retired on a pension of £10,888 p.a. in today's terms, taking no tax free cash.

Assuming inflation is over 3% annually, his pension will be indexed at 3%. Pension at start of year 2 is 103% of £10,888.

$$\frac{103}{100} \times 10,888 = £11,215 \text{ p.a.}$$

Pension at start of year 3 is 103% of £11,215 p.a. = £11,551.
Pension at start of year 4 would have been 103% of £11,551 p.a. = £11,898.
Pension at start of year 5 would have been 103% of £11,898 p.a. = £12,255.

His spouse would therefore receive tax-free cash of £11,898 + £12,255 = £24,153 (the remaining two years of the guaranteed period).

She would also receive a pension based on John's pension at the start of year 4 of half of £11,898 p.a. = £5949 in today's terms. This would then be indexed in the same way as her husband's pension.

If your employer provides a defined benefit pension scheme for you it is very simple for you to calculate your final benefits in today's terms. You simply assume you will work to normal retirement age and using this number of years and your current pensionable salary apply them to the various formulae. It is impossible to create an accurate financial plan until you have these details because only then will you be able to see what additional provision you may have to make and hence what it will cost you. The structure of most pension schemes is two-fold. In the first part the contributions and their growth build up a pension fund which at maturity or normal retirement age will be used to purchase an annuity. There are a few DB schemes which operate differently and in these the pension is paid from the total accumulated fund. Some, especially in the public sector, are even pay as you go schemes like SERPS.

■ Exercise 2.9

Laurence Barnes also works for Potter and Prince Ltd and is a member of the company pension scheme. He is 30 and on an annual salary of £16,000. Calculate:

1 In today's terms the pension he would receive at 65.
2 The lump sum if he decided to take it and the corresponding reduced pension.
3 At 35 his salary has just been increased to £22,000. If he were to die then what would his spouse receive?
4 He retires but dies just over four years later. What does his spouse receive, assuming he took no tax-free cash and inflation has been only 3% p.a.?

■ The money purchase scheme (MPS)

The other type of exempt approved pension scheme is the money purchase scheme or defined contribution scheme. These are also called insured schemes since they are normally run by insurance companies. In this case there is no defined benefit and the pension is not related to final salary apart from ceilings imposed by legislation. This will be dealt with in Chapter 5. There is simply a stipulated amount paid into the pension each month for each employee. This money is invested and its final value will be used to purchase an annuity. Clearly in this version the member is entirely dependent on investment performance over the years and charges those running the pension might make.

At maturity when the annuity is purchased the choice is open at the discretion of the employer. Part of the fund could be used to take a tax-free cash sum which cannot be more than 3/80th of final salary for every year of service or 2.25 × the pension which could have been taken, whichever is the greater. Other options can also be chosen such as indexation and spouses' benefits in the event of death in retirement.

As with the DBS the employer may ask the employee to contribute towards the scheme. Illustrations are usually available of projected benefits at normal retirement date (NRD). Most of these schemes will have an NRD of 60 since the trend is towards the lower age and since this imposes no additional cost on the employer because the final benefits are not guaranteed. Projections will be based

---

The money purchase company pension does not guarantee maturity benefits.

---

on three different assumed investment growths, 6, 9 and 12 per cent. The better funds have performed well and given a growth over 12 per cent per annum over the long term, i.e. 25 years or more. Hence at the moment this is quite a realistic growth to use. Life assurance can be added to these schemes so usually on death in service (DIS) a multiple of salary would be paid as a tax-free lump sum to the spouse. It is also possible to provide DIS pensions for spouses and the better money purchase schemes would include this. If the employee leaves the company he is working for he also leaves the pension scheme but in the case of the MPS his investments will continue to take part in the full growth of the fund.

There are two fundamentally different types of money purchase scheme.

The with-profits scheme

This pension scheme will make use of the sort of with-profits funds described in Chapter 1. The value of the policy at retirement consists usually of three elements:

1 **A minimum guaranteed amount**. This could represent a notional rate of growth on the premiums of anywhere between 2 and 5 per cent depending on the contract. Guarantees like these will be taken into account when assessing the liabilities that these policies represent against the value of underlying assets and will, therefore, play their part in deciding the bonuses that will be declared.
2 **Reversionary bonuses declared every year** plus, if applicable, special reversionary bonuses. These will be added at maturity and are not actually added at the time of declaration. Once declared they cannot be taken away.
3 **The terminal bonus declared and added at maturity**. In recent years the terminal bonus has represented as much as 40 per cent of the final value of the scheme. It is clear that apart from the guaranteed part of the scheme it is impossible to monitor its current value. However, it is possible to request and receive a transfer value which is the amount which would be transferred into another scheme if so desired. It is very difficult to discover the actual charges on these policies.

> **The terminal bonus of a with-profits money purchase company pension scheme could represent as much as 40 per cent of the final fund.**

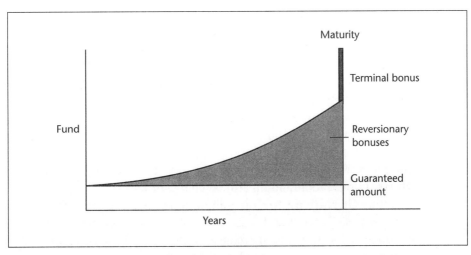

Fund

Maturity

Terminal bonus

Reversionary bonuses

Guaranteed amount

Years

Fig. 2.9 The with-profits pension scheme

In the event of the member's death before retirement the scheme may pay out:

- nothing
- a return of the premiums paid with no interest
- a return of the premiums paid with interest from 3 to 6 per cent per annum
- a return of the 'value' of the fund at the time of death – an amount calculated by the company actuary
- a terminal bonus may be added.

■ The unit-linked scheme

In this scheme the premiums purchase units in the chosen fund or funds. The funds are divided into units and pension premiums purchase a number of these units at the price prevailing at the time. The value of the fund will be the number of units owned times the value of a unit. At retirement an individual fund will have a value calculated in this way. The value of units quoted will be that after charges have been made, i.e. the bid price. Clearly it is possible to monitor the total value of the fund at any time.

The final value of the fund will be entirely the result of the investment performance the company achieves and the charges it makes.

There is usually a choice of funds and switching between them can be done at small cost. Also the fund or funds to which premiums are allocated can be changed at any time at the policy holder's wish.

The funds available will be exactly those described in Chapter 1. This time the structure put around them will be the pension which will mean that growth in the funds and income will be totally free of all UK taxes. It may be a good idea at this point to go back to Chapter 1 and work through both these funds and the criteria for choice again. Especially important is the use of the deposit fund as an instrument for consolidation. In other words, the main purpose of this fund is for switching into four or so years from retirement to avoid the risk of a sudden drop in the stock markets.

The charges with respect to the funds will be those already described. The pension structure will often vary overall charges to produce different charge structures. Thus a monthly (or annual) scheme charge of £3 to £6 (£36 to £72) may be added to cover additional administration costs. Sometimes additional management charges are applied to the amount invested in the first year or two of investment or any increase in investment. This could be between 3½ and 7 per cent per annum. To balance this, management charges on investments made from year three on will be removed. This could be very valuable since in later years an overall annual management charge of 1½ per cent on a large fund of say £200,000 would represent an annual charge of £3000.

Another alternative is to reduce allocation to investment in the first year or two to as low as 35 per cent and thereafter make no management charges. The period of reduced allocation usually relates to the term of the policy, the longer terms having the longer period of reduced allocation.

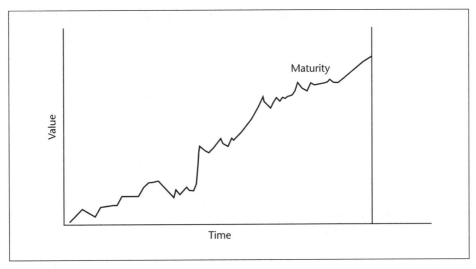

Fig. 2.10 The unit-linked pension scheme

The growth in the value of the unit-linked pension scheme could look something like this which makes the point that values can go down as well as up and this is one of the main differences between the unit-linked and the with-profits policy.

■ Additional voluntary contribution pension scheme (AVC)

Since the Social Security Act 1986 it has been mandatory that companies run these schemes to enable their pension scheme members to make additional contributions into a pension in order to enhance the final payout. These schemes are primarily money purchase schemes (MPS) although a very few of the older ones are DBS. An individual can make annual personal investments up to 15 per cent of total income. This includes the income equivalent of such benefits provided by the company as cars, medical insurance, etc. These are called P11D benefits. Thus if an individual is required to invest say 3 per cent per annum of salary into his company pension, he would be able to put 12 per cent per annum into the company AVC, thus making a total of 15 per cent. It is important to note that the mandatory 3 per cent of salary will relate to pensionable salary, i.e. usually salary minus LEL. This will mean that there will be an eligibility greater than 12 per cent of total salary. (See Case Study 2.1, p. 96.) These contributions are deducted from gross salary after NIC deductions. Thus tax relief at the highest rate paid is received immediately the contribution is made. Contributions cannot continue if the policy holder leaves the company. There is no facility with this scheme for commuting part of the pension for tax-free cash. Contributions cannot continue if the policy holder leaves the company but in the case of the MPS his investments will continue to take part in the full growth of the funds.

■ The free-standing additional voluntary contribution scheme (FSAVC)

The FSAVC is in fact free standing in that it is not connected or tied in any way to any company pension the investor may be in. In other words it is a personal investment made into the FSAVC of choice, available from an insurance company. It is an additional contribution because it can only be made by existing members of a company scheme. It is certainly voluntary. It is money purchase and has the same two-fold structure that the majority of other pension schemes have, i.e. build up a final fund and use this to purchase an annuity. Regular contributions can be made but so too can one-off singles, as a result of bonuses for example. There is no facility with this scheme for commuting some of the pension for tax-free cash. The policy holder can take it with him or her if he or she changes companies and continue to invest in it, always assuming he or she becomes a member of the new company's pension scheme.

For those in a company scheme, who have done their calculations and discovered the scheme will not provide the total financial independence required and therefore further investment is needed, the FSAVC could be the right investment. It should be carefully compared with the benefits offered by the company's additional voluntary contribution scheme. The criteria on fund choice in Chapter 1 should be valuable here.

Charges can be accurately compared by asking for illustrations of projected funds since, although insurance companies are all obliged to quote the same rates of fund growth, they will use their own particular charges.

Plans for the future will form part of a decision on whether to invest into an AVC or an FSAVC since, for example, if it is intended to work abroad for a number of years when it will not be possible to invest in a pension then a pension with lower or no upfront charges would probably be best.

Some companies offer to match investment into an AVC up to the maximum total allowed for each individual of 15 per cent of income. This, of course, is an enormous advantage and will beat anything that could be achieved with investment into an FSAVC since the company offer will immediately double the investment and the FSAVC investment performance would have to be almost miraculous to equal that. Again the annual total personal investment allowed is 15 per cent of income which can include the monetary equivalent of P11D benefits, i.e. such things as a car, petrol allowance, company medical insurance, etc. Also, pensionable salary, as we said earlier, often does not include that salary below the lower earnings level and this can be included in the calculation.

> The free-standing additional voluntary contribution pension scheme can be freely taken with you from company to company.

FSAVC premiums are paid net of basic rate tax, at 23 per cent in the tax year 1997/98. This means for a monthly contribution of £100 into the scheme £77 is paid by the investor per month. This is called premium relief at source (PRAS). For higher rate tax payers the remaining 17 per cent of tax relief would be given by change of code. So on the monthly investment of £100 a further £17 per month would be returned by way of tax relief. In other words for a monthly cost of £60 the money invested into an FSAVC is £100 per month.

So in order to complete your financial independence calculations you need to get a projection of what your additional personal investment could produce (see Table 2.15). You will be able to get this, tailored to your own situation, from any insurance company offering FSAVC contracts or running AVC contracts for companies. As we said earlier these will vary because although all companies must use growth rates of 6, 9 and 12 per cent their charges will be different.

Life assurance can be added to the FSAVC and premiums for this will attract tax relief in the same way. The amount of life assurance which can be added is governed by the rules on exempt approved company schemes. This will be dealt with in detail in Chapter 5.

At retirement the fund is used to buy an annuity. There is a considerable choice of type of annuity. Also, most insurance companies will offer an open market option, meaning that an accumulated pension fund can be used to purchase an annuity from another insurance company in order to get the best annuity on offer at the time.

Table 2.15 Typical pension projections

Regular investment into pension £100 per month gross								
Years	5	10	15	20	25	30	35	40
Fund at a growth of 12%	7240	19,200	39,400	73,400	130,000	227,000	404,000	713,000

Single contribution of £1000 into a pension								
Years	5	10	15	20	25	30	35	40
Fund at a growth of 12%	1530	2570	4310	7200	12,100	20,300	34,050	57,000

NB: Most good funds have averaged a growth of over 12% p.a. over the last 25 years

[Please note that in all cases using pension figures gross premiums will be used unless otherwise stated.]

Typical types of annuity

The choice of annuity is wide. Single life, level, non-guaranteed means the pension will remain level and die with the pensioner. Single life, indexed, non-guaranteed means the pension will increase by a specified percentage each year. Single life, indexed, guaranteed – the pension will be guaranteed for a number of years, e.g. 5, 10. This means that if death occurred before the specified length of guarantee, the pension still to be paid up to the end of the guarantee period would be paid on death to dependants, in the case of the 5 year guarantee as a tax free lump sum and in the case of the 10 year guarantee in annual taxable instalments. Joint life, indexed, guaranteed: at death of the first life the pension would continue at a percentage of its level at death for a dependant. This could be up to 100 per cent. Pensions can be paid monthly, quarterly, annually in advance or in arrears.

Any combination of these variables is available (see Table 2.16).

Table 2.16 Typical costs of annuities at age 60 paid monthly in arrears
[Yield is gross so that, for example, if the yield is 6% p.a. then £100 of fund would buy a pension of £6 p.a. The pension would then be taxed as earned income.]

Annuities	Men	Women
Single life, level, non-guaranteed	9.16%	8.17%
Single life, level, guaranteed for 5 years	9.08%	8.14%
Single life, indexed at 5% p.a., non-guaranteed	5.78%	4.81%
Single life, indexed at 5% p.a., guaranteed for 5 years	5.74%	4.79%
Joint life, indexed at 5% p.a., non-guaranteed and 50% to continue at death of first life, male 3 years older than female	4.83%	4.61%

The annuity rates quoted in Table 2.16 are actual rates for the fiscal year 1997/98. It is important to note that illustrations of projected pensions received from insurance companies will be using annuity rates considerably more optimistic than these. The Personal Investment Authority (PIA) currently make this mandatory. It is linked to the ruling that assumed average earnings index figures must always be exactly 3 per cent below the assumed growth rates, hence if a yearly 12 per cent growth rate is being considered then the AEI linked to this must be 9 per cent per annum. This sort of differential has hardly ever been the case over the last 25 years as actual investment growths have exceeded AEI figures by as much as 10 per cent per annum. To get a better projection it seems a good idea to use an indexing figure for contributions of say 5 per cent per annum which will be closer to the AEI and then apply annuity rates, such as those in Table 2.16, to the fund produced.

Annuity rates will be linked to the gilt gross redemption yield usually for gilts of 15 to 20 years' term. The gross redemption yield takes into account the final capital sum received. As this yield figure grows so will annuity rates, in direct proportion. Annuity rates offered by different companies are volatile and the actual companies offering top rates will vary from week to week. Therefore most assurance companies today offer an open market option meaning that once the policy matures the policy holder can choose a different company from which to buy the annuity with no penalty.

The eventual income which can be guaranteed from a pension fund can, in fact, be improved on by taking maximum tax-free cash and buying what is known as a purchased annuity which is taxed more favourably (dealt with in Chapter 6).

Inflation

We have seen earlier that inflation will play a major part in financial independence calculations so Table 2.17 should prove useful.

Table 2.17 The role of inflation in financial independence calculations

Inflation at 5% p.a. Years	1	2	3	4	5	6	7	8
Factor by which costs will increase	1.05	1.10	1.16	1.22	1.28	1.34	1.41	1.48
Years	9	10	11	12	13	14	15	16
Factor by which costs will increase	1.55	1.63	1.71	1.80	1.89	1.98	1.99	2.18
Years	17	18	19	20	21	22	23	24
Factor by which costs will increase	2.29	2.41	2.53	2.65	2.79	2.93	3.07	3.23
Years	25	26	27	28	29	30	31	32
Factor by which costs will increase	3.39	3.56	3.73	3.92	4.12	4.32	4.53	4.76
Years	33	34	35	36	37	38	39	40
Factor by which costs will increase	5.00	5.25	5.52	5.79	6.08	6.39	6.70	7.04

Hence, for example, at inflation of 5 per cent annually over ten years costs will increase by a factor of 1.63 so what would cost £100 now in ten years will cost £163, an increase of 63 per cent. If total financial independence in today's terms were £10,000 a year then in ten years' time it would need to be £10,000 × 1.63 = £16,300 per annum.

Another way of looking at it is that an annual pension of £20,000 projected in ten years by a pension scheme, with an average rate of inflation of 5 per cent per annum over those years would be worth, in today's terms, £20,000 per annum divided by 1.63 = £12,269.94. It is clear what a threat inflation represents, especially to fixed incomes.

Table 2.17 confirms the efficacy of the Rule of 70 – since 70 divided by 5 = 14 prices will double every 14 years. The table gives a factor of 1.99, approximately equal to 2, for 15 years and 3.92, approximately equal to 4, for 28 years.

■ **Case Study 2.1**

Sally Deerhurst is 30. She earns £16,500 p.a. and has a contracted out defined benefit company pension scheme based on sixtieths, with an NRA of 65. Pensionable salary is defined as salary minus the lower earnings level of NIC. Her company pension is indexed at 5% p.a. She has to contribute 3% of pensionable salary.

Pensionable salary = 16,500 – 3224 (the LEL) = £13,276 p.a.
Pension at 65 in today's terms = 35/60 × 13,276 = £7744.33 p.a.

She wants to be financially independent by age 60 and this for her, in today's terms, is £11,000 p.a. She thinks inflation will average 5% annually over the long term. At age 60 she will have worked for this company for 30 years. In fact if she retires before the NRA there could be a penalty and she will not get the full 30/60ths of final salary. She will have to discuss this with her company. However, we can get an approximate answer by assuming she will get 30/60ths of final salary. Since we are concerned with values in today's terms we can use current salary, which is already in today's terms. Hence pension in today's terms at 60 is 30/60 × 13,276 = £6638 p.a. Therefore her shortfall is 11,000 – 6638 = £4362 p.a., in today's terms. She needs, therefore, to make additional contributions into her company's AVC scheme or into an FSAVC to give her the additional £4362 indexed at 5% p.a. This investment will mature in 30 years' time and she thinks inflation will average 5% p.a. over the long term.

Our Rule of 70 says 70 divided by 5 = 14, so prices will double every 14 years. So in 28 years (nearly the 30 for which she will invest) prices will quadruple.

Table 2.17 gives us a factor of 4.32 times.

Hence if she needs £4362 annually in today's terms she will need 4.32 × 4362 at age 60 = £18,844 p.a. at age 60.

Sally decides she will want a pension indexed at 5% p.a. to cope with the aspect of inflation. She does not feel she needs a guaranteed period. Table 2.16 shows this particular annuity has a yield of 4.81%. This tells us that £4.81 p.a. is produced by £100.

Hence £18,844 p.a. will be produced by,

$$\frac{18,844}{4.81} \times 100 = £391,767$$

Many people are not easy with arithmetic and so I suggest just using this formula,

$$\text{Required fund} = \frac{\text{required pension}}{\text{annual yield per £100}} \times 100$$

To produce a fund of £391,767 in 30 years' time, Table 2.15 tells us that a fund of £227,000 is produced by £100 per month.

Hence a fund of £391,767 is produced by,

$$\frac{391,767}{227,000} \times 100 \text{ per month} = £172.58 \text{ per month gross}$$

$$\text{Contribution needed} = \frac{\text{fund needed}}{\text{fund produced by £100 per month}} \times 100$$

She already makes a personal contribution of 3% of £13,276 (pensionable salary) = £398.28 p.a. She is allowed to contribute a total of 15% of £16,500 (total salary) = £2475 p.a. which leaves her £2475 – £398.28 = £2076.72 p.a. = £173.06 per month gross. We can see then that her £172.58 per month gross is within limits and she will be able to achieve the level of financial independence at 60 which she wants. In fact, at age 65 she will also receive the state basic pension which in today's terms is £3242.40 p.a. so her financial independence will be enhanced. It is worth noting that her additional personal contributions of £172.58 gross only, in fact, cost her £132.89 per month because of tax relief.

■ Case Study 2.2

Tom Tasker is 42. He has been with his current company five years. It has just decided to start a money purchase company pension scheme. Tom earns £25,000 p.a. and thinks inflation will average 5% over the long term. The company has decided to invest £150 per month into the pension scheme on his behalf. Tom has a family and a mortgage and decides that at 60 his family will no longer be dependent upon him and his mortgage will be paid off. He therefore wants to be financially independent at age 60 on £15,000 p.a. in today's terms. From Table 2.15 we use age 40 to get an approximate answer as this is the age Tom is closest to.

£100 per month produces a fund of £73,400 in 20 years, at an annual growth of 12%.

From Table 2.16 an annuity guaranteed for 5 years and indexed at 5% p.a. would yield 5.74%. Hence,

£100 yields £5.74 p.a.

£73,400 would yield $\dfrac{73,400}{100} \times 5.74 = £4213$ p.a.

Pension from fund = $\dfrac{\text{fund}}{100} \times$ yield p.a. per £100

Table 2.17 tells us that inflation of 5% for 20 years produces a factor of 2.65. Hence, a pension of £4213 p.a. in 20 years will be worth in today's terms,

$\dfrac{4213}{2.65} = £1590$ p.a.

The company is investing £150 per month. This will produce a pension in today's terms of,

$\dfrac{150}{100} \times 1590 = £2385$

Pension produced = $\dfrac{\text{investment p.a.}}{100} \times$ pension produced by £100 per month

Tom's shortfall is £15,000 – £2585 = £12,615 p.a.

To produce this he would need a contribution of,

$$\frac{12,615}{1590} \times 100 \text{ per month} = £793 \text{ p.a. in today's terms}$$

Contribution needed

$$= \frac{\text{pension needed}}{\text{pension produced in today's terms by £100 per month}} \times 100$$

He is limited to a personal investment of 15% of income, i.e. 15% of £25,000 p.a. =

$$\frac{15}{100} \times £25,000 = £3750 \text{ p.a.} = £312.50 \text{ per month}$$

This additional investment would produce a pension of,

$$\frac{£312.50}{100} \times £1590 = £4969 \text{ p.a.}$$

$$\text{Pension produced in today's terms} = \frac{\text{contribution}}{100} \times \frac{\text{pension produced in today's}}{\text{terms by £100 per month}}$$

His shortfall is now £15,000 – £2385 – £4969 = £7646 p.a.

He just cannot make his objective and cannot achieve his required total financial independence at age 60. He did not start contributions early enough. Referring to Table 2.17 shows that if he continued to invest for a further five years his pension would more than double. Hence he will achieve financial independence somewhere between 60 and 65. Do not forget that at 65 he will also have his old age pension which is £3274.40 p.a. in today's terms. He will also have his SERPS which will represent approximately 17.5% of his income in today's terms, i.e. £4325.00. He decides to reset his sights and go for financial independence at age 65, which means he can make a smaller personal investment, which lightens the burden the larger investment would have represented.

However, he has not been able to achieve his wish for financial independence at age 60. It is never too early to start planning for this.

It is never too early to start planning for financial independence.

If you are a member of an exempt approved company pension scheme you will now be able to complete your calculation for total financial independence. You may like to do this now or perhaps limber up first by working through Exercise 2.10

■ **Exercise 2.10**

Natalia Prescot is 35. She earns £18,000 p.a. with Petersfield Tiles Ltd. She has worked for the company for two weeks and is already a member of the company pension scheme. This is a DB scheme based on sixtieths of final pensionable salary with NRA 60.

Pensionable salary is basic salary minus LEL. She has to make contributions of 3% p.a. of pensionable salary.

Financial independence for her in today's terms is £10,000 p.a. She hopes to achieve this by age 60. She thinks annual inflation will average 5% over the long term.

Calculate:

1 Her company pension at age 60 in today's terms.
2 Her shortfall in today's terms.
3 The shortfall this will represent at age 60.
4 Using an annuity indexed at 5% p.a. and guaranteed for 5 years (she plans to marry), calculate the fund she will need.
5 Calculate the pension contribution she will have to make into an AVC or FSAVC to achieve this.
6 Check that this is possible.

Retirement annuity contracts (RAC) and personal pension schemes (PPS)

The retirement annuity is the forerunner of the personal pension scheme. These pensions were also called 'self-employed deferred annuities' while in fact they were available to anyone with an earned income which was not already being pensioned. This, of course, included employees. The RAC was introduced in the Income and Corporation Taxes Act (ICTA) 1970 under Sections 226–28, later incorporated in ICTA 1988, and because of this were often called Section 226 schemes. Finance (No.2) Act 1987, also incorporated later in ICTA 1988, introduced the personal pension scheme (PPS) which started in July 1988. They are similar in that contributions attract tax relief and investments grow free of all UK taxes. At retirement the fund is used to buy an annuity which is taxed as earned income. Part of the annuity can be commuted for a tax-free lump sum. In the case of the PPS the maximum will be 25 per cent of the fund. The RAC limits it to 3 times the residual pension after the cash is taken with an overall maximum of £150,000 unless the policy was effected before 17 March 1987. The annuity used is level, non-guaranteed, paid annually in arrears, thus giving the largest pension and therefore the biggest tax-free lump sum. The investor is then free to take the annuity of his choice.

Since July 1988 it has not been possible to commence a new RAC. Those who already have them are able to continue premiums, may even increase them or make single contributions to the scheme, but they may not change them by adding life insurance or waiver of contribution option (see later). For those who have no company pension the PPS is the current available vehicle for their pension planning. It has many similarities with the RAC, but there are differences. Both are treated in this section because some readers will already be investing in an RAC. It therefore seems that the most productive way of dealing with them both is to describe the PPS and where differences arise treat that at the time.

Since tax relief is given on the contributions the amount one may invest is limited. This is done in two ways:

1 A limit on the percentage of income which can be invested.
2 A limit on the amount of income which can be pensioned, which in the fiscal year 1997/98 stood at £84,000. This is meant to increase in line with the Retail Prices Index (RPI) and started 6 April 1989 at £60,000. Thus someone currently earning £100,000 can only invest a percentage of £84,000.

Premiums for life assurance receive tax relief if included in a personal pension scheme or retirement annuity contract.

Life cover can be included in the pension contract and that part of the premium diverted to this also attracts the same tax reliefs. The maximum which can be paid for this is 5 per cent of earnings which is included in the overall maximum (see Table 2.18).

Table 2.18 Maximum contributions possible to PPS

Age attained at beginning of tax year	Percentage of earnings	1997/98 maximum contributions for earnings of £84,000+
35 or less	17.5	£14,700
36–45	20.0	£16,800
46–50	25.0	£21,000
51–55	30.0	£25,200
56–60	35.0	£29,400
61–74	40.0	£33,600
Life cover	5.0	£4200

■ Example 2.17

a) A self-employed person age 25 on 3 February 1997, earns £15,000 p.a. and could invest a maximum of $17\frac{1}{2}$% of £15,000 = £3062.50 p.a.

If this person wanted to spend £450 p.a. on life assurance within the pension, i.e. 3% of NRE then only $14\frac{1}{2}$% of NRE, i.e. £2175 p.a. would be left for pension investment.

b) A self-employed person age 53 on 1 January 1997 earns £90,000 and could therefore invest a maximum of 30% of £84,000, £25,200 p.a.

In the case of the RAC, investment is limited in only one way, by percentage of income which can be invested. This is an enormous advantage to the higher earner since there is no earnings cap applied to investment (see Table 2.19).

Table 2.19 Maximum contributions possible to existing RACs as a percentage of earnings

Age attained at beginning of tax year	Percentage of earnings
50 or less	17.5
51–55	20.0
56–60	22.5
61 or over	27.5
Life assurance	5.0

There is nothing to stop a contributor to an RAC investing in a PPS as well. However, if this happens the contributor's maximum overall contributions are immediately affected by the earnings cap.

■ Example 2.18

Adrian Walters earns £30,000. He was 36 on 17 January 1997. He is currently investing in an RAC at £2000 p.a. He has just completed his financial plan and sees that he has to increase his pension scheme contributions as much as possible.

Maximum possible into RAC 17½% of £30,000 = £5250 p.a.
Maximum possible into PPS = 20% of £30,000 = £6000 p.a.

At this stage then he should put an additional £4000 p.a. into a PPS in order to maximise his contributions. This fixes his pensionable income at £84,000 but at this stage it does not have a negative effect. He must keep a check on this as his income increases.

■ Example 2.19

Fiona Shepherd was 44 on 14 February 1997. She is a securities dealer with a merchant bank, earning £110,000 p.a. She is currently investing £1000 p.a. into an RAC. She has been so busy with her career that she has only recently completed her financial plan. She realises she desperately needs to do something about eventual total financial independence and certainly needs to invest the maximum she possibly can into pensions.

Maximum possible into RAC is 17½% of £110,000 = £19,250 p.a.
Maximum possible into PPS = 20% of £84,000 = £16,800 p.a.

In this case she should clearly increase her RAC and not invest into a PPS.

If you are already contributing to an RAC you need to calculate the advantage or disadvantage in also investing in a PPS.

It is important for you if you have an RAC to know whether you should increase it or continue it at current level and, in addition, start contributions into a PPS. In each age bracket there will clearly be a point at which the two possibilities will be equal, i.e. the breakpoint. This breakpoint will change as you get older.

■ Example 2.20

Dilys Jones was 49 on 17 March 1997. She has an RAC and in order to help with her financial plan needs to know the breakpoint between PPS and RAC for her particular age, i.e. at what salary would the amounts she could invest be equal?

Maximum into PPS = 25% of £84,000 = £21,000

She is allowed to invest 17½% of total salary into an RAC. When will this equal £21,000?

$$\text{Total salary} \times 17\tfrac{1}{2}\% \qquad = 21,000$$
$$\text{Total salary} \times 0.175 \qquad = 21,000$$
$$\text{Total salary} = \frac{21,000}{0.175} \qquad = 120,000$$

In other words if she is earning more than £120,000 she can invest more by increasing her RAC.

■ Exercise 2.11

Hamish McCallum was 51 on 3 January 1997. He is already investing into an RAC. Calculate the breakpoint for his particular age.

Table 2.20 Breakpoints

Age	0–35	36–45	46–50	51–55	56–60	61–74
Breakpoint	84,000	96,000	120,000	126,000	130,667	122,182

Thus at any given age for an income above the breakpoint more money can be invested in an RAC than can be contributed to a PPS.

If you are an RAC contributor it is extremely important to know the breakpoints before starting a PPS.

For the high earner who has an existing RAC this should be treasured like gold. It enables him or her to request the return of more and more of the money he or she has paid to the Inland Revenue and is totally and utterly legal. There are many people who could afford to do this who for some reason do not. It should be noted that in any year investing even a minimal amount into a PPS causes salary to be capped that year with respect to contributions into not only the PPS but also the RAC.

If you do have an RAC you need to mastermind any use of a PPS and only invest in one in the years when your income is below the breakpoint unless other conceived advantages of the PPS outweigh the advantage of being able to invest more money. In this situation the question of charge structure will be paramount since if you commence a regular contribution PPS with upfront charges and then have to stop future contributions, i.e. make it paid up, you will have paid those charges unnecessarily.

The income on which pension contributions are based is net relevant earnings (NRE). For the employed person this will include basic salary, overtime, bonuses and the salary equivalent of benefits in kind, or P11D benefits, such as a company car, medical insurance, etc.

For the self-employed NRE are the profits for the year minus business expenses and capital allowances, in other words the before tax profit.

■ Tax relief

All contributions to the RAC are paid gross and tax relief is claimed back by an adjustment of tax code in the case of the employee and by a reduction in before tax profit by the self-employed. In the case of the PPS it is exactly the same situation as for the self-employed, but for the employee premiums are paid net of basic rate tax, which is 23 per cent currently in the fiscal year 1997/98. Thus if the contributor wished £100 per month to go into his or her PPS he or she would contribute £77 and the £23 per month would be claimed back by the insurance company from the Inland Revenue and added to his or her contribution. If he or she were a higher rate tax-payer, currently 40 per cent, the rest of the tax relief, i.e. 17 per cent, would be received by an adjustment in his or her tax code. Remember this is exactly the same for the FSAVC.

The employed person has a cashflow advantage since he or she has to find less each month than the self-employed for the same total investment. The self-employed person would get his or her relief by way of a reduction in tax paid at the time he or she would normally pay tax on 31 January and 31 July each year.

The PPS and RAC will always be MPS and can be with profits or unit linked as described earlier and there will be exactly the same range of funds and charge structures as those found in the FSAVC. Regular and/or single contributions will be available. There will usually be an indexing facility available for the premiums. Contracts today are very flexible, allowing variation of premiums up or down, and enabling stopping and restarting contributions. Although all of these facilities are available they are primarily there to accommodate fluctuations in a working career and best results will be obtained by tailoring your future pension contributions as accurately as possible. It is always important to study charging structures in the light of future plans. For example, someone planning to work abroad for a period in the near future would not really want to invest in a pension whose charges were more upfront, although for the person intending regular contributions till retirement this method of charging can be the most advantageous.

Life assurance can be included in the contract and is limited to premiums representing no more than 5 per cent per annum of NRE. Although tax relief is available on these premiums making the cost less expensive, it should be clearly understood that premiums used for life assurance cannot be used for investment and thus less advantage is being taken of the growth in the funds being free of all UK taxes.

■ Benefits in kind or P11D benefits

The most usual of these is the company car available for private use. The taxable benefit is currently 35 per cent of the list price. This is reduced by one-third where there are at least 2500 business miles per annum and by a further one-third where annual business mileage is at least 18,000 miles.

Where private petrol is supplied by the employer this is also treated as a P11D benefit which, in the tax year 1997/98 was,

Engine size	Petrol	Diesel
Up to 1400cc	£800	£740
1400 to 2000cc	£1010	£740
More than 2000cc	£1490	£940

These figures apply regardless of the amount of fuel supplied.

In the case of living accommodation, if the employer owned the property, the taxable benefit was the gross annual value for rating purposes. This treatment continues to apply for properties on existing rating lists. In other cases, since the abolition of domestic rates the Inland Revenue makes an estimate of what that rateable value would have been. Where the property is rented by the employer the assessable amount of taxable benefit is the greater of the actual rent paid and the rateable value.

In the case of premiums paid for such things as medical insurance the taxable value is simply the annual premiums paid.

■ Example 2.21

Alexander Chapman earns £35,000 p.a. His company provides him with free accommodation in a property whose gross rateable value is £1000 p.a. He has a company car, list price £23,000, and free medical insurance costing the company £1100 p.a. He is glad he has this since he has to drive at least 20,000 business miles every year.

	Net relevant earnings
Salary	35,000
P11D benefits:	
Car 23,000 × 35% = 8050	
8050 × $\frac{1}{3}$ = 2683	2683
Free accommodation	1000
Medical insurance	1100
Total	£39,783

■ **Exercise 2.12**

Betty Rawlinson has an annual salary of £36,000, a company car (list price £18,000), free accommodation (rateable value £1200, on which her employer pays the rent of £6000 p.a.) and medical insurance for which the company pays £850 yearly. She does 10,000 business miles p.a.

Calculate her net relevant earnings on Form 2.5.

■ **Form 2.5 NET RELEVANT EARNINGS ANALYSIS**

Name	Year
	Net relevant earnings
Salary	
P11D benefits:	
Car	
Free accommodation	
Medical insurance	
	———————
Total	———————

If you are employed you might now like to calculate your own NRE using Form 2.6.

■ **Form 2.6 NET RELEVANT EARNINGS ANALYSIS**

Name	Year
	Net relevant earnings
Salary	
P11D benefits:	
Car	
Free accommodation	
Medical insurance	
	———————
Total	———————

■ Maturity

The proceeds of the PPS can be taken by way of pension or tax-free cash and reduced pension without necessarily retiring from work. In the case of the PPS this can be done at any time between 50 and 75. The ages for the RAC are 60 to 75. The tax-free cash from the PPS will be 25 per cent of the value of the fund, in the case of the RAC the amount is three times the residual pension after the cash is taken.

Most contracts are constructed in such a way that the taking of benefits can be phased. For example a policy holder deciding he or she wants to work only four days a week could supplement the possible decrease in income by taking only part of his or her pension. A little later he or she could take a further instalment and so on. It is not possible to delay taking benefits beyond the age of 75. Most insurance companies offer an open market option which allows the purchase of an annuity from another company which may be offering better terms at the time.

> The proceeds of a personal pension scheme can be taken from age 50 on.

■ What happens to your pension fund if you die before maturity?

If you were to die before taking the proceeds of your pension, the insurance company is allowed to pay the whole of the value of the fund, tax free, into your estate. Not all contracts will do this however and payouts may vary as follows:

1 no return (this is very rare)
2 return of contributions only
3 return of contributions with interest credited at usually around 4 per cent per annum
4 return of total fund.

Thereafter it would be governed by your will, which is treated in some detail in Chapter 3. Probate has to be granted before your estate can be distributed and there might be a liability for inheritance tax (IHT). Both of these problems can be solved simply by writing your RAC or PPS in trust. A flexible trust is used for this purpose. This trust will specify an immediate beneficiary or beneficiaries to whom the benefits would go, on the death of the policy holder, if not changed before his or her death. There would also be a number of potential (reserve) beneficiaries to whom the death benefit might go if the policy holder decides before his or her death, or the trustees decide after his or her death. Thus beneficiaries may be changed, within these two classes, either to exclude the immediate beneficiary or not. The pension remains under the control of the policy holder and cannot be assigned and will revert to him or her when he or she requires the benefits.

As mentioned earlier it is possible to include life assurance on the pension policy and this is dealt with in more detail in Chapter 3.

It is important to mention here that the exempt approved company pension scheme will usually be written in trust automatically. The trustees will either be the body corporate of the company or a number of directors of the company. As a result of the Maxwell incident concerning the Mirror Group pension scheme the Pensions Act 1995 has decreed that employees must now be represented among the trustees. The AVC and the FSAVC are also automatically written in trust and in this case the trustees would be the insurance company running the scheme. In the case of all these schemes this allows death benefits to be paid directly to the beneficiaries bypassing the estate and therefore potential inheritance tax.

■ Medical disability and waiver of contribution (WOC)

> In certain circumstances if you become medically unable to work the insurer will waive your pension premiums but your scheme will continue to be credited with them right up to retirement.

Becoming medically unable to work with respect to loss of income and its replacement has been treated in some detail earlier. However, the question remains, 'What about pension contributions?' If the benefit under the permanent health insurance or income protection plan is paid from a personal policy it is free of tax and is not treated as earned income. Thus, even if there was a wish to continue to pay contributions to an RAC or PPS it would not be possible since there would be no NRE. If the benefit is paid from a company policy then the income is actually salary and the continuation of pension premiums could be considered. However, it is unlikely, with a reduced income, that this would be found affordable. The answer is the waiver of contribution.

The waiver of contribution is an enormously valuable option since it guarantees the pension in the event of becoming medically unable to work. A small additional premium, somewhere between 3 and 6 per cent of the original premium, is charged for this facility. If medical inability to work happens, then after a deferment period of three to six months, the premiums are waived by the insurer but the scheme continues to be credited with them. They are also indexed if this was part of the contract.

■ Case Study 2.3

William Rhodes, who attained the age of 25 in March 1997, wants to invest £100 a month into a PPS with selected retirement age 55. He opts for indexation at 3% p.a. and pays the extra premium of £3 per month to include waiver of contribution with a deferment period of three months.

After three years he has a heart attack and can never work again. After the deferment of three months his waiver of contribution latches in and his premiums are credited to his pension scheme and also indexed. Remembering that his pension premiums are indexed at 3% p.a. he will have paid a total of £121.08 gross for the option of waiver. In return for this his premiums will be credited and indexed at 3% p.a. right up to his 55th birthday, approximately £55,557.

The extremely beneficial effect of adding the waiver of premium benefit to an RAC or PPS is clear. Since it guarantees a pension against the effect of medical inability to work, it might well have been called the pension guarantee. This benefit is not available under the company pension AVC or FSAVC. It is an enormous advantage for those who are making their pension provision using an RAC or PPS and should certainly be seriously considered in one's financial plan.

■ Pension guarantee policy

What about those in company pensions for whom no provision is made for continuing pension premiums in the event of medical inability? Is there anything they can do? A critical illness policy might be considered as a pension guarantee policy.

■ Example 2.22

Diana Pullen is 40 and looking forward at age 60 to an annual pension of £20,000 provided by her company scheme. In the event of her becoming medically unable to work the company would pay her full salary for six months and thereafter 60% of pensionable salary which will actually be the proceeds of a company PHI policy.

Unfortunately no further premiums would go into her pension which will, of course, severely restrict what she will receive at age 60. As her benefit from the PHI policy will be paid as salary and therefore she will pay tax and NIC contributions on it, she does not feel she would be able to contribute anything into a pension herself.

She decides to look at a critical illness policy to guarantee her pension. A cover of £100,000 fully indexed in line with the Average Earnings Index (AEI) and including the waiver of contribution (WOC) benefit would cost approximately £80.30 per month. As the benefit is inflation proofed this can be considered to be £100,000 in today's terms whenever it might be paid out. This invested, for example, in unit trusts could be considered to produce an annual indexed income of 5%, i.e. £5000 p.a. Her annual pension in today's terms would be £7538 so she has managed to guarantee a sizeable portion of her pension. She may feel she can afford now to increase this guarantee. It is extremely important at this juncture to emphasise the point that the benefit from a permanent health insurance will come to an end. At age 60 income could suddenly disappear. It is therefore crucial in financial planning to be crystal clear about the situation at this point, when the critical illness policy can be like a lifebelt to a drowning man.

A PHI policy will come to an end. At age 60 income could suddenly disappear. A pension guarantee policy could be invaluable.

You may wish to work through your own situation with respect to this contingency when you have done your financial independence planning.

If you are not currently in a pension scheme or are in a group personal pension scheme you are now in a position to complete your calculations for total financial independence.

GPs and dentists

GPs and dentists are in a unique position in that, unless they are totally in private practice, they work for the National Health Service and are actually members of the National Health Sponsored Superannuation Scheme (NHSSS) (an exempt approved pension scheme) but yet are considered to be self-employed. Hence they are members of a company pension scheme but are self-employed. Such a person is required to make personal contributions to the NHSSS representing 6 per cent of NHS earnings. These contributions are tax relievable at the highest rate of tax paid. However, a GP or dentist is also able to make further pension provision by investing into a PPS and before July 1988, into an RAC. There are two ways in which this can be done:

1 By pensioning any non-NHS earnings and privately earned income.

However, the figure for private earnings is not the actual figure. The figure is arrived at by a formula, i.e. total earnings minus 100/6 of NHS pension contributions. It is this figure on which the eligibility is assessed for PPS contributions.

■ Example 2.23

A GP has total earnings assessed in the tax year 1997/98 of £50,000. His NHS pension contributions are £2400. He was 40 on 12 March 1997.

$$2400 \times \frac{100}{6} = 40,000$$

Hence his private earnings are deemed to be £50,000 – £40,000 = £10,000 p.a. He is therefore eligible to invest 20% of £10,000 = £2000 into a PPS.

---

2 By giving up the tax relief on the 6 per cent invested into the NHSSS the GP or dentist is allowed to repension up to the whole of his or her earned income.

■ Example 2.24

In the case of Example 2.23 we can see that he could now invest £10,000 into a PPS and, of course, receive tax relief on it at the highest rate he pays.

It is important to note that the contributions themselves to the NHSSS are not given up, but merely the tax relief on them.

> ## ■ Exercise 2.13
>
> Petra Pollard has total earnings in the tax year 1997/98 of £65,000. Her NHS pension contributions are £3000 p.a. She was 34 on 14 June 1997. Calculate how much she could invest into a PPS using each method.

This unique concession is enormously advantageous and should ensure beyond doubt that this sector of society will reach financial independence.

Is it tax efficient? Using the case in Example 2.23 the tax relief would be,

$$(40\% \times £2400) + (40\% \times £2000) = £960 + £800 = £1760$$

In the case in Example 2.24 it is,

$$40\% \times £10,000 = £4000$$

In method two the whole of the income does not have to be repensioned, but it is clearly not tax efficient if the extra investment does not at least mean that no tax relief is lost.

Using Example 2.23 the GP is losing tax relief on £2400, hence additional investment into PPS must be at least £2400, which means a break even from the tax point of view and an additional £2400 invested.

Late starters

It cannot be stressed enough how crucial it is to start planning for total financial independence as early as possible. Late starters may find themselves in the position of Tom Tasker in Case Study 2.2 (p. 97) who had to work five years longer than he intended. It could even be worse than that. Financial planning is about reality and sometimes reality is tough, so avoid shocks and start early.

> It is crucial to start planning for total financial independence as early as possible.

However, that said, the Inland Revenue have made some provision for catching up.

■ Carry forward of unused eligibility or relief

> You can go back and sweep up all or part of the pension contributions you could have made in the last six years and pay them now with full tax relief.

This facility enables contributions missed from previous years to be made up. It is possible to go back six fiscal years and pick up any unused pension eligibility for those years. In order to do this the maximum possible pension contributions in the current year have to have been made. First, unused eligibility in the tax year six years before is swept up, then five years before, then four years before and so on.

■ Example 2.25

Mavis McTor was 49 on 4 March 1997. She has only just decided to make contributions to a PPS. She earns £30,000 p.a. and has just been left a small bequest of £10,000. She wants to put all of this into a PPS.

Consulting Table 2.18 (p. 100) she sees she can contribute £7500 in tax year 1997/98. However, in 1991/92, six years before, she earned £25,000 and made no PPS contribution. At the beginning of that tax year she was 43 and therefore could have invested 20% of £25,000 = £5000 into a PPS. She can therefore opt to carry £2500 of this past eligibility into the current tax year and make a pension contribution of £10,000 fully tax relievable. Tax relief for a contribution carried forward is given at the rate in force at the time of payment.

■ Exercise 2.14

Tom Bates was 36 on 1 April 1997. He earns £20,000 p.a. He wants to start contributions into a PPS with a bang and puts in £8000. In tax year 1991/92 he earned £12,000 and in tax year 1992/93 £12,500.

Calculate how he can arrange to invest the full £8000 into a PPS in tax year 1997/98.

You are not allowed to invest in any one year more than total income in that year, ICTA 1988. This would, anyway, not be very tax-efficient. Part of an income, an amount equal to the personal allowance, is not taxed anyway. Carry forward of unused relief has to be approved by the Inland Revenue and so Form PP42 has to be completed and submitted to the Revenue if you are self-employed and to the provider of your pension contract if you are employed.

If you are employed and a higher rate tax payer the form has to go to the Inland Revenue with a copy to the insurer.

> **Tax relief for a contribution carried forward is given at the rate in force at the time of payment.**

Those in group personal pension schemes are also eligible for carry forward as long as the relevant contributions are made personally. It is not available in respect of contributions paid by an employer.

■ Case Study 2.4

Mary O'Sullivan was 47 on 23 January 1997. Her income and pension contributions are shown in Table 2.21. Her salary is £30,000 p.a. and she is currently contributing £2000 p.a. to a PPS.

In the present year she could contribute a further £5500 (£7500 − £2000). Then, if she wished, she could carry forward £5400 from the tax year 1991/92, then £5000 from the tax year 1992/93 and so on.

> **If you do not use your pension eligibility for six years back, then you lose it.**

It is important to point out that if she does not use the eligibility of £5400 from tax year 1991/92 by the end of the current tax year, she will lose it since she will then only be able to go back as far as the tax year 1992/93.

Table 2.21 Worked example of income and pension contributions (1)

			Details of carry forward			
	1	2	3	4	5	6
Income tax year	1991/1992	1992/1993	1993/1994	1994/1995	1995/1996	1996/1997
Net relevant earnings non-pensionable sources	27,000	27,500	28,000	29,000	29,000	30,000
A Maximum relief available	5400	5500	5600	5800	5800	7500
B Payments made under PP schemes, RA contracts etc	nil	500	1000	1000	1000	2000
C Unused relief available (A−B)	5400	5000	4600	4800	4800	5500

We can see that she has scope using carry forward to invest a further £35,600. Since her income is £30,000 she is not allowed to invest more than this, but even if she could it would be terribly tax inefficient since she would receive no tax relief at all on £10,605 of it, i.e. £5600 exceeding her income, plus £4045, the personal allowance on which she has already had tax relief. Therefore if she desperately wanted to invest this amount of money she should invest part this year and part next.

■ **Exercise 2.15**

Peter Sands was 31 on 4 March 1997. His current annual salary is £20,000, and has been the same since tax year 1993/94. Before that, for the previous five years it was £17,000 p.a. He has been investing £1200 p.a. gross into a PPS since 6 April 1992.

Calculate the maximum which could be invested in the current tax year using unused reliefs.

Would it be wise to do this?

You might now like to calculate your own situation if carry forward applies to you.

■ **Carry back provisions**

This process can be refined further by the use of carry back provisions. Part or all of the contribution may be carried back to the tax year preceding the year of payment. This means it will be treated for tax purposes exactly as if it had been paid in the year to which it is carried back and the maximum contribution will be that for the maximum pertaining in that year. This could, of course, include any unused eligibility for the six years previous to the year to which the contribution has been carried back. For example if a contribution paid in the tax year 1997/98 were carried back to the tax year 1996/97 and happened to bring the total deemed paid in that year to more than the maximum allowable, carry forward from tax year 1990/91 could be used to justify this. Hence by the use of the carry back provision we can now go back seven years to sweep up unused eligibility or relief. Also, instead of spreading the contribution and hence the tax relief between the current tax year and the next, it can be spread between the current tax year and the previous one. Thus the tax relief is available much earlier by way of tax rebate.

It is not possible to carry back more than one year except in the situation where there were no net relevant earnings in that particular year, when contributions can be carried back to the previous year. Hence in the case of a situation like this a contribution paid in 1997/98 could be carried back to the tax year 1995/96. In this case missed eligibility could be swept up going as far back as 1989/90.

■ Example 2.26

Blodwin Davis was 39 on 27 March 1997. Her salary in 1997/98 is £26,000 p.a. She has just increased her annual PPS investment to £2000 p.a. She has just inherited £30,000 and considers using this towards her financial independence. Her salary and pension contribution history is shown in Table 2.22.

In the tax year 1990/91 her annual salary was £19,500 and no pension contribution was made. Hence unused eligibility in that year was £3412.50. By using carry back this can also be swept up. In the year 1997/98 she will still have eligibility of £3200 left after she has made her contribution of £2000.

Table 2.22 Worked example of income and pension contributions (2)

	Details of carry forward					
	1	2	3	4	5	6
Income tax year	1991/1992	1992/1993	1993/1994	1994/1995	1995/1996	1996/1997
Net relevant earnings non-pensionable sources	20,000	23,000	25,000	25,000	25,000	26,000
A Maximum relief available	3500	4025	4575	5000	5000	5200
B Payments made under PP schemes, RA contracts etc	nil	nil	nil	1500	1500	1500
C Unused relief available (A−B)	3500	4025	4575	3500	3500	3700

Hence her total eligibility is:

Year	1990/91	1991/92	1992/93	1993/94	1994/95	1995/96	1996/97	1997/98
£	3412.50	3500.00	4025.00	4575.00	3500.00	3500.00	3700.00	3200.00

= £28,412.50

Clearly she must carry some back into tax year 1996/97 in order to be able to go back to year 1990/91. In order to do this she must contribute the maximum possible in 1996/97, i.e. another £3700. It is important not to lose any eligibility so the whole £3412.50 should be swept up. This means at least £3700 + £3412.50 = £7112.50 should be carried back.

In 1996/97 personal allowance £3765

Tax	£0–£3900	20%
	£3900–£25,500	24%
	Over £25,500	40%

Looking at the tax situation in 1996/97 the basic rate was 24%. It is only 23% in 1997/98. Hence it would be important to put as much relieved against the 24% rate as possible. In 1996/97 she paid 24% tax on £26,000 – £3765 – £3900 = £18,335, i.e. income minus personal allowance in that year minus taxed at 20% in that year. She has already made a contribution of £1500 in 1996/97. Hence she should carry back £18,335 – £1500 = £16,835.

This will be relieved at 24% and she will get an immediate tax rebate of £4040.40.

The total amount of her income in the tax year 1997/98 taxed at 23% is £26,000 – £4045 – £4100 = £17,855. She has already made a contribution of £2000 leaving £15,855. She has eligibility left of £26,412.50 – £16,835 = £9577.50. Hence she should make this contribution since all of it will be relieved at 23%.

It is clear that carry back can be extremely valuable to someone who was paying higher rate tax in the previous year but only basic rate in the current year since pension contributions could achieve 40 per cent tax relief rather than 23 per cent.

■ **Exercise 2.16**

Patrick O'Connel was 47 on 1 April 1997. His annual income is £30,000. His total PPS contribution for 1997/98 will be £3000. Previous figures are as follows and in 1990/91 from an income of £20,000 he invested £1000 into his PPS. If he carries a contribution back into the tax year 1996/97 calculate the total eligibility he could now make use of in the fiscal year 1997/98.

Decide on the most tax-efficient way he should spread a contribution of this amount between this year and the previous.

			Details of carry forward			
	1	2	3	4	5	6
Income tax year	1991/1992	1992/1993	1993/1994	1994/1995	1995/1996	1996/1997
Net relevant earnings non-pensionable sources	20,000	22,000	24,000	26,000	28,000	30,000
A Maximum relief available	4400	4400	4800	5200	5600	7500
B Payments made under PP schemes, RA contracts etc	1000	1000	2500	1700	3000	3000
C Unused relief available (A−B)	3000	3400	2300	3500	2600	4500

Carry back has also to be approved by the Inland Revenue and Form PP43 used. Self-employed would send this to the tax inspector, employees on basic rate tax to the insurer and higher rate employees would send it to the tax inspector with a copy to the insurer.

For self-employed and higher rate tax employees a further form, PP120, must accompany either Form PP42 or PP43 and this must be sent to the tax inspector.

■ The self-invested personal pension (SIPP)

The self-invested personal pension scheme or plan (SIPP) is by definition a PPS and is therefore governed by all the rules and regulations applicable to the PPS. A much wider range of investment is possible and it can even borrow money to buy commercial property. It will be dealt with in Chapter 5.

■ Deferred annuity purchase

Since the 1995 Pensions Act it is no longer necessary initially to purchase an annuity. This can be deferred to age 75 with an income paid from the pension fund. This is treated in Chapter 6.

■ The income withdrawal facility

This is another way of deferring the taking of an annuity and in many ways is more flexible. It will be discussed fully in Chapter 6.

Contracting out of SERPS

It is possible to contract out of SERPS and invest what would have been part of the national insurance contribution of both the employer and the employee either into a company scheme or a PPS depending on the main pension scheme.

■ Contracting out of SERPS via a defined benefit company scheme

It has been possible to contract out with this type of scheme since 6 April 1978 as a result of the Social Security Act 1975. This decision would be taken by the employer when setting up the scheme. It would apply to all members of the scheme and, therefore, for all those in DB schemes they are already contracted out of SERPS or not. In other words there was and is no personal choice in such schemes. Members of contracted out schemes pay lower national insurance contributions and so will the employer (see Table 2.23).

Table 2.23 Reduced NIC for a contracted out DB pension scheme

Earnings		Contracted in rates		Contracted out rates		
Weekly (£)	Yearly (£)	Employee	Employer	Employee	Employer	
					% on first £62	% on remainder
0–61.99	0–3224	nil	nil	nil	nil	nil
62–109.99	3224–5720	2% of £62	3%	2% of £62	3	nil
110–154.99	5720–8060	plus	5%	plus	5	2
155–209.99	8060–10,920	10% of	7%	8.4% of	7	4
210–465	10,920–24,180	£62–465	10%	£62–£465	10	7
465 plus	24,180 plus	–	10%	–	10	7/10

> **An employee in a contracted out defined benefit company pension scheme pays 1.6% less national insurance contribution.**

This amounts to a rebate in NIC on band earnings of employee 1.6 per cent, employer 3 per cent. These amounts must be invested into the scheme. It is then mandatory that the pension scheme takes over the responsibility of paying a pension equivalent to SERPS. This is called guaranteed minimum pension and it is included within the total pension paid out by the scheme, not in addition to it.

For those in a contracted in scheme then SERPS will be in addition to whatever the pension will pay. This is an important point to clarify when studying the benefits of a company scheme. Benefits under GMP are similar to SERPS, but very slightly different.

Original basis

- ■ Retirement in 1997/98 or earlier: 1.25 per cent of total surpluses (same in SERPS).
- ■ Retirement in 1998/99 or later: 25 per cent/N of the total surpluses (it can be seen that this is 25 per cent of the average surplus whereas SERPS would have applied to the best 20 years).

Revised basis

As a result of the Social Security Act 1986 and commencing on 6 April 1988:

- Retirement in 1997/98 or earlier: 1.25 per cent of the surpluses for years 1978/79 to 1987/88 inclusive plus 1 per cent of the surpluses for the tax years 1988/89 onwards.
- Retirement in 1998/99 onwards: 25 per cent/N of the surpluses for the tax years 1978/79 to 1987/88 inclusive; plus 20 per cent/N of the surplus for the tax years 1988/89 onwards.

Where N is the number of contracted out tax years in the member's working life after 5 April 1978. (It can be seen that there was no sliding scale introduced here.)

The benefit could be paid at whatever the retirement age is for that particular company scheme, which could be from 60. The benefit in payment must be increased by the RPI or 3 per cent if lower. However, for benefits accruing from 6 April 1997, the increase must be in line with the RPI or 5 per cent if lower. A widow or widower would be paid half what the spouse would have been paid. With this sort of pension the member has no choice and could not therefore eventually contract back into SERPS at a later date. A member has the choice to opt out of the whole company pension scheme but not just the GMP part of it.

■ Contracting out of SERPS via a contracted out money purchase scheme (COMPS)

As a result of the Social Security Act 1986 it has been possible since 1 July 1988 to contract out of SERPS using a COMPS. Here again the employee will pay 1.6 per cent less NIC on band earnings and the employer 1.5 per cent less. The employer will have to pay this into the COMPS. In addition to this the Department of Social Security (DSS) will pay into the scheme an age-related bonus. Table 2.24 shows the total payments into the COMPS.

Table 2.24 COMPS total age-related rebates as a percentage of NIC including bonuses

Age last birthday as at 5 April 1997	1997/98	1998/99	1999/2000	2000/01	2001/02
15	3.1	3.2	3.2	3.3	3.3
20	3.4	3.4	3.5	3.5	3.6
25	3.6	3.7	3.8	3.8	3.8
30	3.9	4.0	4.0	4.1	4.2
35	4.3	4.4	4.4	4.5	4.6
40	5.2	5.3	5.3	5.4	5.5
45	8.0	8.1	8.2	8.3	8.5
50+	9.0	9.0	9.0	9.0	9.0

For example for a person who is 30 on 5 April 1997 the age-related bonus in 1999/2000 will be 4.0−3.1 = 0.9 per cent of NIC, since the ordinary rebate is 3.1 per cent. These contributions will purchase protected rights and at maturity must be used to purchase a unisex, unistatus joint life annuity which must increase at RPI or 3 per cent if lower. This must inevitably lower the purchasing power of that part of the fund, since the unisex, unistatus annuity will be more expensive than other annuities one might have wished to purchase. However, being joint life it follows that if one spouse dies the remaining spouse continues to receive the total pension. Those protected rights accruing after 6 April 1997 must be used to purchase an annuity increasing at RPI or 5 per cent if lower. Benefits from protected rights can be taken at the normal retirement age of the company pension scheme.

It is clear that there is no guarantee here and the pension resulting from protected rights contributions will be better or worse than SERPS purely as a result of the investment performance and charge structure of the particular scheme. It should also be noted that SERPS in payment has no ceiling on the indexing.

Using certain investment growth rate assumptions the results of contracting out of SERPS or staying in can be compared. There is a break even point after which it is better to contract back into SERPS. This will occur around age 50 for men and age 40 for women in the tax year 1997/98. Contracting back into SERPS from a COMPS will be at the discretion of the employer.

■ Contracting out using a personal pension scheme (PPS)

This time the choice is entirely the individual's, who will apply to the DSS through a provider of PPS to contract out of SERPS. Both the employee and the employer will continue to pay NIC at full rates. The DSS will pay into the PPS a rebate from the NIC contributions of the employee 1.5 per cent, from the employer 1.6 per cent. This time the employee's rebate will be grossed up re basic rate tax. Age-related bonuses will also be paid into the PPS in exactly the same way as for COMPS. Once again these contributions are called protected rights and at maturity must be used to purchase exactly the same annuity as described above for COMPS. These can be taken at age 60.

Table 2.25 PPS total age-related rebates as a percentage of NIC including bonuses

Age last birthday as at 5 April 1997	1997/98	1998/99	1999/2000	2000/01	2001/02
20	3.6	3.7	3.7	3.8	3.8
25	3.9	3.9	4.0	4.0	4.0
30	4.2	4.2	4.3	4.3	4.3
35	4.5	4.6	4.7	4.7	4.8
40	5.4	5.5	5.6	5.6	5.7
45	8.2	8.3	8.4	8.6	8.7
50+	9.0	9.0	9.0	9.0	9.0

Rebates are bigger in the case of the PPS route if contracting out, so as expected, with bigger protected rights going into the pension, the break even point is now around age 53 for men and age 44 for women. Contracting out of SERPS through a PPS can also be done by employees who are members of a company pension scheme as long as the scheme is not already contracted out, and hence, in this case, final total pension will be the proceeds of the company pension plus the pension derived from the protected rights payments. If at any time you are running your own limited company you will be able to choose the route which gives you the best benefit. (For details see Chapter 5.)

Flowchart for pensions

The whole question of pensions is a complex web of possibilities so perhaps a schematic overview (Fig. 2.11) will help you to position yourself before you proceed further.

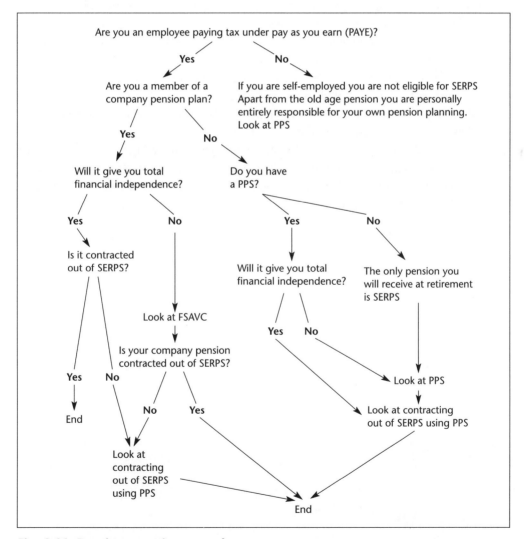

Fig. 2.11 Pension overview at a glance

■ Case Study 2.5

Verona Prescott was 30 on 18 March 1997. Her salary is £18,000 p.a. She has a contracted out company pension based on sixtieths and indexed at 3% p.a. or RPI, whichever is the lower. Normal retirement age is at 60. She contributes 3% of pensionable salary, i.e. salary minus the LEL. She has done no financial planning and has no savings. She rents a small flat for £300 per month. If she became medically unable to work her company would pay her full salary for six months but then nothing. She decides to create a financial plan.

The first thing she needs to know is her net income so she uses an income tax and national insurance contribution form.

Now she knows exactly what her spendable income is, exactly what she is currently living on. The next thing to do is a budget analysis so she uses Form 2.8.

Clearly she is living on a tight budget and has very little to spare. She feels she needs to save some of her income to cater for possible future needs and she also sees how very vulnerable she is to the disaster of becoming medically unable to work. Using the formula described earlier in the chapter she sees she could be insured for £8452 p.a. This would be paid free of all taxes. She would also get £3247.40 annually from the state and as this would be below her personal allowance she would pay no tax on it. Hence her total income would be £11,700 p.a.

Thankfully she sees she could survive on this. She is advised that a typical premium would be £18.83 per month or £4.35 per week. This leaves her £33.64 per week.

She sees that at age 60, in today's terms, her pension would give her $30/60\text{ths} \times (18,000 - 3224) = \frac{1}{2} \times 14,776 = 7383$ p.a. gross.

Her position is not easy. She clearly needs more pension. Ideally she needs to guarantee her pension and she needs to build up a contingency fund. She has £33.64 per week to spare. If starting her financial plan has done nothing else it has probably made the reality clear to her that she needs seriously to assess her financial position, examine her prospects and put effort into bettering her situation because although Verona is reasonably comfortable in her present state and enjoys life she can do relatively little financial planning and her future could be bleak.

Once again we come across the truth that the practice of financial planning is the art of compromise and so for the present she decides to split the £33.64 per week between additional pension contributions and a contingency fund.

■ Form 2.7 INCOME TAX AND NIC ANALYSIS

INCOME TAX			
Name Verona Prescott		*Year* 1997/98	
	£	*Remaining income £*	*Tax £*
Gross income	18,000 p.a.		Nil
Gross contribution to pension paid personally*	3% of (18,000−3224) = 443.28	17,556.72	Nil
Personal allowance	4045	13,511.72	Nil
Income taxed at 20%	4100	9411.72	820.00
Income taxed at basic rate 23%	9411.72	Nil	2164.70
Income taxed at higher rate 40%			
Total	18,000		3014.70
Less married couple's allowance			
Total tax payable			
* Some pension contributions paid personally are net of basic rate tax. For the purposes of this form this would need to be grossed up.			

NATIONAL INSURANCE CONTRIBUTION (NIC) (Employed)			
	£	*Remaining income £*	*NIC £*
Gross income	18,000	18,000	Nil
Income up to LEL £3224 p.a. NIC at 2%	3224	14,776	64.48
Income up to UEL £24,180 p.a. minus £3224 p.a., the LEL NIC at 10%	14,776	Nil	1477.60
Total	18,000		1542.08

NATIONAL INSURANCE CONTRIBUTION (NIC) (Self-employed)
Flat rate paid if income over £3480 p.a. £6.15 p.w.
On profits between £7010 and £24,180 p.a. 6.0%
Total
Income after tax and NIC deductions 18,000−3014.70−1542.08 = 13,443.22 p.a.

■ **Form 2.8 BUDGET ANALYSIS**

Name	Verona Prescott		Year	1997/98	
Income				Capital	Capital
Source		*Amount £ p.a.*		*Assets £*	*Liabilities £*
Salary		18,000		None	None
Total p.a. gross		18,000			
Total p.a. net of tax and NIC		13,443.22			
Expenditure		*£ p.w.*			*Net income £*
Food, drink and toiletries		55.00			
Rental/mortgage payments		69.23			
Heating, lighting and cooking		10.00			
Transport		29.00			
Clothes		25.00			
Entertainment		20.00			
Books and journals		6.00			
Telephone		6.00			
Other outgoings					
Total p.w.		220.23			258.52
p.a.		11,451.96			13,443.22
Surplus p.w.	37.99	Deficiency	p.w.	[	]
p.a.	1975.48		p.a.	[	]

■ **Case Study 2.6**

Rajkumar Singh earns £40,000 p.a. running his own business as a sole trader. On his 35th birthday he decides it is crucial that he thoroughly review his financial planning. He has a permanent health policy producing a benefit of £10,000 p.a. indexed in line with RPI. He has been investing £85 per month gross in a PPS for the last five years. Mistakenly he set the retirement age at 65 because he did not really understand the implications of this at the time. He feels he will definitely not want to go on working past 60.

At least he is very clear about his outgoings, which he knows to be £15,000 p.a. Rajkumar's situation is worked out in Forms 2.9 and 2.10.

■ Form 2.9 INCOME TAX AND NIC ANALYSIS

INCOME TAX			
Name Rajkumar Singh	*Year*	1997/98	
	£	*Remaining income £*	*Tax £*
Gross income	40,000		Nil
Gross contribution to pension paid personally*	1020	38,980	Nil
Personal allowance	4045	34,935	Nil
Income taxed at 20%	4100	30,835	820
Income taxed at basic rate 23%	22,000	8835	5060
Income taxed at higher rate 40%	8835	Nil	3534
Total	40,000		9414
Less married couple's allowance			
Total tax payable			

* Some pension contributions paid personally are net of basic rate tax. For the purposes of this form this would need to be grossed up.

NATIONAL INSURANCE CONTRIBUTION (NIC) (Employed)			
	£	*Remaining income £*	*NIC £*
Gross income			
Income up to LEL £3224 p.a. NIC at 2%			
Income up to UEL £24,180 p.a. minus £3224 p.a., the LEL NIC at 10%			
Total			

NATIONAL INSURANCE CONTRIBUTION (NIC) (Self-employed)	
Flat rate paid if income over £3480 p.a. £6.15 p.w.	319.80
On profits between £7010 and £24,180 p.a. 6.0%	1030.20
Total	1350.00
Income after tax and NIC deductions 40,000−9414−1350 = 29,236 p.a.	

■ Form 2.10 LIFETIME FINANCIAL PLAN ANALYSIS

Name Rajkumar Singh	Date 14 December 1997
Date of birth (DoB) 12 December 1962	smoker/non-smoker N/S
Employed/self-employed SE	Time with business 8 years
Income p.a. gross £40,000	Income p.a. net of taxes and NIC £29,235
Annual outgoings £15,000	Surplus/deficiency p.a. £14,236
Regular savings from net income	None
If I become medically unable to work what would my income situation be for the first 6 months?	Receipts would continue for 4 to 5 months and then dry up
For the second 6 months?	Permanent health insurance – £10,000 p.a. indexed at RPI
Thereafter?	Permanent health insurance continues to age 60
What is the maximum income which I could have?	65% of £40,000−£3247.40 = £22,753 p.a.
Approximate cost of increasing my cover to this	22,753−10,000 = 12,753 From Table 2.6 $\dfrac{12,753}{10,000} \times 13.50 = 17.22$ p.m.
Pension type	PPS
Personal contribution	£85 p.m.
Maximum I am allowed to contribute	$17^1/_2$% of £40,000 = £7000 p.a. or £583.35 p.c.m.
Retirement age	65
Projected pension fund (MPS or PPS) at retirement age	£227,000 × 85/100 = 192,950 from Table 2.15
Projected pension at retirement age (DBS)	
At what age do I want total financial independence?	60
Pension fund (MPS or PPS) adjusted to financial independence age	£130,000 × 85/100 = £110,500 p.a. from Table 2.17 NB: In reality probably less as a penalty for taking benefits early is likely
Pension (DBS) adjusted to financial independence age	

■ Form 2.10 (continued)

Type of annuity required	Single life, non-guaranteed, indexed at 5% p.a.
Pension this would produce	5.78% of £110,500 = £6387 p.a.
Assumed rate of inflation long term	5%
Pension in today's terms	$\dfrac{6,387}{3.39} = 1884$ p.a. from Table 2.17
What is total financial independence for me in today's terms?	£20,000 p.a.
Shortfall	£18,116 p.a.
Shortfall at financial independence age, taking inflation into account	£18,116 × 3.39 = £61,413 p.a. from Table 2.17
Fund needed to produce this pension	$61,413 \div \dfrac{5.78}{100} = £1,062,508$
Pension contribution needed to produce this fund at a growth of 12% p.a.	$\dfrac{1,062,508}{130,000} \times 100 = £817$ p.m. from Table 2.17

Decisions: 1 Start saving 10% of net income, i.e. £2923 p.a. for a contingency fund.
2 Take out the additional permanent health cover.
3 Invest a further £583 – £85 = £498 per month gross into a PPS with retirement age 60.

His surplus of £14,236 p.a. will therefore be reduced by £2923 p.a. contingency fund.

£17.22 × 12 = £206.64 p.a. PHI premium
£498 × 12 = £5976 p.a. gross pension
= £3585.60 p.a. net of 40% tax
Total £6715.24 p.a.

leaving a surplus of £7520.76 p.a.

He therefore decides on a critical illness policy to cover him to age 60, sum assured £100,000 indexed plus waiver of contribution. This would produce a further income of £5000 p.a. indexed for the rest of his life (premium from Table 2.8).

Rajkumar has left his financial planning late – he cannot invest the needed amount into pension. However, he could use carry forward and carry back to enhance his contribution. Also in 1999–2000 he will be able to increase his contributions to 20% of net relevant earnings.

Rajkumar should seriously consider adding waiver of contribution to his pension even though this will reduce the final pension by a small amount.

> **Do look after your financial health in this age and start to plan as early as possible.**

We see over and over again how important it is to start a financial plan as early as possible, especially from the point of view of achieving total financial independence.

Do look after your financial health in this age and start to plan as early as possible.

You may like to use the following forms to do your own lifetime financial plan for the age of work.

■ Form 2.11 BUDGET ANALYSIS

Name		Year		
Income			Capital	Capital
Source		Amount £ p.a.	Assets £	Liabilities £
Total p.a. gross				
Total p.a. net of tax and NIC				
Expenditure		£ p.w.	Net income £	
Food, drink and toiletries				
Rental/mortgage payments				
Heating, lighting and cooking				
Transport				
Clothes				
Entertainment				
Books and journals				
Telephone				
Other outgoings				
Total p.w. p.a.				
Surplus p.w. p.a.	Deficiency	p.w. p.a.	[[	]]

■ Form 2.12 INCOME TAX AND NIC ANALYSIS

INCOME TAX		
Name	Year	
	£	Remaining income £ Tax £
Gross income		
Gross contribution to pension paid personally*		
Personal allowance		
Income taxed at 20% Income taxed at basic rate 23% Income taxed at higher rate 40%		
Total		
Less married couple's allowance		
Total tax payable		

* Some pension contributions paid personally are net of basic rate tax. For the purposes of this form this would need to be grossed up.

NATIONAL INSURANCE CONTRIBUTION (NIC) (Employed)		
	£	Remaining income £ NIC £
Gross income		
Income up to LEL £3224 p.a. NIC at 2%		
Income up to UEL £24,180 p.a. minus £3224 p.a., the LEL NIC at 10%		
Total		

NATIONAL INSURANCE CONTRIBUTION (NIC) (Self-employed)
Flat rate paid if income over £3480 p.a. £6.15 p.w.
On profits between £7010 and £24,180 p.a. 6.0%
Total
Income after tax and NIC deductions

■ Form 2.13 NET RELEVANT EARNINGS ANALYSIS

Name	*Year*
	Net relevant earnings
Salary	
P11D benefits:	
Car	
Free accommodation	
Medical insurance	
	_____
Total	
	_____

■ **Form 2.14 LIFETIME FINANCIAL PLAN ANALYSIS**

Name	Date
Date of birth (DoB)	Smoker/non-smoker
Employed/self-employed	Time with business
Income p.a. gross	Income p.a. net of taxes and NIC
Annual outgoings	Surplus p.a.
Regular savings from net income	
If I become medically unable to work what would my income situation be for the first 6 months?	
For the second 6 months?	
Thereafter?	
What is the maximum income which I could have?	
Approximate cost of increasing my cover to this	
Pension type	
Personal contribution	
Maximum I am allowed to contribute	
Retirement age	
Projected pension fund (MPS or PPS) at retirement age	
Projected pension at retirement age (DBS)	
At what age do I want total financial independence?	
Pension fund (MPS or PPS) adjusted to financial independence age	
Pension (DBS) adjusted to financial independence age	
Type of annuity required	
Pension this would produce	
Assumed rate of inflation long term	
Pension in today's terms	

■ **Form 2.14 (continued)**

What is total financial independence for me in today's terms?
Shortfall
Shortfall at financial independence age, taking inflation into account
Fund needed to produce this pension
Pension contribution needed to produce this fund at a growth of 12% p.a.

Decisions:

Comments:

SUMMARY

In this age we have worked through the following:

1 The three important questions of financial planning which have to be answered. We have asked and answered two of them: What happens if I become medically unable to work? What happens if I live too long?

2 The consequences of becoming medically unable to work over a prolonged period and of sustaining a critical illness.

3 Policies which can cater for these contingencies and also state benefits.

4 Medical insurance.

5 Redundancy and unemployment and policies related to these states.

6 Total financial independence and the effect of inflation.

7 All types of pension including company pension schemes and additional voluntary contribution schemes, free-standing additional voluntary contribution schemes, retirement annuity contracts and personal pension schemes, annuities, deferred annuities and self-invested pension plans.

8 State pension provisions and contracting out of the state earnings-related pension scheme.

References

1 Department of Social Security [DSS] Statistics 1994.

2 Conservative Research Department, Central Office, March 1997.

3 Regional Trends 30, 1995 edition.

4 Cancer Research Campaign 1997.

ANSWERS

■ Exercise 2.1

He must be given 12 weeks' notice (maximum number of weeks notice).

- ■ Years worked while 41 or more = 13
- ■ Years worked while his age was 22 to 40 = 3
- ■ A week's gross pay = £403.84
- ■ However the maximum amount which can be counted is £210.

His redundancy payment will be

$$(3 \times 1\frac{1}{2} + 13 \times 1) \times £210 = 17\frac{1}{2} \times £210 = £3675$$

■ Exercise 2.2

$$70 \div by\ 7 = 10$$

Costs double every 10 years.

Hence in 30 years they will have multiplied by 8.

■ Exercise 2.3

1 Benefit is 65% of £35,000 – £3247.20:

$$= £22,750 - £3247.20$$
$$= £19,502.80\ p.a.$$

2 *See form on page 133*

3 Total benefit = £19,502.80 p.a. + £3247.40 p.a. = £22,750.20 p.a.

4 Benefit is 22,750.20/25,017.92 × 100% = 90.94% of her net income.

5 Joan is 38. The nearest age on Table 2.4 (p. 50) is 40. Benefit of £19,502.80 is nearest to a benefit of £20,000. Hence premium =

$$\frac{19,502.80}{20,000} \times 91.58 = £69.80\ per\ month.$$

As a percentage of her net income this is,

$$\frac{69.80 \times 12}{25,017.92} \times 100\% = 3.35\%$$

■ Exercise 2.5

Maximum cover = 597 + 25% of 597 = £746.25 per month.

$$Premium = \frac{746.25}{100} \times 5.90$$
$$= £44.03\ per\ month$$

■ **Exercise 2.3 (continued)**

INCOME TAX			
Name Joan Tucker		*Year* 1997/98	
	£	*Remaining income £*	*Tax £*
Gross income	35,000		
Gross contribution to pension paid personally*			
Personal allowance	4045	30,955	Nil
Income taxed at 20%	4100	26,855	820
Income taxed at basic rate 23%	22,000	4855	5060
Income taxed at higher rate 40%	4855	Nil	1942
Total	35,000		7822
Less married couple's allowance			
Total tax payable			

* Some pension contributions paid personally are net of basic rate tax. For the purposes of this form this would need to be grossed up.

NATIONAL INSURANCE CONTRIBUTION (NIC) (Employed)			
	£	*Remaining income £*	*NIC £*
Gross income	35,000		
Income up to LEL £3224 p.a. NIC at 2%	3224	31,776	64.48
Income up to UEL £24,180 p.a. minus £3224 p.a., the LEL NIC at 10%	20,956	10,820	2095.60
Total	24,180		2160.08

NATIONAL INSURANCE CONTRIBUTION (NIC) (Self-employed)
Flat rate paid if income over £3480 p.a. £6.15 p.w.
On profits between £7010 and £24,180 p.a. 6.0%
Total
Income after tax and NIC deductions   35,000 − 7822 − 2160.08 = £25,017.92

■ Exercise 2.6

SERPS benefit = (income − lower earnings limit) × number of years up to fiscal year 1987/88 × 23%/45.

　Plus (income − lower earnings limit) × number of years from fiscal year 1987/88 to fiscal year 2027/28 × 25%/45

$$= 11,726 \times 5 \times \frac{25\%}{45} + 11,726 \times 40 \times \frac{20\%}{45}$$

$$= 325.72 + 2084.60$$

$$= 2410.32$$

Old age pension = £3247.20

　Total state pension benefit = £5657.52 which is 37.72% of her final income.
　The calculation is 5657.52/15,000 × 100% = 37.72%.

■ Exercise 2.7

He is not eligible for SERPS as he is self-employed. His old age pension = £3247.20 p.a. which is 12.03% of his final salary.
　The calculation is 3247.20/27,000 × 100% = 12.03%.

■ Exercise 2.8

SERPS benefit =　band earnings (upper earnings limit − lower earnings limit) × number of years up to fiscal year 1987/88 × 25%/22.

　Plus band earnings × number of years from fiscal year 1987/88 to fiscal year 2003/2004 × 23.5%/22

$$= (24,180 - 3224) \times 6 \times \frac{25\%}{22}$$

$$+ (24,180 - 3,224) \times 16 \times \frac{23.5\%}{22}$$

$$= 20,956 \times 6 \times \frac{0.25}{22} + 20,956 \times 16 \times \frac{0.235}{22}$$

$$= 1428.82 + 3581.57 = 5010.39$$

Old age pension = £3,247.20.

　Total state pension benefit = £8257.59 which is 15.01% of her final income.
　The calculation is 8257.59/55,000 × 100% = 15.01%.

■ Exercise 2.9

1　Pensionable salary = (16,000 − 3224) = £12,776.
　　Pension in today's terms = $^{35}\!/_{60} \times 12,776 = £7452.67$ p.a.

2　Lump sum = $^{3}\!/_{80} \times 35 \times 12,776 = £22,358$.
　　Pension reduction = 22,358/9 = £2484.22 p.a.
　　Hence his reduced pension is £4968.45 p.a.

3 Spouse would receive:
  ■ Tax-free cash of $3 \times (£22,000 - 3224) = £56,328$.
  ■ Pension of $\frac{1}{2} \times \frac{1}{60} \times 35 \times (22,000 - 3224) = £5476.33$ p.a.

4 Laurence retires on a pension in today's terms of £7452.67 p.a.
   Pension will be indexed at 3% p.a., hence pension at start of year 2 is,

$$103\% \text{ of } £7452.67 = \frac{103}{100} \times 7452.60 = £7676$$

Pension at start of year 3 is,

$$\frac{103}{100} \times 7676 = £7906$$

Pension at start of year 4 is,

$$\frac{103}{100} \times 7906 = £8143$$

Pension at start of year 5 is,

$$\frac{103}{100} \times 8143 = £8387$$

His spouse would therefore receive tax-free cash of £3387 (the remaining year of the guaranteed period).
   She would also receive a pension of $\frac{1}{2} \times 8387 = £4195.50$ p.a. in today's terms, indexed at 3% p.a.

■ Exercise 2.10

1 Pensionable salary = 18,000 − 3224 = £14,776 p.a.
   Pension, at 60, in today's terms = $\frac{30}{60} \times 14,776 = £7388$ p.a.

2 Shortfall = £10,000 − £7388 − £2612 p.a.

3 If inflation averages 5% p.a. then Table 2.17 (p. 95) tells us in 25 years the factor is 3.39. Hence shortfall in 30 years will be $3.39 \times 2612 = £8855$ p.a.

4 The annuity chosen yields 4.79%.
   A pension of £4.79 p.a. is produced by a fund of £100.

5 Fund needed $= \dfrac{\text{pension needed}}{\text{annual yield per £100}} \times 100$

$$= \frac{11,283.84}{4.79} \times 100 = £235,571$$

6 Using Table 2.15 (p. 93), £130,000 is produced in 25 years by a pension of £100 p.a.

Contribution needed $= \dfrac{\text{fund needed}}{\text{fund produced by £100 per month}} \times 100$

$$= \frac{235,571}{130,000} \times 100$$

$$= £181.21 \text{ per month gross}$$

She will pay this PRAS so contribution will be £181.21 less 23% of £181.21

$= 181.21 - 23/100 \times 181.21$

Hence the PRAS contribution is £181.21 – £41.68 = £139.53 per month net.

7 She is allowed to contribute 15% of income = 15% of 18,000

$= \dfrac{15}{100} \times 18,000 = £2700 \text{ p.a.}$

She currently contributes 3% of 14,776,

$= \dfrac{3}{100} \times 14,776 = £443.28 \text{ per month}$

Eligibility left is £2700 – £443.28 = £2256.76 p.a. = £188.06 per month gross.
Hence it is possible for her to contribute £181.51 per month gross.

■ **Exercise 2.11**

Maximum into PPS = 30% of £84,000 = £25,200.
He is able to invest 20% of his total salary into an RAC.
When will this equal £25,200?

Total salary × 20%	= 25,200
Total salary × 0.2	= 25,200
Total salary = $\dfrac{25,200}{0.2}$	= 126,000

Hence breakpoint is £126,000.

■ **Exercise 2.12**

NET RELEVANT EARNINGS ANALYSIS

Name	Betty Rawlinson	*Year*
		Net relevant earnings
Salary		£36,000
P11D benefits:		
Car		
18,000 × 35% = 6300		
6300 × ⅔ = 4200		4200
Free accommodation		6000
Medical insurance		850
		———
Total		£47,050
		———

■ **Exercise 2.13**

Method 1: NHS earnings = 100/6 × 3000 = £50,000 p.a.
  Hence earnings are deemed to be £15,000 p.a. She can invest 17½% of this into a PPS = £2625 p.a.
Method 2: She gives up the tax relief on NHS pension contributions of £3000.
  She can then invest into a PPS 17½% of £65,000 = £11,375 p.a.

■ **Exercise 2.14**

In tax year 1991/92 he could have invested into a PPS 17½% of £12,000 = £2100.
  In tax year 1992/93 he could have invested into a PPS 17½% of £12,500 = £2187.50.
  He can invest in 1997/98 20% of £20,000 = 20/100 × 20,000 = £4000.

  Thus he can opt to carry forward to tax year 1997/98 an eligibility of £2100 from tax year 1991/92 and £1900 of his £2187.50 eligibility from tax year 1992/93, making a total contribution of £8000 in tax year 1997/98.

■ **Exercise 2.15**

He could carry forward a total of £13,950.
  In the current year 1997/98 he still has unused eligibility of £2300. Hence total = £16,150. As his annual income is £20,000 this would be allowed.
  However, he has a personal allowance of £4045 so only £15,955 of his income is taxable. He would then hardly be wise to invest the whole £16,250.

■ **Exercise 2.16**

Details of carry forward						
	1	2	3	4	5	6
Income tax year	1991/1992	1992/1993	1993/1994	1994/1995	1995/1996	1996/1997
Net relevant earnings non-pensionable sources	20,000	22,000	24,000	26,000	28,000	30,000
A Maximum relief available	4400	4400	4800	5200	5600	7500
B Payments made under PP schemes, RA contracts etc	1000	1000	2500	1700	3000	3000
C Unused relief available (A−B)	3000	3400	2300	3500	2600	4500

In year 1990/91 he has unused eligibility of £3000.
In year 1997/98 he has unused eligibility of £4500. Thus total eligibility is £26,800.
In 1996/97 he is taxed at 40% p.a. on,

$$£30,000 - £3765 - £25,500 = £735$$

He is taxed at 24% on £25,500 – £3900 = £21,600.

He should, therefore, make a total contribution in 1996/97 of,

£21,600 + £735 = £22,335

He has already contributed £3000. He should therefore carry back £19,335, leaving an additional contribution of £7445 in 1997/98.

He therefore contributes £26,800 in 1997/98 and carries back to 1996/97 £19,335 of that.

CHAPTER 3

THE AGE OF
MARRIAGE

Birth and education	Work	Marriage	Parenthood	Career development	Retirement	Old age

FINANCIAL PLANNING AT A GLANCE –
THE AGE OF MARRIAGE

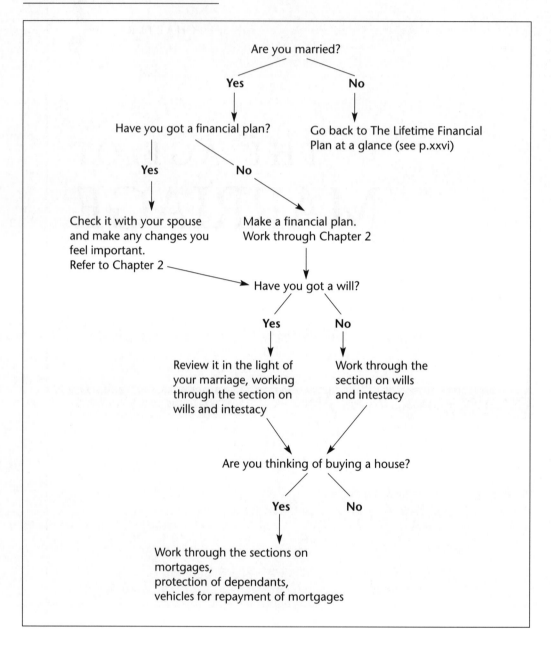

Are you married?

Yes — Have you got a financial plan?

No — Go back to The Lifetime Financial Plan at a glance (see p.xxvi)

Yes — Check it with your spouse and make any changes you feel important. Refer to Chapter 2

No — Make a financial plan. Work through Chapter 2

Have you got a will?

Yes — Review it in the light of your marriage, working through the section on wills and intestacy

No — Work through the section on wills and intestacy

Are you thinking of buying a house?

Yes — Work through the sections on mortgages, protection of dependants, vehicles for repayment of mortgages

No

CONTENTS

In this age the following is discussed:

INTRODUCTION

Now you are married. You have entered an age of life in which you are closely associated with another person. Your life is entwined with someone else as it has never been before. No doubt many of your personal objectives will be retained but now you are likely to have joint aims, to want things for another person as well as for yourself, to want to support and be supported by another person.

> **What happens if I become medically unable to work? What happens if I die too soon? What happens if I live too long?**

And all this is true of your financial plan. It is even more important that it should cater for the negative contingencies of life because now if you become medically unable to work, for example, your state will eventually affect someone else as well as yourself; if your plan is not designed to bring you total financial independence at the age of your choice this will affect someone else as well as yourself.

Thus if life is to be shared with someone else there will probably be a wish to share and discuss financial plans together and to make sure that they complement and enhance each other. I expect you will both want to be properly financially planned; you will both want to have answered the three core questions to the satisfaction of both of you, i.e. What happens if I become medically unable to work? What happens if I die too soon? What happens if I live too long? Why not go back to Chapter 2 and work through it together?

BUYING A HOUSE TOGETHER

Now there will be joint financial responsibilities. If you have not already done so you will probably want to purchase a house. Hopefully your joint contingency funds will provide a deposit. You may feel there is an immediate need to start rebuilding these funds. But now you will probably need a mortgage, to borrow money in order to buy your home. It could be important to investigate the whole field of mortgages, to study the details of variable rates of interest, fixed rates, capped rates, discounts and cash-backs, repayment mortgages, endowment linked or pension linked etc. All these aspects are discussed in detail later in this chapter.

> **There are several vehicles suitable for the repayment of a mortgage.**

Besides paying interest on a mortgage the capital borrowed needs eventually to be repaid. In the case of a repayment mortgage some capital will be paid back every month as well as interest. With an interest only mortgage the capital can be repaid at the end of the term with some sort of savings plan or vehicle for repayment. This vehicle could be an endowment policy, a pension, unit trust, investment trust, open ended investment company fund, personal equity plans (PEP) or friendly society savings plan.

Most lenders will want the borrowers to indemnify them against loss of money in the event that the property has to be repossessed and sold quickly in order to recover their loan. This will involve a mortgage guarantee policy.

They will also require that buildings insurance is put into effect to insure against loss of value of the property due to damage of any sort and, of course, in particular to insure against the possibility that the building could be totally destroyed. This type of insurance will often be offered as part of a block arrangement lenders will have with a general insurance company.

It would also be wise to insure contents, i.e. belongings which form the contents of the home. Lenders will not usually make this form of insurance mandatory as it will not affect them, for example, should valuable belongings be burgled. Once again, however, lenders may offer this type of insurance and will sometimes reduce the rate of interest on the mortgage should this offer be taken up, suggesting that they will be making a profit from so doing. It would be wise to do the calculations and decide whether it is better to insure with the lender or some other insurer of your choice.

> **Do not forget the upfront charges you will have to pay for a mortgage.**

Certain upfront charges will have to be paid when the mortgage is negotiated. There are stamp duty, valuation fee, and solicitor's fee, currently around £1200 to £1800.

You will be able to claim some tax relief on the interest payments on your mortgage and this is now given upfront under the system of mortgage interest relief at source (MIRAS).

Most lenders will require you both to have life assurance covering the amount you have borrowed. Even if they do not require it, it would be wise for you to have it since if one of you dies the other will be left with full responsibility for making the mortgage payments, which without a partner's income could constitute a very heavy burden. It is also a great gift to leave a partner an unencumbered home. Life assurance is dealt with in detail later in this chapter.

Something often forgotten in this age is making a will, providing your last will and testament. If you have not done this and you die, then you die intestate. It is often mistakenly thought that the estate will pass directly to the spouse but this is not the case. Information on intestacy can be found later in this chapter.

You might also consider an accident, sickness and unemployment (ASU) policy to cover the mortgage payments.

The income protection policy or accident, sickness and unemployment (ASU) policy would provide an income but even so the mortgage will hang like a millstone around your neck. How lovely it would be without it. A critical illness policy could completely pay off the mortgage in such an event. I well remember a client telling me that his first thought on becoming conscious after a heart attack was, 'Thank goodness I no longer have a mortgage'. For details of critical illness policies, turn back to Chapter 2. There is some additional information later in this chapter.

MORTGAGES

A mortgage is a particular type of loan that it is always associated with a domestic property as the collateral. Its purpose would be to enable the purchase, or improvement of such a property and even to raise capital for other purposes such as purchase of commercial property, injection of capital into a business, school fees or consolidation of other loans.

A mortgage will be negotiated with a building society, bank or some other specialised institution. The money lent will have been invested in a deposit account or purchased on the money market. In each case lenders will add a margin to make their profit. The borrower is responsible for two things: paying interest on the loan and paying back the capital, either over the term of the loan or at the end of the term.

DETAILED INFORMATION AND ANALYSIS

■ Mortgage interest relief at source (MIRAS)

The Finance Act 1967 (assistance for house purchase and improvement in Great Britain) introduced the concept of tax relief on mortgage interest payments. Tax relief was originally given on the interest on the total loan and it was at the highest rate paid by the mortgagor (borrower). It was claimed by the borrower from the Inland Revenue at the end of each fiscal year and a certificate of interest paid had to be produced by the lender for the borrower to send to the Inland Revenue.

From the fiscal year 1974/75 tax relief was limited to the interest payable on up to £25,000 of a mortgage. This was lifted to £30,000 in 1983 and at the same time the relief became available at source, i.e. mortgage interest relief at source (MIRAS). This meant that the interest was paid net of tax relief and the lender had to collect the rest from the Inland Revenue. This relief was available whether the mortgagor was actually paying tax or not. From 6 April 1991 the tax relief was restricted to basic rate, from 6 April 1994 to 20 per cent and from 6 April 1995 to 15 per cent.

■ Example 3.1

In 1984 the gross interest chargeable on Julie Watson's mortgage of £25,000 was £340 monthly. This was paid under MIRAS so, because she was a basic rate tax payer (30%) at the time, she paid her interest net of tax, i.e. she paid 70% of £340 = £238 monthly.

Had she been paying this loan in 1982 she would have paid her interest at £340 monthly but would have received back her tax relief in the way described earlier.

Limits on the amount of a mortgage qualifying applied originally to the individual borrower but since 1 August 1988 the limit generally applies to the property. Thus an unmarried couple borrowing £80,000 jointly to purchase a home would have each been entitled to claim tax relief on the interest paid on up to £30,000. This meant that tax relief on the interest paid on up to £60,000 of the loan was given. Relief was not so available to each of the partners in a marriage as they could only claim relief on up to £30,000 of a mortgage. This difference was often referred to as the 'morality tax'. After 1 April 1988 tax relief was only available on the interest on £30,000 of the loan however many people were purchasing the property together.

Before 6 April 1988 tax relief was also given for loans raised to improve property.

■ Example 3.2

A mortgage of £20,000 taken out in 1985 received tax relief on all the interest paid since it was under £30,000. When a further £5000 was added in order to fit a new kitchen tax relief was given on the full £25,000 since the total loan was still under £30,000.

Had this refurbishment been done in 1989 then tax relief would have been available only on the initial £20,000.

Availability of MIRAS

MIRAS is allowed if the following conditions are satisfied:

1 The interest must be relevant loan interest. This means that the loan must be for the purchase of property, land, caravan or houseboat in the UK which is used wholly or substantially as the borrower's only or main residence.
2 The borrower must be a qualifying borrower. In other words he pays relevant loan interest.
3 The lender must be a qualifying lender. This will include such establishments as building societies, local authorities and authorised insurance companies. Banks have to be authorised by statutory instrument issued by the Treasury. Most of the larger banks and specialist mortgage companies have been authorised.

MIRAS is currently available on the interest on up to £30,000 of a mortgage at the rate of 15%.

If a mortgagor is moving from one house to another but cannot sell the first house, then MIRAS is given on the mortgages against both houses for up to 12 months. Since March 1993 MIRAS will continue for 12 months in respect of a mortgage against a property where the owner has moved into rented accommodation.

The tax implications of selling a home

When a home or main residence is sold it will usually have made a capital gain but there is exemption to capital gains tax (CGT) because it was a main residence.

This tax relief can only be claimed on one property at a time and the selling of a second home, not considered to be the main residence, could attract a potential liability to capital gains tax.

However, on moving out of or into a main residence there is considerable flexibility. A delay of 12 months between purchase of a home and taking up residence does not prejudice its exemption from CGT, the property is still treated as a main residence. This period can even be extended for a further 12 months if there are good reasons for residence not being taken up, such as building work being necessary or an unavoidable delay in selling the former home. Similarly in moving from a main residence, even if the owners are not living in the property for up to three years before sale the exemption is not prejudiced. Thus if there is difficulty in selling the property which has been moved from there is considerable leeway with respect to capital gains tax (see Fig. 3.1).

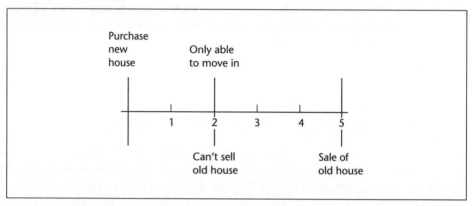

Fig. 3.1 Leeway for capital gains tax liability in buying and selling property

For a general discussion of capital gains tax turn to Chapter 5.

The capital repayment mortgage

With this sort of loan, interest is paid every month and some capital. Thus as the capital borrowed gets less the interest will get less. This would normally result in the payments changing every month or every year, depending on the frequency of the lender reducing the capital on which the interest is paid. This was considered clumsy and inconvenient for the borrower, and lenders adopted the method of totalling interest paid plus capital and simply dividing this by the number of months in the term of the loan to produce a constant monthly payment. This resulted in less capital being repaid in the earlier years than in the later years so that initially there was considerable tax relief which tailed off towards the end of the loan. The profile of the loan would have looked like that in Fig. 3.2.

The introduction of MIRAS appears to have complicated matters and most

Table 3.1 Typical profile of a capital repayment mortgage

Each month during year	MIRAS payment £	Actual net cost £	Capital repaid £	Mortgage o/s at year end £
1	423.99	423.99	72.49	59,130
2	423.99	423.99	78.00	58,194
3	423.99	423.99	83.93	57,187
4	423.99	423.99	90.31	56,103
5	423.99	423.99	97.18	54,937
6	423.99	423.99	104.56	53,682
7	423.99	423.99	112.51	52,332
8	423.99	423.99	121.06	50,879
9	423.99	423.99	130.26	49,316
10	423.99	423.99	140.16	47,634
11	423.99	423.99	150.81	45,825
12	423.99	423.99	162.27	43,878
13	423.99	423.99	174.60	41,782
14	423.99	423.99	187.87	39,528
15	423.99	423.99	202.15	37,102
16	423.99	423.99	217.52	34,492
17	423.99	423.99	234.05	31,683
18	423.99	423.99	251.83	28,661
19	425.27	425.27	270.97	25,409
20	428.36	428.36	291.57	21,911
21	431.68	431.68	313.73	18,146
22	435.26	435.26	337.57	14,095
23	439.10	439.10	363.23	9736
24	443.25	443.25	390.83	5046
25	447.70	447.70	420.53	0
	128,190.30	128,190.30	60,000.00	

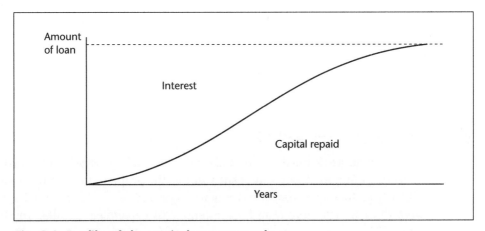

Fig. 3.2 Profile of the capital repayment loan

lenders have adopted a system of applying this smoothing process to the loan over the period until the loan goes below £30,000 and then, because the amount of tax relief will alter as the loan decreases, they revert to a payment which will vary every month or year.

One extremely valuable improvement over recent years is that the borrower can ask for a complete profile of his or her mortgage over the term showing the monthly payment to be made each successive year, the amount of capital repaid and the capital remaining to be paid.

Table 3.1 shows a typical example for a mortgage of £60,000 over a term of 25 years with the full £30,000 qualifying for MIRAS of 15 per cent and an interest rate of 7.60 per cent per annum.

It can be seen that in the first five years £5063 of the capital is repaid while in the last five years the figure is £21,911, giving rise to the same profile shown in Figure 3.2.

Interest only mortgage

This is just what it says it is. The lender insists only that interest is paid. He leaves it entirely to the borrower how the capital is eventually paid off. Hence on a mortgage of £60,000 with MIRAS on the full £30,000 and an interest rate of 7.6 per cent the monthly payment would be £351.50 per month. This would continue until some of the loan was repaid in which case the monthly payment would reduce, or until the whole loan was repaid. With such a loan it is important to check the situation every year so that time does not go by with very little of the mortgage being paid off. It may help cashflow in the early days when this could be a problem but it is always wise to plan carefully for how long this is needed and how eventually the loan will be repaid.

■ Interest only mortgage with a mandatory vehicle for repayment of capital

In this type of loan the lender insists on interest payments and also a recognised vehicle of repayment of capital designed to repay the loan at the end of the term. This could be an endowment, unit trusts, investment trusts, open ended investment company fund shares, personal equity plans, friendly society investment or pension.

Mortgage guarantee policy

This is sometimes known as mortgage indemnity policy. Most lenders will allow borrowing of up to 95 per cent of the value of the property to be purchased. Some will only go to 90 per cent, a very few will lend 100 per cent. For very large loans most will lend no more than 80 per cent. This percentage is called the loan to value (LTV) ratio.

Most lenders will seek to lay off some of the risk of a mortgage when it represents a large proportion of the value of the property, usually where it is over 70 to 75 per cent. They do this because if there is a failure to keep up mortgage payments then the lenders are no longer making a profit on the loan. They will therefore repossess the property and then do not want it on their hands, making no profit. So they will seek to sell it off quickly in what is called a forced sale. If they are insured

> **Do not forget you could be asked to pay £1000 or more upfront for a mortgage guarantee policy.**

for that part of the loan over 75 per cent of the value of the property they will be happy to sell it for 75 per cent of the full value as long as they can sell quickly, recover the loan and lend it again.

The risk is laid off by the purchase of a mortgage guarantee policy (MGP). There is a one-off payment for this policy which the borrower will pay, although often the lender will allow the premium to be added to the mortgage. A typical cost for this policy would be 7 per cent of the amount.

■ Example 3.3

Alistair Brown borrows £81,000 to buy a property for £90,000, putting down a deposit of £9000. The lender insists on a MGP for anything over 75% of the value of the property at a premium of 7%.

Alistair has borrowed $\dfrac{81,000}{90,000} \times 100\% = 90\%$ of the value of the property.

This is 15% over the 75% level. Hence he must take out an MGP on 15% of £90,000,

$$\frac{15}{100} \times 90,000 = £13,500$$

The cost will be 7% of £13,500,

$$\frac{7}{100} \times 13,500 = £1155$$

It is clear that this can be a rather large charge, especially if the lender does not add it to the loan and it has to be paid upfront. You should therefore make very sure that you consider this aspect when doing your calculations.

■ Exercise 3.1

Archibald Waters borrows £95,000 to buy a property for £100,000. The lender insists on an MGP for anything borrowed over 70% of the value of the property. The cost is 6%.

Calculate the actual cost of the MGP.

Buildings insurance

Buildings insurance will cover the main structure of the building and such things as baths and toilets, fitted kitchens and bedroom cupboards and interior decorations. Policies usually extend to cover garages, greenhouses and garden sheds. Boundary walls, fences, gates, patios, paths, drives and swimming pools may not be covered and therefore policies need checking carefully.

Most policies cover damage to the home by:

- storm and flood
- lightning
- fire
- earthquake
- theft
- riot and malicious persons
- subsidence, heave and landslip
- falling trees or branches
- aircraft or things falling from them
- breakage or collapse of aerials
- impact by vehicles or animals
- escape of oil from fixed heating installation
- escape of water from tanks or pipes.

Most policies add additional facilities such as,

- alternative accommodation if the property cannot be lived in
- liability to damages claimed against the owner, as owner, for injury to a person or his property with a usual upper limit of £1 million
- underground pipes and cables supplying gas, water, oil or electricity and sewage pipes are insured against accidental damage
- glass in doors, windows and skylights.

Excesses are usually written into the policy making the homeowner responsible for paying a certain amount towards the cost of a claim. Sometimes this will apply to all claims, sometimes only to those of a special nature. One excess which is almost ubiquitous is damage caused by subsidence, heave or landslip and this could be as much as £1000. Other common exclusions are damage caused by frost, sonic booms, war and radiation contamination.

The maximum any insurer will pay out is called the sum insured and this will be, not as often thought, the value of the property, but the cost of rebuilding it. This will be different from the full value since it does not take into account the land on which the property stands.

An idea of this cost can be gained from Table 3.2.

Second floors are usually calculated at three-quarters the full cost to rebuild. To use Table 3.2 we first measure total floor area. All houses will consist of floor areas broken up into rectangles as shown in Fig. 3.3.

Simply measure the length and breadth of each rectangle and add them together. The same must be done for the first floor which may be different in shape. Let us look at the property in Fig. 3.4.

Table 3.2 Typical insurance costings on a property

January 1997 costings – £/ft² gross external floor area

		Pre-1920			1920–1945			1946–1979			1980–Date		
		Large	Medium	Small	Large	Medium	Small	Large	Medium	Small	Large	Medium	Small
Detached house	Region 1	74.50	79.50	80.00	70.50	74.50	76.00	59.00	63.50	65.50	57.50	57.50	61.50
	2	67.50	72.50	72.50	64.50	67.50	69.50	53.50	58.00	59.50	52.50	52.50	56.00
	3	63.00	67.50	67.50	60.00	63.00	64.50	49.50	54.00	55.50	49.00	48.50	52.00
	4	60.00	64.50	64.50	57.00	60.00	61.50	47.50	51.50	53.00	46.50	46.50	50.00
	Typical area ft²	3450	1700	1300	2550	1350	1050	2550	1350	1050	2400	1400	950
Semi-detached house	Region 1	72.00	73.50	74.00	76.50	74.00	74.00	55.50	58.50	62.50	60.50	61.00	65.50
	2	65.50	67.00	67.00	69.50	67.00	67.50	50.50	53.00	56.50	55.00	55.50	59.50
	3	61.00	62.00	62.50	65.00	62.50	62.50	47.00	49.50	52.50	51.00	51.50	55.50
	4	58.00	59.50	60.00	62.00	60.00	60.00	45.00	47.50	50.50	49.00	49.00	53.00
	Typical area ft²	2300	1650	1200	1350	1150	900	1650	1350	1050	1600	900	650
Detached bungalow	Region 1				74.50	69.00	71.50	63.00	63.50	66.50	64.50	65.00	67.00
	2				67.50	63.00	65.00	57.00	58.00	60.50	58.50	59.00	61.00
	3				63.00	58.50	60.50	53.00	54.00	56.50	54.50	55.00	56.50
	4				60.00	56.00	58.00	51.00	51.50	54.00	52.00	52.50	54.00
	Typical area ft²				1650	1400	1000	2500	1350	1000	1900	950	750
Semi-detached bungalow	Region 1				76.00	73.50	71.00	60.00	61.50	66.00	62.50	70.00	73.50
	2				69.00	66.50	64.50	54.50	56.00	60.00	56.50	63.50	66.50
	3				64.00	62.00	60.00	50.50	52.00	56.00	52.50	59.00	62.00
	4				61.50	59.50	57.50	48.50	49.50	53.50	50.50	56.50	59.50
	Typical area ft²				1350	1200	800	1350	1200	800	950	550	500
Terraced house	Region 1	78.50	77.00	77.00	76.00	76.50	76.00	55.00	60.00	66.50	62.00	64.00	63.50
	2	71.50	70.00	70.00	69.50	69.50	69.00	50.00	54.50	60.50	56.50	58.00	58.00
	3	66.50	65.50	65.00	65.00	65.00	64.50	46.50	50.50	56.00	52.50	54.00	54.00
	4	63.50	62.50	62.00	62.00	62.00	61.50	44.50	48.50	53.50	50.50	51.50	51.50
	Typical area ft²	1650	1350	1050	1350	1050	850	1650	1300	900	990	750	4650

Regions: **1 London Boroughs and Channel Islands* 2 South East:** Bedfordshire, Berkshire, Buckinghamshire, Essex, Hampshire, Hertfordshire, Kent, Oxfordshire, Surrey, East Sussex, West Sussex; **Scotland, North West 3 East Anglia, Northern, South West, Yorkshire and Humberside 4 East Midlands, West Midlands, Northern Ireland**, Wales**
* Building costs in the Channel Islands tend to be as high as those in London Boroughs but they are affected by particular local conditions.
** Building costs in Northern Ireland are considerably lower than in the rest of the UK and may be 20% below the costs given for Region 4.
You should seek local advice if your home is in the Channel Islands or Northern Ireland.
Source: ABI from figures provided by the BCIS and the RICS.

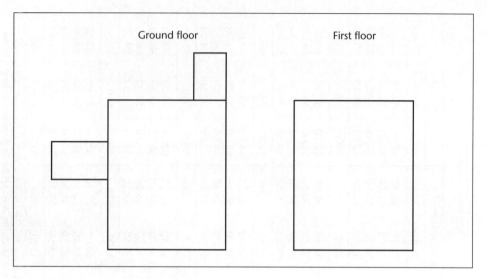

Fig. 3.3 Floor area broken into rectangles

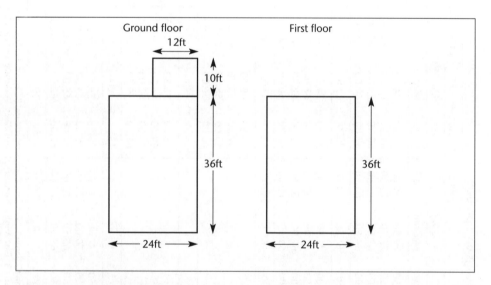

Fig. 3.4 External floor area

The area of the ground floor is,

$$24 \times 36 + 10 \times 12 = 864 + 120 = 984 \text{ sq ft}$$

Area of first floor is,

$$24 \times 36 = 864 \text{ sq ft}$$
$$\text{Total external floor area} = 984 + 864 = 1848 \text{ sq ft}$$

Let us say the house is small, located in Surrey and built in 1985. The cost of rebuilding will be $1848 \times 56 = £103,488$.

If there is an integral garage it will already have been taken into account. If not then it too will need to be measured and added to the total external floor area.

Finally an estimate for the cost of rebuilding outbuildings, walls, floors, patios, etc. would have to be made and added to the cost.

It would be wise to have the policy indexed and to review the situation every three years or so.

The figures in Table 3.2 are based on houses of an average quality finish, and with single glazing. If the house is higher quality with double glazing and a luxury kitchen, for example, then adjustments would have to be made.

They are definitely unsuitable for houses,

- built of materials other than brick with more than three storeys or with basements or cellars
- with special design functions
- containing hazardous materials such as asbestos
- which are considered historic or are listed.

For any of these situations expert professional advice from a chartered surveyor would need to be taken.

■ Example 3.4

The measurements of Leonard and Gloria Winter's semi-detached house in Wales, built in 1938 are shown in Fig. 3.5.

External area of,

Ground floor = $24 \times 50 + 22 \times 10 = 1200 + 220 = 1420$ sq ft
First floor = $24 \times 50 + 12 \times 10 = 1200 + 120 = 1320$ sq ft
Second floor = $24 \times 50 = 1200$ sq ft
Garage = $10 \times 14 = 140$ sq ft
Total floor area = $1420 + 1320 + (^3/_4 \times 1200) + 140 = 3780$

Consulting Table 3.2 we see a medium size house costs £60 per sq ft to rebuild. Hence rebuilding costs would be $3780 \times 60 = £226,800$.

They estimate that garden walls and patio would cost a further £12,000 to rebuild. They therefore need a policy with a sum assured of £238,800. They decide that they will have this indexed.

■ Exercise 3.2

Use Table 3.2 to estimate the rebuilding costs of your property or the one you may be contemplating buying.

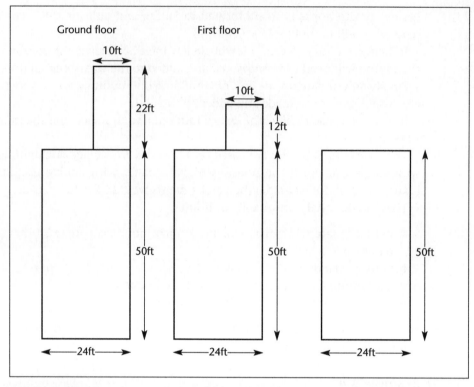

Fig. 3.5 Measurements of the Winters' house

Contents insurance

Typically contents insurance will cover the contents of the home against the effects of:

- theft
- fire
- flood
- burst pipes
- storm
- lightning
- falling trees
- explosion
- collision, riot, vandalism.

Different policies will add extras such as:

- loss of metered water
- loss of freezer contents
- loss of contents in the ope
- automatically increasing cover during Christmas and for a period covering a wedding.

Apart from the usual contents, valuables also covered could include:

■ jewellery, gemstones, pearls, gold and silver or other precious metals
■ curios, collections of stamps, coins or medals
■ furs
■ works of art, pictures, musical instruments
■ photographic equipment, watches, clocks.

There will usually be a limit for a claim on any single article, say anywhere between £1000 and £5000.

Some further options may need an increased premium or be automatically covered. These are such things as covering personal possessions taken out of the house to anywhere in the world. Once again there will be an overall limit for this cover with, in addition, a single object limit. Thus, for example, an overall limit could be £10,000 with a single object limit of £2500. Such things as losing money or the misuse of credit cards can also be covered. Accidental damage usually requires an additional premium and this would cover such things as the dropping and breaking of a vase, or a cupboard in the kitchen falling, damaging a work surface and breaking things in it.

More esoteric items such as legal fees for the family can also be covered.

Some insurance companies may offer legal advice helplines and the provision of tradesmen to carry out emergency repairs. They will also almost certainly include cover for liability, as the occupier of the property, to domestic servants and the public. This cover is usually in the millions of pounds.

New for old will often be a feature so, for example, a rug damaged by leaking pipes would be replaced by a similar brand new rug, no matter the age of the damaged rug.

Stamp duty

Do not forget you will have to pay 1% of the value of your property, upfront, if it costs over £60,000.

A duty of 1 per cent is paid by the purchaser on any property purchased for over £60,000. Thus on a purchase of up to £60,000 no duty is paid. On a purchase, for example, of £60,100 duty of £601 is paid. This is another large upfront charge.

Valuation costs

The lender will commission a valuation of the property by a surveyor to ensure the property is worth what you propose to pay and that there are no hidden problems such as dampness or dry rot. You will have the option of paying for a more detailed valuation if you wish so that you are totally satisfied there is nothing wrong with the property (see Table 3.3).

Table 3.3 Typical valuation costs

Purchase price (£000s)	25	30	40	50	60	75	80	100	125	150
Valuation fees	145	145	145	145	180	180	180	180	220	220

Purchase price (£000s)	175	200	250	300	350	400	450	500	750	1000
Valuation fees	255	255	290	325	◄———		by negotiation		———►	

■ Example 3.5

Beatrice Finlay earns £20,000 p.a. and has saved £4000. She has been told she can borrow 3 × £20,000 = £60,000, so decides she can buy a property for £64,000. However, the lender tells her there will be an upfront charge for an MGP of 7% of anything borrowed over 70% of the purchase price and that the valuation fee will be £180.

She lists her upfront charges.

MGP: If she borrows £60,000 on a price of £64,000 she will have borrowed,

$$\frac{60,000}{64,000} \times 100\% = 93.75\% \text{ of the purchase price}$$

MGP will therefore be paid on 23.75% of £64,000,

$$\frac{23.75}{100} \times 64,000 = £15,200$$

At a cost of 7% of 15,200,

$$\frac{7}{100} \times 15,200 = £1064$$

Solicitor's fees	£1200
Stamp duty 1% of £64,000 = $\frac{1}{100} \times 64,000 =$	£ 640
Valuation fee	£ 180
MGP	£1064
Total	£3084

Luckily she had worked all this out before she had gone too far with negotiating the mortgage.

She now approaches the situation differently.

Capital in hand	£4000	
Solicitor's fees		£1200
Valuation fee		£ 145
No stamp duty (she will buy below £60,000)		
Assume MGP		£1000
Total		£2345

She can only afford a deposit of £1655. She will need a 100% mortgage which will leave her some cash in hand.

Term of mortgage

Traditionally, this is 25 years but can be as little as five years or as much as 40 years.

The lifetime mortgage

Some lenders will now allow you to keep your mortgage for your lifetime and only require repayment when you die and your house is sold. You would need to demonstrate the necessary level of income not only while you are working but also in retirement. This type of loan will remove the extra cost of a repayment loan or vehicle of repayment. It is extremely rare and usually applies to older people with little possibility of repaying the loan. It is sometimes used as a means of raising capital to enhance income (see Chapter 7).

Multiples of income

A lender will need to be convinced that the mortgage payments can actually be afforded. He will therefore limit the loan to certain multiples of income. In the fiscal year 1997/98 most lenders allowed a mortgage equal to 3 times first income plus 1 times second income or 2½ times joint income, whichever was the greater. Some lenders lend on larger multiples, especially if the mortgagors are in safe professions where the incomes are likely to increase reasonably rapidly. Bonus, overtime and commissions will be treated differently, but if these are seen to be regular or, indeed, even guaranteed, most lenders will allow 50 per cent to be added to income.

> **Usually a lender will consider at most 50 per cent of bonuses, overtime etc. when assessing income.**

Income will need to be proved by production of the last three payslips or last P60 or employer's letter or a selection of these. In the case of the self-employed or someone running his own limited company (i.e. has 20 per cent or more shares and is considered to be a controlling director) the last three years' audited accounts will need to be produced.

∎ Example 3.6

Grant and Trudy Ferguson want to borrow as much as possible to buy the best house they can. Grant has a basic annual income of £20,000 with guaranteed overtime of £5000. Trudy has an annual income of £15,000.

Grant will be considered to have an annual income of,

$$£20,000 + \frac{1}{2} \times £5000 = £22,500 \text{ p.a.}$$

They could borrow,

$$3 \times £22,500 + 1 \times £15,000 = £67,500 + £15,000 = £82,500$$
or
$$2\frac{1}{2} \times (£22,500 + £15,000) = 2\frac{1}{2} \times £37,500 = £93,750$$

Hence the most they can borrow is £93,750. Of course, they may wish to find a lender who will offer higher multiples.

> ### ■ Exercise 3.3
>
> Petrona and George Weston wish to borrow as much as they can to buy the best house possible. Petrona earns £30,000 p.a. basic plus guaranteed overtime of £4000. George is working part time and earns £6000 p.a. What is the most they can borrow?

In the case of someone running his or her own limited company and paying himself or herself by way of dividends to avoid large payments of national insurance contributions some lenders will consider the whole income for the purposes of a mortgage.

■ Other references

Usually other references are taken from establishments such as banks, previous mortgagees (lenders) or landlords. A credit check is almost always done to see that there are no bad debts.

The non-status mortgage

Some lenders will allow borrowings of up to 80 per cent LTV with no proof of income whatsoever, although in some circumstances they may need a letter from a chartered or certified accountant confirming ability to service the mortgage.

Guarantor mortgages

In a situation where it is felt more money is needed than incomes will allow the lender will sometimes accept a guarantor. This is someone who is ready to become legally responsible for making the mortgage payments if the borrowers fail to do so. In this case the guarantor will be checked for his or her ability to make the mortgage payments. If the guarantor already has a mortgage then income requirements will need to be such as to cover both mortgages. Thus a guarantor earning £60,000 per annum with an existing mortgage of £100,000 would be able to service a total mortgage of three times 60,000 = £180,000. Hence he would be able to guarantee a mortgage of £80,000.

> **It is possible to borrow more than the usual multiples if a willing guarantor can be found.**

Variable interest rate mortgage

This type of mortgage will be charged interest at the rate prevailing with the lender at the time. This rate will usually be closely connected to the bank base rate and as that varies so too will the mortgage rate. This sort of mortgage is called a variable rate mortgage.

Table 3.4 Typical variable mortgage rates

Date	% rate	Date	% rate	Date	% rate	Date	% rate
1.2.78	8.50	1.12.84	11.875	1.2.89	13.50	1.1.93	8.55
1.7.78	9.75	1.2.85	13.00	1.11.89	14.50	1.3.93	7.99
1.12.78	11.75	1.4.85	14.00	1.3.90	15.10	1.1.94	7.64
1.1.80	15.00	1.9.85	12.75	1.11.90	14.50	1.10.94	8.10
1.2.81	14.00	1.4.85	12.00	1.4.91	13.75	1.2.95	8.35
1.5.81	13.00	1.6.86	11.00	1.5.91	12.95	1.10.95	7.99
1.11.81	15.00	1.11.86	12.25	1.7.91	12.45	1.1.96	7.74
1.1.82	13.50	1.5.87	11.25	1.8.91	11.95	1.2.96	7.49
1.9.82	12.00	1.12.87	10.30	1.10.91	11.50	1.4.96	7.25
1.12.82	10.00	1.5.88	9.80	1.3.92	10.95	1.8.96	6.99
1.7.83	11.25	1.8.88	11.50	1.6.92	10.55	1.1.97	7.25
1.4.84	10.25	1.10.88	12.75	1.11.92	9.99	1.6.97	7.60
1.8.84	12.75	1.12.92	9.29	1.12.92	9.29		

The fixed rate mortgage

> **During the period of a fixed rate mortgage it is possible to budget exactly, and there is protection from nasty surprises if rates go up.**

In this case the lending rate is fixed over a number of years regardless of the changes in the variable rate. Usual terms for the fixed rate period are one to five years, although occasionally longer terms can be negotiated. If the variable rate goes up the borrower is better off and vice versa. However, whatever happens there is the advantage of knowing that for a number of years no changes in the rate can be suffered and it is therefore possible to budget exactly for the mortgage payments.

Referring to Table 3.4 it can be seen that a fixed rate taken out on 1 December 1982 for five years at 10.5 per cent would have been very good news, whereas a fixed rate of 9 per cent over five years from 1 June 1992 would have been regretted. An arrangement fee is usually charged.

The discounted rate mortgage

This is a variable rate mortgage but with a discount aspect. This means that the lender will charge 1 or 2 per cent less than the variable rate for a period of time. Thus if there is a discount of 2 per cent per annum over two years and the rate starts off at 7.5 per cent per annum payments will be made at a rate of 5.5 per cent per annum. If during the two years the variable rate changes, say to 8 per cent per annum the payment rate will change to 6 per cent per annum. An arrangement fee is usually charged.

The cashback mortgage

With this sort of mortgage once the purchase is completed the lender will give the borrower a cheque for a percentage of the loan. This could typically be 5 per cent. Hence if the negotiated loan is for £100,000 then on completion a cheque for £5000 will be received by the borrower. Payments will be at the usual variable rate. This cashback could be very useful since, as we have seen, upfront charges can be high including such things as stamp duty, mortgage indemnity policy, solicitors' fees and valuation. An arrangement fee is usually charged.

The low start mortgage

Here the lender allows payments which are less than the actual variable rate for a number of years. However, the interest not paid is added to the loan and interest is charged on that also. Unless some projected figures on the potential build up of debt are produced there can be a very nasty shock at the end of the first few years. An arrangement fee is usually charged.

A typical example of this type of mortgage for an amount of £60,000 over 25 years, interest only, MIRAS on the full amount of £30,000 and interest at 7.60 per cent would be actual charge £351.50 per month.

The borrower is allowed to pay the lower amount of £278.50 per month in the first five years. The profile is shown in Table 3.5.

Table 3.5 Low start mortgage: profile

At year	Net monthly payment (£)	Outstanding mortgage (£)
1	278.50	61,123
2	278.50	62,125
3	278.50	63,206
4	278.50	64,373
5	278.50	65,632
6 onwards	387.17	65,632

Imagine not seeing the figures in Table 3.5 before the loan is commenced.

The level payment mortgage

Here an interest rate is established at outset as the actual payment, but not the true charge, to continue for a number of years, say 10 per cent per annum for 10 years. If the actual rate charged is more, then the interest not paid is added to the loan and itself attracts interest. If the actual rate is less then the additional amount paid decreases the outstanding loan. This type of mortgage has the same dangers as the low start mortgage. However, it does have the advantage that it is possible to budget exactly for the period of the level payment. Do bear in mind that at the end of the 10 years very much more than the initial negotiated loan could be owed. An arrangement fee is usually charged.

As a typical example of this, had a borrower started a level payment mortgage on 1 May 1987 at say 11 per cent per annum. Fig. 3.6 shows how this would have related to the actual rate over 10 years until 30 April 1997.

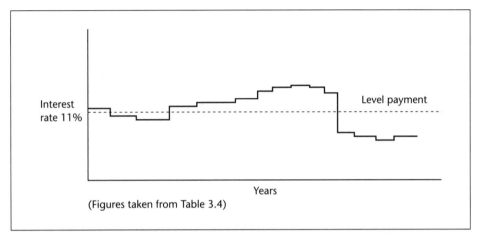

Fig. 3.6 The level payment mortgage

The capped rate mortgage

This is a variable rate mortgage but the rate is never allowed to go higher than the capped rate, although it can drop with any decreases in rate. A one-off upfront fee, which purchases the cap, is charged for this. Figure 3.7 illustrates the concept.

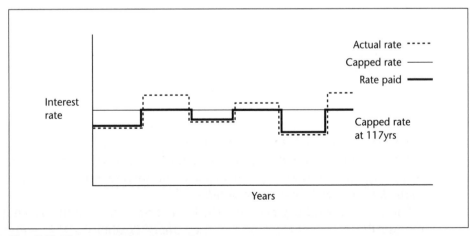

Fig. 3.7 The capped rate mortgage

The capped and collared rate mortgage

This is exactly the same as the capped mortgage with the additional arrangement that the rate can never drop below the collar rate. There is also a one-off upfront fee in this case.

All sorts of combinations of these types of mortgage are on the market and there are some very esoteric versions available.

The adaptable mortgage

This sort of mortgage is tailored exactly to the client's changing needs. It is basically a variable rate mortgage. It could start with a graduated payment, in which the client will choose a level of payment, usually not less than a certain proportion of the actual charge and with an overall minimum percentage payment. Payments would then increase annually over a period of five years, say, and then revert to the full rate.

A typical example on a mortgage of £60,000 over 25 years, interest only, with MIRAS on the full £30,000 and an interest rate of 7.60 per cent would be actual monthly charge of £351.50.

Suppose the borrower wanted to pay at a rate of 4.00 per cent in the first year, increasing by 0.5% each year, until in the 6th year the payment reverted to the full rate of 7.60 per cent. The profile can be seen in Table 3.6.

Table 3.6 Adaptable mortgage: profile

At Year	Net monthly payment (£)	Payment rate (%)	Outstanding mortgage (£)
1	171.50	4.00	62,237
2	196.50	4.50	64,339
3	221.50	5.00	66,296
4	246.50	5.50	68,096
5	271.50	6.00	69,728
6 onwards	413.11	7.60	69,728

If the payments are less than the actual rate the difference will be added to the loan and will itself attract interest. If they are more they will be used to reduce the loan. At the end of the period the loan would switch to the full rate.

Another version could be the level payment described earlier. The added facility is that the client chooses his or her own level payment within the same sort of restrictions as described under the graduated payment.

A payment holiday will usually be available for up to say three months, during which no interest whatsoever will be paid. This interest will, of course, be added to the loan and will itself attract interest.

But the method of payment and the level of payment within a given method can usually be renegotiated and thus the extreme flexibility of this mortgage will satisfy at all times the changing needs of the client.

With all loans which involve a potential increase in debt because of deferred interest payment the original loan to value ratio (LTV) will be considerably less than usual, catering for the potential increase in debt and ensuring that it has no chance of becoming greater than the value of the property or a reasonable percentage of this.

Furthermore, any life assurance required or particular vehicle for repayment will have to cater for the potential increase in debt.

Typically policies could be required designed to pay off 110 to 120 per cent of the initial loan on death or maturity.

OTHER ASPECTS OF A MORTGAGE

Accurate illustration of possible debt position

In the past those using a deferred payment of interest mortgage have sometimes had an extremely nasty shock when they have become aware how much more than the original loan they owed after a period of time. Lenders will usually provide detailed illustrations showing possible debt position over a period of time so that an informed and clear decision can be taken on whether or not to enter into such a loan. They will also run checks every year to see that the loan is not growing too rapidly, and will inform the borrower of these.

> **If you defer interest payments in any way to help cashflow you could get a nasty shock in five or more years.**

Capital raising

Many lenders will allow capital raising with a mortgage. This will usually only apply with a remortgage when there is extra equity in the property. The value of a property may have grown, for example, to £120,000 and still carry only a mortgage of £90,000. It would now be possible to remortgage for, say, £114,000 (95 per cent of the current value of the property) using the additional £24,000 capital for other purposes such as injection into a business, towards the purchase of another property, school fees, or consolidation of other debts. The advantage of this is that the rate of interest will usually be better than for other types of loan, being charged at the original mortgage rate or at worst with a differential of up to 1 per cent per annum. It usually also places the consolidated debt on a longer-term basis with correspondingly smaller monthly outgoings.

The drawdown facility

Sometimes capital raising goes together with a drawdown facility which means that having negotiated the total amount of capital raising this does not have to all be taken upfront but can be drawn down in partial amounts over a period of time. A cheque book is usually issued and instalments of the negotiated loan can be called upon whenever needed. This can be especially useful for the payment of school fees, treated in Chapter 4.

Redemption penalty charges

With all types of mortgage which offer a special facility such as a fixed interest loan or a cashback there will usually be a penalty to pay if part or all of the loan is redeemed before a certain time. Thus with a typical cashback, having taken the 5 per cent, if the loan is then paid back, for example, within five years the borrower will be obliged to return the 5 per cent. With a typical fixed rate over five years if the loan is redeemed within six years the borrower will be obliged to pay a penalty of, for example, six months interest.

> **If you are negotiating a special deal on your mortgage remember the penalties payable on early redemption.**

Commercially the whole point of offering a special deal is to lock the borrower into that particular lender for a period of time.

■ Example 3.7

James and Carol Davis decide to purchase a house. Their details appear in Form 3.1.

■ Form 3.1   MORTGAGE ANALYSIS FORM

Names: James and Carol Davis	
1st income	20,000 p.a.
2nd income	17,000 p.a.
3 × 1st + 1 × 2nd	77,000
$2\frac{1}{2}$ × (1st + 2nd)	92,500
Maximum mortgage available	92,500
Assuming LTV 95% maximum cost of property	92,500 divided by 0.95 = 97,368
MGP on average say 7% over 70%	7% of 25% of 97,368 = 7% of 24,342 = 1704
Solicitor's fees	1500
Stamp duty	974
Valuation	180
Total cost £ Cash needed 101,726 − 92,500 = 9226	101,726

■ Form 3.2 MORTGAGE ANALYSIS FORM

Names:	
1st income	
2nd income	
$3 \times 1\text{st} + 1 \times 2\text{nd}$	
$2\frac{1}{2} \times (1\text{st} + 2\text{nd})$	
Maximum mortgage available	
Assuming LTV 95% maximum cost of property	
MGP on average say 7% over 70%	
Solicitors' fees	
Stamp duty	
Valuation	
Total cost £	
Cash needed £	

They do not have this amount of cash, they therefore consider,

1 Finding a lender who will add the MGP to the loan.
2 Looking for a lender who will offer bigger multiples of income.
3 Looking for a cashback loan, e.g. a cashback of 5% would produce a further £4625 and reduce the cash needed to £4601.
4 Looking for a 100% mortgage.
5 Buying a less expensive house, thus reducing deposit, MGP, stamp duty and valuation.

They actually have £3200 in the bank. They find a lender who will add the MGP to the loan and who will give them a cashback of 5%, i.e. £4625. This reduces the cash they need to £9226 – 1704 – 4625 = 2897. This will leave them £303 to cover moving expenses and other incidentals.

James and Carol already have some furniture from their years of living in rented accommodation. They will probably furnish their new home to their own satisfaction in the next few years. They have solved the question of negotiating the right mortgage for their purchase. They must, of course, give some thought to making sure they can maintain the payments. This is usually not a problem as the outgoing of two rental payments will be replaced by one mortgage payment. They can, of course, be absolutely sure by completing a budget analysis form and an income and national insurance form. This would anyway be a wise step enabling them to budget exactly the financial aspects of their new life.

■ Exercise 3.4

Wah Pong and Lee Ping Peng decide to buy their first home. They want an LTV of 95%. Wah earns £16,000 p.a. and Lee £19,000. They have £3500 in the bank. Use Form 3.2 to work out costs etc. for this. Assume solicitor's fees are £1500. Assume MGP has to be paid upfront. If they do not have enough cash what might make it possible for them to buy a property?

When you decide to buy a house you may find the Mortgage Analysis Form 3.2 useful.

WILLS AND INTESTACY

It is extremely important to write a will since if you die intestate the consequences for your dependants can be serious, as you will see from the intestacy tables below.

Table 3.7 Intestacy tables

ENGLAND AND WALES

Married couple – with children

Spouse receives:	■ All the personal belongings (car, furniture, jewellery, etc)
	■ £125,000 absolutely*
	■ A 'life interest', i.e. the income only, in half the balance, for the rest of the life of the spouse

| Children receive (shared equally): | ■ Half the balance when they attain the age of 18 or marry, if earlier |
| | ■ The remainder of the estate when spouse dies |

Married couple – no children

Where there is a living parent, brother, sister, nephew or niece:

Spouse receives:	■ All the personal belongings
	■ £200,000 absolutely*
	■ Half the balance absolutely*
Relatives receive:	■ Half the balance to parents, but if no living parent to brothers and sisters (with nephews and nieces stepping into their parent's shoes if the parent is dead)

Where there is no living parent, brother, sister, nephew or niece:

| Spouse receives: | ■ Everything absolutely* |

Single person

Estate passes to:	■ Children; but if none:
	■ Parents; but if none:
	■ Brothers, sisters (nephews and nieces step into parents' shoes); but if none:
	■ Grandparents; but if none:
	■ Uncles and aunts (cousins step into their parents' shoes); but if none:
	■ The Crown

NORTHERN IRELAND

Married couple – with children

Spouse receives:	■ All the personal belongings (car, furniture, jewellery, etc)
	■ £125,000 absolutely*
	■ Half the balance, where there is one child, or one third of the balance, where there is more than one child

| Children receive (shared equally): | ■ Half or two-thirds of the balance depending on whether one or more children survive |

Table 3.7 (continued)

Married couple – no children
Where there is a living parent, brother, sister, nephew or niece:

Spouse receives:
- All the personal belongings
- £200,000 absolutely*
- Half the balance absolutely*

Relatives receive:
- Half the balance to parents, but if no living parent to brothers and sisters (with nephews and nieces stepping into their parent's shoes if the parent is dead)

Where there is no living parent, brother, sister, nephew or niece:

Spouse receives:
- Everything absolutely*

Single person

Estate passes to:
- Children; but if none:
- Parents; but if none:
- Brothers, sisters (nephews and nieces step into parents' shoes); but if none:
- Grandparents; but if none:
- Next of kin; but if none
- The Crown

---

* Absolutely = without condition or limitation

The law in Scotland is different, the key element being the system of prior rights and legal rights. In the event of intestacy these rights apply.

Prior rights

These are the rights of the surviving spouse to certain property and money from the deceased's estate. They have priority over other claims on the estate, except costs and expenses, and apply only where there is no will.

A spouse is entitled to the following prior rights:

- **Dwelling house** – The spouse is entitled to ownership of the house (up to a value of £110,000) in which they were residing at the date of the spouse's death. If the value of the house is greater than this figure, then the spouse would be entitled to money instead of the value of the house.
- **Furniture and plenishing** – The spouse is entitled to furniture and plenishing up to the value of £20,000. Furniture and plenishing includes most of the contents of the house excluding personal items such as jewellery and cars or assets not owned outright by the deceased.
- **Money** – The spouse is entitled to £50,000 if there are no surviving children or £30,000 where there are.

Legal rights

These are the rights of the spouse and children to a share of the property whether or not a will has been made. Legal rights apply to moveable property which is any property, including investments and life assurance policies, other than land and buildings.

If the spouse is the only survivor then he or she is entitled to half the moveable estate after payment of prior rights. If the spouse is also survived by a child then the spouse is only entitled to a third of the moveable property, again after payment of prior rights.

If there is a surviving spouse then the children are entitled to a third of the moveable property shared equally, but if the children are the only survivors then they are entitled to a half share, again shared equally.

Free estate

Once the prior rights and any legal rights have been paid the balance of the moveable property is added to the deceased's heritable property or heritage. This balance is called the free estate.

The free estate passes in the order shown:

1 Children.
2 Parents and brothers and sisters (half taken by parents and half by the brothers and sisters. If no parents, then brothers and sisters take all, and vice versa).
3 Surviving spouse.
4 Uncles and aunts.
5 Grandparents.
6 Brothers and sisters of the grandparents.
7 Remoter ancestors.
8 The Crown, if no relatives can be found.

It is worth noting that the spouse appears only third in the list below children, parents and brothers and sisters. This is because the spouse is arguably provided for adequately under prior rights and legal rights.

Nowadays a simple will can be produced inexpensively by solicitors, will agencies and insurance companies.

LIFE ASSURANCE

Most lenders do not like to be left with an unredeemed mortgage in the event of the death of the mortgagor. They therefore insist that life assurance is taken out on the life of the borrower or borrowers. Some lenders do not so insist but it would seem extremely important if there is a dependant, such as a spouse, to make sure your life is covered for the amount of the loan. Life assurance can be taken out on a single life or on joint lives, the sum assured payable on the first death, i.e. joint life first death policies. There are various types of life assurance details of which follow. However in most cases they will include several automatic benefits and some which can be included optionally. Not all these options will necessarily be applicable to the mortgage situation but will be extremely valuable in other cases.

Automatic and optional benefits

■ Increasing the sum assured

The sum assured of an existing policy can usually be increased at any time during its term on producing further medical evidence and paying the increased premium relevant to the age at which the increase is made. This saves the extra cost of taking an additional policy and paying additional policy charges.

■ Terminal illness

With some life assurance policies a terminal illness benefit is included which means that if a terminal illness (one that will result in death within the next twelve months) is diagnosed, then the policy will immediately pay out. This can be a valuable facility since it removes money worries at a tremendously difficult time, allowing one's affairs to be left in proper order.

■ Mortgage increase option

There are often other facilities included such as a mortgage increase option. This means that if the mortgage is increased there is the facility to increase the life insurance to cover the increased mortgage with no need to produce any further medical evidence. In other words whatever the state of health at the time the policy holder would be treated as a standard life for that particular increase. At this point it would also usually be possible to increase the term of the life assurance if so desired.

■ Special event benefit

Some of these policies also allow an increase in cover and/or lengthening of term without any further medical evidence on the occasion of some special event such as:

- ■ marriage
- ■ birth of children
- ■ adoption
- ■ divorce
- ■ inheritance which gives rise to an increased potential inheritance tax.

It will be seen later that all of these events could give rise to the need for increased life assurance cover.

■ Indexation benefit

At the commencement of the policy the applicant can choose to have the benefit level or indexed. Indexation could be in line with the Retail Prices Index (RPI) or the National Average Earnings Index (AEI) or a fixed percentage. On increasing the cover at each anniversary no further medical evidence would be required. The increase in premium would be that related to the age of the policy holder at the time.

■ Waiver of contribution option

For a small increase in premium this option would guarantee that should the policy holder become medically unable to work all premiums would be waived. There would usually be a deferred period like three months from the incidence of the disability before premiums were waived but then those premiums paid during the deferment period would be refunded. The premiums would usually be waived while the disability persisted and if necessary to the end of the term of the policy,

> **Waiver of contribution protects your life assurance payments in the event of you becoming medically unable to work.**

but not later than the 65th birthday. It is extremely important to note that this facility would only operate if the medical inability to work took place while the policy holder was in gainful employment. This is another point which is sometimes not clearly understood. In the case of joint life policies the policy holders would have the choice of to whose life the waiver of contribution option should apply. This choice would be made at the commencement of the policy. It is important to note that should the waiver of contribution option and indexation option both be included, and if the policy holder became medically unable to work, not only would the premiums be waived but the cover would continue to be indexed at each anniversary and no premiums would be required.

■ The renewable option

When a term policy comes to an end this option allows renewal of the life assurance for a further term equal to the first without production of any further medical evidence. The new premium will, of course, reflect the increase in age at the time. This could be an extremely valuable option were the policy holder to become seriously ill towards the end of the term of the life assurance with the prognosis of death shortly after the end of the term. Clearly the renewable option could be activated. This type of insurance will be more expensive than straight term.

■ Conversion option

This option allows the conversion of a term policy to any other type of life assurance policy offered by the company, such as whole of life. The new premium will, of course, be that applicable to the age at the time of conversion but, once again, no further medical evidence will be required.

Types of life assurance

■ Reducing term life assurance

In the case of a capital repayment loan the debt will decrease over the term as explained. It is therefore possible to purchase life assurance where the death benefit or sum assured reduces in line with the debt over the term of the loan. The term of this life assurance would equal that of the loan and the cover would cease at the end of the term. This is, of course, why the life assurance is called term. Typical premiums are shown in Table 3.8.

However, rates will vary between companies, some will be more expensive and some will be less. The table shows that rates in general will be considerably more expensive for a smoker.

Table 3.8 Typical premiums for reducing term (sum assured £100,000 over 25 years)

Single life

	Men Monthly premium			Women Monthly premium		
Age	Non-smoker £	% increase for smoker	% increase for WOC	Non-smoker £	% increase for smoker	% increase for WOC
20	11.20	5.4	2	8.64	5.4	2
25	11.41	17.3	2	9.06	20.8	2
30	12.63	40.1	2	10.47	31.3	2
35	16.38	64.1	2	13.00	46.8	2
40	18.81	78.3	3	15.34	59.8	4
45 (15 years)	23.03	85.1	3	17.88	78.6	4

Joint life payable on first death, woman three years younger than man

	Monthly premium			
	Non-smoker £	% increase for smoker (both lives)	% increase for WOC on man	% increase for WOC on woman
Man's age				
20	16.02	2.4	2	2
25	16.12	16.6	2	2
30	17.90	37.7	2	2
35	22.98	58.3	2	2
40	26.48	72.6	3	4
45 (15 years)	31.96	80.7	3	4

■ Example 3.8

Marianne Proctor is 28 and a smoker. She wants to cover her capital repayment loan of £73,000 with reducing term assurance and include WOC.

Using Table 3.8 the nearest age to 28 is 30.

The premium for a non-smoker for a sum assured of £73,000 will be,

$$\frac{73,000}{100,000} \times 10.47 = £7.64 \text{ per month}$$

Increase for smoker is 31.3% of 7.64 = £2.39, hence contribution is 7.64 + 2.39 = £10.03 per month.

WOC will cost 2% of £10.03 = £0.20. Total premium is £10.23 per month.

■ Example 3.9

John Taylor is 26 and Linda Taylor is 22. John is a smoker, Linda is not. They want to cover their mortgage of £58,000 with reducing term and WOC on Linda's life as she is the better earner.

Using Table 3.8, the nearest age to John is 25. Linda is 3 years younger than this. As John is a smoker we will use smoker rates, even though Linda is not a smoker. This is as near as we can get with the information we have.

The first difference will make our premium cheaper than it should be. The three year gap in ages tallies with the tables. The last difference will make it more expensive. However, the premium we calculate will give us an approximate value. More accurate figures will have to be obtained from a consultant or insurance company.

Premium for two non-smokers:

$$\frac{58,000}{100,000} \times 16.12 = £9.35 \text{ per month}$$

The increase for smoker rates:

$$16.6\% \text{ of } 9.35 = \frac{16.6}{100} \times 9.35 = £1.55$$

Total so far = £10.90 per month.

WOC will cost an additional 2% of 10.90:

$$\frac{2}{100} \times 10.90 = £0.22$$

Hence total cost of premium is £11.12 per month.

■ Exercise 3.5

Mark Prentice is 28 and his wife Pauline is 24. They are both smokers. They wish to cover their capital repayment loan of £62,000 with reducing term assurance with WOC on Mark's life. Calculate the total premium.

Straight term assurance

In the case of an interest only loan the debt will remain constant. The life cover would therefore remain the same over the term of the loan. If lumps of capital are paid back during the course of the loan the sum assured of the term assurance could be reduced correspondingly. With both reducing term and straight term assurance there is no investment aspect, which is why it is relatively cheap. On death it pays out, on survival the policy holder gets nothing back. There is often a confusion over this point, people thinking that their term assurance will pay off the loan (see Table 3.9).

Table 3.9 Typical premiums for straight term (sum assured £100,000 over 25 years)

Single life

	Men Monthly premium			Women Monthly premium		
Age	Non-smoker £	% increase for smoker	% increase for WOC	Non-smoker £	% increase for smoker	% increase for WOC
20	11.31	35.1	2	8.98	35.6	2
25	12.10	63.7	2	9.30	56.0	2
30	15.02	78.9	2	11.24	73.6	2
35	21.24	92.1	2	14.52	91.2	2
40 (20 years)	27.90	92.1	3	16.60	102.5	4
45 (15 years)	35.38	121.1	3	21.78	99.6	4

Joint life payable on first death, woman three years younger than man

	Monthly premium			
Man's age	Non-smoker £	% increase for smoker (both lives)	% increase for WOC on man	% increase for WOC on woman
20	15.94	43.7	2	2
25	17.30	67.7	2	2
30	21.36	84.7	2	2
35	30.12	98.4	2	2
40 (20 years)	37.52	115.3	3	4
45 (15 years)	48.92	124.2	3	4

■ Renewable term

This is a straight term policy but has the added facility that at the end of the term it can be renewed for a further term without the necessity to submit any further medical evidence. Normally all options existing on the policy will continue into subsequent terms. The premiums will be those applicable to the age of the policy holder at the time of renewal. There is usually a limit on the number of renewals that can take place. For example, if the new term fell after the policy holder's 60th birthday, this will be the last renewal and it would only be possible up to age 75 (see Table 3.10).

Table 3.10 Typical premiums for straight renewable term (sum assured £100,000 over 10 years)

Single life

	Men Monthly premium			Women Monthly premium		
Age	Non-smoker £	% increase for smoker	% increase for WOC	Non-smoker £	% increase for smoker	% increase for WOC
20	11.26	55.9	2	8.60	46.6	2
25	11.48	54.9	2	8.76	51.3	2
30	12.78	52.4	2	9.52	80.2	2
35	17.58	52.9	2	10.56	100.2	2
40	23.78	77.8	3	15.56	80.9	4
45	36.98	81.1	3	22.42	88.5	4

Joint life payable on first death, woman three years younger than man

	Monthly premium			
	Non-smoker £	% increase for smoker (both lives)	% increase for WOC on man	on woman
Man's age				
20	16.16	63.7	2	2
25	16.42	62.9	2	2
30	18.06	69.1	2	2
35	23.62	76.8	2	2
40	32.46	91.1	3	4
45	50.40	91.5	3	4

■ Example 3.10

Rebecca Winter's 20 year renewable term policy reaches the end of its current term when Rebecca is 70. She could renew for a term of five years, without needing to produce any further medical evidence, if she so wished.

■ Convertible term

This is also a straight term policy but this time it has the facility that at any time up to the end of the term it can be converted without any further medical evidence into any of the other types of life assurance policy offered by the particular insurance company. For example, it could be converted to whole of life (see later). The premiums for the new policy will be those for that policy at the age of the policy holder at the time (see Table 3.11).

Table 3.11 Typical premiums for straight convertible term (sum assured £100,000 over 10 years)

Single life

	Men Monthly premium			Women Monthly premium		
Age	Non-smoker £	% increase for smoker	% increase for WOC	Non-smoker £	% increase for smoker	% increase for WOC
20	10.96	55.6	2	8.06	53.2	2
25	11.20	55.5	2	8.22	58.7	2
30	12.46	54.5	2	8.76	88.8	2
35	17.12	56.2	2	9.90	108.3	2
40	23.16	80.2	3	14.16	95.9	4
45	35.70	85.8	3	20.62	101.6	4

Joint life payable on first death, woman three years younger than man

	Monthly premium			
Man's age	Non-smoker £	% increase for smoker (both lives)	% increase for WOC on man	on woman
20	15.36	67.6	2	2
25	15.62	67.4	2	2
30	17.16	74.5	2	2
35	22.40	83.1	2	2
40	30.86	97.5	3	4
45	47.90	99.0	3	4

■ Renewable convertible term life assurance

This straight term carries the facilities from both the previous types so that either it could be converted, or renewed and later converted if so wished (see Table 3.12).

■ Straight term life assurance written under pension legislation

This could be stand-alone life assurance or it could be linked to pension invest-ment. Clearly the premiums will be the same as those for straight term except that this time the premiums will attract tax relief. This will make the actual cost less. Also because the earliest retirement age is 50 we cannot have a 25 year term for a 20 year old, it will have to be at least 30 years. Clearly joint life policies are not possible in this case (see Table 3.13, p. 178).

Table 3.12 Typical premiums for straight renewable convertible term (sum assured £100,000 over 10 years)

Single life

| | Men | | | Women | | |
| | Monthly premium | | | Monthly premium | | |
Age	Non-smoker £	% increase for smoker	% increase for WOC	Non-smoker £	% increase for smoker	% increase for WOC
20	12.28	56.5	2	9.24	49.6	2
25	12.60	54.1	2	9.48	54.9	2
30	14.06	45.5	2	10.26	84.6	2
35	19.50	43.1	2	11.62	101.9	2
40	26.72	66.3	3	17.16	75.7	4
45	41.56	66.9	3	24.62	83.0	4

Joint life payable on first death, woman three years younger than man

| | Monthly premium | | | |
| | Non-smoker £ | % increase for smoker (both lives) | % increase for WOC | |
Man's age			on man	on woman
20	17.46	69.2	2	2
25	18.20	67.1	2	2
30	19.36	78.9	2	2
35	24.10	76.4	2	2
40	35.24	70.3	3	4
45	52.70	79.0	3	4

It is always worth bearing in mind that premiums paid for life assurance written into a personal pension scheme will take up part of total eligibility which cannot then be used for investment. Premiums paid for life assurance in a company pension scheme do not take up part of eligibility although the sum assured is limited to four times remuneration.

■ Whole of life life assurance

This form of life assurance policy is literally what it says it is. It is a policy which can go on for the whole of life. It will not come to an end unless the policy holder dies or cashes it in. It has no set term. Its only application to mortgages will be in the case of a lifetime mortgage when the lender may insist on life assurance and if not it may be decided that it is valuable to have. And so a whole of life policy would insure the policy holder for the whole of his or her life.

Table 3.13 Typical premiums for straight term written under pension legislation (sum assured £100,000)

Single life

Men Age	Non-smoker £ Gross	Basic rate taxpayer £	Higher rate taxpayer £	% increase for smoker	% increase for WOC
			Monthly premium		
20 (30 years)	12.00	9.24	7.20	35.1	2
25	12.10	9.32	7.26	63.7	2
30	15.02	11.57	9.01	78.9	2
35	21.24	16.35	12.74	92.1	2
40 (20 years)	27.90	21.48	16.74	92.1	3
45 (15 years)	35.38	27.24	21.23	121.1	3
Women Age					
20 (30 years)	8.98	6.91	5.39	35.6	2
25	9.30	7.16	5.58	56.0	2
30	11.24	8.65	6.74	73.6	2
35	14.52	11.18	8.71	91.2	2
40 (20 years)	16.60	12.78	9.96	102.5	4
45 (15 years)	21.78	16.77	13.07	99.6	4

There will usually be a small investment aspect although it should in no way be seen as an investment policy. This will mean that should the policy be cancelled and it has been in effect long enough there would be a cash in value which the policy holder would receive.

■ Sum assured continuation

It is possible to retain life assurance cover while paying no premiums.

A benefit of the investment aspect is the sum assured continuation. This means that premiums can be stopped but the sum assured continue in operation. The costs for keeping the policy holder insured under this policy would be taken regularly from the built up value of the policy until there is nothing left. This could mean that in financially difficult times the life assurance could be maintained although no premiums would be paid. Premiums would be started again when the financial situation improved.

Table 3.14 Typical premiums for whole of life policy (sum assured £100,000)

Single life

Age	Men Monthly premium			Women Monthly premium		
	Non-smoker £	% increase for smoker	% increase for WOC	Non-smoker £	% increase for smoker	% increase for WOC
20	18.88	35.1	2	13.48	21.1	2
25	24.98	44.6	2	17.78	28.3	2
30	34.68	62.4	2	24.28	39.1	2
35	48.38	84.5	2	33.68	51.6	2
40	68.98	105.3	3	47.48	64.5	4
45	98.38	149.5	3	67.08	98.8	4

Joint life payable on first death, woman three years younger than man

Man's age	Monthly premium			
	Non-smoker £	% increase for smoker (both lives)	% increase for WOC on man	on woman
20	23.98	45.9	2	2
25	31.68	59.1	2	2
30	44.38	82.9	2	2
35	61.98	112.0	2	2
40	88.18	131.6	3	4
45	125.78	184.7	3	4

■ Example 3.11

Peter O'Donal was 30 on 1 September 1997. He decided he needed a whole of life policy with a sum assured of £100,000, premium £34.68. After paying this for 15 years he was made redundant, had no income protection and could no longer keep up the premiums. The sum assured continuation option allowed him, rather than cashing in the policy, to be covered for £100,000 sum assured without paying any further premiums for another 19 years. In other words for a monthly cost of £34.68 for 15 years (= 34.68 × 12 × 15 = £6242.40) he has been covered for 34 years. Averaged out on a monthly basis this would be,

$$\frac{6242.40}{34 \times 12} = £15.30$$

Referring to Table 3.9 (p. 174) we see that 23 years of straight term cover would have cost £15.02 per month. Whole of life may be harder on cashflow initially but can work out over the long term about the same with the added flexibility of a whole of life policy. It is important to consider such options before making a decision.

■ Early cash facility

There is often an early cash facility on these policies. This enables the policy holder to take some cash out of the policy while maintaining premiums and therefore the life assurance cover. This would be useful if a need for cash arose.

The whole of life policy will usually make available the various options possible such as indexing, mortgage increase option, special event option and waiver of contribution option. It can, of course, be written as a single life policy, or as a joint life first death policy payable on the death of either partner. There is, however, a joint life second death version payable on the death of the last life assured which makes it an ideal policy for the amelioration of inheritance tax. This aspect will be treated in Chapter 5.

Clearly the whole of life policy is going to be considerably more expensive than term assurance.

Table 3.15 Typical premiums for low start or enhanced cover whole of life (sum assured £100,000 reducing to £55,000 at the end of 10 years)

Single life

| | Men | | | Women | | |
| | Monthly premium | | | Monthly premium | | |
Age	Non-smoker £	% increase for smoker	% increase for WOC	Non-smoker £	% increase for smoker	% increase for WOC
20	14.53	51.4	2	12.38	45.2	2.5
25	18.28	53.2	2	14.16	48.4	2.5
30	22.56	66.7	2	17.58	51.0	2.5
35	30.34	58.0	2	23.14	52.2	2.5
40	42.18	63.1	3	29.52	52.5	4
45	60.52	68.6	3	41.24	61.0	4

Joint life payable on first death, woman three years younger than man

| | Monthly premium | | | |
| | Non-smoker £ | % increase for smoker (both lives) | % increase for WOC | |
Man's age			on man	on woman
20	19.98	63.4	2	2.5
25	22.54	68.9	2	2.5
30	29.80	71.2	2	2.5
35	40.38	73.8	2	2.5
40	55.86	75.3	3	4
45	73.36	76.7	3	4

If the reduced figure chosen is less than £55,000 the premiums would be lower and vice versa.

■ The low start or enhanced cover whole of life policy

This policy offers a way of achieving the level of cover required but with a premium which is initially lower than the true whole of life. The policy will have a lower underlying level of whole of life cover which will be supplemented in the first ten years to the higher level required. At the end of the ten years the sum assured will revert to the lower underlying level of sum assured. The premiums will remain the same throughout. At the end of ten years the policy holder will have various choices.

1 The policy can be left where it is with its underlying level of whole of life sum assured (Fig. 3.8). Table 3.15 shows typical premiums in such a situation.
2 By paying increased premiums at the beginning of the eleventh year the underlying level can be increased by any amount up to the full initial level of sum assured. The policy would then continue for the whole of life at this level (Fig. 3.9).
3 The level of enhanced sum assured applicable during the first ten years can be maintained for a further ten years. At the end of the second ten years the same choices would be available (Fig. 3.10).

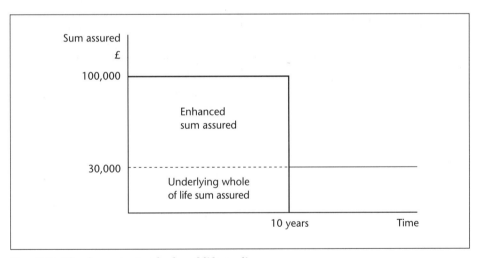

Fig. 3.8 The low start whole of life policy

At any time during the initial or subsequent ten years of enhanced cover the underlying level of whole of life cover could be increased by increasing the premiums. In which case the new underlying level of whole of life cover would come into effect at the end of the ten years. Since the increased premiums will relate to the age of the policy holder at the time, the earlier the underlying level of whole of life cover is increased the cheaper it will be (Fig. 3.11).

The whole of life policy can be extremely flexible.

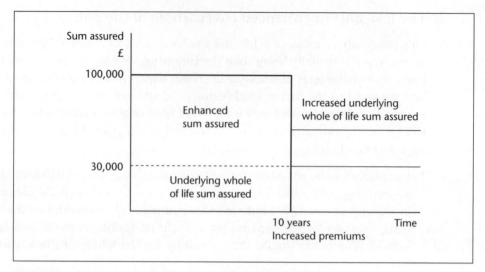

Fig. 3.9 Increased level of underlying sum assured

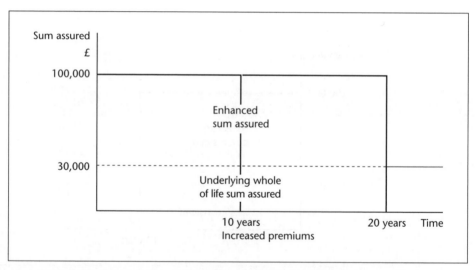

Fig. 3.10 Maintaining the enhanced sum assured for a further 10 years

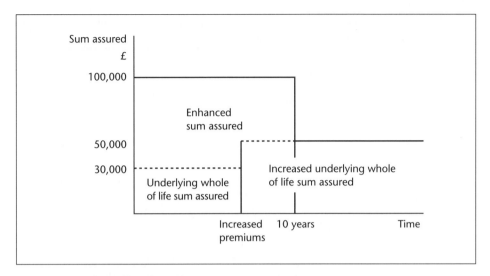

Fig. 3.11 Increasing the underlying level of whole of life sum assured at any time during the first 10 years

Indexed premiums

There is a further possible sophistication which is the facility to index the premiums without indexing the cover. This will result in the underlying whole of life element increasing each year until it reaches the enhanced level when the indexing could then cease.

CRITICAL ILLNESS ASSURANCE

Critical illness is treated fully in Chapter 2, where it is used to enhance permanent health insurance or as a pension guarantee policy. However its use in the mortgage situation is invaluable. In the aftermath of suffering a critical illness what a blessing it would be to know the mortgage was gone and the house unencumbered. Endowment policies will usually admit to the adding of critical illness cover but if the vehicle for repaying the mortgage is not an endowment it can, of course, be taken out separately or added to the life assurance.

Whole of life life assurance plus critical illness is dealt with in Chapter 2.

Reducing term critical illness assurance

In the case of the capital repayment mortgage a further type of critical illness cover is needed and this is reducing term critical illness in which the cover will reduce in line with the reducing outstanding amount of mortgage (see Table 3.16).

Table 3.16 Typical premiums for reducing term critical illness (sum assured £100,000 reducing over 25 years)

Single life

Age	Men Monthly premium			Women Monthly premium		
	Non-smoker £	% increase for smoker	% increase for WOC	Non-smoker £	% increase for smoker	% increase for WOC
20	21.68	Nil	2	24.38	Nil	2
25	21.68	25.9	2	24.38	19.5	2
30	23.69	72.9	2	25.98	52.3	2
35	34.25	77.7	2	34.75	58.8	2
40	48.29	72.7	3	44.99	63.8	4
45	65.96	71.4	3	59.26	63.4	4

Joint life payable on first death, woman three years younger than man

Man's age	Monthly premium			
	Non-smoker £	% increase for smoker (both lives)	% increase for WOC on man	on woman
20	40.68	Nil	2	2
25	40.68	12.8	2	2
30	42.38	56.4	2	2
35	56.78	69.7	2	2
40	77.47	69.2	3	4
45	104.78	69.7	3	4

Reducing term critical illness plus life assurance

These policies will pay out on either the event of a critical illness or death. It is important to be clear that they will not pay out on both, critical illness and then death (see Table 3.17).

Table 3.17 Typical premiums for reducing term critical illness plus life assurance (sum assured £100,000 reducing over 25 years)

Single life

	Men Monthly premium			Women Monthly premium		
Age	Non-smoker £	% increase for smoker	% increase for WOC	Non-smoker £	% increase for smoker	% increase for WOC
20	25.62	Nil	2	26.42	Nil	2
25	25.62	24.2	2	26.42	15.8	2
30	27.64	69.0	2	27.79	48.0	2
35	39.43	77.5	2	36.14	61.4	2
40	54.29	74.6	3	47.08	64.6	4
45	73.68	74.0	3	62.16	65.5	4

Joint life payable on first death, woman three years younger than man

	Monthly premium			
	Non-smoker £	% increase for smoker (both lives)	% increase for WOC on man	on woman
Man's age				
20	46.52	Nil	2	2
25	46.70	11.7	2	2
30	48.27	50.8	2	2
35	63.42	69.5	2	2
40	85.18	70.0	3	4
45	114.46	70.8	3	4

VEHICLES FOR REPAYING THE MORTGAGE

The endowment policy

An endowment policy is a vehicle for repaying a mortgage within a certain term. It therefore has a heavy investment aspect and is designed to build up enough value to repay the mortgage at the end of the term. If the endowment does better than the assumptions originally made the maturity value may exceed the amount of mortgage owed and the extra amount would be paid back to the policy holder tax free. It must be remembered that the endowment fund has been taxed internally throughout its life in exactly the same way as the life funds described in Chapter 1, so any tax advantage would simply be the difference between the tax rate paid by the policy holder and the taxes charged in the life fund. Clearly this difference is considerably more for the higher rate tax payer. Just as a reminder, life funds pay tax at 24 per cent on capital gains and 20 per cent on income, but actual tax is less because capital gains can usually be deferred into the future and certain expenses incurred through the running of the fund can be offset against tax on income. In the case of the unit-linked policy the policy holder is often allowed to use the endowment policy to pay off the mortgage early if original assumptions have been exceeded.

The endowment policy also has a life assurance aspect such that if the policy holder dies before the policy matures the mortgage would be paid off. In other words there is a guaranteed sum assured. The life assurance will be reducing term so designed that at any time during the term of the policy the life assurance plus the value of the investment will equal the guaranteed sum assured (see Fig. 3.12).

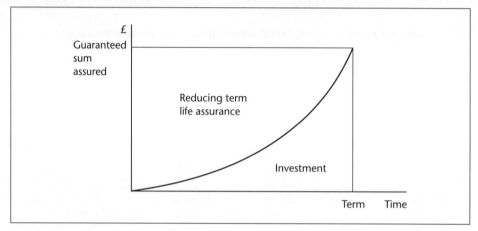

Fig. 3.12 The endowment policy

■ Versions

There are two versions of the endowment policy: the single life policy written on the life of one person and the joint life policy written on the life of two people. In this case either the investment aspect of the endowment policy would eventually pay off the mortgage or it would be paid off on the occurrence of the death of either of the lives assured.

> It could be invaluable to be able to increase your policy without further medical evidence if you increase your mortgage.

■ Options and benefits

The endowment policy will carry all the usual benefits which apply to life assurance policies, some automatic on most policies and some optional. Some like the mortgage increase option could be invaluable.

Table 3.18 Typical premiums for an endowment policy (sum assured £100,000 over 25 years, assuming investment growth of 10% p.a.)

Single life

Men	Monthly premium				
Age	Non-smoker £	% increase to add critical illness cover	Smoker £	% increase to add critical illness cover	% increase for WOC
20	128.60	4.0	132.42	5.1	2
25	133.99	3.0	138.16	6.8	2
30	139.32	6.7	145.14	12.8	2
35	144.70	13.1	154.42	23.6	2
40 (20 years)	220.32	12.0	232.96	21.6	3
45 (15 years)	360.74	9.0	377.46	16.4	3

Women	Monthly premium				
Age	Non-smoker £	% increase to add critical illness cover	Smoker £	% increase to add critical illness cover	% increase for WOC
	126.06	5.2	128.26	5.8	2
25	128.56	6.5	131.74	7.8	2
30	131.62	8.9	136.42	11.5	2
35	135.32	12.6	142.74	16.9	2
40 (20 years)	210.16	9.7	219.36	13.5	4
45 (15 years)	349.16	6.8	360.44	10.0	4

Joint life payable on first death, woman three years younger than man

Man's age	Monthly premium					
Age	Non-smoker £	% increase to add critical illness cover	Smoker £ (both lives)	% increase to add critical illness cover	% increase for WOC on man	% increase for WOC on woman
20	131.46	8.4	137.24	9.6	2	2
25	138.16	8.9	144.96	12.2	2	2
30	146.42	12.8	155.94	19.7	2	2
35	154.84	21.0	170.32	32.4	2	2
40 (20 years)	231.94	18.4	251.82	29.1	3	4
45 (15 years)	360.76	9.1	377.52	16.4	3	4

■ Critical illness option

It is usually possible to add critical illness cover to the endowment. Clearly an additional premium would be payable for this option. Details on critical illness cover can be found in Chapter 2.

■ Payment holiday

It is sometimes possible to stop paying contributions in the event of the policy holder experiencing financial difficulties. This is usuallly allowed for up to twelve months. During this time the costs of the policy are met from its cash value. Life cover and, if included, critical illness cover will be maintained. When premiums commence again at the end of the twelve months no further medical evidence is required. Clearly activating such an option will lengthen the original term of the policy.

■ Cashing in

The endowment policy will not begin to acquire any substantial value for a number of years. Thus if it is cashed in early it could be of very little value.

■ Partial cash withdrawal

With some policies a partial cash withdrawal is allowed when the policy has acquired a certain value. This will usually result in the term of the policy being lengthened but could be helpful in times of financial difficulty. If the policy is assigned to a lender permission to increase the term of the mortgage will have to be granted.

Table 3.18 gives typical premiums and shows how inexpensive it is to add critical illness cover to this type of policy compared to a stand-alone policy.

The low start endowment policy

Low start versions of the endowment policy are available. For a given sum assured and projected maturity value they will allow the plan holder to pay less than the true cost of the premiums in the early years. The premiums will, however, increase at each anniversary until after usually five years they will remain constant at a value higher than the ordinary premium would have been. They will then continue at this level for the rest of the life of the policy. No further medical evidence is sought at the times of the increases. A typical such policy, over a 25 year period, would start at a premium 60 per cent of the true premium but this premium would increase by 25 per cent of the original premium at the start of years two to five. It would therefore reach a premium of 120 per cent of the ordinary policy premium and remain at this level for the rest of the life of the policy (see Fig. 3.13).

> An endowment policy which starts low will mean bigger premiums eventually.

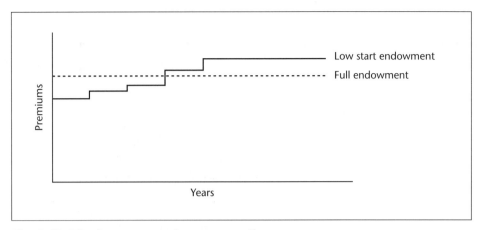

Fig. 3.13 The low start endowment policy

With-profit versions of the endowment

■ The non-profit endowment

This policy guarantees the sum assured to be paid on death or maturity. It will not partake in reversionary bonuses or terminal bonuses. Because it is guaranteed, the final value will represent a liability against the value of the underlying fund at outset and it will therefore be a more expensive policy.

■ The with-profits endowment

This endowment is also sometimes referred to as the full endowment policy. Once again the sum assured at outset is guaranteed whether on death or maturity but this time the policy enjoys the benefit of sharing in the reversionary and terminal bonuses. Because of this premiums will be higher than the non-profit endowment but there should be a tax-free surplus for the policy holder at maturity and also, depending on the contract, on death (see Fig. 3.14).

■ The low-cost with-profits endowment

Of all the versions of with-profits endowments this is by far the least expensive and is therefore the most popular. It consists of two parts, one guaranteed and the other not. Thus an endowment designed to produce a final maturity value of £60,000 might have £30,000 of this guaranteed.

The second part of the policy partakes in reversionary bonuses and the terminal bonus and so it is hoped the full £60,000, or perhaps more, will be available at maturity. Of course, there is no guarantee of this. In order to make this more certain the full amount of reversionary bonuses to be added by maturity is estimated and premiums are calculated on just 80 per cent of these making the maturity value up to the full £60,000. Decreasing term assurance plays its part to

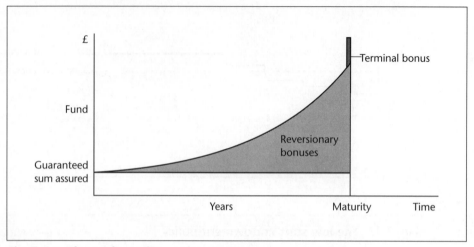

Fig. 3.14 The with-profits endowment

make sure that on death the full amount would be paid. As bonuses are added to this second part of the policy this life assurance decreases by the same amount. Depending on the contract a terminal bonus would also be added.

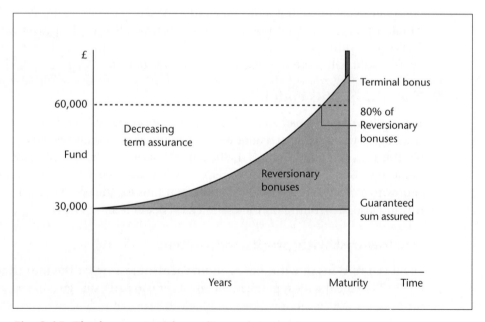

Fig. 3.15 The low cost with-profits endowment

If the policy is cashed in early its value would in no way reflect the value of the declared reversionary bonuses, as explained earlier. Furthermore, there would be no terminal bonus.

These policies often have a review written in which takes place after ten years and then every five years. This tells the investor whether the policy is on track to produce the amount required. If not premiums can be adjusted.

The unit-linked endowment policy

The investment aspect of this policy will be the life funds discussed in Chapter 1. The life assurance aspect will be reducing term assurance. The policy is designed so that the value of the investment at any one time plus the value of the reducing term will be equal to the sum assured which would be paid out on death (see Fig. 3.16).

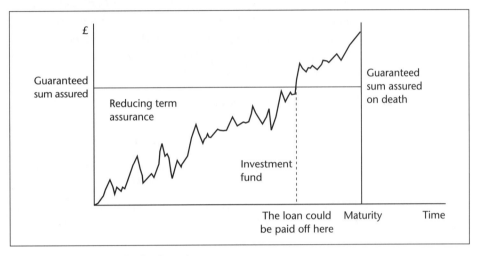

Fig. 3.16 The unit-linked endowment

In some cases the charges will be exactly those for the life funds plus perhaps a monthly plan charge of £3 to £5. In others an upfront charge will take over such as a very low allocation of units or even none at all in the first months and combined with this the management charge on the life funds would be waived.

The value of the policy at any time will be the bid value of the underlying units.

In the case of this policy, as mentioned earlier, if the investment value achieves the full guaranteed sum assured before the end of the term the policy can be used to pay off the mortgage early. If it is continued for the whole term then the mortgage will be paid off and the policy holder will receive the additional sum tax free in his or her hands.

PEP-related mortgage

A typical projection for a PEP to produce £100,000 over 25 years, assuming an annual investment growth of 12 per cent, would be £85.92 per month. There will be lower and higher projections on the market due to companies using their own changing structure in the projection.

Pension-related mortgage

A mortgage could also be paid off by using the tax-free cash available from a pension.

COMPARISON OF DIFFERENT METHODS OF REPAYING THE MORTGAGE

■ Example 3.12

Oliver and Deirdre Pearson are considering a mortgage of £60,000 at a variable rate of 7.6% annually over a term of 25 years. They decide to have life assurance on a joint life first death policy which would pay out on the death of either one. They are both 25 years old, and both are non-smokers. They decide to compare the various vehicles for repayment of the mortgage (see Table 3.19).

Table 3.19 Numerical comparison of vehicles of repayment

Method	Total mortgage payments over the 25 years		Total life assurance (LA) payments or investment or both		Total payment over the 25 years
	Monthly	Total over the 25 years	Monthly	Total over the 25 years	
Repayment increases steeply from year 19 on	423.99	128,190	(LA) 9.24	2772 p.a.	130,962
Endowment	351.50	105,450	(Endow) 84.58	25,314	130,764
PEP	351.50	105,450	(LA) 11.84	3552	
			(PEP) 51.55	15,465	124,467
Pension Basic rate tax payer	351.50	105,450	(LA) 11.84	3552	
			(Pension) 39.69	11,907	120,909
Pension Higher rate tax payer		105,450	(LA) 11.84	3552	118,266
			(Pension) (actual cost) 30.88	9264	

There are some important points to make about the different methods of repaying the mortgage:

1 Mortgage payments are net of MIRAS. The repayment route involves repayment of capital over the 25 years. The other routes are interest only.
2 Premiums for vehicles of repayment are all typical premiums. There will always be cheaper and dearer on the market.

3 The endowment has been quoted on a joint life first death basis. The PEP and pension have been quoted on a single life although if these policies were shared it would result in an increase in premium of no more than £4 per month.

4 The pension in the case of basic rate tax payers is quoted net of basic rate tax relief, PRAS. In the case of higher rate tax payers the true cost of the premium is quoted net of higher rate tax. In each case the actual amount which would be invested is £51.55 per month.

5 The policy holders are assumed to have a pension already and the premiums quoted are those needed to produce a fund to replace the tax-free cash taken out of the pension to pay off the mortgage. For a policy holder with no existing pension four times the premium would be required since a total fund of £240,000 would be needed in order to take out £60,000 in tax-free cash (see personal pension schemes and retirement annuity contracts in Chapter 2). This larger fund would, of course, result in £180,000 left in the policy to produce a pension for the investor.

6 The growth rate assumed for the PEP and pension is 12 per cent per annum which, as the endowment is taxed at somewhere between 20 and 23 per cent less expenses, would result in a net growth rate of somewhere between 9.24 and 9.6 per cent. For the endowment the actual growth rate used is 9.25 per cent.

Table 3.20 provides a non-numerical comparison of repayment options.

Table 3.20 Descriptive comparison of vehicles of repayment

	Tax relief on vehicle premium	Tax on growth and income of fund	Tax free on maturity
Capital Repayment	Capital repayments attract no tax relief	No income or growth	Not applicable
Endowment	None	20% on income less expenses 23% on growth	Total (i.e. no further tax, fund has already been taxed)
PEP	None	Free of all UK taxes	Free of all UK taxes
Pension	Tax relief at highest rate paid	Free of all UK taxes	PPS 25% of fund tax free RAC approximately 23% of fund tax free Company pension could be as much as 100% of the fund tax free (See Chapter 5)

■ Comparison of different methods of repaying the mortgage

Fig. 3.17 shows investment in different vehicles of repayment.

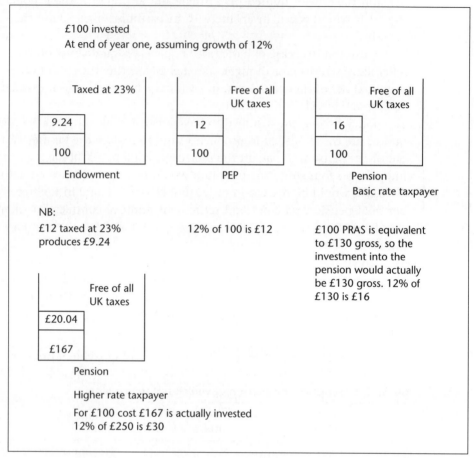

Fig. 3.17 Comparison of vehicles of repayment

Figure 3.18 shows personal pensions for basic and higher rate tax payers.
Hence £100 invested grows at the end of one year to:

Endowment	£109.24
PEP	£112.00
Pension basic rate tax payer	£146.00
Pension higher rate tax payer	£187.04

NB: For the basis of this illustration I have ignored the charges which would, in fact, be roughly the same in each case.

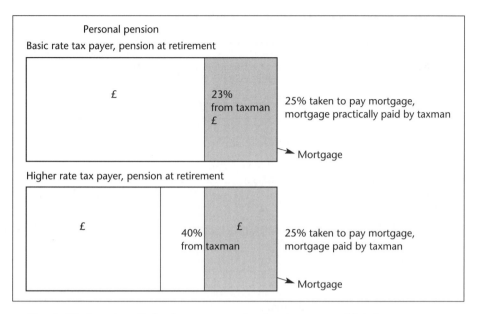

Personal pension

Basic rate tax payer, pension at retirement

£ | 23% from taxman £ | 25% taken to pay mortgage, mortgage practically paid by taxman

Mortgage

Higher rate tax payer, pension at retirement

£ | 40% from taxman | £ | 25% taken to pay mortgage, mortgage paid by taxman

Mortgage

Fig. 3.18 Pension-linked mortgage for basic rate and higher rate tax payer

■ Case Study 3.1

Amanda and Martin Jenkins have just got married. They decide to discuss in full their respective financial plans and to investigate the purchase of a home. Because Martin is the higher earner and likely to hit the higher rate tax band before Amanda, they have decided that he should take all the married couple's allowance. The core details of their financial life are as follows:

Martin needs to contribute £502 per month into a pension scheme to achieve his total financial independence objective. His eligibility is limited to £365 per month. When he is 36 his eligibility lifts to 20% p.a. He could also consider using carry forward and carry back to contribute a lump sum.

With these details on the table they discuss what would happen if they became medically unable to work. Amanda would have an income of £6502 p.a., but once Martin's lump sum of £10,000 was gone he would have nothing. They decide it is crucial that Martin starts an income protection policy at the maximum benefit of £13,002 p.a.

Using Table 2.4 (p. 50), and an age of 35, which is the nearest to Martin's age, we see the premium would be to age 60, fully indexed with six months deferment:

$$\frac{13,002}{10,000} \times 13.50 = £17.55 \text{ per month}$$

with three months deferment

$$\frac{13,002}{10,000} \times 24.38 = £31.70 \text{ p.a.}$$

■ Comparison of different methods of repaying the mortgage

■ Form 3.2 INCOME TAX AND NIC ANALYSIS

INCOME TAX			
Name Amanda Jenkins	*Year* 1997		
	£	*Remaining income £*	*Tax £*
Gross income	15,000		
Gross contribution to pension paid personally*	353.28	14,646.72	Nil
Personal allowance	4045	10,601.72	Nil
Income taxed at 20%	4100	6501.72	820.00
Income taxed at basic rate 23%	6501.72	Nil	1495.40
Income taxed at higher rate 40%			
Total	15,000		2315.40
Less married couple's allowance			
Total tax payable			

* Some pension contributions paid personally are net of basic rate tax. For the purposes of this form this would need to be grossed up.

NATIONAL INSURANCE CONTRIBUTION (NIC) (Employed)			
	£	*Remaining income £*	*NIC £*
Gross income	15,000		
Income up to LEL £3224 p.a. NIC at 2%	3224	11,776	64.48
Income up to UEL £24,180 p.a. minus £3224 p.a., the LEL NIC at 10%	11,776	Nil	1177.60
Total	15,000		1242.08

NATIONAL INSURANCE CONTRIBUTION (NIC) (Self-employed)
Flat rate paid if income over £3480 p.a. £6.15 p.w.
On profits between £7010 and £24,180 p.a. 6.0%
Total
Income after tax and NIC deductions   15,000 − 2315.40 −1242.08 = 11,442.52

∎ Form 3.3 LIFETIME FINANCIAL PLAN ANALYSIS

Name Amanda Jenkins	*Date* 1997
Date of birth (DoB) 3 November 1972	Smoker/non-smoker N/S
Employed/self-employed Employed	Time with business 2 years
Income p.a. gross £15,000 p.a.	Income p.a. net of taxes and NIC £11,442.52
Annual outgoings p.a. £10,600 (including £138.72 p.a. for PHI)	Surplus p.a. £842.52
Regular savings p.a. from net income	£300 p.a.
If I become medically unable to work what would my income situation be for the first 6 months?	Full salary
For the second 6 months?	PHI policy £6502 p.a.
Thereafter?	PHI policy £6502 p.a. to age 60
What is the maximum which I could have?	£6502 p.a.
Approximate cost of increasing my cover to this	Not possible – on maximum
Pension type	Defined benefit occupation scheme
Personal contribution 3% p.a. of pensionable salary = £353.28 p.a. Pensionable salary is gross salary – LEL	
Maximum I am allowed to contribute 15% of £15,000 = $\frac{15}{100} \times 15,000 = £2250$ p.a.	
Retirement age	65
Projected pension fund (MPS or PPS) at retirement age	
Projected pension at $\frac{42}{60} \times (15,000 - 3224) = \frac{42}{60} \times 11,776 = 8243$ p.a. retirement age (DBS)	
At what age do I want total financial independence?	60
Pension fund (MPS or PPS) adjusted to financial independence age	
Pension (DBS) adjusted to to financial independence age	$^{37}/_{60} \times 11,776 = 7262$ p.a. There would be a penalty for taking early retirement which would reduce the pension

■ Comparison of different methods of repaying the mortgage

■ **Form 3.3 (continued)**

Type of annuity required	Single life, indexed at 5% p.a. guaranteed for 5 years (yield 4.79% p.a.)
Pension this would produce	
Assumed rate of inflation long term	5% p.a.
Pension in today's terms	£7262 p.a. since the DBS allows calculation in today's terms, as explained in Chapter 2
What is total financial independence for me in today's terms?	£10,000 p.a.
Shortfall	£10,000 – £7262 = £2738 p.a.
Shortfall at financial independence age, taking inflation into account	£2738 p.a. × 5.52 = £15,114 (inflation factor 5.52)
Fund needed to produce this pension	£15,114 divided by $\frac{4.79}{100}$ = £315,532
Pension contribution needed to produce this fund at a growth of 12% p.a.	$\frac{315,532}{404,000} \times 100$ = £78.10 p.m. gross PRAS $\qquad$ = £60.14 p.m. net

■ Form 3.4 INCOME TAX AND NIC ANALYSIS

INCOME TAX			
Name Martin Jenkins	Year 1997		
	£	Remaining income £	Tax £
Gross income	25,000		
Gross contribution to pension paid personally*	1200	23,800	Nil
Personal allowance	4045	19,755	Nil
Income taxed at 20%	4100	15,655	820.00
Income taxed at basic rate 23%	15,655	Nil	3600.65
Income taxed at higher rate 40%			
Total	25,000		4420.65
Less married couple's allowance 15% of 1830			274.50
Total tax payable			4146.15

* Some pension contributions paid personally are net of basic rate tax. For the purposes of this form this would need to be grossed up.

NATIONAL INSURANCE CONTRIBUTION (NIC) (Employed)			
	£	Remaining income £	NIC £
Gross income			
Income up to LEL £3224 p.a. NIC at 2%			
Income up to UEL £24,180 p.a. minus £3224 p.a., the LEL NIC at 10%			
Total			

NATIONAL INSURANCE CONTRIBUTION (NIC) (Self-employed)	
Flat rate paid if income over £3480 p.a. £6.15 p.w.	319.80
On profits between £7010 and £24,180 p.a. 6.0% $17,170 \times \dfrac{6}{100} = 1030.20$	
Total	1350.00
Income after tax and NIC deductions $25,000 - 4146.15 - 1350 = £19,503.85$	

■ Comparison of different methods of repaying the mortgage

■ Form 3.5 LIFETIME FINANCIAL PLAN ANALYSIS

Name Martin Jenkins	Year 1997	
Date of Birth (DoB) 14 August 1963	Smoker/non-smoker Smoker	
Employed/self-employed Self-employed	Time with business 5 years	
Income p.a. gross £25,000	Income p.a. net of taxes and NIC	£19,503
Annual outgoings p.a. £12,000 including £924 net pension contribution paid gross at £1200 p.a.	Surplus p.a.	£7503
Regular savings p.a. from net income	£2000	
If I become medically unable to work what would my income situation be for the first 6 months?	Receipts could continue for about two months. Contingency fund is currently £10,000	
For the second 6 months?	Nil	
Thereafter?	Nil	
What is the maximum which I could have	£13,002 p.a.	
Approximate cost of increasing my cover to this		
Pension type	Personal pension scheme (PPS)	
Personal contribution £100 p.m. gross = £1200 p.a. (for last 5 years)		
Maximum I am allowed to contribute 17½% of 25,000 = $\frac{17.5}{100} \times 25,000$ = £4375 p.a. = £365 monthly		
Retirement age	60	
Projected pension fund (MPS or PPS) at retirement age	Using Table 2.13 nearest age is 30 hence fund = £227,000 approximately	
Projected pension at retirement age (DBS)		
At what age do I want total financial independence	60	
Pension fund (MPS or PPS) adjusted to financial independence age	£227,000	
Pension (DBS) adjusted to financial independence age		
Type of annuity required	Single life, indexed at 5% p.a. guaranteed 5 years (yield 5.74% p.a.)	
Pension this would produce	£227,000 × $\frac{5.74}{100}$ = £13,030 p.a.	
Assumed rate of inflation long-term	5% p.a.	

■ Form 3.5 (continued)

Pension in today's terms	Factor is 3.92 hence $\frac{13,030}{3.92}$ = £3324 p.a.
What is total financial independence for me in today's terms?	£20,000 p.a.
Shortfall	£16,676 p.a.
Shortfall at financial independence age, taking inflation into account	$16,676 \times 3.92$ = £65,370 p.a.
Fund needed to produce this pension	65,370 divided by $\frac{5.74}{100}$ = £1,138,850
Pension contribution needed to produce this contribution fund at a growth of 12% p.a.	Martin has 28 years to age 60. The nearest on the table is 30 years, hence pension contribution $\frac{1,138,850}{227,000} \times 100$ = £502 p.m. gross approximately

In view of the facts they decide on the three month deferment.

They also decide that Martin should lift his pension contribution to the maximum allowed, i.e. £365 per month gross. Because he cannot achieve his financial independence objectives, they decide Amanda should contribute the maximum possible to either her company AVC or an FSAVC,

$$£2250 - £353.28 = £1896.72 \text{ p.a. or } £158.06 \text{ per month gross}$$

$$PRAS = \frac{77}{100} \times £158.06 = £121.71 \text{ per month net}$$

They then address the question of buying a house.

They have enough in their contingency funds to afford this but it would help if they can find a lender who will add the MGP to the loan. This would leave a more substantial amount in the funds.

They find a 5 year fixed rate at 7.65% with MGP added to the loan and an arrangement fee of £250.

Because Martin is not going to achieve his financial independence objective they decide not to do a pension-linked mortgage and settle on PEP related over a 25 year period.

Interest at 7.65% including full MIRAS =	£608.82 per month
PEP investment =	£ 85.92 per month
Total	£694.74 per month

Before going further, they now just check on their income and outgoings.

■ **Comparison of different methods of repaying the mortgage**

■ **Form 3.6 MORTGAGE ANALYSIS FORM**

Names:	Amanda and Martin Jenkins
1st income	£25,000
2nd income	£15,000
$3 \times 1st + 1 \times 2nd$	$3 \times £25,000 + £15,000 = $ £90,000
$2\frac{1}{2} \times (1st + 2nd)$	$2\frac{1}{2} \times (£25,000 + £15,000) = £100,000$
Maximum mortgage available	£100,000
Assuming LTV 95% maximum cost of property	£100,000 divided by $\frac{95}{100}$ = £105,263
MGP on average say 7% over 70%	7% of 25% of £105,263 = 7% of £26,316 = £1842
Solicitor's fees	£1500
Stamp duty	£1053
Valuation	£180
Total cost	£109,838
Cash needed £109,838 – £100,000 =	£9838

	Net income	Outgoings
Amanda	£11,443	£10,600 including £6000 p.a. rental
Martin	£19,504	£12,000 including £7200 p.a. rental
Total	£30,947	£22,600

Adjustments to outgoings due to financial planning decisions.

Amanda plus £1460.52 (pension) minus £6000 rental
Martin plus £380.40 (IPP) minus £7200 rental plus £4296.60 (pension net cost)
Joint plus £8336.88 (mortgage)
Total adjustment plus £1201.68 p.a.

	Net income	Outgoings
Final situation	£30,945 p.a.	£23,801.68 p.a.
Surplus	£7145 p.a.	

The actual surplus is probably considerably better than this as there will be other savings such as only one heating, cooking and lighting bill.

They now look at the question, 'What happens if I die?'

As a result of this they take out joint life first death term assurance to cover the mortgage. Using Table 3.9 (p. 174), they see the nearest age to Martin's is 35. The difference between this and Amanda's age is ten, whereas the table quotes three years. Also they are both non-smokers. All these factors will make the actual premium less than the nearest we can get.

Premium $= 30.12 + 98.4\%$ of 30.12

$$= 30.12 + \frac{98.4}{100} \times 30.12$$

$$= 30.12 + 29.64 = £59.76 \text{ per month}$$

Then Amanda suggests they put WOC on Martin's life:

$$2\% \text{ of } £59.76 = \frac{2}{100} \times 59.76 = £1.20 \text{ per month}$$

Hence total cost is £60.96 per month. This will cost them £731.52 p.a. and in order to be really secure they take a critical illness policy each to cover the mortgage. They decide to include WOC just in case they develop something like rheumatism which would prevent them from working properly but would not constitute a critical illness and, besides, the addition of WOC is so cheap.

Using Table 2.6 (p. 52), Amanda is approximately 25 so using that age,

Premium = £22.40 per month
Additional premium for WOC = 2.5% of 22.40 = £0.56
Total premium = £22.96 per month

The nearest age for Martin is 35,

Premium for non-smoker £52.16 per month
Additional premium for smoker rates = 54.2% of 52.16

$$= \frac{54.2}{100} \times 52.16 = £28.27 \text{ per month}$$

Total premium so far = 52.16 + 28.27 = £80.43 per month

Additional premium for WOC = 2% of 80.43

$$= \frac{2}{100} \times 80.43 = 1.61$$

Total premium = 80.43 + 1.61 = £82.04

They also need to build up their contingency fund again and decide to save £2000 p.a.

Total additional outgoings are:

Life assurance		$60.96 \times 12 =$	£731.52 p.a.
Critical illness	Amanda	$22.96 \times 12 =$	£275.52 p.a.
	Martin	$82.04 \times 12 =$	£984.48 p.a.
Contingency fund			£2000.00 p.a.
Total			£3991.52 p.a.

This still leaves them with a surplus of £3153 p.a. They decide to complete their financial planning with a pension guarantee policy for Amanda and reduce Martin's pension investment slightly by including WOC in the total figure feeling that this makes their financial planning totally safe and secure and brings them both financial health in their current age.

Premium for Amanda for sum assured £200,000 of critical illness over 35 years to take her to age 60 – using Table 2.4 once again the nearest we can get is 25 years so the actual premium would be more. They might, of course, decide to take the policy to 25 years and then use the renewability option. This would, of course, mean more expensive premiums since Amanda would be 50 by then.

Premium = £45.92 since cover is twice as much as before. This will be £551.04 p.a. still leaving them a surplus of £2602 p.a. which should allow them to redecorate and suitably furnish their new house over the next few years.

You may like to use the following forms to analyse your own situation.

■ Form 3.7 INCOME TAX AND NIC ANALYSIS

INCOME TAX			
Name		Year	
	£	*Remaining income £*	*Tax £*
Gross income			
Gross contribution to pension paid personally*			
Personal allowance			
Income taxed at 20% Income taxed at basic rate 23% Income taxed at higher rate 40%			
Total			
Less married couple's allowance			
Total tax payable			
* Some pension contributions paid personally are net of basic rate tax. For the purposes of this form this would need to be grossed up.			
NATIONAL INSURANCE CONTRIBUTION (NIC) (Employed)			
	£	*Remaining income £*	*NIC £*
Gross income			
Income up to LEL £3224 p.a. NIC at 2%			
Income up to UEL £24,180 p.a. minus £3224 p.a., the LEL NIC at 10%			
Total			
NATIONAL INSURANCE CONTRIBUTION (NIC) (Self-employed)			
Flat rate paid if income over £3480 p.a. £6.15 p.w.			
On profits between £7010 and £24,180 p.a. 6.0%			
Total			
Income after tax and NIC deductions			

■ Comparison of different methods of repaying the mortgage

■ **Form 3.8 INCOME TAX AND NIC ANALYSIS**

INCOME TAX			
Name		Year	
	£	Remaining income £	Tax £
Gross income			
Gross contribution to pension paid personally*			
Personal allowance			
Income taxed at 20% Income taxed at basic rate 23% Income taxed at higher rate 40%			
Total			
Less married couple's allowance			
Total tax payable			

* Some pension contributions paid personally are net of basic rate tax. For the purposes of this form this would need to be grossed up.

NATIONAL INSURANCE CONTRIBUTION (NIC) (Employed)			
	£	Remaining income £	NIC £
Gross income			
Income up to LEL £3224 p.a. NIC at 2%			
Income up to UEL £24,180 p.a. minus £3224 p.a., the LEL NIC at 10%			
Total			

NATIONAL INSURANCE CONTRIBUTION (NIC) (Self-employed)
Flat rate paid if income over £3480 p.a. £6.15 p.w.
On profits between £7010 and £24,180 p.a. 6.0%
Total
Income after tax and NIC deductions

■ Form 3.9 LIFETIME FINANCIAL PLAN ANALYSIS

Name	Date
Date of birth (DoB)	Smoker/non-smoker
Employed/self-employed	Time with business
Income p.a. gross	Income p.a. net of taxes and NIC
Annual outgoings	Surplus p.a.
Regular savings from net income	
If I become medically unable to work what would my income situation be for the first 6 months?	
For the second 6 months?	
Thereafter?	
What is the maximum which I could have?	
Approximate cost of increasing my cover to this	
Pension type	
Personal contribution	
Maximum I am allowed to contribute	
Retirement age	
Projected pension fund (MPS or PPS) at retirement age	
Projected pension at retirement age (DBS)	
At what age do I want total financial independence?	
Pension fund (MPS or PPS) adjusted to financial independence age	
Pension (DBS) adjusted to financial independence age	
Type of annuity required	
Pension this would produce	
Assumed rate of inflation long term	
Pension in today's terms	
What is total financial independence for me in today's terms?	

■ **Form 3.9 (continued)**

Shortfall
Shortfall at financial independence age, taking inflation into account
Fund needed to produce this pension
Pension contribution needed to produce this fund at a growth of 12% a p.a.
Comments:
Decisions:

■ Form 3.10 LIFETIME FINANCIAL PLAN ANALYSIS

Name	Date
Date of birth (DoB)	Smoker/non-smoker
Employed/self-employed	Time with business
Income p.a. gross	Income p.a. net of taxes and NIC
Annual outgoings	Surplus p.a.
Regular savings from net income	
If I become medically unable to work what would my income situation be for the first 6 months?	
For the second 6 months?	
Thereafter?	
What is the maximum which I could have?	
Approximate cost of increasing my cover to this	
Pension type	
Personal contribution	
Maximum I am allowed to contribute	
Retirement age	
Projected pension fund (MPS or PPS) at retirement age	
Projected pension at retirement age (DBS)	
At what age do I want total financial independence?	
Pension fund (MPS or PPS) adjusted to financial independence age	
Pension (DBS) adjusted to financial independence age	
Type of annuity required	
Pension this would produce	
Assumed rate of inflation long term	
Pension in today's terms	
What is total financial independence for me in today's terms?	
Shortfall	

Comparison of different methods of repaying the mortgage

Form 3.10 (continued)

Shortfall at financial independence age, taking inflation into account
Fund needed to produce this pension
Pension contribution needed to produce this fund at a growth of 12% p.a.
Comments:
Decisions:

Form 3.11 MORTGAGE ANALYSIS FORM

Names:
1st income
2nd income
$3 \times 1st + 1 \times 2nd$
$2\frac{1}{2} \times (1st + 2nd)$
Maximum mortgage available
Assuming LTV 95% maximum cost of property
MGP on average say 7% over 70%
Solicitor's fees
Stamp duty
Valuation
Total cost
Cash needed

SUMMARY

In this age we have worked through the following:

1 The importance of checking your financial plan and discuss it with your spouse. It is important that your financial plans complement one another.

2 Before you go house hunting use Form 3.1 to calculate how much you are likely to be able to borrow and how much cash you will need for upfront charges and deposit. Now you know the sort of house you can afford and the sort of mortgage you need.

3 Writing a will.

4 The position if you were to die, became medically unable to work, or were made redundant. This will tell you what additional policies you feel you need.

ANSWERS

■ **Exercise 3.1**

Archibald has borrowed 95%.
  Hence he must purchase an MGP to cover 20%.
  20% of £100,000 is £20,000.
  The cost is 6% of £20,000 =

$$\frac{6}{100} \times 20,000 = £1200$$

■ **Exercise 3.3**

Petrona will be considered to earn £30,000 p.a. + $\frac{1}{2} \times$ £4000 = £32,000 p.a.
  They could borrow 3 × £32,000 + £6000 = £102,000 or,

$$2\tfrac{1}{2} \times £38,000 = £95,000$$

Hence the most they could borrow would be £102,000.

■ Exercise 3.4

MORTGAGE ANALYSIS FORM

Names:	Wah Pong and Lee Ping Peng
1st income	£19,000 p.a.
2nd income	£16,000 p.a.
$3 \times$ 1st $+ 1 \times$ 2nd	£73,000
$2\frac{1}{2} \times$ (1st + 2nd)	£87,500
Maximum mortgage available	£87,500
Assuming LTV 95% maximum cost of property	87,500 divided by $\frac{95}{100}$ = $\frac{87,500}{0.95}$ = £92,105
MGP on average say 7% over 70%	7% of 25% of 92,105 = 7% of 23,026 = $\frac{7}{100} \times 23,026$ = £1612
Solicitor's fees	£1500
Stamp duty	1% of 92,105 = $\frac{1}{100} \times 92,105$ = £921
Valuation	180
Total cost	£96,318
Cash needed	96,318 − 87,500 = £8818

If they take a 5% cashback loan with a lender who will add the MGP to the loan, this will save them 5% of £87,500 + £1612 =

$$\frac{5}{100} \times £87,500 + £1612$$
$$= £4375 + £1612 = £5987$$

They now only need £2831 cash. Hence after purchase they are left with £669 in the bank.

■ Exercise 3.5

Using Table 3.8 (p. 172) the nearest age to Mark is 30. Difference in ages will now be 6 years, making our figure less than it should be.

$$\text{Premium for non-smokers} = \frac{62,000}{100,000} \times 17.90 = £11.10 \text{ per month}$$

$$\text{Increase for smoker rates} = 37.7\% \text{ of } £11.10$$
$$= \frac{37.7}{100} \times 11.10 = £3.07$$

Total so far = 11.10 + 3.07 = £14.17 per month

Increase for WOC = 2% of 14.17 = $\frac{2}{100} \times 14.17$ = £0.28 100

Total premium = £14.45 per month

CHAPTER 4

THE AGE OF
PARENTHOOD

Birth and education	Work	Marriage	Parenthood	Career development	Retirement	Old age

FINANCIAL PLANNING AT A GLANCE –
THE AGE OF PARENTHOOD

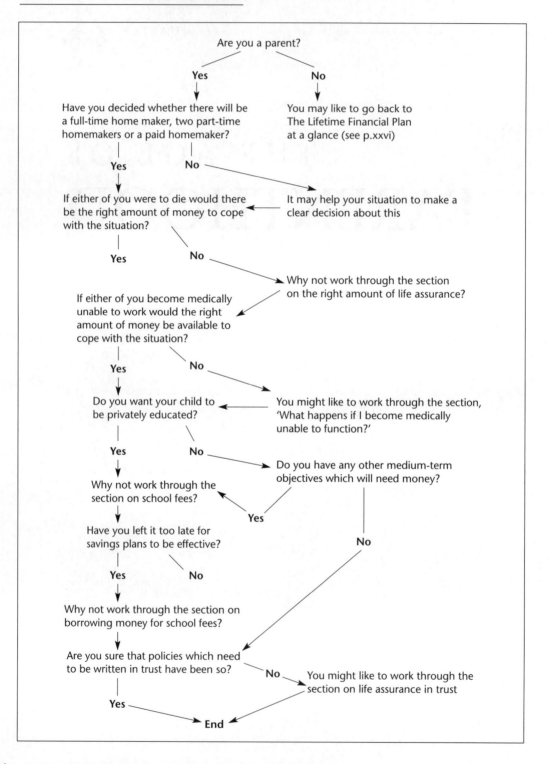

CONTENTS

In this age the following is discussed:

- a child to be cared for by either:
  - one parent who gives up gainful employment and becomes the full-time homemaker
  - both parents part time
  - a paid nanny/housekeeper
  - a single parent
- the right amount of life assurance
- life assurance in trust
- trusts
- family income benefit assurance
- reversion to settlor
- what happens if you become medically unable to function
- the single parent
- school fees
- borrowing money to pay for school fees
- saving for other medium-term objectives

INTRODUCTION

Thoughts turn to the financial implications of this new age. Financial life has been planned according to the first three ages and there is a feeling of financial security. Core questions have been answered to full satisfaction. Now, yet again, the situation has changed and it might be wise to revisit these questions and answer them in the light of the new situation.

Clearly the advent of a child will entail extra expense and place an added strain on the budget. However, if all current outgoings connected with financial planning can be maintained then the answer to 'What happens if I live too long?' should remain the same.

What about the question, 'What happens if I die too soon?' Hopefully the existing plan would ensure that the mortgage would be paid off and spouse would be left with an unencumbered house.

Before proceeding beyond this point we must discuss and decide on the future approach to gainful employment in the light of parenthood.

Your child will need constant looking after. This will mean that either you employ someone to perform that function while both of you continue your work as before, or one of you gives up work entirely to look after your home and child, or both of you work less and take turns looking after things at home, or indeed some mixture of these possibilities. Whichever you choose you will have less money available because you will either be paying someone a salary or earning less. And on top of all this, what happens then if one or both of you die?

> A paramount objective of financial planning is to put the right sum of money into the right hands at the right time.

If one of you dies the other is left with less income or indeed none, if the only breadwinner has died. 'That we shall die we know; 'tis but the time.'[1]

The answer to the problem is clearly life assurance that would provide a tax-free cash sum you could either use or invest to produce an income, or a mixture of these two possibilities. You will find details on the different types of life assurance in Chapter 3.

Your objective will be to put the right sum of money into the right hands at the right time. The right time is at death and clearly life assurance will do this. What about the right amount?

THE RIGHT AMOUNT OF LIFE ASSURANCE

Let us assume the decision is one breadwinner with spouse looking after the home and bringing up the family full time. This means that he or she will not be able to return to paid employment for at least 16 years, assuming a child of 16 can reasonably look after himself or herself – it could be longer.

But suppose the breadwinner dies. Is spouse immediately to return to work? In

If you die is it not important to leave your spouse financial choices?

this case the child suddenly loses both parents and is cared for by a stranger or strangers. Would it not at least be better to give your spouse choices. In other words to put the right amount of money into his or her hands at this time.

The homemaker spouse could be out of gainful employment for at least 16 years, the time needed for a child to become able to care for himself or herself. Assuming a working life is 40 years, this is 40 per cent of that life. The chances of achieving total individual financial independence for that person will be severely limited. Hence if the breadwinner dies it would seem logical to give spouse total financial independence immediately. The right amount of life assurance is what will achieve this.

If the breadwinner dies is it not important to give the spouse total financial independence immediately?

What is total financial independence in this situation? We will see later that the maximum pension allowed by current legislation is two-thirds of final income. It is unlikely that there will be dependent children when that pension matures, whereas death could occur while the children are young.

It seems reasonable then to suggest that immediate total financial independence would be at least 70 per cent of current income. Therefore what is needed is a cash sum to be invested in such a way as to produce that income indexed in line with inflation. We have seen earlier that this means a cash sum invested on the stock market through pooled investments which would produce an annual income of approximately 5 per cent indexed. If the yield is to be one-twentieth (5 per cent) of the cash sum then the cash sum must be 20 times the yield. If the yield is only to be 70 per cent of income, then the cash sum needed will be 14 times income. For example if annual income is £20,000 then 70 per cent of this is,

A reasonable sum assured to protect spouse and family would appear to be fourteen times salary.

$$\frac{70}{100} \times 20,000 = £14,000 \text{ per annum}$$

A cash sum of $14 \times 20,000 = £280,000$ at a yield of 5 per cent per annum will produce,

$$\frac{5}{100} \times 280,000 = £14,000 \text{ per annum}$$

In the same way, had we decided that immediate total financial independence was 60 per cent of salary then the cash sum needed would be twelve times income.

Hence, whatever percentage of income we decide on we simply multiply that percentage by 20 to find the multiple of income needed. For example, 80 per cent of income would be produced by a cash sum of,

$$20 \times \frac{80}{100} = 16 \text{ times income}$$

■ Example 4.1

John and Amanda Tyler have just produced their first child. They decide that John will be the breadwinner as his salary and prospects are better and Amanda will look after home and child full time. John is 25, a non-smoker and earning £20,000 p.a. They decide immediate total financial independence for Amanda would be 70% of present income. John, therefore, needs life assurance with a sum assured of 14 × 20,000 = £280,000. Looking at the tables in Chapter 3 we see the various costs are:

	Approximate monthly premium
25 year term	£33.88
10 year renewable term	£32.14
10 year convertible term	£31.36
10 year renewable and convertible term	£35.28
Pension linked (basic rate taxpayer)	£26.10
Whole of life	£67.94
Low start (sum assured reducing to £154,000 after 10 years)	£51.18

This gives some idea of the order of cost and so John and Amanda would be able to make their decision. Indexation could be added to any of these policies making sure that the sum assured would keep pace with inflation. The sum assured would increase by a small amount each year and the increase in premium would relate to a premium for the increased sum assured, costed in line with John's age at the time. Also, each time the shorter-term policies were renewed, or if they were converted, there would be an increase in premium. The addition of the waiver of contribution benefit would be invaluable, since if John becomes medically unable to work, although his company would pay him 60% of income indexed to age 60, with this considerably reduced salary life assurance premiums could be under threat.

The 25 year term would only take John to age 50 whereas his pension is designed to mature at age 60. They would probably also want to look at a 35 year term.

There are many permutations of life assurance contracts which could be used such as 17 year renewable term which takes John to 59 at the end of the second term. For a full analysis it would be necessary to obtain other quotes.

■ Example 4.2

Sally and Peter Brightwater decided at the birth of their daughter, Penelope, that Sally would be the breadwinner since her income and prospects were better. Peter would care for the home and family. Peter is 33 years old. Sally is 31, a smoker and earning £25,000 p.a. She has a company pension which provides life assurance of four times pensionable salary, i.e. salary minus the lower earnings limit (LEL). They have done their calculations carefully in the event of Sally dying, including the fact that the mortgage would be paid off and Sally would not be there to feed and clothe and that they want Peter to be immediately financially independent.

They have decided that 65% of current salary would solve the potential problem. They therefore need a total sum assured of 13 times salary,

$$20 \times \frac{65}{100} = 13, \text{ i.e. } 13 \times 25{,}000 = £325{,}000$$

Sally's pension policy would already pay out $4 \times (25{,}000 - 3224) = 4 \times 21{,}776 = £87{,}104$. They therefore need, in addition to this, $£325{,}000 - 87{,}104 = £237{,}896$.

The various costs will be, using age 30, the nearest we can get to Sally's age:

	Approximate monthly premium
25 year term	£46.42
10 year renewable term	£40.81
10 year convertible term	£39.35
10 year renewable convertible term	£45.06
Pension linked (basic rate taxpayer)	£35.73
Whole of life	£80.35
Low start (sum assured reducing to £130,843 after 10 years)	£63.15

Typical calculation for straight term written under pension legislation,
    Premium for basic rate, non-smoker:

$$\frac{237{,}896}{100{,}000} \times 8.65 = £20.58 \text{ per month}$$

Increase for smoker rate:

$$73.6\% \text{ of } 20.58 = \frac{73.6}{100} \times 20.58 = £15.15 \text{ per month}$$

Total = £20.58 + £15.15 = £35.73 per month.

The last two examples show how the tables can produce a range of costs. This could be refined with further quotes and a totally informed decision made to put this piece of the financial plan in place.

■ **Exercise 4.1**

Alex and Janet McGregor have decided, now that their son Duncan has arrived, that Janet will become a full-time mother and homebuilder. Alex is a non-smoker and has a company pension which, on death, would give Janet twice pensionable salary and half the pension Alex would have received had he completed his service with the company to retirement at 60. The pension is built on sixtieths and pensionable salary, which is salary minus the LEL. Alex is 34, has just started with the company and is earning £30,000 p.a. They decide Janet would need 70% of salary were Alex to die.

   Work out what sum assured is needed and cost the different types of cover.

LIFE ASSURANCE IN TRUST

We have decided on the right time and we have decided on the right amount. Have we really put this money into the right hands? If the breadwinner dies then most certainly the spouse needs the money. In the cases we have examined the money would funnel into the breadwinner's estate and, on grant of probate, would go to the homemaker. There would be no tax liability since there is none between spouses (see inheritance tax (IHT) in Chapter 6). However, there could be some delay while waiting for probate to be granted. We will deal with this shortly when we discuss trusts.

Suppose the spouse dies too? What if they are both killed in the same car accident? Again the money would funnel into their estate once probate was granted. However, there is now a considerable difference because in this instance there would be an IHT liability.

Looking at Example 4.2, let us say the house is worth £150,000, contents, car, jewellery, etc. worth another £20,000. The £87,104 would go straight to Penelope, bypassing the estate because all company pensions are in the trusteeship of the company. Because of the trust it would go to Penelope free of inheritance tax. However, the sum assured of £237,896 would funnel into the estate which would now be worth:

House	£150,000
Contents	£ 20,000
Life assurance	£237,896
Total	£407,896

Once probate had been granted, the estate would pass to Penelope, their daughter, and she would be liable for IHT. Anything over £215,000 would be taxed at 40 per cent. Hence inheritance tax would be 40 per cent of £407,896 – 215,000 =

$$\frac{40}{100} \times 192,896 = £77,158$$

Instead of their daughter getting the full estate, £77,158 would go to the taxman.

This problem can be totally solved by the simple expedient of putting this life assurance into a flexible trust. Their daughter would be the beneficiary but Peter would be a reserve beneficiary. Thus if only Sally died the £250,648 would be paid directly to Peter. However, if they both died together the money would go straight to Penelope with no tax implications. In each case it would not be necessary to wait for grant of probate.

> It is always wise to consider putting life assurance into trust.

The trust has therefore accomplished two very important results. Any tax liability that might have occurred has been wiped out and the delay in receiving the money while waiting for grant of probate has been eliminated. Thus it is always wise to consider putting life assurance into trust.

What if the spouse looking after the home were to die? What are the choices of the spouse who is earning the income? He or she could change to part-time work and look after the home and family part time. In which case income is reduced and job prospects seriously prejudiced. He or she could continue to work full time and employ someone full time to look after the home and family.

Whatever the decision it is clear that money is needed. In this case we do not need to make the surviving spouse totally financially independent immediately since he or she will continue with his or her career. The requirement in this situation is different. We simply need to provide enough cash to pay someone to look after the home and family until the youngest child is, say, 16. In the fiscal year 1997/98 it would have cost £18,000 to £20,000 annually to employ someone full time to look after a home and family. To cover this for 16 years we would need to start off with cover of at least £18,000 × 16 = £288,000. However, every year which goes by the total cover needs to be less and so, just as with the mortgage a reducing term policy will solve the problem. Once again the policy should be in a flexible trust.

> If the housewife or housebusband dies cash may be necessary to employ someone to do that job.

The possible problem of the cost of this employee increasing over the years with normal rises in salary would be covered at least in the early years by placing the cash sum on deposit. The interest gained would cover possible increases in salary payable. It might, however, be safer and simpler to index the policy).

Typical premiums for reducing term assurance can be found in Table 4.1.

■ Example 4.3

In the case of John and Amanda in Example 4.1 we need reducing term assurance on the life of Amanda of £288,000 reducing by £18,000 over a period of 16 years. Amanda is 27 years old and a non-smoker. Using Table 4.1 the nearest age to Amanda is 25.

$$\text{Premium} = \frac{288,000}{100,000} \times 7.92 = £22.81 \text{ per month}$$

Clearly there is no point in including WOC because Amanda is not in gainful employment and therefore WOC would not pay out.

■ Example 4.4

In the case of Sally and Peter in Example 4.2 we need term assurance on the life of Peter of £288,000 reducing by £18,000 annually over a period of 16 years. Peter is a non-smoker. Using Table 4.1 the nearest age to Peter is 35.

$$\text{Premium} = \frac{288,000}{100,000} \times 12.59 = £36.26 \text{ per month}$$

Table 4.1 Typical premiums for reducing term life assurance (sum assured £100,000 over 16 years)

Single life

	Men Monthly premium			Women Monthly premium		
Age	Non-smoker £	% increase for smoker	% increase for WOC	Non-smoker £	% increase for smoker	% increase for WOC
20	9.79	4.8	2	7.82	2.4	2
25	9.99	17.8	2	7.92	9.4	2
30	11.48	17.1	2	8.49	22.1	2
35	12.59	33.9	2	9.76	44.0	2
40	17.76	71.2	3	13.17	55.4	4
45	24.30	87.8	3	18.69	78.1	4

Joint life payable on first death, woman three years younger than man

	Monthly premium			
	Non-smoker £	% increase for smoker (both lives)	% increase for WOC on man	on woman
Man's age				
20	13.80	34.0	2	2
25	13.97	14.7	2	2
30	15.69	17.0	2	2
35	17.76	73.4	2	2
40	22.77	67.4	3	4
45	33.72	83.1	3	4

■ Exercise 4.2

Using the information in Exercise 4.1 calculate the cost of the necessary reducing term life assurance on Janet who is 29 and a smoker.

TRUSTS

It is thought that a form of trust started as far back as the Crusades when a crusader would leave his lands in the care of some trusted friends for the eventual benefit of his children should he not return. This was done to safeguard his property against acquisition by the local lord. Eventually the courts came to uphold the representation of the 'trustees' against the lords and to ensure that those trustees did, in fact, look after the interests of the children.

The modern day trust faithfully mirrors this process. The person 'declaring' the trust and gifting assets into it is called the settlor, or in Scotland the truster. These assets are thus out of his or her estate and held by the trustees for the benefit of the trust's beneficiaries. The settlor himself or herself will automatically be a trustee and he or she will appoint others who are required, at all times, to act in the interest of all the trust beneficiaries. The beneficiaries are those who could or will benefit from the trust.

The sorts of trusts relevant to the subjects treated in this book are flexible, interest in possession trusts and sometimes, in the case of pensions, a form of discretionary trust, but one not carrying the disadvantage of ten yearly or exit tax charges. The flexibility comes in the power of appointment which allows beneficiaries to be changed and also trustees. There will normally be current beneficiaries, those appointed by the settlor when the trust is declared and potential beneficiaries from among whom new appointments can be made.

These trusts are used for life assurance policies, either regular premium or single, and pension policies. This makes management by the trustees very simple since income is not produced. If it were, it would have to be paid out to the current beneficiaries, who are those with an interest in possession, and who are of course, liable to income tax. In these cases gifts to the trust are either made in the form of regular premiums or as a lump sum. These gifts are lifetime transfers and, as such, subject to inheritance tax (IHT). In the case of regular premiums exemptions will apply since they will normally come under annual exemptions or normal expenditure exemption. Lump sums will be potentially exempt transfers (PET), in which case the doner will have to live for seven years before they become actual exempt transfers. For a detailed treatment of IHT, see Chapter 6. If, however, there is any reservation of benefit on the part of the settlor the transfer will not be potentially exempt. Making himself or herself a beneficiary would be a reservation of benefit and therefore care must be taken that this does not happen. In other words, except in exceptional cases, there must be no possibility of a reversion of the benefit to the settlor.

There will be cases where it is extremely important that the benefit can revert to the settlor. These will be described later in the book and it will be seen how reversion can be made possible without triggering the gift with reservation rules and therefore prejudicing the potentially exempt status of the transfer. There are two extremely important advantages attaching to the use of trusts:

1 The gift to the trust will be outside the settlor's estate and if the gift is, or becomes, free of IHT, whatever comes out of the trust for the beneficiaries will be totally free of IHT.
2 This benefit is already out of the settlor's estate so there can be no question of having to wait for grant of probate, which could be six months or more after death.

■ Example 4.5

Hank Peters takes out a life assurance policy to protect his family. He puts this into a flexible trust asking his wife, Michelle, and his brother, Zeb, to be trustees.

He appoints his children, Cyril and Rosalind, as current beneficiaries with a share of 50% of the sum assured each.

The potential beneficiaries will normally be:

1 Children, grandchildren, great-grandchildren (and the spouses of any of these) of the person(s) declaring the trust.
2 The spouse of the person declaring the trust.
3 The life or lives assured (but not the settlor) and any spouse, child, grandchild or great-grandchild of the life or lives assured.
4 Any current beneficiary.
5 Anyone else the settlor may wish to include.

Five years later Hank dies. The children are still both under ten. The two remaining trustees now have to decide to whom the sum assured should be paid. They have, of course, always kept themselves conversant with Hank's wishes and therefore pay out the money to Michelle. It is paid immediately with no requirement for a grant of probate and it is, as it would have been without the trust in this case, free of IHT, as there is no IHT between spouses. It is, however, necessary for there to be two remaining trustees left at this point in order to be able to appoint the benefits to a spouse. There has, however, been an appointment away from the children and hence a transfer is deemed to have taken place. It is unlikely they will not live for a further seven years when this will have become an actual exempt transfer.

Had Hank and Michelle been killed together in, say, a car accident Zeb could have paid the money directly to the children free of IHT and with no grant of probate necessary. Usually these flexible trusts allow as long as 79 years from declaration of the trust to make the final decision. As the children are minors he would probably retain it in the trust until they are older, releasing only sufficient funds for their upkeep and education.

In the case of a third child arriving before Hank died the trustees at time of death would appoint him or her as a current beneficiary, with all children to receive, say, an equal share. This would again constitute an appointment away from Cyril and Rosalind and be subject to the same considerations as above.

FAMILY INCOME BENEFIT ASSURANCE

This is an alternative to reducing term assurance. On death it would pay out an annual sum assured over the term of the policy. Hence an equivalent to those discussed above would be a policy which on death would pay out £18,000 per annum until the end of the term of 16 years. Because the money is paid out over a period of time the premiums will be cheaper.

In either of the other versions of the decision about caring for the home and family, both continue to work either full time or part time. Hence it is unlikely that in the event of the death of one the other would need to achieve total financial independence immediately. The given situation will dictate the solution and it will have to be decided whether it is a case of providing total financial independence for a surviving spouse or providing enough money to pay someone to look after the home and family. In these versions both spouses are in the same situation so the type of policy would usually be a joint life first death plan.

■ Example 4.6

Vincent and Amelia Plimford have four children, the youngest is two days old. They take turns to start and finish work in time to take their children to and from school and collect the childminder. So far this does not seem to have affected the career path of either or damaged their prospects in any way. They are earning a little less than they would if they were not constrained in this way, and there is also the cost of the childminder. If either one should die the requirement for the surviving spouse would be to pay for a full-time person to look after the home and family for 16 years. Vincent is 35 and Amelia 32. They require term assurance on both lives of 16 × £18,000 = £288,000, reducing by £18,000 p.a. over 16 years. They are both non-smokers.

Using Table 4.1 we see that the ages of 35 and 32 fit perfectly. Hence the premium =

$$\frac{288,000}{100,000} \times 17.76 = £51.15 \text{ per month}$$

Does this, however, cover all potential problems due to potential death? What if Vincent and Amelia are both killed in a car accident? Will they have written wills, appointed executors and guardians? The policy would pay up to £288,000 into their estate depending on when the car accident happened. Their house would be unencumbered and pass to the children, as would their other possessions. Let us say the car accident happened in year five of the policy. It would now pay out £216,000. Since the policy is not in trust it would pay into the estate. Let us say the house and other assets of the estate are worth a further £170,000. (The mortgage would have been paid off by their mortgage-related life assurance.) Hence total estate passing to the children would be £386,000. The inheritance tax payable would be £68,400 (see Chapter 6). This would leave £317,600 to pass to the children. No doubt this would be enough to cover the guardians' expenses and still leave money to pass eventually to the children.

If this event happened later then the reducing term assurance would pay less but the children would be older and dependent on this money for a shorter time. The value of the estate, probably by now greater, would also pass to them.

'Ah,' you will say, 'but the policy should be written in trust therefore totally bypassing the estate and going directly to the children thus saving any potential inheritance tax.'

REVERSION TO SETTLOR

The Finance Act 1986 introduced rules for gifts with reservation, any such gift becoming liable to inheritance tax. Thus the settlor of a life assurance policy gifting it by trust will be avoiding inheritance tax. If the trust were to make provision for the proceeds of the life assurance to revert to the settlor then the gift would fall foul of the rules for gifts with reservation, since this reversion would constitute a reservation. Thus in most cases a trust making such a reservation would defeat the purpose of enabling the avoidance of inheritance tax.

The problem, then, with a joint life policy is that both lives are settlors. If they then put this policy into trust for their children the trust cannot include the possibility of the proceeds of the life assurance reverting to either of the lives. If then only one of them were to die it would be essential that the other receive those proceeds and if the policy had been written in trust this would not be possible.

In the case of a joint life first death policy the proceeds, on the death of one of the lives assured, are automatically paid to the survivor.

■ Example 4.6 – Part two

There are only two possibilities: a single life policy on each parent written in trust for the children which could still go to the other parent if, as is most likely, they do not die at the same time. Now if they were both killed in a car accident there would be no inheritance tax to pay since the value of the estate would be £170,000, below the level at which IHT has to be paid.

Using Table 4.1 Vincent's age fits exactly.

$$\text{Premium} = \frac{288,000}{100,000} \times 12.59 = £36.26 \text{ per month}$$

They decide Vincent should have WOC at an additional cost of,

$$2\% \text{ of } £36.26 = \frac{2}{100} \times 36.26 = £0.73$$

Hence total premium = £36.26 + 0.73 = £36.99 per month.
The nearest age to Amanda is 30, hence,

$$\text{Premium} = \frac{288,000}{100,000} \times 8.49 = £24.45 \text{ per month}$$

The proceeds of a policy written in trust cannot revert to the settlor.

Hence total premium cost for both = £36.99 + 24.45 = £61.44. Or leave it as a joint life first death policy and accept a possible payment of inheritance tax. After all the odds against both parents dying at the same time are very high and the process of financial planning is the art of compromise.

■ **Exercise 4.3**

Grant and Isobel Hammond have three children, the youngest is five days old. Grant is 36 and Isobel 30. Grant earns £40,000 p.a. while Isobel looks after the home and family. Grant is self-employed, they have not done any serious financial planning before and have no life assurance apart from that protecting their mortgage. They are both non-smokers. What steps re life assurance would it be wise for them to take?

WHAT HAPPENS IF I BECOME MEDICALLY UNABLE TO FUNCTION?

The last question to consider is, 'What happens if I become medically unable to function?' If you have both planned your finances according to the first three ages of the book then it is likely you will both have an income protection policy and probably the mortgage will be protected with critical illness cover. However, depending on how you decide to proceed after the birth of your first child it would be wise to look at this again. If you have decided that one spouse will be the breadwinner and the other will look after the home and family, then the situation has fundamentally changed. The spouse who is now not earning is no longer eligible for an income protection policy and, in fact, if a claim were made while not in gainful employment the policy would not pay out.

> An income protection policy will only pay out if you are in receipt of earned income.

Yet if this spouse becomes medically unable to function an enormous financial problem would be created. In fact it would be financially worse than the problem created by death. It would be necessary to employ someone to look after the home and family in addition to spouse.

Anything less would considerably exacerbate the problem because if the breadwinner were to give time to this during the working day it would seriously decrease his or her earning power, his or her potential and his or her future plans for the eventual total financial independence of the couple. It is clearly important to consider critical illness cover on spouse over and above what might already be in force to protect the mortgage (see Tables 4.2 and 4.3).

■ **Example 4.7**

Priscilla and George Martin have just produced their first child, William. They are both 35 years old and smokers. They have decided that Priscilla will become the breadwinner on a current salary of £30,000 annually and George will look after the home and family. George's income protection policy has had to be cancelled and Priscilla's would pay tax free £16,253 p.a. They have covered the question of possible death in each case. Their mortgage is covered with life assurance and critical illness on both lives.

Table 4.2 Typical premiums reducing term critical illness (sum assured £100,000 over 16 years)

Single life

	Men Monthly premium			Women Monthly premium		
Age	Non-smoker £	% increase for smoker	% increase for WOC	Non-smoker £	% increase for smoker	% increase for WOC
0	18.38	Nil	2	20.82	Nil	2
25	18.38	21.2	2	20.82	15.5	2
30	19.44	65.5	2	21.95	44.9	2
35	27.36	76.0	2	28.08	57.6	2
40	41.09	72.9	3	38.49	63.9	4
45	60.59	70.8	3	54.38	62.4	4

Joint life payable on first death, woman three years younger than man

	Monthly premium			
	Non-smoker £	% increase for smoker (both lives)	% increase for WOC on man	on woman
Man's age				
20	34.30	Nil	2	2
25	34.30	70.3	2	2
30	35.39	48.7	2	2
35	45.68	67.1	2	2
40	66.05	68.7	3	4
45	95.97	69.1	3	4

If George were to become medically unable to function they would need to employ someone to look after the home and family and probably also George. They make enquiries and discover they would probably need to pay at least £20,000 p.a. for this service. Ideally they need at least 16 × £20,000 = £320,000 of critical illness cover written on George's life, since they consider that William would be self-sufficient at 16. However, at the end of 16 years Priscilla has a further 9 years to work in an increasingly demanding job. She cannot therefore look after George, although no doubt on retirement she would be able to. It is therefore still necessary to employ someone to look after George, clean the house, and shop, etc. at a cost of, say, £10,000 p.a. In other words the money needed is £20,000 p.a. for 16 years and then £10,000 for a further 10 years. In other words 25 × £10,000 = £250,000 term critical illness reducing by £10,000 p.a. over 25 years and an additional 16 × £10,000 = £160,000 reducing by £10,000 p.a. over 16 years.

Using Table 4.2 George's age fits exactly.

Table 4.3 Typical premiums reducing term critical illness plus life assurance (sum assured £100,000 over 16 years)

Single life

| | Men | | | Women | | |
| | Monthly premium | | | Monthly premium | | |
Age	Non-smoker £	% increase for smoker	% increase for WOC	Non-smoker £	% increase for smoker	% increase for WOC
20	20.58	Nil	2	22.33	Nil	2
25	20.58	21.2	2	22.33	14.0	2
30	22.05	64.6	2	23.36	43.5	2
35	30.66	76.0	2	29.71	56.7	2
40	45.89	73.2	3	40.48	63.3	4
45	67.75	73.9	3	57.02	65.3	4

Joint life payable on first death, woman three years younger than man

| | | Monthly premium | | |
| | Non-smoker £ | % increase for smoker (both lives) | % increase for WOC | |
Man's age			on man	on woman
20	38.10	Nil	2	2
25	38.16	9.9	2	2
30	39.57	45.4	2	2
35	50.14	66.8	2	2
40	72.36	68.7	3	4
45	105.12	70.9	3	4

Premium for non-smoker $\dfrac{160,000}{100,000} \times 27.36 = £43.78$ per month

Additional premium for smoker rate = 76% of 43.78,

$\dfrac{76}{100} \times 43.78 = £33.27$ per month

Total premium for £160,000 cover reducing by £10,000 p.a. over 16 years = £43.78 + £33.27 = £77.05 per month.

Using Table 3.17 (p. 185),

Premium for non-smoker $\dfrac{250,000}{100,000} \times 34.25 = £85.63$ per month

Additional premium for smoker rate = 77.1% of 85.63 = $\dfrac{77.1}{100} \times 85.63$ = £66.02

Total premium = £85.63 + 66.02 = £151.65 per month

■ **What happens if I become medically unable to function?**

■ **Form 4.1 INCOME TAX AND NIC ANALYSIS**

INCOME TAX			
Name Priscilla Martin		*Year* 1997	
	£	*Remaining income £*	*Tax £*
Gross income	30,000		
Gross contribution to pension paid personally*			
Personal allowance	4045	25,955	Nil
Income taxed at 20%	4100	21,855	820.00
Income taxed at basic rate 23%	21,855	Nil	5026.65
Income taxed at higher rate 40%			
Total			5846.65
Less married couple's allowance 15% of £1,830			274.50
Total tax payable			5572.15

* Some pension contributions paid personally are net of basic rate tax. For the purposes of this form this would need to be grossed up.

NATIONAL INSURANCE CONTRIBUTION (NIC) (Employed)			
	£	*Remaining income £*	*NIC £*
Gross income	30,000		
Income up to LEL £3224 p.a. NIC at 2%	3224		64.48
Income up to UEL £24,180 p.a. minus £3224 p.a., the LEL NIC at 10%	20,956		2095.60
Total			2160.08

NATIONAL INSURANCE CONTRIBUTION (NIC) (Self-employed)	
Flat rate paid if income over £3480 p.a. £6.15 p.w.	
On profits between £7010 and £24,180 p.a. 6.0%	
Total	
Income after tax and NIC deductions	30,000 – 5572.15 – 2160.08 = £22,267.77
Net spendable income	22,267

What if Priscilla becomes medically unable to function? Her income protection policy will pay out £16,253 p.a. tax free. The state will pay her £5704.40 p.a. (see Chapter 2). This is £1659.40 over the personal allowance so tax of 20% of £1659.40 = £331.88 p.a. will be paid. Hence the family's income will be £16,253 + £5704.40 – £331.88 = £21,626 p.a.

Carrying out the income tax and NIC analysis in Form 4.1 we see that in normal circumstances the family's net spendable income is £22,267 p.a. Bearing in mind that if Priscilla does suffer a critical illness the mortgage is paid off, that particular outgoing would cease and the family would be better off than before the event.

Protection is the foundation of financial planning.

Had none of this cover been in place the family could have had to exist on £5704.40 – 331.88 = £5372.52 p.a. with a mortgage probably in the region of £400 per month = £4800 still to pay annually, an utterly impossible situation.

I think this shows how crucially important it is not only to protect the payment of the mortgage properly since it is probably everyone's biggest outgoing, but also to put in place all the other aspects of financial planning. You never know what life will throw at you, what lies around the corner and, if one of these disasters overtakes you and you are unplanned the ensuing financial problems could be unbearable.

You never know what life will throw at you.

It is clear that protection is the foundation of financial planning.

If I had my way I would write the word 'insure' upon the door of every cottage and upon the blotting book of every public man, because I am convinced for sacrifices which are inconceivably small, families and estates can be protected against catastrophes which would otherwise smash them up forever. It is our duty to arrest the ghastly waste, not merely of human happiness, but of national health and strength, which follows when, through the death of the breadwinner, the frail boat in which the family are embarked, founders, and women and children and estates are left to struggle in the dark waters of a friendless world.[2]

If you are both working and employing a nanny to look after house and family you have a different situation. If one of you becomes medically unable to work there will be an income, albeit reduced, to come from the income protection policy. You may be able to manage on this or you may feel some additional critical illness cover would be helpful. You will need to cost this and make your individual decision.

■ **Exercise 4.4**

Eileen and Edward Baxter are the happy parents of Gillian, two months old. They are both working and pay a childminder £12,000 p.a. to look after her. Eileen earns £40,000 p.a. and in the event of medical inability to work she would receive full salary for six months and then 65% of salary to age 60. Edward is self-employed and makes a before tax profit of £30,000 p.a. He has a permanent health insurance which would pay out £16,253 p.a., tax free. Eileen is 28, Edward 37. They are both non-smokers. As Eileen is a higher rate taxpayer they have decided that the married couple's tax allowance should go to her.

   Using the tax and national insurance contribution (NIC) analysis forms, answer the question for each of them, 'What happens if I become medically unable to work?' Suggest solutions and cost them.

Try to visualise the financial cost if one of these disasters happened to you.

The other variations of the family situation can all be approached in the same way by trying to visualise what the financial cost would be were one of these disasters to happen to you.

THE SINGLE PARENT

The single parent can depend on no-one else, everything is his or her responsibility. In a sense the potential disasters described earlier could be doubly difficult. If a single parent dies there is no-one to look after the children, so the single parent should make sure that a will is written, guardians are appointed and money is put in the right hands at the right time to ensure that the children will be cared for properly until they are able to earn their own living. This is not a case of making them totally financially independent immediately but of supporting them until they can begin their own financial life. Therefore it would be wise to have an income protection policy, reducing term life assurance, and possibly also reducing term critical illness which could, in fact, be combined with the life assurance to save cost, always bearing clearly in mind that this policy will pay out only once.

■ **Example 4.8**

Ruth Watson at 32 is a single parent with a baby boy, Andrew, three months old. She earns £20,000 p.a., has a capital repayment mortgage of £50,000 with a term of 25 years and is a non-smoker. She has done no financial planning whatsoever, but knows that if she became medically unable to work her company would continue to pay her full salary for six months. She decides she needs a permanent health insurance and using the formula in Chapter 2, calculates the benefit to be 65% of £20,000 – £3247.40,

$$\frac{65}{100} \times 20,000 - 3247.40 = 13,000 - 3247.40 = £9753.$$

Using Table 2.4 (p. 50) the nearest age is 30 and the nearest benefit is £10,000 p.a., hence for a totally indexed benefit with a deferment period of six months.

$$\text{Premium} = \frac{9753}{10,000} \times 2228 = £21.73 \text{ per month}$$

She also decides to cover her mortgage in the event of death or critical illness. Using Table 3.17 (p. 185) we find that,

$$\text{Premium} = \frac{50,000}{100,000} \times 27.79 = £13.90 \text{ per month}$$

She decides to add WOC = 2% of 13.90 = $\frac{2}{100} \times 13.90 = £0.28$. Total premium = £14.18 per month.

Finally she wants to provide £15,000 p.a. for the guardians until Andrew is 16, in the event of her dying or suffering a critical illness. Using Table 4.3 (p. 229) we see,

$$\text{Premium} = \frac{240,000}{100,000} \times 23.36 = £56.06 \text{ per month}$$

She adds WOC at an extra cost of 2% of 56.06 = £1.12 per month. Total premium £56.06 + £1.12 = £57.18 per month.

Now if either of these events happened the mortgage would be paid off and Andrew would be cared for. Finally she writes a will leaving everything to her son and feels secure in the knowledge that she has achieved financial health.

SCHOOL FEES

The advent of the first born will raise the important question of education. It is better to address this shortly after the birth, then there will be no nasty surprises when suddenly five years have gone by and school is imminent.

If school fees are to be paid from current income they are paid from what is left after tax and national insurance has been paid.

The main question to answer is whether it will be state education or private. If it is to be state then there will be very little extra financial planning to do. If it is to be private then it would be wise to think this out carefully. School fees can range from £1200 per annum for day school primary to £12,600 per annum for boarding secondary.[3] They will invariably increase over the years – Fig. 4.1 shows how this has happened in the past.

If they are to be paid from income then they will be paid from an income which has already been reduced by taxes and national insurance contributions.

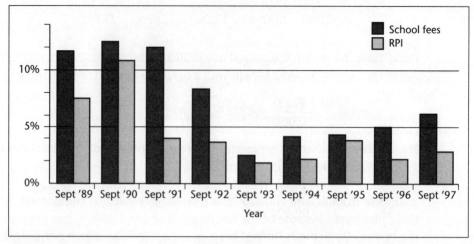

Fig. 4.1 Increase in school fees compared with increase in the Retail Prices Index (RPI)

■ Example 4.9

Adrian and Mary White have decided on private education. They find the annual fees will start at £3000 while their son, John, is a day boy at primary school and will rise to £6000 at his secondary school. Adrian is the breadwinner and as an employee earns £25,000 p.a. gross. After tax and national insurance contribution he is left with £18,418 p.a. net in his pocket. When John is five £3000 p.a. of this will go in school fees, i.e. 16.3%, and when John is eleven this will double, i.e. 33%. Clearly this could become an unbearable burden.

I have seen very high earning clients who could not afford an annual holiday because their two children were boarding at well known public schools.

The answer is preparation, financial planning. Clearly saving has to start at the child's birth. There are at least five years before fees start and if private education is restricted to the secondary stage then there are eleven or even thirteen.

> **You need to start planning for private education no later than the birth of your child.**

We have already worked through investment and savings plans in Chapter 1, Chapter 2 where we studied pensions, and Chapter 3 where saving was linked to the repayment of a mortgage. In this earlier work we went from lump sum investment to regular savings; from deposit accounts, through OEICS, PEPs and pensions to endowment policies. Any of these investments could only help the future payment of fees. However, most people seem to prefer regular saving, which smooths out the fluctuations of the stock market, and also tax efficiency which serves to gear up the investment. The PEP, friendly society investment and pension are totally free of all UK taxes and the pension attracts tax relief on the premiums but is hardly ever suitable as a straight school fees savings plan because the earliest possible maturity is at age 50. The endowment and maximum investment plan carry a measure of tax relief for higher rate tax payers but also most contain life assurance, although this is cut to a minimum in the case of the maximum investment plan. Of course, it would be wise to cover the school fees with life assurance so that in the event of death their availability would be guaranteed. The endowment policy might, therefore, be considered ideal since it contains everything needed in one regular savings policy. In Chapter 3 we compared vehicles for repayment of a mortgage, including life assurance in each case and saw that the PEP method cost considerably less than the endowment because of the tax relief. Probably the PEP plus life assurance is the best method, but is limited because of the amount which can be invested.

> Before putting a child's name down for a school a full financial analysis needs to be done.

What is certain is that there are no magic wands for school fees and any plan which might be promulgated will involve one or more of these forms of investment. In general it is probably better to go for an 11 year period concentrated on secondary education and soldiering on through primary education unaided. This gives the investment a much better chance to produce significant growth. In very general terms a PEP savings plan, assuming an investment growth of 12 per cent per annum, could be expected to produce approximately £17,500 in 11 years with a monthly premium of £100. In the case of Adrian and Mary, assuming that fees go up by 3 per cent per annum, by the time their son John is 11 his secondary school fees will start at £8305:

Age	Year	£
11	1	8305
12	2	8554
13	3	8811
14	4	9075
15	5	9347
16	6	9628
17	7	9917
Total		£63,637

Putting £100 per month into a PEP, starting immediately, will pay for the first two years.

What is clear is that before putting a child's name down for a private school a full analysis has to be done to see if one's wishes are realistic.

Clearly Adrian's income will increase and in 11 years could be very much higher and quite possibly the PEP could be increased over the years to cater for the subsequent years of John's education.

Borrowing money to pay for school fees

There is another approach to school fees which is to borrow money to pay for them and paying only the interest on the loan. This is not such a colossal burden on cashflow. The loan is paid back much later from, say, a pension plan. Clearly this method is at its most efficient when the end of the education coincides as closely as possible with maturity of the pension plan since this cuts down the number of years of paying interest. The most efficient way of raising the loan is through a mortgage on the home coupled with a drawdown facility. If the mortgage is already linked to a pension this can make things very simple.

It could cost less to finance school fees by borrowing.

■ Example 4.10

Nigel and Diana Porter have three children. Their youngest, Doreen, is just 11 and the Porters have decided to send her to a private school for her secondary education. The fees are currently £5000 p.a. They expect her to be there until she is 18. They have made no provision and do not feel they can fund this expense out of their net income. They decide to investigate borrowing the money to do it. Nigel is 40 with a pension which matures at age 55. Their house is worth £200,000 with a mortgage of £100,000. They assume the school fees will increase by 3% p.a.

Hence fees will be,

Age	Year	£
11	1	5000
12	2	5150
13	3	5305
14	4	5464
15	5	5628
16	6	5796
17	7	5970
Total		£38,313

They decide to increase their mortgage to the necessary amount, i.e. to £138,313, the capital raising part to be on a drawdown facility which enables the Porters to draw the right amount each year to pay the fees. At the same time they decide to increase the pension funding to provide an additional £38,313 which will replace the money taken from the tax-free cash element to pay off the additional loan.

Typical increase in pension premiums, assuming investment growth of 12% p.a. would be £177.45 p.a. PRAS.

Thus total outgoings for the school fees to Nigel's 55th birthday are,

Pension $£177.45 \times 12 \times 9 = £19,164.60$

His interest payments at say 7.95% are,

Year 1	7.95% of 5000	=	397.50
Year 1	7.95% of 5000	=	397.50
Year 2	7.95% of 10,150	=	806.93
Year 3	7.95% of 13,455	=	1228.67
Year 4	7.95% of 20,919	=	1663.06
Year 5	7.95% of 26,547	=	2110.49
Year 6	7.95% of 32,343	=	2571.27

Years 7, 8 and 9
(NB: This does not now change as he will stop paying fees at the end of year 7)

3 × 7.95% of	38,313	=	9137.65
Total			£17,915.57

Total cost £37,080.17

You can imagine that Nigel and Diana were very pleased with this. Of course, if Nigel had needed to start a personal pension scheme from scratch to do this, four times the premium would have been necessary since only 25% can be taken in tax-free cash. But 3 × £38,313 = £114, 939 would have been left in the fund to buy a pension for Nigel.

Apart from anything else it is quite startling when you start calculating the total cost of education how very much it is. If your house is perhaps the biggest purchase you will ever make it could well be that purchasing education for your children will be the second largest.

SAVING FOR OTHER MEDIUM-TERM OBJECTIVES

It is clear that early planning is advisable for any probable expenditure in the future that may be needed. This could include such things as a daughter's wedding, helping children to buy houses, something special and expensive that you yourself may want for yourself in the future. All the financial planning discussed will apply in the same way to these things.

■ Case Study 4.1

Neill and Linda Melville have just produced their second child, Primrose. Her brother Tudor is two years old. The Melvilles have done no financial planning whatsoever. Neill is 37, employed by a multinational and earns £35,000 p.a. Linda was in advertising but gave up work to look after the home when Tudor was born. She is 32. They are both non-smokers. They have just bought a new house for £150,000 and have a

■ Form 4.2 INCOME TAX AND NIC ANALYSIS

INCOME TAX

Name	Neill Melville		Year	1997	

	£	Remaining income £	Tax £
Gross income	35,000		
Gross contribution to pension paid personally*	5% of 35,000 $= \frac{5}{100} \times 35,000$ = 1750	33,250	Nil
Personal allowance	4045	29,205	Nil
Income taxed at 20%	4100	25,105	820
Income taxed at basic rate 23%	22,000	3105	5060
Income taxed at higher rate 40%	3105	Nil	1242
Total	35,000		7122
Less married couple's allowance 15% of 1830			274.50
Total tax payable			6847.50

* Some pension contributions paid personally are net of basic rate tax. For the purposes of this form this would need to be grossed up.

NATIONAL INSURANCE CONTRIBUTION (NIC) (Employed)

	£	Remaining income £	NIC £
Gross income	35,000		
Income up to LEL £3224 p.a. NIC at 2%	3224	31,776	64.48
Income up to UEL £24,180 p.a. minus £3224 p.a., the LEL NIC at 10%	20,956	10,820	2095.60
Total			2160.08

NATIONAL INSURANCE CONTRIBUTION (NIC) (Self-employed)

Flat rate paid if income over £3480 p.a. £6.15 p.w.	
On profits between £7010 and £24,180 p.a. 6.0%	
Total	
Income after tax and NIC deductions	35,000 – 6847.50 – 2160.08 = 25,992.42
Net spendable income	25,992 – 1750 = £24,242

■ **Form 4.3 LIFETIME FINANCIAL PLAN ANALYSIS**

Name Neill Melville		*Date* 1997	
Date of birth (DoB) 2 September 1960		Smoker/non-Smoker	N/S
Employed/self-employed Employed		Time with business 1 year	
Income p.a. gross £35,000		Net spendable income	£24,242
Annual outgoings £18,000		Surplus p.a.	£6242

Regular savings from net income £2400	
Contingency fund None Recently used as deposit on home	
If I become medically unable to work what would my income situation be for the first 6 months?	Full salary
For the second 6 months?	Nothing
Thereafter?	Nothing
What is the maximum income which I could have?	65% of 35,000 – 3247.40 $= \frac{65}{100} \times 35,000 - 3247.40$ $= 22,750 - 3247.40 = £19.502$ p.a.
Approximate cost of increasing my cover to this	Using Table 2.4, the nearest age is 35 and the nearest benefit is 20,000 p.a. Premium $\frac{19,502}{20,000} \times 24.18 = £21.58$ p.m. fully indexed with a deferment period of six months
Am I contracted out of SERPS and how?	No
What do I expect to get from SERPS in today's terms and when?	Using Table 2.12, £4181 p.a. at 65 unless I contract out
What do I expect to get from the basic state pension in today's terms and when?	£3247.40 p.a. at 65
Pension type	Company money purchase
Personal contribution	£1750 p.a. = £145.83 p.m.
Maximum I am allowed to contribute	15% of 35,000 = $\frac{15}{100} \times 35,000 = £5250$ p.a. = £437.00 p.m.
Retirement age	60
At what age do I want total financial independence	60
Pension (DBS) at financial independence age in today's terms	

■ Form 4.3 (continued)

Pension fund (MPS or PPS) at financial independence age	Total contribution 3500 p.a. = £291.67 p.m. Using Table 2.13, nearest period is 25 years $\text{Fund} = \dfrac{291.67}{100} \times 130,000 = £379,171$
Type of annuity required and yield (MPS or PPS)	Joint life, 50% for spouse, 5% indexed, guaranteed 5 years, yield 4.82% p.a.
Pension this would produce (MPS or PPS)	$379,171 \times \dfrac{4.82}{100} = £18,276$ p.a.
Assumed rate of inflation long term and factor	Inflation 5% p.a. Factor 3.07
Pension in today's terms (MPS or PPS)	$\dfrac{18,276}{3.07} = £5953$ p.a.
Pension benefit for spouse and death in retirement	$50\% \times 5953 = £2977$ p.a.
What is total financial independence for me in today's terms?	£23,000 p.a.
Shortfall	23,000 − 5953 = £17,047
Shortfall at financial independence age, taking inflation into account	17,047 × 3.07 = £52,334 p.a.
Fund needed to produce this pension	$\dfrac{52,334}{4.82} = £1,085,768$
Pension contribution needed to produce this fund at a growth of 12% p.a.	Using Table 2.15, nearest period is 25 years $\text{Premium} = \dfrac{1,085,768}{130,000} \times 100 = £835$ p.m. gross
Amount of mortgage, rate of interest and monthly payment	£100,000 7.6% p.a. £715
Vehicle for repayment	Capital repayment
Life assurance linked to mortgage	Reducing term over 25 years, sum assured £100,000 on Neill's life
Critical illness cover linked to mortgage	None
Additional life assurance	None
Additional critical illness cover	None
Investments	PEP in Neill's name £6000, 1994
Savings plans	None
The basis of my will	No will

repayment mortgage over 25 years of £100,000. Neill has been with his current company for one year. He has an occupational company pension which is a money purchase scheme. The company contributes 5% p.a. of salary and so does Neill. Neither Neill nor Linda has any previous pension schemes.

With the information in Forms 4.2 and 4.3 before them Neill and Linda see immediately that, although they have identified their age correctly, they need to go back and work through the relevant sections of previous chapters. Once they have done that they sit down together to discuss the making of their lifetime financial plan.

Discussion

1 What happens if Neill becomes medically unable to work?

■ They need to take the PHI policy urgently. This would give a benefit of £19,502 p.a. tax free. Together with the state benefit of £3247.40 + £1942.20 (adult dependant) + £343.20 (age allowance) = £5532.80 p.a.

This represents £1487.80 more than the personal allowance and therefore the tax would be £297.56, less married couple's allowance of 15% of £1830 = £274.50, which brings the tax to £23.06.

Hence total net income = £19,502 + 5532.80 – 23.06 = £25,011.74 p.a.

Net spendable income before the event = £24,242. So, in fact, they would be slightly better off.

Cost = £21.38 per month.

■ Pension contributions would cease and when Neill became 60 the PHI policy would cease and they would be in real financial difficulty. They need to consider a pension guarantee policy (critical illness cover). A sum assured of £300,000 would produce an increasing income of £15,000 p.a. This should be indexed to keep pace with inflation.

Using Table 2.8 (p. 66), premium, including WOC, = £159.61 per month 25 year term.

2 What happens if Linda becomes medically unable to function?

■ They would need to employ a nanny/housekeeper for 16 years till Primrose is 16, at say £18,000 p.a. but then in a reduced capacity, at say £10,000 p.a., for another seven years until Neill retires. It is important for them to consider critical illness cover on Linda. They need £10,000 p.a. for 23 years, i.e. sum assured £230,000 reducing annually by £10,000 over 23 years and £8000 p.a. for 16 years, i.e. sum assured £128,000 reducing by £8000 p.a. over 16 years. The nearest we can get by using Tables 3.8 (p. 172) and 4.2 (p. 228) is,

23 year term, premium = £59.74 per month
16 year term, premium = £28.09 per month

3 What happens if Neill dies too soon?

- It would be extremely important to make Linda immediately financially independent with an increasing income starting at 70% of their current salary. For this we need a sum assured of £490,000 on Neill's life.

    Using Table 3.9 (p. 174) we get an approximate cost for straight term including WOC of £106.16 per month.

- The mortgage would be paid off thus releasing a considerable outgoing.

4 What happens if Linda dies too soon?

Again they would need to employ a nanny/housekeeper. This time for 16 years. They need to consider reducing term life assurance. They need £288,000 over 16 years.

Using Table 4.1 (p. 222) the approximate premium is £24.45 per month.

5 What happens if they live too long?

- Neill's pension is drastically short of their objective for total financial independence. The maximum needs to be invested, i.e. a further £291.17 per month gross, which as a higher rate tax payer would actually cost £174.70 per month.

- His level of eligibility is not enough to contribute the sort of sums needed to achieve their objective. He could see if he could negotiate with his company to take a reduction in salary in order for their putting more into his pension. This area will be dealt with in more detail in Chapter 5.

- They feel that if Neill dies in retirement 50% of the pension is not sufficient for Linda. This means recalculating the whole situation and putting even more into the pension. Their pension situation is drastic and Neill must try to negotiate something with his employer.

6 They need to start rebuilding their contingency fund.

7 They would like Primrose and Tudor to go to private school if possible.
The next step is to cost all this and to see what can be afforded.
The proposed additional costs so far are:

Neill

PHI	£21.38 per month =	£ 256.56 p.a.
Pension guarantee	£159.61 per month =	£1915.32 p.a.
Life assurance	£106.16 per month =	£1273.92 p.a.
Pension	£174.70 per month =	£2096.40 p.a.

Linda

Reducing term critical illness	£59.74 per month	= £ 716.88 p.a.
Reducing term life assurance	£28.09 per month	= £ 337.08 p.a.
	£24.45 per month	= £ 293.40 p.a.
Total		£6089.56 p.a.

Their annual outgoings are £18,000. Their current surplus is £6242, hence they would now only have a surplus of £152 p.a.

They will have to compromise. Ideally they also need to start rebuilding their contingency fund which went on house purchase; they would also feel easier if they both had critical illness cover for the mortgage and Linda had life assurance for it; and they also want to send Primrose and Tudor to private school.

'The process of financial planning is the art of compromise.' They will now have to exercise that art. They decide that protection is of primary importance.

They will take all the protection policies but not increase Neill's pension contribution at this time. This means the total cost of their financial planning is reduced to £3993.16 annually giving them a net surplus of £2249 which they feel must go to their contingency fund.

Having now seen their financial situation so clearly, they decide that Neill must put all his efforts into increasing his income. He decides he must stay with his current company another year but starts to quietly look around to see what is available. If he does not do this then they will have considerable problems when he reaches retirement age.

You may like to use the following forms to complete your own lifetime financial plan for this age.

■ Form 4.4 INCOME TAX AND NIC ANALYSIS

INCOME TAX			
Name		Year	
	£	Remaining income £	Tax £
Gross income			
Gross contribution to pension paid personally*			
Personal allowance			
Income taxed at 20% Income taxed at basic rate 23% Income taxed at higher rate 40%			
Total			
Less married couple's allowance			
Total tax payable			

* Some pension contributions paid personally are net of basic rate tax. For the purposes of this form this would need to be grossed up.

NATIONAL INSURANCE CONTRIBUTION (NIC) (Employed)			
	£	Remaining income £	NIC £
Gross income			
Income up to LEL £3224 p.a. NIC at 2%			
Income up to UEL £24,180 p.a. minus £3224 p.a., the LEL NIC at 10%			
Total			
NATIONAL INSURANCE CONTRIBUTION (NIC) (Self-employed)			
Flat rate paid if income over £3480 p.a. £6.15 p.w.			
On profits between £7010 and £24,180 p.a. 6.0%			
Total			
Income after tax and NIC deductions			
Net spendable income			

■ Form 4.5 LIFETIME FINANCIAL PLAN ANALYSIS

Name	*Date*
Date of birth (DoB)	Smoker/non-smoker
Employed/self-employed	Time with business
Income p.a. gross	Income p.a. net of taxes and NIC
Annual outgoings	Surplus p.a.
Regular savings from net income	
If I become medically unable to work what would my income situation be for the first 6 months?	
For the second 6 months?	
Thereafter?	
What is the maximum income which I could have?	
Approximate cost of increasing my cover to this	
Pension type	
Personal contribution	
Maximum I am allowed to contribute	
Retirement age	
Projected pension fund (MPS or PPS) at retirement age	
Projected pension at retirement age (DBS)	
At what age do I want total financial independence?	
Pension fund (MPS or PPS) adjusted to financial independence age	
Pension (DBS) adjusted to financial independence age	
Type of annuity required	
Pension this would produce	
Assumed rate of inflation long term	
Pension in today's terms	
What is total financial independence for me in today's terms?	

■ **Form 4.5 (continued)**

Shortfall
Shortfall at financial independence age, taking inflation into account
Fund needed to produce this pension
Pension contribution needed to produce this fund at a growth of 12% p.a.
Comments
Decisions

SUMMARY

In this age we have worked through the following:

1 The advent of a child, the added expense it brings and the need for major decisions about its care. Will one of you become a full-time homemaker? Will you both work less and care for the child between you or will you employ a nanny?

2 The implications of death and medical inability to function. These carry greater implications than before and need to be thoroughly analysed. Not only does the right amount of money need to be forthcoming at the time but it needs to go into the right hands.

3 Medium-term financial objectives such as the payment of school fees. It is wise to plan as far in advance as possible as a child's education fees can be the second most expensive purchase you will ever make.

References

1. *Julius Caesar*, Act III, Scene 1, William Shakespeare.

2. Winston Spencer Churchill.

3. The Independent Schools Information Service 1997.

ANSWERS

■ Exercise 4.1

The company pension would pay an income to Janet of,

$$\tfrac{1}{2}\times \frac{26}{60}\times(30{,}000-3224)=\frac{13}{60}\times26{,}776=£5801\ \text{p.a.}$$

This represents $\dfrac{5801}{30{,}000}\times100\%=19.3\%$ of Alex's salary.

Janet will need a further $70-19.3=50.7\%$. The sum assured needed will, therefore, be,

$$20\times\frac{50.7}{100}\times\text{salary}=10.14\times\text{salary}$$

Hence sum assured needed $=10.14\times30{,}000=£304{,}200$. The company pension will produce $2\times(30{,}000-3224)=2\times26{,}776=£53{,}552$.

They will need life assurance on Alex's life of $£304{,}200-£53{,}552=£250{,}648$.

The various costs are, using 35 as the nearest we can get to Alex's age,

	Approximate monthly premium
25 year term	£64.61
10 year renewable term	£53.48
10 year convertible term	£52.08
10 year renewable convertible term	£59.32
Pension linked (basic rate taxpayer)	£49.74
Whole of life	£147.17
Low start (sum assured reducing to £167,310 at the end of 10 years)	£92.29

■ Exercise 4.2

We will need £288,000 sum assured on Janet reducing by £18,000 annually over 16 years. Using Table 4.1 (p. 222) the nearest age to Janet is 25.

$$\text{Premium}=\frac{288{,}000}{100{,}000}\times7.92=£22.81\ \text{per month}$$

The additional cost for smoker rate $=9.4\%$ of 22.81,

$$\frac{9.4}{100}\times22.81=£2.14\ \text{per month}$$

Total premium $=22.81+2.14=£24.95$ per month.

■ **Exercise 4.3**

If Grant were to die it would be important for Isobel to reach total financial independence immediately. They decide this would be 70% of current income. Hence they need life insurance on Grant's life of $20 \times 70/100 \times$ current salary $= 14 \times 40,000 = £560,000$.

Using Table 4.1 the nearest age to Grant is 35.

$$\text{Premium} = \frac{560,000}{100,000} \times 12.59 = £70.50 \text{ per month}$$

It would be wise to have WOC on this which would cost an additional 2% of £70.50 $= 2/100 \times 70.50 = £1.41$ per month.

Hence total premium $= 70.50 + 1.41 = £71.91$ per month.

If Isobel died Grant would need to employ a nanny/housekeeper at a cost of £18,000 p.a. Hence they need reducing term life assurance on Isobel of $16 \times 18,000 = £288,000$ reducing by £18,000 p.a. over 16 years. Using Table 4.1 Isobel's age of 30 fits exactly.

$$\text{Premium} = \frac{288,000}{100,000} \times 8.49 = £24.45 \text{ per month}$$

■ Exercise 4.4

INCOME TAX AND NIC ANALYSIS

INCOME TAX			

Name Eileen Baxter		Year 1997	
		Before becoming medically unable to work	

	£	Remaining income £	Tax £
Gross income	40,000		
Gross contribution to pension paid personally *			
Personal allowance	4045	35,955	Nil
Income taxed at 20%	4100	31,855	820
Income taxed at basic rate 23%	22,000	9855	5060
Income taxed at higher rate 40%	9855	Nil	3942
Total	40,000		9822
Less married couple's allowance 15% of £1,830			274.50
Total tax payable			9547.50

* Some pension contributions paid personally are net of basic rate tax. For the purposes of this form this would need to be grossed up.

NATIONAL INSURANCE CONTRIBUTION (NIC) (Employed)

	£	Remaining income £	NIC £
Gross income	40,000		
Income up to LEL £3224 p.a. NIC at 2%	3224	36,776	64.48
Income up to UEL £24,180 p.a. minus £3224 p.a., the LEL NIC at 10%	20,956		2095.60
Total			2160.08

NATIONAL INSURANCE CONTRIBUTION (NIC) (Self-employed)

Flat rate paid if income over £3480 p.a. £6.15 p.w.	
On profits between £7010 and £24,180 p.a. 6.0%	
Total	
Income after tax and NIC deductions	40,000 – 9547.50 – 2160.08 = £28,292.42
Net spendable income	£28,292

Exercise 4.4 (continued)

INCOME TAX

Name	Eileen Baxter			Year	1997

After becoming medically unable to work

	£	Remaining income £	Tax £
Gross income 65% of 40,000 = $\frac{65}{100} \times 40,000$ = 26,000			
Gross contribution to Pension paid personally *			
Personal allowance	4045	21,955	
Income taxed at 20%	4100	17,855	820.00
Income taxed at basic rate 23%	17,855		4106.65
Income taxed at higher rate 40%			
Total			4926.65
Less married couple's allowance 15% of £1830			274.50
Total tax payable			4652.15

* Some pension contributions paid personally are net of basic rate tax. For the purposes of this form this would need to be grossed up.

NATIONAL INSURANCE CONTRIBUTION (NIC) (Employed)

	£	Remaining income £	NIC £
Gross income	26,000		
Income up to LEL £3224 p.a. NIC at 2%	3224	22,776	64.48
Income up to UEL £24,180 p.a. minus £3224 p.a., the LEL NIC at 10%	24,180 3224 20,956		2095.60
Total			2160.08

NATIONAL INSURANCE CONTRIBUTION (NIC) (Self-employed)

Flat rate paid if income over £3480 p.a. £6.15 p.w.			
On profits between £7010 and £24,180 p.a. 6.0%			
Total			
Income after tax and NIC deductions	26,000 − 4652.15 − 2160.08 = 19,187.77		
Net spendable income	£19,188		

Thus in the event of Eileen becoming medically unable to work her net spendable income would drop from £28,292 to £19,188, p.a. In addition to this the Baxters would now probably have to employ someone full time to look after Gillian and Eileen at a cost of £20,000 p.a. They would not then need the childminder so the additional cost would be £8000 p.a. They need to provide an additional income of £8000 p.a. for 16 years until Gillian is 16 and to replace the lost income of £28,292 – 19,188 = £9104 p.a. at least until Edward retires at 60, i.e. 23 years. Hence they need reducing term critical ill-ness on Eileen's life of £9104 × 23 = £209,392 reducing by £9104 p.a. over 23 years and £8000 × 16 = £128,000 reducing by £8000 p.a. over 16 years.

Using Table 3.12 (p. 177) and Table 4.2 (p. 228) the nearest age to Eileen's is 30 and the nearest term to 23 years is 25. Premium for sum assured £209,392,

$$\frac{209,392}{100,000} \times 25.98 = £54.40 \text{ per month}$$

It would be wise to include WOC on this for a further 2% of 54.40:

$$\frac{2}{100} \times 54.40 = £1.09$$

Total premium = £55.49 per month.
    Premium for sum assured £128,000,

$$\frac{128,000}{100,000} \times 21.95 = £28.10 \text{ per month}$$

Additional premium for WOC = 2% of 28.10,

$$\frac{2}{100} \times 28.10 = £0.56$$

Total premium = £28.66 per month.

INCOME TAX AND NIC ANALYSIS

INCOME TAX			
Name Edward Baxter		Year 1997	
		Before becoming medically unable to work	
	£	Remaining income £	Tax £
Gross income	30,000		
Gross contribution to pension paid personally *			
Personal allowance	4045	25,955	Nil
Income taxed at 20%	4100	21,855	820.00
Income taxed at basic rate 23%	21,855	Nil	5026.65
Income taxed at higher rate 40%			
Total	30,000		5846.65
Less married couple's allowance			
Total tax payable			

* Some pension contributions paid personally are net of basic rate tax. For the purposes of this
   form this would need to be grossed up.

NATIONAL INSURANCE CONTRIBUTION (NIC) (Employed)			
	£	Remaining income £	NIC £
Gross income			
Income up to LEL £3224 p.a. NIC at 2%			
Income up to UEL £24,180 p.a. minus £3224 p.a., the LEL NIC at 10%			
Total			

NATIONAL INSURANCE CONTRIBUTION (NIC) (Self-employed)	
Flat rate paid if income over £3480 p.a. £6. 15 p.w.	319.80
On profits between £7010 and £24,180 p.a. 6.0%	1030.20
Total	1350
Income after tax and NIC deductions	30,000 − 5846.63 − 1350 = 22,803
Net spendable income	£22,803

If Edward became medically unable to work his PHI policy would produce £16,253 p.a. tax free.

From the state he would get £3247.40 p.a. plus age allowance of £343.20 p.a. and dependant child allowance of £514.80 p.a. His total allowances would therefore be,

£3247.40 + £343.20 + £514.80 = £4105.40 p.a.

Since the personal allowance is £4045 p.a. the amount falling into the 20% tax bracket is,

£4105.40 – £4045 = £60.40 p.a.

The tax on this will be,

$$\frac{20}{100} \times 60.40 = £12.08 \text{ p.a.}$$

Hence Edward's net spendable income is,

£16,253 + £4105.40 – £12.08 = £20,346.32 p.a.

His net spendable income before the event was £22,803 p.a. Therefore he is now £22,803 – £20,346 = £2457 p.a. worse off.

He and Eileen would need to employ a full time nanny/housekeeper at £20,000 p.a. (£8000 p.a. more than they currently pay a childminder) at least until Gillian is 16, but probably also until Eileen retires in 32 years time. They decide to replace the lost income, which when rounded up amounts to £2500. Cover needed is therefore,

£8000 + £2500 = £10,500 p.a.

over a 32 year period,

£10,500 × 32 = £336,000.

They therefore need a sum assured on Edward of £336,000, reducing by £10,500 p.a. over 32 years.

Using Table 3.12 (p. 177), the nearest age to Edward's is 35, with a term of 25 years:

Premium = 336,000/100,000 × 34.25 = £115.08 per month.

Adding WOC the additional premium is 2% of 115.08,

2/100 × 115.08 = £2.30 per month.

Therefore the total premium is £115.08 + £2.30 = £117.38 per month.

CHAPTER 5

THE AGE OF
CAREER
DEVELOPMENT

Birth and education	Work	Marriage	Parenthood	Career development	Retirement	Old age

FINANCIAL PLANNING AT A GLANCE –
THE AGE OF CAREER DEVELOPMENT

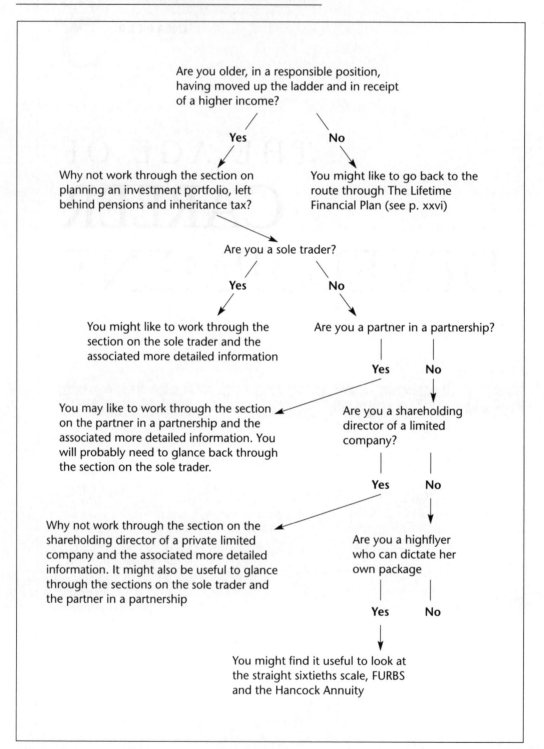

Are you older, in a responsible position, having moved up the ladder and in receipt of a higher income?

Yes

No

Why not work through the section on planning an investment portfolio, left behind pensions and inheritance tax?

You might like to go back to the route through The Lifetime Financial Plan (see p. xxvi)

Are you a sole trader?

Yes

No

You might like to work through the section on the sole trader and the associated more detailed information

Are you a partner in a partnership?

Yes   **No**

You may like to work through the section on the partner in a partnership and the associated more detailed information. You will probably need to glance back through the section on the sole trader.

Are you a shareholding director of a limited company?

Yes   **No**

Why not work through the section on the shareholding director of a private limited company and the associated more detailed information. It might also be useful to glance through the sections on the sole trader and the partner in a partnership

Are you a highflyer who can dictate her own package

Yes   **No**

You might find it useful to look at the straight sixtieths scale, FURBS and the Hancock Annuity

CONTENTS

In this age the following is discussed:

Contents

INTRODUCTION

In this age you have moved up the ladder: you are in a responsible position, have a higher income, and are older. You may be an employee, holding no shares in the company for which you work. You may hold enough shares to have a say in the running of the company and the major decisions. You may be a partner in a partnership. You may be a sole trader running your own business. Whichever one of these you are, if you have achieved financial health in the previous ages then from that point of view your lifetime financial plan will need only the fine tuning dictated by changes in income, changes in job or changes in legislation or investment climate.

Let us look at the many implications of this new age. Hopefully pension contributions are those necessary to achieve the total financial independence desired at the chosen age. They may, of course, be the maximum allowed but still not enough to achieve that objective. Perhaps then it would be wise to look at other forms of investment which might supplement the pension. It might be the time to turn back to Chapter 1 and work through the investment section again. Now is the time to plan the investment portfolio, to balance it and to link it to personal objectives. As with so many things the answer is compromise and spread. It is never wise to have just one sort of investment.

PLANNING AN INVESTMENT PORTFOLIO

The contingency fund, the 25 to 50 per cent of net earned income, will take care of any short-term requirements. We are therefore looking at medium- to long-term investment. We have the choice of gilts, equities, investment property, different geographical areas, investments pooled or straight onto the stock market, safer or more risky, onshore or offshore investments, greater or lesser tax efficiency.

For someone resident and ordinarily resident in the UK the tax treatment of offshore investment is very similar except in the case of offshore investment bonds and in this case the growth and income of the investments in the bond roll up totally free of all UK taxes. This is why they are sometimes called 'gross roll-up funds'. (See offshore investment bonds later.)

The growth and income of an offshore investment bond 'roll up' totally free of all UK taxes.

Investment in other geographical areas has the added variable of exchange rates, which can cause considerable problems. Between June 1991 and August 1992 the US. market rose by approximately 12 per cent. During the same period the UK market fell 5 per cent. Unfortunately during that period the dollar fell against sterling by over 20 per cent making the value of £100 of investment grow by 12 per cent to £112 and then reducing that by 20 per cent,

$$£112 - \frac{20}{100} \times 112 = £112 - £22.40 = £89.60$$

a loss of over 10 per cent.

Fund managers will often use a process called hedging to protect the fund from the dangers of changing exchange rates. This is a complex process using futures but results in the foreign fund, to all intents and purposes, being designated in sterling and thus safe from currency fluctuations. There is, of course, a cost for using this process that will have to be balanced against the potential benefit. This results in some funds having no hedging, some being partially hedged and some totally. Before investing this could be a useful piece of information to obtain about any particular fund being used.

It may have a bearing on geographical decisions to note that of the total world stock market at the end of 1995 the US accounted for 43 per cent, Japan 24%, Europe 16 and the UK 9 per cent.

It might help to follow these 6 points when designing an investment portfolio:

1 Put the larger proportion of the investment in the UK (assuming UK residency).
2 Use pooled investments. The risk factor is lower than that with a small investment portfolio invested directly in equities on the stock market.
3 Have a reasonable proportion of the investment in gilts, national savings and property.
4 Make use of the tax advantages of TESSAs and PEPs. Think especially about corporate bond PEPs with a view to tax-free income in retirement.
5 For those who are likely to be higher rate tax payers in retirement consider investment bonds, especially the guaranteed equity bond.
6 Consider savings plans which can produce a tax-free income in the hands of the investor and friendly society investments which are very tax efficient.

A typical portfolio then, which, of course, will be built up over the years, could look like this:

- ■ **Geographical spread** (see Fig. 5.1):
  - – UK   60 per cent
  - – USA   18 per cent
  - – Europe   8 per cent
  - – Far East (including Japan)   10 per cent
  - – emerging economies   4 per cent

- ■ **Risk/safety**: a good 70 to 80 per cent in good safe blue chip-type shares invested through pooled investments such as the funds of OEICs to cut charges to a minimum. This would include maximum possible into PEPs for tax advantages, possibly bonds for those who expect to be higher rate tax payers in retirement. Possibly also a maximum investment plan from which income can be taken tax free in the investor's hands without the constraint of the 5 per cent annual limit. Gilts, corporate bonds, possibly TESSAs and national savings such as the indexed-linked savings certificates 10 to 15 per

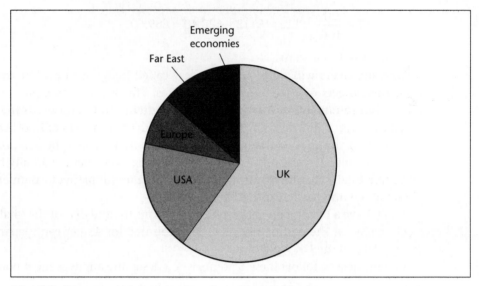

Fig. 5.1 Investment proportions by geographical area

cent. At the riskier end, but with the possibility of a much higher return, special pooled investments might be considered such as emerging economies, special situations, where investment is into companies in special situations which may produce high growth or go badly down, similar more risky investments would be smaller companies and recovery situations.

■ **Property:** 10 to 15 per cent (see Fig. 5.2). Again it would be wise to do this through pooled investment and again the OEIC would keep charges to a minimum.

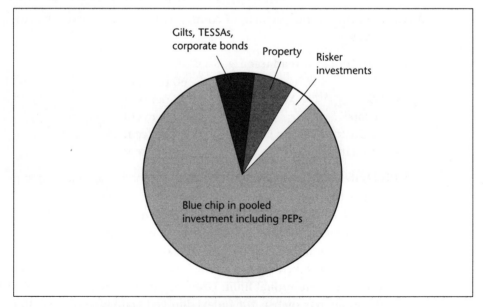

Fig. 5.2 Investment proportions by type of investment

An investment portfolio is very much a matter of the personality of the investor and it is only he or she who can decide on the constituents. It may help to form your own objectives if you write down your attitude to the following eight points. The first four we have already seen in Chapter 1:

- the term of the investment
- accessibility
- tax aspects
- asset-backed or not
- degree of risk
- pooled investments or non-pooled
- geographical area
- income or growth.

There is one observation to be made about the last point. For income to be taken from a 'growth' investment it will have to be taken by encashment and will therefore be subject to capital gains tax (CGT) rather than income tax. However, unlike the tax on income, there are two allowances which can be used, indexation and the personal annual CGT allowance which, in the fiscal year 1997/98, was £6500. Thus a certain amount each year can be taken from these investments tax free.

> A certain amount of capital gain can be taken from an investment each year totally free of all UK taxes.

This is true of practically any investment producing a capital gain, which is encashed. CGT does not apply to gilts. (CGT is treated later in the chapter).

Other investments carrying considerable tax advantages which could be considered are enterprise investment schemes (EIS), venture capital trusts (VCT), investment on the alternative investment market (AIM) and enterprise zone property trusts. However, all of these do have a considerable degree of risk. (Details later in the chapter.)

The family home as an investment

Because your home is where you live you may not often think of it as an investment. However, when it is sold any gain which is made is totally free of all UK taxes. It might, therefore, in this age, be worth considering a home that is more expensive than previously decided on, but one that is still affordable, with the plan in mind that at retirement it will be sold in favour of a smaller less costly property, leaving excess funds to be invested to enhance retirement income.

> One's own home can also be a very tax-efficient investment.

Left behind pensions

It might also, in this age, be worth considering any pensions which have been left behind from previous employment. If these were money purchase then they should be partaking in the full growth being achieved by the fund. If they were defined benefit then it is mandatory for them to be increased only by 5 per cent a year. It might be a good idea to talk to whoever runs your current scheme and ask for an analysis to be done to see whether a forecast of growth is better leaving them where they are or moving them, either to the current pension scheme or into a personal pension scheme. This is done very carefully and there is no fear of making a vastly wrong decision since no company will accept a transfer unless the analysis clearly shows it to be beneficial to the client.

Whether they are moved or not care should be taken that the managers of previous pensions know your current address at all times and contact is not lost.

At this age there may have been an inheritance and so decisions on investment would be even more relevant.

The share exchange scheme

The inheritance may have been received in the form of a small share portfolio and if, on reworking through Chapter 1 you decide to go for pooled investments there will be the problem and cost of selling the shares in order to reinvest. Many companies offer a share exchange scheme which enables the investor to exchange his or her shares in return for pooled investments. This considerably cuts down the costs of selling and if the insurance company decides to keep some of the shares there will be no dealing costs whatsoever. It must be noted, however, that although this is an exchange, shares will be deemed to have been disposed of for the purposes of capital gains tax and there will, therefore, be a liability to this tax. Care needs to be taken with this point.

Inheritance tax

The problem of inheritance tax can be solved by life assurance.

There may have been an inheritance tax (IHT) liability. This might have raised the whole question of IHT which is dealt with in more detail in Chapter 6. However, it could be very relevant in the current age to work through the section on IHT for two reasons:

1 Its amelioration by use of the will trust depends on investment in bonds and may well have a bearing now on the development of an investment portfolio.
2 The solution by the use of life assurance will depend on paying premiums which will be very much less in this age than they will be later.

Table 5.1 will demonstrate this point. Having calculated potential IHT liability, it remains only necessary to take out a joint life second death whole of life policy and put this in trust for those who will become liable for the tax. The sum assured will be payable to the beneficiaries free of all UK taxes and can be used to pay off the IHT (see Table 5.1).

■ Example 5.1

Brian Winter and his wife, Victoria, have recently received an inheritance on which considerable IHT had to be paid. They decide to look at the potential liability for their children and calculate it to be currently £100,000. As they expect further inheritances and that the value of their estate will grow they decide to take out a policy for £200,000. They are both non-smokers, Brian is 46 and Victoria is 41.

Using Table 5.1 the nearest ages to this are 45 and 42. The premium will be,

$$\frac{200,000}{100,000} \times 35.08 = 70.16 \text{ per month}$$

They decide to put WOC on Brian which adds a further 3% of £70.16 = $3/100 \times 70.16$ = £2.10 per month

Total monthly premium = £72.26. They decide they will index this every year to keep pace with inflation. It is interesting to note that the annual cost is £867.12,

$$\frac{867.12}{200,000} \times 100\% = 0.43 \text{ of 1\% of the potential tax of £200,000}$$

which they have insured. Thus they have solved their potential IHT problem by annual payments of less than ½% of the potential tax; they would have to pay this premium for 231 years before they had paid out £200,000, which all makes it a pretty good bargain,

$$231 \times 867.12 = £200,305$$

When Brian is 55 he is made redundant. He decides to start his own business. Over the years he pours in capital. Things go very badly, using up all their capital. The strain tells badly on Victoria and a few months after Brian's 65th birthday she dies. Luckily Brian has a small pension from his earlier employment, but a much smaller estate attracting no IHT liability whatsoever. He decides he no longer needs the policy they took out for IHT. He calls the insurance company and finds its cash in value is £54,200. This is a very welcome surprise and wisely invested brings him a little more comfort in retirement.

■ Exercise 5.1

Why not calculate your own IHT using Table 5.1 and see how much it would cost to deal with it.

Table 5.1 Typical premiums for whole of life, second death life assurance (sum assured £100,000)

[Women are 3 years younger than men in all cases.]

Man's age	Monthly premium non-smoker	% increase for smoke (both lives)	% increase for WOC on man	% increase for WOC on woman	Cash in values £		
					Both alive	Wife only alive	Husband only alive
30	14.48	21.0	2	2.5	After 10 years		
					1250	3750	7650
					At male's age 65		
					15,400	22,500	34,700
35	18.98	26.0	2	2.5	After 10 years		
					1450	3280	6420
					At male's age 65		
					15,000	20,500	29,500
40	25.08	29.8	3	4	After 10 years		
					2090	4550	8820
					At male's age 65		
					14,100	19,600	28,700
45	35.08	32.2	3	4	After 10 years		
					3070	6380	12,100
					At male's age 65		
					12,400	17,900	27,100
50	49.18	35.8	4.5	6	After 10 years		
					4570	8980	16,500
					At male's age 65		
					9990	15,600	25,000
55	70.18	34.2	Usually not available		After 10 years		
					6840	12,600	22,200
					After 20 years		
					25,100	33,500	45,300
60	102.88	31.0	Usually not available		After 10 years		
					9930	17,300	28,800
					After 15 years		
					20,300	29,000	41,300
65	148.78	26.7	Usually not available		After 10 years		
					14,300	23,500	36,400

Up to this point all topics already discussed will be relevant to all those in the age of career development; from here on there will be differences according to different career situations.

For the employee with no control over the business in which he or she works all relevant matters have been discussed. For the employee who has some control over his or her remuneration package the topics of straight sixtieths company pensions, funded unapproved retirement benefit schemes and the Hancock Annuity treated later in the chapter could be important.

THE SOLE TRADER RUNNING HIS OR HER OWN BUSINESS

Approved company pension scheme for spouse

If your spouse is not in gainful employment it might be worth your employing him or her for a small part of the week and paying him or her around £3000 per annum. Reference to the tax and NIC tables in Chapter 2 will show that this figure is within the personal allowance and therefore no tax will be paid, but it is also below the LEL so no NIC will be paid by either the employee or the employer. Hence it would be worth reducing your own income by £3000 and switching it to spouse, thus removing all potential tax and NIC from it. The Inland Revenue will expect to see that spouse is employed in such a way that the payment of £3000 per annum is relevant.

Each person is eligible for the personal allowance and that will not change in retirement so it would also be a good idea for spouse to be receiving an income when retired otherwise the personal allowance is wasted. As a sole trader an occupational pension scheme can be put in place for employees and, as we shall see later, the percentages allowed are very much more generous than either the free-standing additional voluntary contribution or the personal pension scheme. Hence it would be an excellent idea to run such a pension scheme for spouse. This will be totally tax relievable against profit and benefit should also be tax free in retirement as it is unlikely to exceed the personal allowance. Details on investment limits for occupational pension schemes will be found later in this chapter.

■ **Example 5.2**

Callum Treadwell is 42 and runs a successful business as a sole trader. His before tax profit is £41,250. He invests the maximum into a PPS which is £8250 p.a. This means he is still taxed on £33,000. Hence he is in the higher rate tax bracket. His wife, Ursula, is 40 and looks after the home and family. Callum decides that she could answer the phone and do some general work for a few hours each day. For this he pays her £3000 p.a. This reduces his income to £30,000 p.a. and puts him into the basic rate tax bracket.

■ Form 5.1 INCOME TAX AND NIC ANALYSIS

INCOME TAX			
Name Callum Treadwell		*Year* Before	
	£	*Remaining income £*	*Tax £*
Gross income	41,250		
Gross contribution to pension paid personally*	8250	33,000	
Personal allowance	4045	28,955	Nil
Income taxed at 20%	4100	24,855	820
Income taxed at basic rate 23%	22,000	2855	5060
Income taxed at higher rate 40%	2855		1142
Total	41,250		7022
Less married couple's allowance 15% of £1830			274.50
Total tax payable			6747.50

* Some pension contributions paid personally are net of basic rate tax. For the purposes of this form this would need to be grossed up.

NATIONAL INSURANCE CONTRIBUTION (NIC) (Employed)			
	£	*Remaining income £*	*NIC £*
Gross income			
Income up to LEL £3224 p.a. NIC at 2%			
Income up to UEL £24,180 p.a. minus £3224 p.a., the LEL NIC at 10%			
Total			

NATIONAL INSURANCE CONTRIBUTION (NIC) (Self-employed)	
Flat rate paid if income over £3480 p.a. £6.15 p.w.	319.80
On profits between £7010 and £24,180 p.a. 6.0%	1030.20
Total	1350.00
Income after tax and NIC deductions	41,250 – 6747.50 – 1350 = 33,152.50
Net spendable income	33,213 – 8250 = 24,903

■ Form 5.2 INCOME TAX AND NIC ANALYSIS

INCOME TAX			
Name Callum Treadwell	*Year*	After	
	£	*Remaining income £*	*Tax £*
Gross income	41,250 – 3000 = 38,250		
Gross contribution to pension paid personally*	8250	30,000	
	1500 (Ursula)	28,500	Nil
Personal allowance	4045	24,455	Nil
Income taxed at 20%	4100	20,355	820
Income taxed at basic rate 23%	20,355	Nil	4681.65
Income taxed at higher rate 40%			
Total	41,250		5501.65
Less married couple's allowance 15% of £1830			274.50
Total tax payable			5227.15

* Some pension contributions paid personally are net of basic rate tax. For the purposes of this form this would need to be grossed up.

NATIONAL INSURANCE CONTRIBUTION (NIC) (Employed)			
	£	*Remaining income £*	*NIC £*
Gross income			
Income up to LEL £3224 p.a. NIC at 2%			
Income up to UEL £24,180 p.a. minus £3224 p.a., the LEL NIC at 10%			
Total			
NATIONAL INSURANCE CONTRIBUTION (NIC) (Self-employed)			
Flat rate paid if income over £3480 p.a. £6.15 p.w.			319.80
On profits between £7010 and £24,180 p.a. 6.0%			1030.20
Total			1350.00
Income after tax and NIC deductions	38,250 – 5227.15 – 1350 = 31,672.85		
Net spendable income	31,673 + 3000 – 8250 – 1500 = 24,923		

Personal allowance	£4045
Tax at 20%	£4100
Tax at 23%	£22,000
Total	£30,145

Higher rate tax is paid on any income above this.

Ursula now raises the question of retirement and an occupational pension is set up for her at £1500 p.a. or £125 monthly. Referring to Table 5.8 (p. 344), we see this is the maximum allowed at her age and with annual remuneration of £3000. Let us be clear that the premium is contributed by the business in addition to her income.

We have jumped ahead here to the section on company pension schemes revenue limits for maximum contributions. You may like to take the annual £1500 maximum pension contribution on trust at this stage and work through that section later, or turn to that section now, work through it, and then come back to this example.

As can be seen from Table 2.15 (p. 93), this would produce a fund of,

$$\frac{125}{100} \times 73,400 = £91,750$$

at age 60 and using a single life, non-guaranteed, indexed at 5% p.a. annuity with a yield of 4.81% p.a. this would produce a pension of £91,750 × 4.81/100 = £4413 p.a.

If we assume annual inflation at 5% p.a. the personal allowance would be £4045 × 2.65 (using Table 2.17, p. 95) = £10,719 when Ursula takes her pension. It would therefore be totally tax free. Using Forms 5.1 and 5.2, which show the position before and after the introduction of an income and pension for Ursula we see that in spite of paying £1500 p.a. for a pension, net spendable income has increased by £24,923 − £24,903 p.a. = £20 p.a. We can only conclude that Callum and Ursula are extremely happy to have £20 more p.a. to spend plus a pension contribution of £1500 p.a. at no cost to them whatsoever.

> In certain circumstances it is possible to increase one's spendable income by virtue of accepting a free annual pension contribution.

■ Exercise 5.2

Duncan Graham produces a before tax profit of £28,000 p.a. selling and servicing aquarium equipment. Having talked to Callum Treadwell, one of his clients, he decides to employ his wife, Janet, in the business on an income of £3000 p.a. and put in an occupational pension for her. Janet is 38.

Using Table 5.6 and Table 2.15, calculate the fund that a maximum contribution, paid monthly, would produce at age 60. Using an annuity (Table 2.16, p. 94), of single life, non-guaranteed, level, calculate the pension this would produce. Assuming long-term inflation of 5% p.a. use Table 2.17 to see whether Janet's pension income would be within the personal allowance when she is 60.

Using Form 5.3 work out the before and after net spendable income situation.

■ **Form 5.3 INCOME TAX AND NIC ANALYSIS**

INCOME TAX			
Name		*Year*	
	£	*Remaining income £*	*Tax £*
Gross income			
Gross contribution to pension paid personally*			
Personal allowance			
Income taxed at 20% Income taxed at basic rate 23% Income taxed at higher rate 40%			
Total			
Less married couple's allowance			
Total tax payable			
* Some pension contributions paid personally are net of basic rate tax. For the purposes of this form this would need to be grossed up.			
NATIONAL INSURANCE CONTRIBUTION (NIC) (Employed)			
	£	*Remaining income £*	*NIC £*
Gross income			
Income up to LEL £3224 p.a. NIC at 2%			
Income up to UEL £24,180 p.a. minus £3224 p.a., the LEL NIC at 10%			
Total			
NATIONAL INSURANCE CONTRIBUTION (NIC) (Self-employed)			
Flat rate paid if income over £3480 p.a. £6.15 p.w.			
On profits between £7010 and £24,180 p.a. 6.0%			
Total			
Income after tax and NIC deductions			
Net spendable income			

Clearly if before tax profit is well into the higher rate tax bracket it could be advantageous to pay spouse more than £3000 per annum. Although this could begin to attract national insurance contributions this will be outweighed by the saving in higher rate tax. Later in this chapter we will see that the 'de minimus' pension contribution rules would make possible higher pension contributions.

_____

Personal allowance for tax purposes does not disappear at retirement.

_____

We might approach this part of financial planning from a different standpoint with the objective of producing for spouse a pension just within what we assume the personal allowance will be at retirement, thus ensuring that the family income in retirement will be as tax efficient as possible. Case Study 5.1 will illustrate this using the de minimus rules for maximum pension contributions. You can either turn to that section now and work through it enabling you to fully understand the case study, or return to the case study and work through that after you have covered the de minimus section in the normal course of your working through this chapter.

■ Case Study 5.1

Jason Cohen runs a retail musical instrument business as a sole trader. His before tax profit is £45,000. His wife, Rachel, is a full-time homemaker and mother. In discussing their lifetime financial plan they feel they would like to make use of Rachel's personal allowance both now and in the future. Rachel is 36 and Jason 39. Personal allowance in the fiscal year 1997/98 is £4045. Using Table 2.17, and assuming long-term inflation will average 5% p.a., they see the inflation factor for a 24 year period, the time for Rachel to reach her 60th birthday, is 3.23. When Rachel is 60 the personal allowance will be $4045 \times 3.23 = £13,065$. Hence for the Cohens to make full use of this Rachel will need a pension of £13,065 indexed at 5% annually. They decide this will be single life, non-guaranteed because they will be making maximum pension provision for Jason.

Table 2.16 tells us the annuity yield will be 4.81%. Hence the fund needed will be,

$$13,065 \div \frac{4.81}{100} = £217,622$$

Using Table 2.15 the nearest term for Rachel is 25 years.

$$\text{Premium needed} = \frac{271,622}{100,000} \times 100 = £271.62 \text{ per month or } £3259.44 \text{ p.a.}$$

Using the de minimus rule the maximum pension premium possible is the lower of 100% of remuneration or £6000 p.a. Hence Jason pays Rachel £3260 annually for various duties in the business which allows the annual investment of £3259.44 (£271.62 a month) into a company pension scheme for Rachel which will give her, at age 60, assuming a growth of 12% p.a., a pension of £13,065 p.a. indexed at 5%, which assuming inflation is 5% annually over the long term will be exactly equal to the personal allowance at that time and therefore totally free of all UK taxes.

What about the current before and after situation?

■ **Form 5.4 INCOME TAX AND NIC ANALYSIS**

INCOME TAX			
Name Jason Cohen		*Year* 1997 Before	
	£	*Remaining income £*	*Tax £*
Gross income	45,000		
Gross contribution to pension paid personally*			
Personal allowance	· 4045	40,955	Nil
Income taxed at 20%	4100	36,855	820
Income taxed at basic rate 23%	22,000	19,855	5060
Income taxed at higher rate 40%	19,855	Nil	5942
Total	45,000		11,822
Less married couple's allowance 15% of £1830			274.20
Total tax payable			11,547.50

* Some pension contributions paid personally are net of basic rate tax. For the purposes of this form this would need to be grossed up.

NATIONAL INSURANCE CONTRIBUTION (NIC) (Employed)			
	£	*Remaining income £*	*NIC £*
Gross income			
Income up to LEL £3224 p.a. NIC at 2%			
Income up to UEL £24,180 p.a. minus £3224 p.a., the LEL NIC at 10%			
Total			

NATIONAL INSURANCE CONTRIBUTION (NIC) (Self-employed)	
Flat rate paid if income over £3480 p.a. £6.15 p.w.	319.80
On profits between £7010 and £24,180 p.a. 6.0% $\dfrac{6}{100} \times 17,170 =$	1030.20
Total	1350.00
Income after tax and NIC deductions 45,000 – 11,547.50 – 1350 = 32,102.50	
Net spendable income £32,102	

■ Form 5.5 INCOME TAX AND NIC ANALYSIS

INCOME TAX			
Name Jason Cohen		*Year* 1997 After	
	£	*Remaining income £*	*Tax £*
Gross income 45,000 – 3260 – 3259.44		38,480.56	
Gross contribution to pension paid personally*			
Personal allowance	4045	34,435.56	Nil
Income taxed at 20%	4100	30,335.56	820
Income taxed at basic rate 23%	22,000	8335.56	5060
Income taxed at higher rate 40%	8335.56	Nil	3334.24
Total	38,480.56		9214.24
Less married couple's allowance 15% of £1830			274.50
Total tax payable			8939.74

* Some pension contributions paid personally are net of basic rate tax. For the purposes of this form this would need to be grossed up.

NATIONAL INSURANCE CONTRIBUTION (NIC) (Employed)			
	£	*Remaining income £*	*NIC £*
Gross income			
Income up to LEL £3224 p.a. NIC at 2%			
Income up to UEL £24,180 p.a. minus £3224 p.a., the LEL NIC at 10%			
Total			

NATIONAL INSURANCE CONTRIBUTION (NIC) (Self-employed)	
Flat rate paid if income over £3480 p.a. £6.15 p.w.	319.80
On profits between £7010 and £24,180 p.a. 6.0%	1030.20
Total	1350.00
Income after tax and NIC deductions 38,480.56 – 8939.74 – 1350 = 28,190.82	
Net spendable income 28,190 + 3260 = £31,451	

■ Form 5.6 INCOME TAX AND NIC ANALYSIS

INCOME TAX			
Name		*Year*	
	£	*Remaining income £*	*Tax £*
Gross income			
Gross contribution to pension paid personally*			
Personal allowance			
Income taxed at 20% Income taxed at basic rate 23% Income taxed at higher rate 40%			
Total			
Less married couple's allowance			
Total tax payable			

* Some pension contributions paid personally are net of basic rate tax. For the purposes of this form this would need to be grossed up.

NATIONAL INSURANCE CONTRIBUTION (NIC) (Employed)			
	£	*Remaining income £*	*NIC £*
Gross income			
Income up to LEL £3224 p.a. NIC at 2%			
Income up to UEL £24,180 p.a. minus £3224 p.a., the LEL NIC at 10%			
Total			
NATIONAL INSURANCE CONTRIBUTION (NIC) (Self-employed)			
Flat rate paid if income over £3480 p.a. £6.15 p.w.			
On profits between £7010 and £24,180 p.a. 6.0%			
Total			
Income after tax and NIC deductions			
Net spendable income			

■ Form 5.7 INCOME TAX AND NIC ANALYSIS

INCOME TAX			
Name		*Year*	
	£	*Remaining income £*	*Tax £*
Gross income			
Gross contribution to pension paid personally*			
Personal allowance			
Income taxed at 20% Income taxed at basic rate 23% Income taxed at higher rate 40%			
Total			
Less married couple's allowance			
Total tax payable			
* Some pension contributions paid personally are net of basic rate tax. For the purposes of this form this would need to be grossed up.			
NATIONAL INSURANCE CONTRIBUTION (NIC) (Employed)			
	£	*Remaining income £*	*NIC £*
Gross income			
Income up to LEL £3224 p.a. NIC at 2%			
Income up to UEL £24,180 p.a. minus £3224 p.a., the LEL NIC at 10%			
Total			
NATIONAL INSURANCE CONTRIBUTION (NIC) (Self-employed)			
Flat rate paid if income over £3480 p.a. £6.15 p.w.			
On profits between £7010 and £24,180 p.a. 6.0%			
Total			
Income after tax and NIC deductions			
Net spendable income			

There will be a slight adjustment this time because although Rachel will pay no income tax on remuneration of £3260 she will pay NIC of 2% of 3224 + 10% of 3,260 – 3224 = 64.48 + 3.60 = £68.08 and Jason will pay 3% of 3260 – 3224 = £1.08, a total between them of £69.16.

Hence net spendable income = 28,190.82 + 3260 – 69.16 = £31,382.

The total effect then is that their net spendable income reduces by £32,102 – £31,382 = £720 p.a. in return for an annual pension contribution of £3259.44 and an additional income of £13,065 p.a., free of all UK taxes, when Rachel is 60.

> ■ **Exercise 5.3**
>
> If you are in this sort of situation you may like to do your own calculations using Forms 5.6 and 5.7.

Commercial property

A sole trader in this age might also be considering the purchase of a property from which to run his or her business. Apart from the usual method of using a commercial loan which is exactly the same in principle as a mortgage, he or she now has the opportunity of this property being purchased by a self-invested pension scheme (SIPP). Details of the SIPP are discussed later in this chapter.

Loan cover

If money has been borrowed for business purposes whether by way of a term loan or an overdraft, most lenders will insist on an assigned life assurance policy, to pay off the loan on death. Even if this is not requested it would, anyway, be wise that such a loan is covered by a life assurance and also a critical illness policy.

Cover for potential redundancy dues

If a business ceases because of the death or critical illness of the owner redundancy payments would be due to eligible employees. It would be wise to calculate this potential liability and also cover this with life assurance and critical illness cover. Details on redundancy can be found in Chapter 2.

The key person

There may be one or more employees who could be considered to be key to the profitability of the business such that if they could not function profit would reduce seriously. This situation can also be covered by life assurance and critical illness assurance, so that, for example, if a key person were to die the life assurance would pay out and funnel money into the business to make up for the potential loss of profit. The key person's status usually satisfies the requirement for an 'insurable interest', providing the sum assured is reasonable with respect to his or her value to the business, and so the policies could be owned by the business and written under a life of another trust enabling the business to pay the premiums and to receive the benefits. Receipt of the policy proceeds on the death or disability of the key person will not usually give rise to a tax liability since any amount received by way of death benefit is mortality profit which is not considered a gain for tax purposes, also receipt of the sum assured in the case of a critical illness policy is free of tax.

> **The death or medical inability of a key person could seriously affect the profitability of a business.**

However, a question does arise as to whether the premiums are tax deductible as a business expense as the policy is a business asset. Principles stated in 1944 by the then Chancellor of the Exchequer, Sir John Anderson, made the premiums tax deductible provided,

- the policy is a short-term assurance, usually with a term not more than five years
- the insurance is intended to meet the loss of profit resulting from the employee's death
- the sole relationship between the policy holder and the life assured is that of employer and employee.

However, what is important is that if premiums are tax deductible then the benefit is taxed as a business receipt, which is clearly to be avoided if possible. It would therefore be important to make sure that the premiums were not tax deductible by making the term of the policy longer than five years, in which case the proceeds are usually free of tax.

> **It is important that the term of a key person policy is more than five years.**

It would always be wise to clarify any particular situation with the local tax inspector.

Sale of business

What about selling the business or purchasing another business in order to expand? The price will ultimately depend on what a buyer is willing to pay. However, some idea of value can be calculated by looking at various factors:

1 Before tax profit record. Is it consistent or does it fluctuate? Has it been steadily increasing? If the business were sold and continued in the same way how long realistically would it take the purchaser to recoup his or her money?
2 The value of the assets.
3 Is there a wide range of clients or does the profit depend mostly on one or two? Clearly in this case a purchase could be risky as the loss of only one of those clients could cause a severe drop in profit. If there is a close relationship between clients and vendor this could increase the vulnerability of the purchaser who may not appeal to those clients in the same way.

4 How long after purchase would the vendor be willing to continue working in the business?

Valuing a business is an extremely complex and difficult process and especially so for a sole tradership. A more detailed discussion is to be found later in this chapter.

A purchaser could potentially pay stamp duty on top of the purchase price. It would be wise to consider this carefully and work through the discussion on it appearing later in this chapter.

Valuing a business is an extremely complex and difficult process.

What about the tax implications? On sale, a capital gain will usually have been made, so what is the tax liability? Certain reliefs such as business retirement relief, indexation and personal allowance of capital gains tax (CGT) could be available. A discussion of CGT is given later in this chapter.

In the case of a large capital gain the sole trader may wish to consider some offshore planning to avoid tax. He or she would need to be non-UK resident when the business is sold or if a UK resident to have set up various suitable offshore instruments. These topics are discussed more fully later in the chapter.

■ Example 5.3

Reena Solanki purchased her business in July 1986 for £100,000 and, after enormous success, at the age of 52, is about to sell it in July 1997 for £10 million.

Increase in RPI	= 61.54%
Revised value of purchase	= £100,000 + £100,000 × 61.54/100
	= £100,000 + 61,540 = £161,540
Capital gain	= £10 million – £161,540
	= £9,838,460
Personal allowance	= £6500
Effective gain	= 9,838,460 – 6500 = £9,831,960

Because she has run the business for 10 years or more and is over 50 she can claim business retirement relief (BRR)

Tax on first £250,000	= Nil
Tax on next £750,000	= 20% of £750,000
	= 750,000 × 20/100 = £150,000
Tax on remaining £8,831,960	= 40% of £8,831,960
	= 8,831,960 × 40/100 = £3,532,784
Total tax	= £3,682,784

Reena might wish to consider some offshore arrangements.

Transfer of business

What about the question of passing the business on to one's children? If the transfer took place during life there would be no liability to capital gains tax because hold-over relief would apply (see later in this chapter). However, the question of transfer tax or inheritance tax still remains and it would be wise to work through the detail of this in Chapter 6. In the fiscal year 1997/98 there was no transfer tax liability on the transfer of a private business.

> **There is no transfer tax or IHT liability on the transfer of a private business.**

If the business passes on death then capital gain is totally rebased or, in other words, wiped out. Furthermore, there is no IHT on a private business currently.

Staff benefits

■ Permanent health insurance

The sole trader in this age will probably have staff. What happens if one of them becomes medically unable to work? What a dilemma! Does he or she go on paying the salary or does he or she, as is more usual, stop after six months. This is a real moral responsibility: just imagine lying awake at night thinking of a member of staff with not enough properly to live on.

The answer could be group permanent health insurance. The benefit would be received by the sole trader as a taxable business receipt but he or she would obtain tax relief on it when paid out as salary and possibly pension contributions. The employee would, of course, pay income tax and NIC on the benefit. As discussed in Chapter 2, 75 per cent of income less the long-term incapacity benefit of £3247.40 per annum can usually be insured plus, if needed, a further amount for pension payments and sometimes NIC payments. Price, of course, will depend on numbers, sex and age.

> **The group PHI net pay scheme can be very beneficial for employees.**

Some idea could be gained by looking at the tables in Chapter 2, totting up the premiums and then in the case of larger numbers of staff taking off 15 to 20 per cent, the sort of discount which is often possible for group schemes. Premiums for group schemes are often calculated on an annual basis in which case unless they are balanced by a changing employee population could steadily increase.

Some insurance companies offer a net pay scheme where the employee will be insured in such a way that the net return from state benefits plus the company policy will result in him or her, receiving up to 90 per cent of his or her net pay before the disabling event. The benefit, paid gross to the employer, is a business receipt in his or her hands but since it is paid out to the employee no tax is paid. It goes through the gross pay scheme ending up in the employee's hands net of tax and NIC. No further tax is paid by the employee.

■ Critical illness cover

It is also possible for an employer to take out a group critical illness policy for the benefit of his or her employees. Once again premiums are likely to be discounted for larger numbers in the scheme. The benefit is totally tax free in the hands of the employee, although the premiums paid by the employer are treated as a P11D benefit for the employee.

■ Medical insurance

Group medical insurance policies can also be arranged for employees subject to the same tax treatment as group critical illness policies.

On all these staff benefit schemes the employer will generally receive tax relief on the premiums, although this should always be clarified with the local tax inspector.

Most insurance companies will allow a measure of free cover on these schemes, which means that up to a certain benefit level no medical evidence would be required, although pre-existing conditions would be excluded.

■ Pension scheme for employees

The sole trader is able to set up a company pension scheme for his or her employees if he or she so wishes. This could be either an occupational scheme or a group personal pension scheme. It is unlikely he or she would want to embark on a defined benefit scheme because of the long-term guarantees he or she would have to give, which could lead to considerably more expense than initially envisaged. Hence if it were occupational it would be likely to be money purchase. As we saw in Chapter 2, employees could contract out of SERPS through this if they wished. However, because of ease of administration the employer would be much more likely to run a group personal pension scheme into which he or she could make contributions if he or she so wished. Even if no contribution were made by the employer such a scheme would be much more advantageous to the employees than if they were simply making contributions to their own personal pension. This advantage would be obtained by effecting the contribution through 'salary sacrifice', done by the employee 'sacrificing' part of his or her gross income which would then be paid into his or her PPS by the employer.

■ Example 5.4

Walter Redding gives up £100 a month gross from his salary in order that his employer should pay it into his pension. Walter is a basic rate taxpayer. If Walter took the £100 in salary the position would be as follows,

	£100 gross	
Tax		£23
NIC		£10
	£67 net	

Thus Walter would receive £67 net. If the £100 is put into the pension by the employer instead of paying it in salary Walter has given up £67 net and received £100 investment in his pension. Hence £100 investment has cost him £67. His investment has grown immediately by £33,

$$\frac{33}{67} \times 100\% = 49.25\%$$

Had he simply wanted to get £100 into his own PPS by a personal investment this would have cost £77 using premium relief at source (PRAS).

This time his investment would have grown by £23,

$$\frac{23}{77} \times 100\% = 29.87\%$$

When an employer pays £100 salary to an employee he or she also has to pay 10% national insurance contribution, fiscal year 1997/98 (see Chapter 2). To pay £100 into a PPS the employer pays no NIC. It would therefore cost the employer nothing to donate the £10 to Walter's pension.

Now Walter gets an investment of £110 for a cost of £67, an increase of £43 on his investment of £67,

$$\frac{43}{67} \times 100\% = 64.18\%$$

By using 'salary sacrifice' it is possible to make an initial gain on all pension premiums of 64.18 per cent.

An employer could enhance an employee's pension investment at no cost whatsoever to himself or herself by using this method. This could rightly be called the 'no cost company pension' for his or her employees. However, he or she might also wish to make additional contributions.

There are two possible disadvantages to the salary sacrifice system.

1 If salary is reduced then NIC is reduced and hence SERPS or contracted out PPS contributions are reduced. Let us assume Walter is 27 and is contracted out through his PPS. Using Table 2.22 the nearest age is 25. Walter and his employer between them have contributed £20 a month less to NIC. Hence 3.9 per cent of £20 less has been contributed to Walter's contracted out PPS, i.e.

$$\frac{3.9}{100} \times 20 = 78 \text{ pence}$$

This is clearly negligible in view of the enormous advantage.

2 If salary is sacrificed then net relevant earnings (NRE) is decreased and therefore pension contribution eligibility is decreased. Assuming Walter earns £14,000 per annum then at 27 he could invest a maximum of 17½ per cent of £14,000 = 17½/100 × 14,000 = £2450 per annum gross into his PPS.

If his annual income is reduced by £1200 by salary sacrifice his maximum investment is 17½ per cent of £12,800 = £2240 per annum gross.

The enormous investment advantages of salary sacrifice will have to be balanced against reduction in maximum contribution which would always refer to total contribution by whatever route it reaches the PPS, employer or employee, or both.

As we saw in Chapter 2, the employees could contract out of SERPS through a PPS if they so wished. It is also important to note that unless an employee is making a personal contribution (i.e. other than a salary sacrifice) to the Group Personal Pension Scheme, neither carry-forward nor carry-back can be used.

THE PARTNER IN A PARTNERSHIP

Unlike a limited company no formal agreement is needed to form a partnership. It is defined by the Partnership Act 1890 as 'two or more people working together in the same business with a view to profit'. Unless a partnership has instigated its own 'partnership agreement or deed' it is still governed by that act which says for example that all partners are equal and therefore own an equal share of the partnership and hence the profits.

The whole crux of a partnership is that each partner is jointly and severally responsible, which means that any action taken by an individual partner involves all the other partners in responsibility for it. For example if one partner decides to run up debts against the partnership all are responsible. It is clear, then, that a partnership is not lightly to be entered into and adequate checks and balances must be in place. This will usually be done by a partnership agreement or deed which would supersede the 1890 Partnership Act.

Everything which has been said so far will apply to a partner. Even purchase of property by a SIPP can be done as it is possible for each separate SIPP to own part of the property and be responsible for part of the loan. There is no longer the problem of one of the partners retiring considerably earlier than the others and the property having to be sold in order for him or her to receive his or her pension by way of an annuity. The income withdrawal facility treated in Chapter 6 can delay this until the partner is 75 which is usually ample time for the other partners to reach pension age or a suitable time for the sale of a property to arise. There would, however, be a problem if a partner died before taking his or her pension or deferred annuity payments, as in this situation his or her share of the investments would have to be paid to his or her dependants and this could make it necessary to sell the property at a time when the market may make it undesirable, thus affecting the other partners as well as his or her dependants.

No formal agreement is needed to set up a partnership but it is wise not to enter it lightly and to set up a partnership deed early in its life.

One important modification of what has so far been discussed arises in the case of permanent health insurance where it is crucial that the partnership agreement

---

The partnership agreement must take account of any permanent health assurance arrangement.

---

provides, in the event of a partner needing to call upon his or her policy, for a corresponding cancellation or reduction in that partner's share of profits for the period of absence. If this is not done then the Partnership Act 1890 will provide for that partner to continue to take his or her share of the profits, thus cancelling the benefit which otherwise would have been paid and putting a burden on the other partners.

Death of a partner

Like any other business a partnership, over the years, will build up a value just as we saw in the case of the sole trader. What happens if one of the partners dies?

If there is no partnership agreement to say differently, that partner's dependants will be entitled to his or her share of the value of the partnership and, if necessary, the partnership will have to be sold in order to pay that share. A drastic situation!

■ Example 5.5

Peter Brant and John Masters have a successful partnership. It has been running now for five years, is well established making before-tax profits of £160,000. They have a good relationship with their bank and have an overdraft of £50,000. They and their bank manager feel the business must be worth at least £500,000. They sell electrical equipment to companies, John being the technical expert and Peter doing the marketing and sales.

On the way back from a meeting to negotiate a large contract, Peter is killed in a car accident. Peter's wife, Anne, is devastated, as is John.

The death of a partner may lead to loss of confidence in the business by the bank and customers.

John wonders what he will do. Peter had all the contacts, who were all used to dealing with him, but who hardly knew John. Selling is definitely not John's forte. Will he try to employ a good salesman? He rings the company Peter was dealing with and senses reluctance to close the deal, asking if he will be able to continue.

Next day the bank manager rings and reluctantly, in the circumstances, calls in the overdraft.

Anne feels that financially she will be fine because, in addition to their personal financial planning arrangements, Peter has always told her they owned half of a business worth £500,000.

Her solicitor asks her whether there was a partnership agreement because he had no knowledge of one. She rings John and is told there is no such document but, obviously, she will be looked after.

John begins to wonder how he will look after Anne and her children. He can already see it is going to be difficult to survive, apart from paying Anne an income.

The next day Anne rings and, although friendly, tells John her solicitor has said that in law she is entitled to half the value of the business. John cannot help telling her some of his problems. They are overwhelming him. She suggests perhaps the business could borrow £250,000 to pay her. John goes to see his bank manager who tells him the business is no longer truly a going concern and the asset value, stock and a couple of vans, are worth about £80,000. There is no way the bank could advance a loan.

John approaches his biggest competitor and asks if he would buy the business. The competitor knows all the contacts were Peter's so he would only be buying John's technical expertise. He declines but offers John a job.

The end result of this lack of financial planning is that Anne and John have £40,000 each and no business. If the business is terminated in this way redundancy payments will also be due to any employees there may be which would further reduce the cash that Anne and John could expect to receive.

If only they had written a partnership agreement. But even that would not have solved this particular problem. Peter and John would have both wanted Anne to be taken care of financially, as they would John's wife and children in a similar situation. A partnership agreement could have made it possible for Anne simply to own half the business and avoid forcing its sale, but this would not actually have solved anything as she has no expertise which would help this particular situation. No, the only solution is a partnership protection plan.

The partnership protection plan

This plan solves the problem of the disaster which could follow from the death of a partner.

It is designed to put the right amount of money in the right hands at the right time and to ensure that none of the instruments used should in any way prejudice the solution of the problem.

> The partnership protection plan puts the right amount of money in the right hands at the right time.

The right amount of money will be the true value of the partner's share of the partnership valued as a going concern, in other words just before the event of death.

Valuation of a business is treated in some detail later in this chapter. There will, however, be aspects to consider in calculating the value of partner's share which are specific to partnerships:

- the amount standing to the credit of his or her current account and loan account.
- his or her proportionate share of the profit or loss made in the accounting period up to his or her death.
- any repayments made to him or her, or drawings taken by him or her.

This 'value' will have to be calculated, as accurately as possible at the time of death, by an independent expert appointed at the instigation of the plan and recorded in the 'cross-option agreement', the legal document we shall discuss later.

Each partner would then take out life insurance to the value of his or her share of the partnership which would be put in trust for his or her fellow partners, thus ensuring that the money would go into the right hands at the right time, which would be in the event of the death of the partner (see Fig. 5.3).

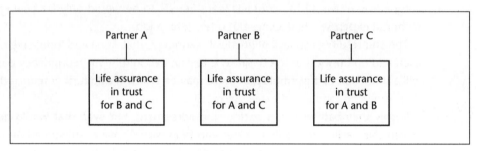

Fig. 5.3 Life assurance in trust for other partners

There will also have to be an estimate of this 'value' at the instigation of the arrangement in order to set the life assurance policies at the right level. It will be extremely important to review this regularly in the light of the potential changing value of the partnership due to its success or failure and inflation. It is not suggested that the expense of a professional valuation would be incurred at this point but rather that accountant's advice and partners' own feelings should produce a sensible value, hopefully as near to fact as possible.

On the death of a partner the money which goes tax free to the remaining partners is used to buy from the deceased partner's dependants his or her share of the partnership. The dependants are satisfied because they have the true value of their share of the partnership and the remaining partners are satisfied because they now own the whole of the partnership.

Including critical illness

Should a partner suffer a critical illness and be unable to fulfill his or her full responsibilities in the partnership a very similar situation will have arisen. It could also be very valuable to cater for this contingency in the partnership protection plan.

In the case of critical illness, a policy is also settled by each partner and written in trust for the others with exactly the same sort of trust. The partners will decide at outset whether moving from this policy is to be subject to the same sort of cross-option agreement or whether in this case it will be the single option of the partner suffering the critical illness.

A more detailed treatment of partnership protection plans will be found later in the chapter.

Reading back through the particular problems that John experienced as a result of Peter's death it is very clear that it would have been very wise to have had key person policies covering both death and critical illness on both partners' lives, which, in this case, would have given John the money to tide him over the various traumatic events which occurred and enabled him to keep the business going and eventually to have made it a success again. It is wise not to lose sight of this aspect when considering a partnership protection plan.

THE SHAREHOLDING DIRECTOR OF A CLOSE COMPANY OR PRIVATE LIMITED COMPANY

A 'close company' is a company under the control of up to five people, or under the control of its directors. A person controls a company if he or she is able to exercise control directly or indirectly over its affairs by owning the greater part of its share capital, voting capital or other capital giving entitlement to more than half the assets on winding up. Most shareholding directors in such a company will have a measure of control over the financial planning of the company.

> **The private limited company is an entity separate from the shareholders who own it.**

This private limited company is an entity separate from the shareholders who own it. Hence any liability is that of the company and not of the directors. It is therefore limited by the resources of the company. The only liability of a shareholding director is to the limited company for any amounts that remain unpaid on any shares he or she holds.

It is the company, not the company's owners, which runs the business. If the business fails the company will fail, but not the shareholders who lose only the value of their shares.

Unlike the sole tradership and partnership which need no formal setting up, a company must be registered which involves the submission of a number of key documents.

Memorandum of association

The memorandum of association acts as the company's charter and enables persons who invest in, or deal with it to establish such facts as,

- its name
- what its objectives are
- the location of its registered office
- the amount of its share capital and how it is divided, e.g. £1000 divided into 1000 shares of £1 each.

Articles of association

The articles of association regulate its internal affairs dealing with such matters as,

- issue and transfer of shares
- alteration of share capital
- holding of meetings and voting rights
- directors' appointments and retirements
- appointment of a company secretary
- declaration of dividends
- accounts
- auditing
- winding up.

Once the business is incorporated or becomes limited it is issued with a certificate of incorporation. The company pays its employees, among which are the shareholding directors, a regular income, possibly the occasional bonus and benefits in kind such as a company car. All of these are taxed under Schedule E and both the employee and employer, the limited company, pay Class 1 national insurance contributions (NIC) on them. The company can also declare dividends to be paid on the shares. These attract income tax but are not liable to NIC.

Corporation tax

The company pays corporation tax on its profits. In the fiscal year 1997/98 this tax was 21 per cent for smaller companies rate on profits up to £300,000 and full rate of 31 per cent for profits of £1,500,000 and more. For profits between these limits a marginal rate of tax is charged.

The way this works is best illustrated by an example.

■ Example 5.6

Equipment Hire Ltd makes profits in its current financial year of £400,000.

Tax at full rate on £400,000 = 31% of £400,000,

$$\frac{31}{100} \times £400,000 = £124,000$$

$$- \frac{1}{40} \times (1,500,000 - 400,000) =$$

$$\frac{1}{40} \times 1,100,000 = £27,500$$

Tax charged = £124,000 − £27,500 = £96,500

■ Example 5.7

Western Airfreight Ltd makes before tax profits of £700,000 in the current financial year.

Tax at full rate on £700,000 = 31% of £700,000,

$$\frac{31}{100} \times £700,000 = £217,000$$

$$-\frac{1}{40} \times (1,500,000 - 700,000) =$$

$$\frac{1}{40} \times 800,000 = £20,000$$

Tax charged = £217,000 − £20,000 = £197,000

The differences in Examples 5.6 and 5.7 illustrate the marginal tax rate, i.e. the actual rate of tax on profit between £300,000 and £1,500,000.

Difference in profit = 700,000 − 400,000 = £300,000

This £300,000 lies in the marginal rate band.

Difference in tax = 197,000 − 96,500 = £100,500

Hence tax on the 300,000 difference = £100,500. A tax rate of

$$\frac{100,500}{300,000} \times 100\% = 33.5\%.$$

Clearly if profits are only marginally over the £300,000 mark it is important to try to bring them down to £300,000 to avoid these higher marginal rates. Although we take a jump in tax rate to 33.5% on entering the marginal rate, the effect on the overall tax rate is to increase it gradually from 21% to 31%, for example overall rate on a profit of £400,000 is,

$$\frac{96,500}{400,000} \times 100\% = 24.1\%$$

Overall rate on a profit of £700,000 is,

$$\frac{197,000}{700,000} \times 100\% = 28.1\%.$$

Thus overall corporation tax rate in the fiscal year 1997/98 will never be above 31 per cent. Salaries paid to employees will be treated as a business expense and therefore not subject to corporation tax but income tax will be paid by the employees. Thus, although profits can be retained in a company after a maximum overall tax rate of 31 per cent, which is lower than the higher

Corporation tax in the fiscal year 1997/98 will never be above 31 per cent.

rate of tax for sole traderships or partnerships, the retained profit can only be got into the hands of the employees by paying further tax. This is a consequence of the private limited company being a separate entity. Thus very careful consideration has to be given to profits at the end of the company year. Apart from regular remuneration paid to employees throughout the year a bonus can be paid or dividends declared. A certain amount of profits retained in a company could increase the value and, on eventual sale, come out with no further tax payable because of allowances such as business retirement relief, treated later in the chapter.

The company pension scheme, also treated later in this chapter, is fully tax relievable against company profits and is not only essential for company directors but has the added advantage of effectively dealing with marginal rates, although this should be considered as a valuable side effect and not a reason in itself for investing in a company pension scheme.

■ Example 5.8

Abim Muomah's private limited company makes a profit of £350,000. The marginal rate of tax on the top £50,000 will be paid at 33.5%, i.e.

$$\frac{33.5}{100} \times 50,000 = £16,750$$

Luckily Abim has decided to set up a company pension for himself at £50,000 p.a. This will mean tax relief of £16,750 hence the net cost of this premium will be only £50,000 − £16,750 = £33,250. It is important to note here that a pension contribution must be paid by the end of the financial year to obtain tax relief for it in that financial year. There is no facility for the approved company pension scheme such as carry back, which is applicable to the personal pension scheme (PPS).

Dividends on shares

A company can pay its shareholders dividends and although these will be taxed as income no NIC will be paid on their receipt. If a company declares dividends then these dividends are paid on the shares of all the shareholders.

■ Example 5.9

Sharon Porter has made profits in her company such that £50,000 can be taken out for her own use. Using Form 5.8 she compares all salary against part in dividends.

She then looks at a salary of £10,000 and a dividend of £40,000. The income tax will, of course, be exactly the same. Let us look at NIC.

We see that her net spendable income has increased by £35,436 − 34,018 = £1418.

What about the company NIC? Referring to Table 2.6 (p. 52),

■ Form 5.8 INCOME TAX AND NIC ANALYSIS

INCOME TAX			
Name Sharon Porter		*Year* 1997	
	£	*Remaining income £*	*Tax £*
Gross income	50,000 salary		
Gross contribution to pension paid personally*			
Personal allowance	4045	45,955	Nil
Income taxed at 20%	4100	41,855	820
Income taxed at basic rate 23%	22,000	19,855	3060
Income taxed at higher rate 40%	19,855		7942
Total			13,822
Less married couple's allowance			
Total tax payable			

* Some pension contributions paid personally are net of basic rate tax. For the purposes of this form this would need to be grossed up.

NATIONAL INSURANCE CONTRIBUTION (NIC) (Employed)			
	£	*Remaining income £*	*NIC £*
Gross income	50,000 salary		
Income up to LEL £3224 p.a. NIC at 2%	3224	46,776	64.48
Income up to UEL £24,180 p.a. minus £3224 p.a., the LEL NIC at 10%	20,956	25,820	2095.60
Total			2160.08

NATIONAL INSURANCE CONTRIBUTION (NIC) (Self-employed)	
Flat rate paid if income over £3480 p.a. £6.15 p.w.	
On profits between £7010 and £24,180 p.a. 6.0%	
Total	
Income after tax and NIC deductions	50,000 – 13,822 – 2160.08 = 34,018
Net spendable income	£34,018

■ **Form 5.9 NATIONAL INSURANCE CONTRIBUTION (NIC) (Employed)**

	£	Remaining income £	Tax £
Gross income	10,000 salary		
Income up to LEL £3224 p.a. NIC at 2%	3224	6776	64.48
Income up to UEL £24,180 p.a. minus £3224 p.a., the LEL NIC at 10%	6776	Nil	667.60
Total			742.08
NATIONAL INSURANCE CONTRIBUTION (NIC) (Self-employed)			
Flat rate paid if income over £3480 p.a. £6.15 p.w.			
On profits between £7010 and £24,180 p.a. 6.0%			
Total			
Income after tax and NIC deductions	50,000 – 13,822 – 742.08 = 35,436		
Net spendable income	£35,436		

		Salary £50,000	Salary £10,000
		NIC	
Slice of salary			
£3224 – 3720	3%	74.88	74.88
£3720 – 8060	5%	217.00	217.00
£8060 – 10,920	7%	200.20	135.80
£10,920 on	10%	3900.00	
Total		4392.08	427.68

There is a difference of £4392.08 – 427.68 = £3964.40. Hence the total NIC saved is £3964.40 + £1418 = £5382.40.

___

Paying dividends instead of salary reduces NIC payments. However this reduces net relevant earnings for the purposes of pension investment.

As usual advantages carry concomitant disadvantages. Dividends do not count as net relevant earnings for the purposes of pension contributions. This could have a serious effect on eventual financial independence. Also some trouble could be encountered in negotiating a mortgage against dividends but lenders will usually accept the full amount if company accounts show them to be regular. It is sometimes difficult to base permanent health insurance benefits against dividends in the case of companies with more than one shareholding director since in the event of a director becoming medically unable to work other directors will still want dividends to be declared. Since if a dividend is declared it will apply to all shareholders this would mean that the director medically unable to work would still be in receipt of an income and therefore unable to collect that part of the benefit equal to the income. Many insurance companies will not provide PHI in these circumstances because of the ensuing difficulties.

Advanced corporation tax (ACT)

Those in receipt of share dividends will pay tax as described in Chapter 1. The company will pay advanced corporation tax on the dividends at 20 per cent of the gross dividend. As its name suggests ACT is treated as an advance payment of corporation tax and can be deducted from mainstream corporation tax liability payable on the profits for the accounting period in which the dividends have been paid. The company must submit a return to the Inland Revenue concerning dividends on a quarterly basis and ACT is payable 14 days after the end of the relevant quarter.

Since the shareholding directors can, within the prevailing legal restraints, decide exactly what the company will do in all aspects, they could decide to pay income up to a level which attracts no NIC payments personally or by the company, i.e. £3224 in the fiscal year 1997/98, and pay all other remuneration in the form of dividends which will attract tax but no NIC payments. A balance between the advantages and the disadvantages described will have to be reached. As we have seen before the practice of financial planning is the art of compromise.

The practice of financial planning is the art of compromise.

Timing of tax payments

The close company will choose an accounting period or financial year. Accounts will be made up for that period and corporation tax is automatically due nine months and one day from the end of that accounting period. Employees' remuneration can be deducted from the profits of the company even though it is not paid and is not taxable income of the individual until it is paid. Provided the remuneration is actually paid within nine months of the company's year end, the company is normally entitled to a deduction from its profits. These delays in payment can be valuable and contrast favourably with ACT which has to be paid within 14 days after the relevant period.

■ Example 5.10

Hygienic Cleaners Ltd has a financial year end 31 December. Income of £50,000 for director A is deducted from the profits of the company for the year ending 31 December 1997. It is not, however, paid until 30 September 1998, although the corporation tax is reduced for the year 1997. The corporation tax is paid on 1 October 1998. This allows a degree of flexibility which could be valuable. For example the funds to pay director A may not be available in 1997 but from the corporation tax point of view they can be deemed to be paid in that year and the relevant pension contributions made against them before 31 December 1997.

A sole trader or partnership also has an accounting period. Accounts are made up for that period and paid in two instalments, one on 31 January falling in the tax year within which the end of the accounting period falls and one on 31 July following. Thus a sole trader having an accounting period ending on 30 April will pay half his tax for the accounting period ending on 30 April 1997 on 31 January 1998 and half on 31 July 1998. This is even more advantageous since half the tax can be delayed up to 9 months and the other half up to 13 months.

In this case there is no question of delaying the payment of remuneration but by the use of carry back (Chapter 2), a pension payment to be set against profit made in the accounting period to 30 April 1997 can be made as late as 5 April 1999.

Treatment of spouse's earnings

The shareholding director can arrange for the company to pay his or her spouse an income in return for duties performed in exactly the same way as the sole trader and an approved company pension can be funded for him or her. However, although it is most rare for the Inland Revenue to dispute the level of profits allocated to a spouse in an unincorporated business, in the case of limited companies a spouse's remuneration is regularly argued as being excessive and not to be allowed in computing profit.

Potential double charge for CGT

A company is assessed for capital gains in exactly the same way as an individual but actually pays corporation tax on the gain. Details of CGT are treated later in this chapter.

■ Example 5.11

A company acquires a commercial property for £150,000 and five years later sells it for £300,000. Suppose the gain to the company after indexation is £120,000, the company will pay corporation tax on this gain. Assuming it pays small companies rate it will pay 21% of £120,000 = £25,200. The profit in the company due to this sale is £150,000. Tax of £25,200 has been paid so the net retained profit is £124,800.

Supposing that two years later the company is sold. The directors will have a personal capital gains tax liability. Part of that gain will come from the earlier retained profit of £124,800. Tax will now be paid again on this at 40%, i.e.

$$\frac{40}{100} \times 124,800 = £49,920$$

Thus there has been a double taxation on the gain in the property value ending up with a tax bill of £25,200 + £49,920 = £75,120 on a gain of £150,000:

$$\frac{75,120}{150,000} \times 100\% = 50.1\%$$

Double taxation could produce overall tax rates of 50.1 per cent or more.

All the financial aspects described in the earlier sectors of this chapter will also apply to the shareholding director of a limited company.

In the case of group PHI, critical illness and medical insurance because the shareholding director is also an employee he or she can be a member of any of these schemes. Because he or she has a measure of control over the company and in the case of PHI and critical illness would be able to boost his or her benefit relative to the other employees, if he or she does this, there could be questions arising on the tax treatment of the premiums paid by the employer. It would be wise to seek clarification on these points from the local tax inspector.

Death of a shareholding director

On death or critical illness of a shareholding director, considerable problems could arise with respect to shares. Although these are similar in principle they are different in detail from those following the death or critical illness of a partner.

As we have said, such a director has shares in a legal entity completely separate from the directors themselves and as such are usually left, in his will, to his dependants. The dependants, normally having very little connection with the company, will wish to realise their value. The problem arises because, although the shares of a close company are relatively easier to sell than other forms of private business, they are still usually difficult to sell. The smaller the proportion of the total shares the more difficult and, in the case of 25 per cent or less, unless the company plans to float, practically impossible.

Twenty-five per cent or less of a close company will be almost impossible to sell.

The corresponding difficulties of the remaining shareholding directors will also vary with respect to the proportion of shares passed to the dependants of the deceased director. The beneficiaries may, knowing nothing of the company, end up with considerable control over it. Hence the proportion of shares held is crucial. A majority shareholding gives day-to-day control over the company. Thus any holding over 50 per cent puts the owner or owners in a position of power.

■ Example 5.12

Valerie Partridge dies leaving 51% of the shares of a very successful limited company to her husband, Christopher, who knows only what Valerie has told him about the company. However, the Partridges have enjoyed a comfortable lifestyle provided by the company and Christopher expects this to continue. The other two minority shareholders, although performing useful roles in the business, can in no way replace the driving force that Valerie represented. The bank calls in loans advanced to the company and several customers leave. At the first directors' meeting Christopher is told by the others he can no longer expect an income in any way equal to what was received before Valerie's death. They feel, to weather the storm, economies in this area will have to be made since Christopher is putting nothing into the company. Christopher, having day-to-day control, overrides the others and accepts only a small reduction in income. He also insists on other changes being made, assuming his conversations with Valerie have given him certain insights about what needs doing. Things go from bad to worse as Christopher continues this regime. More customers are lost and a key employee leaves.

Eventually, seeing that things are not going to work in this way, he decides to cut his losses and sell for whatever he can get. One of the minority shareholders disagrees with Christopher's decision, but he decides to go ahead and sell anyway thinking he has total control. However, he is told by his accountant that because the minority shareholder owns more than 25% of the shares he can block the sale. It is not long before the company deteriorates further and becomes unprofitable. More customers are lost and the situation becomes irretrievable.

It is clear that, although the situation has differences from the partnership scene, the death or critical illness of a controlling director could cause enormous problems.

The share protection plan

The solution is exactly the same as the partnership protection plan but is usually called something like a share protection plan. All aspects of policies written in flexible trusts, the cross-option agreement and valuation of the business will be the same. These topics are all treated in some detail later in the chapter.

The crucial difference is that the value of a certain proportion of the shares will not be that proportion of the total value of the company.

Thus a 20 per cent shareholding of a company whose total value is £500,000 will not be $20/100 \times 500,000 = £100,000$, but considerably less.

A rough guideline is shown below.

Table 5.2 The value of shares in a company

Percentage shareholding	Percentage of whole company value
25 or less	0–10
greater than 25 & less than 50	15–35
50	35–45*
greater than 50 & less than 75	55–65
75–100	75–100

* this will depend on how many other minority shareholders there are.

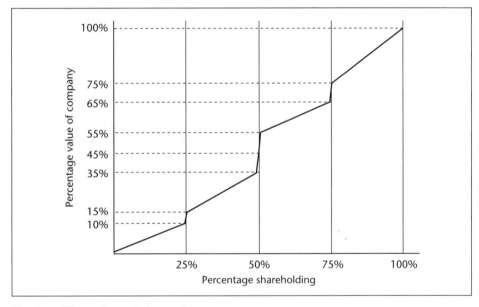

Fig. 5.4 The value of shares in a company

The reasons for this are:

1 A shareholder with 75 per cent or more of a company's voting shares has total control of the company and can effectively do what he or she likes. He or she can elect members to the board without reference to other shareholders and even sell the company.

2 It follows that anyone with 25 per cent or less of the voting shares can be totally ignored from the point of view of decision making.

3 With more than 25 per cent of the voting shares major decisions can be blocked.

4 More than 50 per cent of the voting shares gives day-to-day control of the company including the decision to declare a dividend or pay a salary to a shareholder.

5 Fifty per cent is problematic. If there is only one other shareholder an impasse could arise. These two directors have to agree all the time on any decisions affecting the company. If there are several other shareholders it is unlikely that in the day-to-day running of the company they will all vote against the 50 per cent shareholder.

These differences give rise to different problems arising on the death or critical illness of a shareholder, depending on different configurations of shareholding. These reduce to three main situations, as can be seen in Example 5.13.

■ Example 5.13

Leslie Waters, Yvonne Marchand and Frank Caine own Fetterlane Nurseries Ltd between them. Leslie Waters dies leaving his wife Penelope his shares.

Case 1: All are minority shareholders, e.g. Leslie 35%, Yvonne 30%, Frank 35%

Penelope's problems
- Loss of Leslie's income
- No job
- No dividends
- No power
- Cannot demand salary or dividends
- No buyer for shares
- Decreased value as minority shareholding
- Knows nothing about company
- No company financial planning done
- No knowledge of business

Yvonne's and Frank's problems
- Loss of Leslie, a key person
- Some loss of confidence in company
- No cash to look after widow
- Cost of borrowing too high and difficult anyway
- Cannot afford salary for person not contributing to company
- Widow, in desperation, brings pressure to bear
- Widow could block major decisions
- Widow might just be able to sell to a competitor

Case 2: A two shareholder company, i.e. Leslie 50%, Yvonne 50%

Penelope's problems
- The same as in Case 1 plus
- Can block all Yvonne's decisions causing stalemate and drastic deterioration of company

Yvonne's problems
- The same as in Case 1 plus
- Has to get widow's agreement to every decision
- Widow knows nothing of business but is in a desperate situation
- Would possibly have to work with widow's new husband if she remarried

Case 3: Majority plus minority shareholder, e.g. Leslie 60%, Yvonne 40%

Penelope's problems
- Loss of Leslie's income but she can declare dividends
- She could insist on an income
- However, totally dependent on Yvonne's knowledge of business in general and the company in particular
- Yvonne could demand more from company because of Penelope's dependence
- A better chance of selling but still very difficult
- Sale of whole company could be blocked by Yvonne

Yvonne's problems
- Same as in Cases 1 and 2
- Greater loss of confidence in company as Leslie was known to be in day-to-day control

Case 4: Majority plus minority shareholder, e.g. Leslie 80%, Yvonne 20%

Penelope's problems
- Penelope can do anything she likes with the company but knows absolutely nothing about it
- Yvonne could leave and set up as a competitor
- Yvonne could demand a much better package

Yvonne's problems
- Yvonne's shares are almost worthless
- Almost totally impossible to sell them and, if she could, how much would she get?
- Has no power whatsoever
- Working for someone who knows nothing about the company
- No security whatsoever

Case 5: Minority plus majority shareholder, e.g. Leslie 20%, Yvonne 80%

In this case Penelope is in a totally hopeless position. Yvonne can totally ignore her.

It is crucially important when considering the share protection plan not to lose sight of key director insurance.	Underlying all of this is the loss of what is probably a key director, especially in the case of a majority shareholder. Because he or she no longer participates in the running of the company confidence of the bank manager and customers could be lost. It is worth emphasising this so that it is not lost in the problem of

protecting the share situation. In parallel with the share protection scheme close attention must be given to the key director problem, exactly as described in the partnership situation.

Pensions for the shareholding director

Unlike the ordinary employee who has no control over his or her company's occupational pension scheme, the shareholding directors have total control. They therefore need to know much more about these schemes. In Chapter 2 we described typical defined benefit pension schemes and mentioned final pensions being governed by length of service with the company and sixtieths of final salary. However, in the same way that limitations are put upon the personal pension scheme (PPS) by virtue of the amounts that can be invested, similarly limits are suffered by the company occupational scheme. For someone running the company scheme for himself or herself, he or she will need to be conversant with these limits. The benefits from a company scheme for an ordinary employee will rarely reach these limits but the shareholding director will want to maximise his or her pension by so doing. He or she will want to reach the maximum possible pension which is two-thirds of final remuneration indexed at 5 per cent per annum.

■ Maximum premiums payable to an approved company pension scheme

Maximum benefits of occupational pensions are governed by a succession of finance acts and also guidelines issued by the Pension Schemes Office (PSO) in the form of 'practice notes'.

The approved company pension scheme is treated in considerable detail later in the chapter, however it is important to include at this point an indication of the maximum contributions possible for a director joining such a scheme after September 1994 who has a possibility of completing 20 years of service with his or her company.

Table 5.3 shows the maximum regular contribution levels as a percentage of earnings (restricted to £84,000 for the tax year 1997/98), under new plans set up to provide maximum benefits assuming the member has 20 years or more service at NRA and no other pension plans.

It is interesting to compare this table with the funding limits for a personal pension scheme (PPS) (see Table 5.4).

Table 5.3 Maximum contribution levels as a percentage of earnings

	Males		Females			Males		Females	
Age	NRA 60	NRA 65	NRA 60	NRA 65	Age	NRA 60	NRA 65	NRA 60	NRA 65
20	18	13	21	16	42	48	31	56	37
21	19	14	22	16	43	51	33	60	39
22	19	14	23	17	44	55	35	64	41
23	20	15	23	17	45	59	37	69	43
24	21	15	24	18	46	63	39	74	46
25	22	16	25	18	47	69	41	81	49
26	22	16	26	19	48	75	44	88	52
27	23	17	27	20	49	83	47	97	56
28	24	17	28	20	50	92	51	108	60
29	25	18	29	21	51	103	55	120	65
30	26	19	31	22	52	116	60	136	70
31	27	19	32	23	53	134	65	157	77
32	28	20	33	24	54	157	71	185	85
33	30	21	35	25	55	190	79	223	94
34	31	22	37	26	56	240	89	281	105
35	33	23	38	27	57	322	100	378	119
36	34	24	40	28	58		116		137
37	36	25	42	29	59		136		161
38	38	26	45	30	60		164		195
39	40	27	47	32	61		207		245
40	42	28	50	33	62		278		329
41	45	30	53	35					

Table 5.4 Current maximum contributions possible to PPS

Age attained at beginning of tax year	Percentage of earnings	1997/98 maximum contributions for earnings of £84,000+
35 or less	17.5	£14,700
36–45	20.0	£16,800
46–50	25.0	£21,000
51–55	30.0	£25,200
56–60	35.0	£29,400
61–74	40.0	£33,600
Life cover	5.0	£4200

Note: Life cover can be included in the pension contract and that part of the premium diverted to this also attracts the same tax reliefs. The maximum which can be paid for this is 5 per cent of earnings which is included in the overall maximum.

The shareholding company director who can do 20 years with his or her company can make sure of a maximum pension indexed at 5 per cent per annum equal to two-thirds of his or her final salary.

Let us try to compare the effects of these different funding limits. To do this we will need to simplify matters as we did in Chapter 2, when we tried to get some approximate projections on the basic rate pension and SERPS. Thus let us assume inflation remains constant at 5½ per cent per annum so that remuneration is always equal to the earnings cap. Hence as before we can assume that remuneration remains constant in real terms at £84,000. It will be clear later in the chapter why an inflation rate of 5½ per cent is chosen.

■ Example 5.14

John Price and Zef Proctor were both born on 4 April 1967. John is self-employed and Zef is a shareholding director, both earning £84,000 p.a. They both decide to fund their pensions to the maximum allowed until retirement at age 60, starting 6 April 1997.

John's maximum contributions are:

$17\frac{1}{2}$% of £84,000 for six years to age 36 $= \dfrac{17.5}{100} \times 84,000 \times 6 \quad = £\ 88,200$

20% of £84,000 for ten years to age 46 $= \dfrac{20}{100} \times 84,000 \times 10 = £168,000$

25% of £84,000 for five years to age 51 $= \dfrac{25}{100} \times 84,000 \times 5 \ = £105,000$

30% of £84,000 for five years to age 56 $= \dfrac{30}{100} \times 84,000 \times 5 \ = £126,000$

35% of £84,000 for four years to age 60 $= \dfrac{35}{100} \times 84,000 \times 4 \ = £117,600$

Total $£604,800$

Zef's maximum contributions are:

26% of 84,000 for 30 years to age 60 $\quad = \dfrac{26}{100} \times 84,000 \times 30 = \ £655,200$

Figure 5.5 shows the position of the two pensions. The area under the graph shows total contributions.

■ The shareholding director of a close company or private limited company

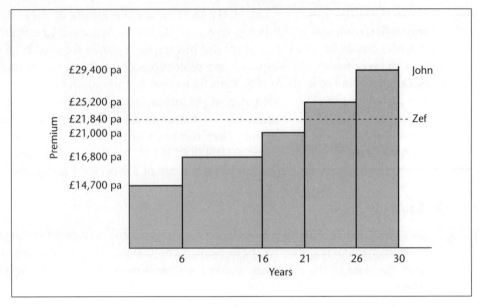

Fig. 5.5 Total possible pension investment for John and Zef

■ **Example 5.15**

Phillipa Brendon and Angela Frost were both born on 4 April 1957. Phillipa is self-employed and Angela a shareholding director, both earning £84,000 p.a. They decide to start pensions on 6 April 1997 and fund them to the maximum possible until they reach retirement at 60.

    Phillipa's maximum contributions are,

20% of £84,000 for six years to age 46 $= \dfrac{20}{100} \times 84{,}000 \times 6 =$ £100,800

25% of £84,000 for five years to age 51 $= \dfrac{25}{100} \times 84{,}000 \times 5 =$ £105,000

30% of £84,000 for five years to age 56 $= \dfrac{30}{100} \times 84{,}000 \times 5 =$ £126,000

35% of £84,000 for four years to age 60 $= \dfrac{35}{100} \times 84{,}000 \times 4 =$ £117,600

Total   £449,400

Angela's maximum contributions are,

50% of £84,000 for 20 years to age 60 $= \dfrac{50}{100} \times 84{,}000 \times 20 =$ £840,000

Figure 5.6 shows graphically the two women's pension position.

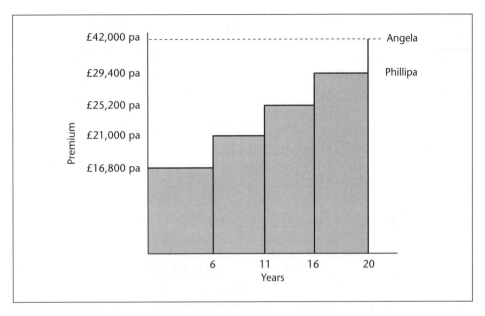

Fig. 5.6 Total possible pension investment for Angela and Phillipa

Clearly the discrepancy between the two sets of limits grows as age increases, the approved company pension allowing very much more to be invested. This is not surprising since the funding limits for the company scheme are designed to produce a maximum pension of two-thirds of final salary indexed at 5 per cent per annum, if the member has completed 20 years' service with the company at whatever age the pension may have been started.

This is an enormous advantage for the shareholding director, who can, of course, choose between an approved company pension or a PPS. It is very unlikely, certainly at the older ages, that the choice would be for the PPS.

The PPS investor could, of course, sweep up the previous seven years' eligibility by using carry forward and carry back.

In John's case this would add to the funding a further $17\frac{1}{2}$ per cent of £84,000 for seven years,

$$\frac{17.5}{100} \times 84,000 \times 7 = £102,900$$

bringing his total to £707,700, better this time than Zef's.

In the case of Phillipa another £102,900 brings her total to £552,300 which is still nowhere near Angela's total.

It is clear, then, that at the older ages there can be no comparison. It is also clear that for those who are not eligible for an approved company scheme because they are sole traders the sooner they start funding their personal pension scheme the better. We saw that at 30 John could still achieve a pension of two-thirds of final income indexed at 5 per cent per annum but that Phillipa at 40 had no chance.

For the older ages there can be no question of the superior benefits of the approved company pension.

It is, of course, less and less likely, today, that anyone would spend as long as 30 years with the same company or have achieved a measure of control in the affairs of the company in which he or she is a worker at the age of 30. There are, of course, exceptions and for those this sort of choice is very relevant.

You may like to use these tables to do the sort of calculations we have been describing for yourself. The real situation will, of course, be different because the variables will be rather more unpredictable. However, this sort of exercise can give additional clarity.

■ Exercise 5.4

Greg Watson and Ralph Broom were both born on 4 April 1977. Greg is self-employed and Ralph is a shareholding director in his father's company. Both Greg and Ralph earn £84,000 p.a. They both start pensions on 6 April 1997 funding them to the maximum until retirement age 60.

Using the parameters in the previous examples, calculate the maximum total contributions which can be made to their respective pension schemes.

It will be seen from the answer to this exercise that it is possible to beat the maximum pension limit of two-thirds of final salary indexed at 5 per cent per annum. Also the discussion of the straight sixtieths scheme will show that this is emminently possible for the high flyer able to dictate his or her own package.

■ The small self-administered scheme

This pension scheme is the company equivalent of the self-invested personal pension (SIPP), allowing the member great freedom in the possible range of investments, even including the shares of the funding company. It has a true loanback facility and can lend to the company up to 50 per cent of the funds. It is treated in detail later in the chapter.

Collecting payments

Collecting money from one's customers is a time consuming and often difficult task, the time lag between sending the invoice and receiving the payment tending to get longer. Often small businesses find themselves financing other companies because debts have not been paid, making it necessary for the selling company to borrow more to keep going. Thus a debt that has not been paid for three months is tantamount to having lost the interest on that money over that period. It could be said it is a loan to the company owing the money at zero interest, sometimes requiring the company owed to run an overdraft larger than would otherwise be necessary. The dilemma is the need to have the money and the importance of retaining the client. A possible answer to these problems is either invoice discounting or factoring which makes a proportion of the debt available immediately on invoicing and in the case of factoring gives the problem of collecting the debt to a company specialising in that particular activity. The subject is treated in more detail later in the chapter.

Expanding the company

The company may have reached a point where to continue increasing profit a considerable expansion of activity may be needed. Perhaps it is realised that customer base could be increased substantially, a new product produced in sufficient numbers could capture a niche market or opening a new factory in Morocco, for example, could reduce costs. All of these things would usually require a considerable injection of money, perhaps beyond existing borrowing potential. This will be the time to consider raising funds through venture capital and perhaps even involving business angels and enterprise investment schemes (EIS), all topics treated later in the chapter.

DETAILED INFORMATION AND ANALYSIS

INVESTMENTS

The Offshore Investment Bond or Gross Roll-Up Fund

As we said earlier the funds inside these bonds roll up free of all UK taxes. Thus, assuming an annual growth, including reinvested income, of 12 per cent per annum and an average tax rate for illustration purposes of 24 per cent, then the offshore bond could grow at 12 per cent per annum and its UK equivalent at 12 per cent – 24 per cent of 12 per cent:

$$12\% - \frac{24}{100} \times 12\% = 12\% - 2.88\% = 9.12\% \text{ per annum.}$$

Thus in ten years an offshore bond investment of £10,000 would have grown to £31,058; its UK equivalent to only £23,935. A considerable advantage.

Any proceeds taken by the investor while still a UK resident are subject to exactly the same tax situation as the UK investment bond, except that any chargeable event triggered would attract, for the higher rate tax payer, tax at the higher rate, and for the basic rate tax payer 23 per cent, no tax having been paid within the bond. Five per cent per annum can be taken over a period of 20 years with no tax liability in the investor's hands.

If the investor were non-resident when a chargeable event was triggered and, for example, taking the whole proceeds, the tax would be subject to the income tax rates of the new country. In the Isle of Man, for example, this is 20 per cent.

The gross roll-up fund can produce a significant advantage in growth.

If the bond holder were between countries, having left the UK and on holiday before reaching his or her new country of residence when the proceeds were taken, then they would be totally free of tax. He or she would then need, of course, to remain in his or her new country for at least one full tax year while holding a permit to work in that country and carrying out that work, or to remain in that country for at least three full tax years. This is dealt with later in this chapter under non-residence.

This could be a very important investment consideration both for the gross roll-up aspect but, also, if there is an intention to leave the UK at some point for the perceived advantages of non-residence.

An even more sophisticated version of this investment is to use the structure as an envelope for a portfolio of other investments often called a portfolio bond. This could give the same tax advantages to a more personal portfolio (see Fig. 5.7).

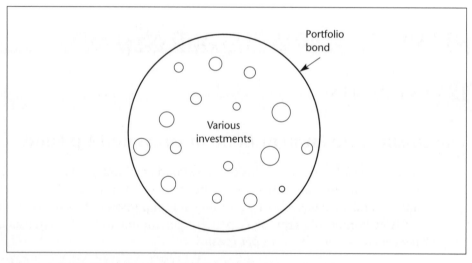

Portfolio bond

Various investments

Fig. 5.7 The portfolio bond as an envelope

The Enterprise Investment Scheme (EIS)

Introduced in the November 1993 Budget and modified in the Finance Act 1995 to increase tax reliefs, this scheme is intended to be an incentive for investment in unquoted trading companies. As long as the investment is held for five years it attracts income tax relief at 20 per cent and on disposal after five years it is totally free from capital gains tax. Should a loss be made relief is available against capital gains tax or income tax.

An additional tax relief can make this a very valuable investment and this is capital gains tax deferral relief. This means that if a capital gain has already been made then an investment into an EIS can be set against that. The EIS must be done within the period one year before and three years after the disposal giving rise to the chargeable gain. At the disposal of the EIS to anyone other than a spouse the deferred gain comes back into charge.

■ Example 5.16

Lee Ping Peng made a net capital gain of £8000 on 3 March 1997. She bought shares in an EIS company on 14 December 1997 for £7000. Her chargeable gain will be £8000 – £7000 = £1000. Lee is a higher rate taxpayer hence she has gained 60% tax relief on her investment, 20% income tax relief and 40% deferral of CGT.

The maximum investment into an EIS is £100,000 per annum.

In any one year up to half the amount invested between 6 April and 5 October can be carried back to the previous tax year subject to a maximum of £15,000. This is allowed up to the full amount being invested for that year.

Although there are excellent tax reliefs with this particular investment it is wise to reflect on the fact that the investment must be in the shares of unquoted companies. Unless the company becomes quoted, winds up or is purchased by a quoted company it could prove very difficult to realise the value of the investment at the end of the five years. The investor may then find himself or herself locked in. The directors of the unquoted company may be reluctant to wind up or sell because of the ensuing loss of their directorships. There is, therefore, a considerable risk element.

The Venture Capital Trust (VCT)

VCTs are companies similar to investment trusts. They were proposed in the November 1993 Budget and the Finance Act 1995 introduced them on 6 April 1995. The VCT must be quoted on the stock exchange and be invested in the shares of unquoted trading companies.

The tax reliefs are the same as for the EIS with two slight differences:

1 Tax relief of 20 per cent is given on dividends from the VCT.
2 Capital gains tax deferral relief is given where the investment is made during the period one year before and one year after the disposal which gave rise to the gain.

The investment must be held for five years to qualify for the tax relief and the maximum investment is £100,000 per annum. Because the investment is made in unquoted companies there is still a considerable risk element but this time it is spread between a number of such companies thus making the risk relatively lower than that of the EIS and being quoted on the stock market could make it easier to sell.

Investment on the Alternative Investment Market (AIM)

Investment in the shares of companies on AIM carries the same advantage of deferral of CGT. There are no other tax reliefs but it does give personal choice. Clearly there is still the risk, described in Chapter 1, that this is not a pooled investment.

The Enterprise Zone Property Trust

These investments are portfolios of properties in designated enterprise zones in which the investor purchases 'units' or 'shares'.

The investment is allowed against income tax to the extent that the money is invested to construct or purchase newly constructed and unused buildings within the enterprise zone. The cost of purchasing the land is not so allowed, i.e. about 4 to 8 per cent of the total investment.

Current rental yields are 6 to $7\frac{1}{2}$ per cent of the gross investment. A disposal of units within 25 years triggers a clawback of some or all of the income tax relief given. This clawback does not arise in the case of the units being gifted.

There is always the risk that the properties could remain empty for a time but sometimes they can be pre-let on a 25 year lease with upward only rent reviews.

The rental income can be set off for tax purposes against any loan raised to purchase units exactly the same as in the case of a straightforward purchase of investment property. Any surplus can be set off against other rental income for the same year or for future years.

It is often difficult to dispose of units as there is no established market for them.

■ Example 5.17

Deirdre Wheeler earns £90,000 annually. She spends £50,000 on shares in an enterprise zone property trust. The land element is 5% and the rental income is $6\frac{1}{2}$% of the gross investment. Tax relief is given on,

$$£50,000 = \frac{5}{100} \times 50,000 = £2500$$

$$£50,000 - £2500 = £47,500$$

Tax relief $= 40\%$ of 47,500,

$$= \frac{40}{100} \times 47,500$$

$$= 19,000$$

Net cost of investment = £50,000 – £19,000 = £31,000.
Rental income = $6.5/100 \times 50,000 = £3250$ p.a.
True percentage yield = $3250/31,000 \times 100 = 10.48\%$.

THE SELF-INVESTED PERSONAL PENSION (SIPP)

As we said earlier a SIPP is by definition a personal pension scheme (PPS) and is therefore governed by all the rules and regulations applicable to the PPS and is, in fact, approved under the Income and Corporation Taxes Act (ICTA) 1988.

The difference is the wide range of investments which can be made. In addition to the funds of the particular insurance company described in Chapter 1, the SIPP can invest in,

- equities, gilts, debentures, etc. quoted on the UK stock market
- securities quoted on the alternative investment market (AIM)
- stocks and shares traded on recognised overseas stock exchanges
- unit trusts, investment trusts and the funds of OEICs within the European Union
- the funds, as described in Chapter 1, of any insurance company in the European Union
- sterling deposit accounts
- commercial property in the UK not bought from a connected person.

It is not possible to invest in,

- residential properties
- loans to the policy holder or any connected person
- personal chattels
- any 'pride in possession' assets such as classic cars, racehorses, yachts or works of art
- any assets owned by a connected person.

A connected person is,

1 A family connection – a spouse or a relative of the policy holder or his or her spouse.
2 A business connection – a partner or any relative of such a person or a company in which the policy holder owns 20 per cent or more of the shares.

This is clearly very much a pension scheme for those who enjoy or have an expertise in building their own investment portfolio. It is a chance to do exactly the same thing within the envelope of the pension structure.

The self-invested personal pension (SIPP) offers a wide choice of investment.

It is possible for the SIPP to borrow money to buy a commercial property. The rental income from the property will then service the loan. If the property is used by the business it will pay the rental. Clearly a suitable deposit would need to be built up in the SIPP and the lender would have a loan criterion reflecting the perceived ability of the SIPP to service the loan.

What are the advantages and disadvantages of this method of purchase?

Advantages

1 The deposit would have been built up from untaxed profit whereas outside the pension it would have been taxed first. It can therefore be built up much more quickly.
2 While the deposit is growing inside the pension it is free of all UK taxes.
3 Rental income is untaxed. However, purchase outside allows rental to be set off against interest payments for tax purposes.
4 There is no CGT liability on sale of property. However, this is largely discounted outside pension by indexation allowance, personal CGT allowance and business retirement relief, all dealt with later in this chapter.
5 Free of inheritance tax on death before retirement if pension in trust but has to be sold at this point which may be at a time when the market is unfavourable. However, a property owned by a business is free of inheritance tax on death and does not have to be sold.
6 However, on retirement the income withdrawal facility, treated in Chapter 6, could be used to defer the sale until property prices improve. Even then an annuity has to be purchased by the 75th birthday of the policy holder.
7 The loan capital is paid back from untaxed profit. However, this could be true outside the pension if a pension linked or PEP linked loan is used.

Disadvantages

1 If it represents a large proportion of the total pension investment there is the considerable disadvantage of lack of spread of investment. The value of one small particular property may suffer adverse growth prospects and there is no spread of investment to balance this.
2 When an annuity is finally taken the property has to be sold. It may be at a time when property prices are depressed.
3 There are many tax benefits in the purchase of commercial property outside the pension which in a sense will be lost if the property is put inside the pension and prevent the use of tax advantages on other sorts of investment which do not have them outside the pension.

This discussion should allow a decision to be made in the light of knowledge.

VALUING A BUSINESS

The only right price for a business is that which a willing buyer is prepared to pay and a willing seller to receive.

The only right price for a business is that which a willing buyer is prepared to pay and a willing seller to receive. Short of actually putting it on the market there is no accurate method of calculating the true value. However, businesses are bought and sold and there are several accepted methods of valuing them. There are also many factors which could modify the first calculated price.

What is crystal clear is that this is a job for experts. Eventually, if the proposition is serious, an expert will have to be employed for, apart from anything else, three year projections of profits and cashflow will have to be prepared and anyway, the valuation process can actually help in grooming a business for sale.

However, anyone wishing to sell or buy will have an idea of what price he or she will take or give. The following points should help to clarify, refine and bring greater reality to that view:

■ Who, and indeed how many people, might want to buy?

■ What prices have been paid for similar businesses?

■ If profitability is heavily dependent on one individual this will considerably impact on value, so will all relevant knowhow in one person's head and no formal management systems in place.

■ While historic and current year figures on profit, loss and cashflow are important it is the future potential which is being bought and sold and therefore forecasts for the next three years, at least, are essential.

■ Past record of achieving projections.

■ The possible changing nature of the company's markets will have a bearing.

■ The extent to which projected growth will be achieved from new products and markets rather than from existing.

■ The general economic outlook.

■ Potential technological innovation.

■ Growing competition.

■ Changing labour costs.

■ Changing raw material costs.

■ Regulatory patterns.

■ Spending patterns.

■ Is this a young, fast growing industry or is it more mature with lower rates of growth?

■ Is it prone to cyclical slumps and, if so, at what point is the cycle in at the moment?

■ Is there enough cash in the business to fund its working capital needs?

■ Has there been the necessary investment in plant and equipment?

■ Profit may have been exaggerated by under investment.

■ Is the business dependent on any key suppliers?

■ Are the suppliers financially secure?

■ Is the business dependent on key customers? Any customer accounting for more than 10 per cent of sales can be regarded as key.

■ Would key customers be likely to continue with the new ownership?

■ Are there contracts to supply key customers and how long have they got to run? Are they reasonable?

■ Are key customers financially stable?

■ Is the presence of the proprietor on the premises minimising costs which would rise if the business were run more remotely?

- Has the company incurred special expenses such as costly cars or aircraft for the chairman?
- Is the business likely to become involved in litigation?
- Could future regulatory procedures lead to fines or other penalties?
- Is the company property costing a reasonable commercial rate?
- How could the market change? IBM, for example, probably found the computer market initially less crowded and competitive than it is today.
- A purchaser might change selling levels; appoint additional staff, such as a financial controller; invite staff to join an existing pension scheme; all changes which will increase costs but be seen as necessary.
- Greater purchasing power may ensue from a sale, rationalisation might take place, e.g. integration of premises, staff and equipment.

The price/earnings (P/E) ratio method

This is the most widely used method of valuation for quoted companies. These ratios are published in the national press and calculated as follows,

$$P/E \text{ ratio} = \frac{\text{price per share}}{\text{earnings per share}}$$

In the case of the close company it is the whole of the company which is of interest. Hence we substitute,

$$P/E \text{ ratio} = \frac{\text{value of the company}}{\text{after tax profit}}$$

This now gives us our basis of valuation:

1 Find a range of comparable quoted companies.
2 Take the P/E values of these companies and adjust them for differences in circumstances to produce the ratio we will use.
3 Ascertain the company's maintainable profitability and prospects.

> The price/earnings (P/E) ratio method is the most widely used method of valuation for quoted companies.

Maintainable profitability is found by taking into account all previous points which may apply to the particular company and restate past, present and projected profits in the light of these to obtain the maintainable profitability. This is the profit the business can be reasonably expected to maintain on an ongoing basis. Thus, value of company = maintainable profitability less tax × adjusted P/E ratio.

■ Example 5.18

	£
Maintainable profits	200,000
Less tax	(66,000)
Maintainable profit after tax	134,000
P/E ratio	8

Value = 134,000 × 8 = £1,072,000

Most investors use the higher rate of corporation tax to parallel the tax rate of the quoted companies whatever the actual tax rate of the close company might be.

It is clear that the P/E ratio measures the number of years it would take to recoup the purchase outlay.

> Business valuation is a complex subject requiring the advice of experts who will often differ from each other.

There is a vast difference between buying shares in a quoted company and those of an unquoted limited company. There is always a market for quoted shares but a close company may be difficult or impossible to sell. This would suggest a reduction in the P/E ratio obtained from comparable quoted companies before its application to unquoted companies.

However, the close company is usually being purchased in its entirety, giving the purchaser total control and thus introducing a 'control' factor thereby lifting the value of the P/E ratio.

If only part of the unquoted company is being purchased then the P/E ratio will have to be considerably adjusted to cater for the degree of control the shares will actually give. This is discussed more fully earlier in this chapter under share protection.

It is clear that this is a very complex subject requiring the help of experts, and even then there will often be differences between their valuations.

STAMP DUTY

Stamp duty was introduced in 1694 and has not been redrafted since the Stamp Act of 1891. It is a tax charged on documents by which certain property is transferred, e.g. the conveyance of a freehold. It is actually charged on the document by which the freehold is conveyed. It is charged on documents implementing the sale of:

- shares and other securities
- freehold land and buildings and the grant on assignment of liens
- certain types of business property, such as goodwill, copyrights, patents and trade marks.

It is the purchaser who pays the duty.

The purchase of a business which is a sole tradership or partnership attracts duty at 1 per cent whereas in the case of the shares of a limited company, quoted or unquoted, the duty is half of 1 per cent.

In the case of land and buildings and business property duty is only paid on purchases over £60,000 and then on the whole purchase price.

Because the stamp duty definition of a sale includes an exchange of property for shares, turning a sole tradership or a partnership into a limited company is treated as a sale of that business in exchange for the shares of the new company. Stamp duty is charged on the value of the shares received. However, no stamped contract is required on transferring a business to an unlimited company so no duty would be payable. The company can later be re-registered as a limited company.

It is the purchaser who pays the stamp duty.

On the sale of property, stamp duty is not charged on that part of the agreed purchase price represented by such things as fixtures and fittings which are left in the property.

A purchaser wishing to buy a new house could reduce stamp duty by buying the land on which he or she would pay stamp duty and then contracting with a builder to build the house, the price of which would not attract the duty.

In the case of a business, if the vendor transfers ownership of plant, machinery and stock in trade to the purchaser physically rather than by conveyance then stamp duty is saved on this part of the sale.

Where prices are high and stamp duty would be considerable one might decide to sign documents outside the UK in which case they need not be stamped, and therefore attract duty, until brought into the UK. The documents are usually left in safe deposit outside the UK. If they need to be brought in, as long as they are stamped within 30 days, no interest or penalty is charged.

It must be said that the whole question of stamp duty is complex and an experienced solicitor should always be consulted.

CAPITAL GAINS TAX (CGT)

If an asset is acquired at a certain value and sold at a higher amount, a capital gain has been made. This gain is potentially taxable and the tax is called capital gains tax (CGT). A major difference between this and income tax is that an allowance is made for inflation in computing the gain. The tax is assessed in the tax year that the gain is made but not paid until 31 January in the following tax year. Thus a gain made and assessed during the tax year ending 5 April 1997 is paid by 31 January 1998.

Rate of CGT

The net amount of capital gain is added to the person's taxable income. The amount of extra income tax which would now have been due is the CGT due.

■ Example 5.19

Rufus Stirling earns £26,000 in the tax year 1997/98. He also makes a capital gain of £10,000.

■ Form 5.10 INCOME TAX AND NIC ANALYSIS

Income tax			
Name Rufus Stirling	*Year*	1997	
	£	*Remaining income £*	*Tax £*
Gross income	26,000		
Gross contribution to pension paid personally*			
Personal allowance	4045	21,955	Nil
Income taxed at 20%	4100	17,855	820.00
Income taxed at	17,855	Nil	4106.65
- -			
basic rate 23%	4145	Add 10,000	
Income taxed at			
higher rate 40%	5855	Nil	2342.00
Total			
Less married couple's allowance			
Total tax payable			
* Some pension contributions paid personally are net of basic rate tax. For the purposes of this form this would need to be grossed up.			

Using Form 5.10 we see that £4145 will be taxed at basic rate and £5855 at higher rate, giving a CGT of £953.35 + 2342 = £3295.35. This becomes due on 31 January 1999.

Annual exemption

The annual exemption for CGT in the tax year 1997/98 stood at £6500.

Each person has an annual exemption which is deducted from total gains made, to arrive at the assessable CGT. This allowance has been increased over the years and in the fiscal year 1997/98 stood at £6500.

Indexation relief

CGT is charged not on a nominal capital gain but on a real one and can therefore be adjusted for inflation, i.e. the increase in the Retail Prices Index (RPI).

■ Example 5.20

Roslyn Croft acquired an asset in July 1989 for £10,000 and sold in July 1995 for £15,000. The nominal gain is £5000. However, referring to Table 5.4 (p. 300), we see that inflation over those years has been,

$$\frac{149.1}{115.5} \times 100\% = 29.1\%$$

In other words the asset would have grown in value 29.1% simply as a consequence of inflation. Hence the acquisition price is rebased in line with this,

$$10,000 + \frac{29.1}{100} \times 10,000 = 10,000 + 2910 = £12,910$$

Hence the real capital gain is £15,000 − £12,910 = £2090.
The gain to be considered for tax purposes is £2090.

Losses

Obviously capital losses can be made as well as gains. These losses can be set off against gains and even carried forward to be set off against future gains. In the case of these brought forward losses, the annual exemption is used before they are applied. In the case of losses and gains in the same year the losses have to be set off against the gains before using the annual exemption.

■ Example 5.21

Sebastian Fisher made capital gains in the tax year 1997/98 of £8000. However, in previous years he had made losses of £6300.

To compute his capital gains he first subtracts the annual exemption of £6500 leaving a gain of £1500. He then uses £1500 of the previous losses to reduce his gain to nil. He still has losses left of £4800 to carry forward. Had he made the losses in the same year the calculation would have been first set off previous losses of £6300 reducing his gain to £1700. Then use £1700 of the allowance to reduce his gain to nil. He has not used all his allowance and the surplus cannot be carried forward. He has used up all his previous losses and has nothing left to carry forward.

■ Example 5.22

Zara Morton purchases shares in July 1989 for £15,000. She sells them in July 1997 for £30,000. She has losses from previous years of £2000.

From Table 5.5 (p. 340) we see that over those years the RPI has increased by,

$$\frac{157.5}{115.5} \times 100\% = 36.4\%$$

Rebasing the cost of the shares we see that they would have increased in value from inflation alone,

$$15,000 + \frac{36.4}{100} \times 15,000 = 15,000 + 5460 = £20,460$$

Hence the real gain has been $30,000 - 20,460 = £9540$.

Deducting the annual allowance of £6500 we get a gain of £3040. Setting off the losses we get a gain of $£3040 - 2000 = £1040$.

As she is a higher rate taxpayer she will pay tax at 40% on this $= 40/100 \times 1040 = £416$.

The gain was made in the tax year 1997/98 so the tax becomes due on 31 January 1999.

Spouse transactions

There is no CGT liability between spouses.

As long as a couple are not permanently separated, there can be no gains or losses on the transfer of any asset between them whether by sale or gift. The asset is treated as passing from one to the other on a no gain no loss basis. The recipient is treated as acquiring it at spouse's cost plus indexation to date.

■ Example 5.23

Barnaby Grant was given shares by his wife in July 1994 which she had bought in July 1986 for £10,000. He sold the shares in July 1997 for £22,000, having made losses in the same year of £3000.

Using Table 5.5, we see the increase in the RPI from July 1986 to July 1994 was,

$$\frac{144.0}{97.5} \times 100\% = 45.1\%$$

Hence when Barnaby received the shares their real value was,

$$10,000 + \frac{45.1}{100} \times 10,000 = 10,000 + 4510 = £14,510$$

From July 1994 to July 1997 the RPI increased by,

$$\frac{157.5}{144.0} \times 100\% = 9.4\%$$

Hence when Barnaby sold the shares their real value was,

$$14,510 + 14,510 \times \frac{9.4}{100} = 14,510 + 1363.94 = £15,873.94$$

The capital gain was therefore 22,000 – 15,873.94 = £6126.06.

He sets off losses of £3000 against this reducing the gain to £3126.06. £3126.06 of the annual allowance wipes this out leaving £3373.94 of the allowance unusable and no losses to carry forward.

It would seem a good idea to time the losses and gains made very carefully if one can.

■ Exercise 5.5

Tina Bramwell buys shares in July 1987 for £10,000 which she sells in July 1997 for £25,000. In July 1990 her husband gives her shares which he had bought in July 1989 for £10,000. She sells these in July 1997 for £18,900. In 1990 she made losses of £3500. Tina earns £25,000 p.a. Compute her CGT.

Restriction of indexation relief

Up until the November 1993 Budget indexation relief could not only create a decrease in gain but also a loss. After the budget, confirmed in the Finance Act 1994, Section 93, it was possible for it only to reduce or extinguish a gain.

■ Example 5.24

Barbara Garston acquired an asset for £4000. When she sold it for £3800 indexation relief had rebased its cost to £4750. Thus, in real terms, she had made a loss of £950. Prior to November 1993 this could have been used but now it simply reduces the gain to nil.

Assets which are specifically exempt from CGT

The main categories of exempt assets are,

1 Chattels which are wasting assets, i.e. they have a useful life expectancy of less than 50 years.
2 Chattels where the sale consideration is less than £6000. There is some alleviation for chattels sold for more.
3 Decorations for valour as long as sold by the original recipient.
4 Foreign currency acquired for personal expenditure outside the UK. This includes money spent on the purchase or maintenance of any property situated outside the UK.
5 Winnings from betting.
6 Compensation or damages for wrong or injury suffered in a profession or vocation.
7 Debts.

8 National savings certificates and non-marketable securities.

9 Gilt edged securities and qualifying corporate bonds and any options to acquire or dispose of such investments.

10 Shares held in personal equity plans.

11 Shares held in pension schemes.

12 Shares in business expansion schemes (BES), the forerunners of enterprise investment schemes (EIS).

13 Shares in enterprise investment schemes (EIS).

14 Shares in venture capital trusts (VCT).

15 Sale of principal private residence.

16 Cars, unless not suitable for use as a private vehicle or commonly used for the carriage of passengers.

17 Woodlands.

18 Gifts to charities, gifts for national purposes to anyone mentioned in the Inheritance Tax Act (IHTA) 1984.

19 Works of art where they are taken by the Inland Revenue in lieu of IHT.

20 Gifts to housing associations; a claim is made by both transferer and the association.

21 Mortgage cashbacks. The Revenue finally conceded this on 21 March 1996.

Main residence exemption

This exemption is available to an individual who realises a gain on the disposal of a property which has been his or her sole residence throughout his or her period of ownership. The land which forms part of the property up to the permitted area is also exempt from CGT. The permitted area is a 1/2 hectare (approximately an acre) but may be more where the land is required for the reasonable enjoyment of the property. Relevant factors here include such things as the extent to which other similar properties have gardens or grounds larger than a 1/2 hectare, the need for an area of land to provide privacy or to provide a buffer between the property and some source of constant noise or disturbance. Another factor is the need to have appropriate facilities and amenities for the property.

Sale of part of the land attached to the property within the permitted area is not subject to CGT as long as the owner is resident in the property at the time or, sells the property at the same time. If, however, part of the land is not sold until later and has development value, there is likely to be a tax charge. A sale of part of a garden greater than 1/2 hectare may attract capital gains tax even when sold while the owner is still in occupation. The owner continuing to live there suggests that this parcel of land was not required for the reasonable enjoyment of the property.

There is no CGT liability on selling a main residence.

■ Availability of the exemption

Main residence exemption is available only on one property for a particular period. However, a delay of up to 12 months between buying a property and occupying it will not affect the exemption. This period can be extended by a further 12 months if there is an unavoidable delay in occupation due for example to an unavoidable inability to dispose of a previous sole residence. The last three years of ownership of a property which has previously been a main residence qualify for exemption whether the owner lives there or not. This is not prejudiced even if the property is let during that time.

Thus the purchase of a new property not moved into for two years, followed three years after the move by the sale of the old property, could still qualify for CGT exemption on both properties.

If two private residences are owned at the same time it is wise to decide which one is to be considered the main residence. If this is not done the commissioners will make the decision and it is not always clear on which basis this is done. It may not necessarily coincide with the owner's wishes. This decision should be made within two years of the purchase of the second house, and can be varied. This could lead to the ownership of two private residences over a period of years, each qualifying for part of that period as the main residence. In this case tax will be charged on a proportion of the capital gain relating to that part when the property was not the main residence.

■ Example 5.25

Malcolm and Nessa Williams have owned a house in London for 20 years. It has been their main residence for 16 years of that time.

The capital gain adjusted by indexation relief is £50,000. Tax is liable on a gain of,

$$\frac{4}{20} \times 50,000 = £10,000$$

■ Running a business in part of the main residence

If part of the main residence has been used exclusively for the running of a business, the exemption does not apply to that part of the gain attributable to that part of the property. This restriction does not apply where that part of the property has been used for personal purposes also. For example, a self-employed journalist using for his or her work a room which also serves as a sitting room.

Bed and breakfasting

There may be a wish or need to sell equity investments at some time in the future. To reduce the potential CGT at that time it might be wise to 'bed and breakfast', making use of any unused annual exemption. This is done by selling near to close of business one day and buying back the same investments at opening of business the next day. Thus the investments are rebased at current value.

■ Example 5.26

Herbert Young sells investments just before the stock market closes on 3 April 1997 realising a gain after indexation relief of £6300. Because the annual exemption for that year was £6300 he pays no CGT and uses up the exemption which would have been lost by the 6 April 1997 if not used. He buys back the equities first thing on 4 April 1997 and luckily finds the price has not moved. He has now considerably reduced future potential CGT on these equities. Hopefully the market will not move the wrong way between the two transactions in most cases and the price might actually reduce producing an added advantage.

There will, of course, be dealing costs and the disadvantage of this expense has to be weighed against the obvious advantage.

Roll-over relief

Relief may be available where an asset used in a business is sold if the seller reinvests in replacement assets used for business purposes. This is roll-over relief. The rolled-over gain is not charged to tax but is deducted from the cost of the new assets.

■ Example 5.27

Samantha Frost sells her business for £300,000 making a gain, after indexation relief, of £100,000. She starts a new business investing £200,000. By claiming roll-over relief she avoids having to pay tax on the gain of £100,000.

Actual cost of new business	£200,000
Less rolled-over gain	(£100,000)
Deemed acquisition cost	£100,000

This relief is really a deferment as is the case of transfers between spouses.

■ Example 5.28

Instead of the above, Samantha invests in a business costing £75,000.

Actual cost of new business	£75,000
Less rolled-over gain	(£75,000)
Deemed acquisition cost	Nil

This means that CGT will still be liable on the residual gain of £25,000.

■ Conditions which need to be satisfied

The asset disposed of must have been used in the business and fall into one of the following categories:

- ■ land and buildings
- ■ fixed plant and machinery
- ■ ships
- ■ goodwill
- ■ milk and potato quotas
- ■ aircraft
- ■ hovercraft, satellites and spacecraft
- ■ the whole business.

The replacement asset must also fall into one of these categories and be acquired within a period one year before the disposal of the original asset and three years after.

■ Assets used by a partnership

If assets owned by a partner are used by the partnership then roll-over relief can be claimed by the partner.

■ A shareholding director owning property used by his or her personal trading company

In this case roll-over relief is available only if the replacement asset is acquired by him or her and used by the same company. For the company to be deemed 'his or her personal trading company' he or she must personally own at least 5 per cent of the voting shares.

The relief is not lost even if he or she is neither a director, nor an employee, nor if he or she charges the company rent.

There are circumstances where a director of a family company sells an asset used by one company and purchases a new asset used by another family company where roll-over relief can still be available. However, this aspect is different and needs professional advice.

■ Reinvestment in unquoted shares

We have seen earlier that investment on the alternative investment market (AIM) carries what we called deferral relief of CGT. This is, in fact, roll-over relief. As a result of the Finance Act 1994 investment in qualifying unquoted trading companies on or after 30 November 1993 also attracts roll-over relief, whether or not the company is on AIM. This applies to any capital gain whether from the sale of business property or not.

A company is qualifying only if it does not carry on a prohibited business such as:

- ■ dealing in land, commodities, futures, shares, securities or other financial instruments

- dealing in goods otherwise than in the course of any ordinary trade of whole-sale or retail distribution
- banking, insurance, money lending, debt factoring, hire purchase, financing or other financial activities
- leasing or receiving royalties or licence fees
- providing legal or accountancy services
- providing services or facilities for any trade carried on by another person (other than a parent company) which consists substantially of activities already described, and in which a controlling interest is held by someone who also has a controlling interest in the trade carried on by the company.

Reinvestment must take place during the period one year before and three years after the disposal which gave rise to the capital gain.

■ Clawback of relief

Relief is clawed back where:

- a company ceases to meet the qualifying rules within three years of the rein-vestment
- the investing individual becomes non-resident in the UK within the three year period.

A company becoming quoted does not prejudice the relief.

Hold-over relief

This relief works in exactly the same way as roll-over relief but since 1989 is applicable only to business property. The relevant legislation is included in Taxes of Capital Gains Act (TCGA) 1992. It applies to gifts of business property from one UK entity to another. In this context business property is defined as:

- an asset used by the transferer in a trade, profession or vocation
- an asset used by the transferer's family company in a trade
- an asset used for a trade by a subsidiary of the transferer's family company
- unquoted shares in a trading company
- quoted shares if the company concerned is the transferer's family company (very unusual)
- agricultural land which qualifies for the inheritance tax agricultural property relief (see later in the chapter).

If instead of selling your business, you wished to gift all or part of it directly to your children or indirectly by making them the beneficiaries of a trust holding part or all of your business, hold-over relief would be available.

> Hold-over relief could be an extremely useful element of financial planning in this age.

This could be an extremely useful part of your financial planning as there is no IHT liability on the transfer of a business or shares in that business.

Capital gains in respect of partnerships

Any capital gain made by a partnership is divided among the partners in accordance with their profit-sharing ratios. Thereafter the tax liability will depend on the personal situation of the partner with respect to other gains, annual allowance, indexing allowance, possible losses, possible roll-over relief or potential business retirement relief, treated later in this section.

A partner selling his or her share of a partnership, of course, makes an individual capital gain which is treated accordingly. However, two other situations can affect all partners from a capital taxes point of view.

Retirement of a partner

The retirement of a partner would necessitate a valuation of the business.

■ Example 5.29

Sharon Tomlinson retires from a solicitors' practice where she has been one of five equal partners. The valuation shows a capital gain of £400,000 for the total partnership. Sharon will be assessed on a fifth share of this and have a CGT liability on a gain of £80,000. The other partners are not treated as having made a disposal. On the contrary they have each made an acquisition of a further 5% share of the partnership for one quarter of £80,000 = £20,000.

Introduction of a new partner

Similarly at the introduction of a new partner a valuation is likely to be done.

■ Example 5.30

Desmond Baron buys into a two partner business valued at £400,000 which is considered to be all capital gain. Desmond is now an equal partner with a third share valued at £133,333. The other two partners are deemed to have made a disposal of half that amount each and are therefore liable to CGT.

Incorporating a sole tradership or partnership

When a business is turned into a limited company a disposal of the business is deemed to have occurred, which would normally attract a CGT liability. However, if certain conditions are met the gain which is deemed to have been made is rolled over into the cost of the shares issued. There is no requirement that the company should be incorporated or resident in the UK. The conditions are:

1 There must be an issue of shares to the former proprietors of the business.
2 All assets of the business must be transferred. Although from the point of view of stamp duty it would be advantageous not to include such things as trade debts, thus paying less stamp duty, this could prejudice the relief.

■ Example 5.31

Pandora Young incorporates her fashion business at a deemed disposal value of £200,000. Since the business was started from scratch the capital gain after indexation relief will also be £200,000. The market value of the shares will be £200,000.

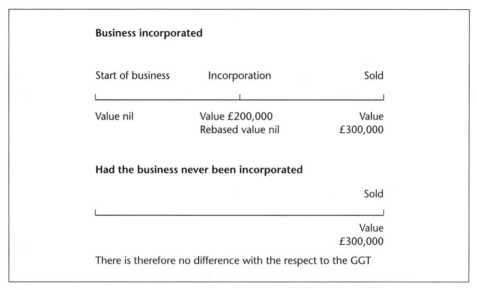

Business incorporated

Start of business	Incorporation	Sold
Value nil	Value £200,000	Value
	Rebased value nil	£300,000

Had the business never been incorporated

		Sold
		Value
		£300,000

There is therefore no difference with the respect to the GGT

Fig. 5.8 The effect of CGT on incorporating a sole tradership

Hence, for CGT purposes the current purchase price of the limited company would be seen to be,

Market value	£200,000
Less rolled-over gain	£200,000
	Nil

She later sells her business for £300,000. The capital gain would still be deemed to be £300,000 i.e. incorporation has made no difference to this.

Business retirement relief (BRR) on the sale of a business

The Taxes of Capital Gains Act (TCGA) 1992, Sections 163–4, makes relief available to the vendor if he or she has been running the business as a sole trader, partner or shareholding director. The vendor must have reached the age of 50 and have been running the business for 10 years. For periods less than 10 years a corresponding proportion of relief is available. The relief is also available to those retiring before 50 for reasons of ill health.

> On selling a business the first £250,000 of gain could be totally free of CGT.

Total relief is available on the first £250,000 of the gain and half of the gain is relieved on the next £750,000.

■ Example 5.32

Oswald Jenkins, a higher rate tax payer, sells his business for £450,000 at age 60 after running it for 20 years. The gain after indexation relief and annual allowance is £340,000.

Using BRR	
Tax on first £250,000 gain	Nil
Tax on remaining £90,000 gain at 20% = 20/100 × 90,000	£18,000
Total tax	£18,000

■ Example 5.33

Regina Manwell, a higher rate tax payer, sells her business at age 65 having built it up from scratch over a period of three years. She receives £100,000.

Using BRR	
Tax on first $^3/_{10}$ths of £250,000 = £75,000	Nil
Tax on next £25,000 at 20% = 20/100 × 25,000 =	£5000
Total tax	£5000

■ Exercise 5.6

Morris Waller sells his share of Falcon Masonry Ltd for £500,000, in July 1997 at age 55. He has been a shareholding director for 11 years. He originally bought his shares for £100,000. He made losses three years earlier of £50,000.
Using all reliefs available to him calculate his CGT liability.

■ Exercise 5.7

If you are thinking of selling your own business why not calculate the potential CGT you will pay?

Gains may arise in different tax years if for example payments are staggered or different businesses are sold. BRR limits, in this case, will apply to the total gain.

Personally owned property used by a partnership or limited company

An individual who is either a partner in a partnership or a shareholding director in a limited company may personally own property or other assets used by the partnership or company. Retirement relief may be claimed in respect of such property or other assets if the following conditions are satisfied:

1 The disposal of the property must take place as part of the individual's disposal of his or her share of the business.
2 The property must have been in use by the business at the time of the above disposal or at the time the business ceased.
3 The property must have been used for part or the whole of the time the individual owned it:
    – for the purposes of the business carried on by the partnership or company
    – for the purposes of another business carried on by the owner or by a partnership of which the individual was a member
    – for the purposes of another incorporated business.

Relief may be restricted where the individual has charged rent.

If a full market rent has been charged then no BRR will be available. For lesser rents a proportion may be allowed, for example, if a rent of half the market amount is charged then half the BRR would be allowed.

The owner of the property could, of course, be recompensed by higher salary which would not prejudice BRR in any way. However, income tax and NIC would have to be paid, whereas in the case of rental income it can be set off against interest payments on any loan used for the purchase of the property and no NIC is payable.

Reducing CGT

If assets are to be sold on which a capital gain will be made:

1 Transfer assets to spouse first to make use of two annual allowances of £6500 (the allowance relevant to the tax year 1997/98).
2 Transfer assets to spouse first to maximise the proportion of the gain at the lower rate.

■ Example 5.34

Rex Bradbury wishes to sell shares on which a capital gain of £30,000 will be made. His taxable income after personal allowances is £35,000, his wife, Pauline's, is £14,000.

If he sells the shares he can claim the annual allowance of £6500, thus paying CGT of 40% on a gain of £23,500,

$$\text{Tax} = \frac{40}{100} \times 23,500 = £9400$$

If he transfers shares to Pauline first with a potential gain of £12,100, she will simply take on that gain. She claims annual allowances of £6500, leaving a gain of £5600.

This will all be taxed at 23% since £14,000 + £5600 = £19,600, which is all within the basic rate tax band,

$$\text{Tax} = \frac{23}{100} \times 5600 = £1288$$

He will be left with a gain of £17,900. Subtracting the annual allowance of £6500 leaves him with a gain of £11,400 on which he will pay tax at 40%,

$$\text{Tax} = \frac{40}{100} \times 11,400 = £4560$$

Total tax now paid by the family is 1288 + 4560 = £5848.

This is a saving of 9400 – 5848 = £3552.

3 Bed and breakfast whichever unused annual allowances exist. This will save future tax.
4 Make sure to claim for capital losses.
5 With an asset which has become of negligible value and cannot be sold the Revenue may be persuaded that a loss is allowable.

THE PARTNERSHIP PROTECTION PLAN

This plan is designed to solve the disastrous problems which can follow the death or critical illness of a partner.

It puts money into the hands of the surviving partners enabling them to purchase the deceased partner's share of the partnership from his or her dependants. The surviving partners end up owning between them the whole business and the dependants will have cash representing the value of the deceased partner's share. It should not be forgotten that in most cases, in order to overcome a period of loss of confidence in the business, the remaining partners will need an injection of money at this time. This will be supplied by a key person life insurance and critical illness policies which should be taken on each partner.

Thus the right amount of money has been put into the right hands at the right time. It is vitally important to ensure that the instruments used to bring this about will not prejudice this in any way.

The right amount

A reasonably accurate estimate of the value of the business and the value of each partner's share of this is needed. There are some guidelines earlier in the chapter. But, although it is not suggested that the expense of a full professional valuation should be contemplated at this stage, some help from the business accountant and solicitor will usually be needed. This valuation should be reviewed each year because of the almost inevitable progressive change in the value of the business.

Policies

Life assurance and critical illness policies should be taken on each partner with sums assured equal to the value of his or her share of the partnership.

Trusts

These policies should be put into trust for the other partners. This is the first instrument and very great care must be taken in order that this is done in the best way possible.

The choice of trust will be very important. It may be thought that a simple inflexible trust would do. However this would take no account of potential future needs necessitating a change in the arrangement such as,

- retirement of a partner
- introduction of a new partner
- amalgamation of the firm with another.

A flexible trust will be needed to cope with these points as it will be possible to make necessary changes to beneficial interests, i.e. change the beneficiaries, deal with retirement and appointment of trustees. In other words it will carry a power of appointment. In spite of this power of appointment a flexible trust can be such that it is not a discretionary trust. This is important since a discretionary trust is taxed every 10 years. This taxation occurs because there is no inheritance tax liability on the death of a beneficiary since none are specifically appointed in this form of trust. The theory is that a generation is approximately 30 years and the 10 yearly charge will thus approximate eventually to any potential inheritance tax liability.

Having arrived at the flexible trust it is important not to fall foul of the 'gift with reservation' rules introduced in the Finance Act 1986, which say, in very simple terms, that if a benefit is reserved when making a gift, then the gift is not free of transfer tax or IHT (see IHT Chapter 6). If the settlor is included in the list of beneficiaries a benefit has been reserved, because he or she could benefit from his or her own gift, yet the settlor must be included in the list of potential beneficiaries if the degree of flexibility required is to be achieved. The Revenue has confirmed that provided the arrangement is commensurate with no gratuitous intention, a 'commercial arrangement' for example, it will not be liable to inheritance tax. Where this exemption applies the 'gift with reservation' rules will not. The trust includes the settlor in the list of potential beneficiaries but limits the beneficiaries to those

It is important not to fall foul of the 'gift with reservation' rules.

directly involved in the partnership i.e. present and future partners. No members of the settlor's family are included, hopefully making the trust the required commercial arrangement. However, this is a very complex area and expert advice must be taken since the commercial arrangements exemption cannot be guaranteed.

An alternative to own life in trust would be for each of the partners to insure the other partners' lives on a life of another basis. In order to do this an insurable interest must be shown, i.e. a financial interest in the death or critical illness of a partner. This is manifestly the case. Thus partner A would own a policy on the life of B and one on the life of C. These policies would pay out to A. The only advantage would appear to be that where there is an inequality of cost due to age differences etc., then each partner bears the cost of the policies which could eventually benefit himself or herself. However, the considerable disadvantages include,

- future flexibility is considerably reduced
- in the case of three or more partners the number of policies could become cumbersome.

The legal document – the cross-option agreement

This document ensures that the exchange of money for the deceased partner's share of the business takes place effectively with no danger of prejudicing such things as business property relief, treated in detail in Chapter 7.

The last thing to ensure is that in the event of a death the arrangement actually operates. For this to happen a separate legal document must be produced, this is called a 'cross-option agreement' or 'double option agreement' or 'put and call option agreement'. We must be very careful not to prejudice business property relief (BPR) for IHT which allows a business to pass, on death, with no IHT liability. BPR is given to relieve the IHT burden on business and because of the difficulty of selling a private business at a realistic price at what will almost certainly be an unfavourable time for sale. Hence a business subject to a binding contract for sale will not be eligible for such relief. Inland Revenue Statement of Practice SP IC18, 13 October 1980, on inheritance tax is relevant.

Business relief from inheritance tax 'buy-and-sell' agreements

The Inland Revenue understand that it is sometimes the practice for partners or shareholder directors of companies to enter into an agreement (known as a 'buy-and-sell' agreement) whereby, in the event of the death before retirement of one of them, the deceased's personal representatives are obliged to sell and the survivors are obliged to purchase the deceased's interest or shares, funds for the purchase being frequently provided by means of appropriate life assurance policies.

In the Inland Revenue's view such an agreement, requiring as it does a sale and purchase and not merely conferring an option to sell or buy, is a binding contract for sale within paragraph 3(4) of Schedule 10 to the Finance Act 1976. As a result the inheritance tax business relief will not be due on the business interest or shares.

The Revenue accepts that an option is not a binding contract for sale and cross-option agreements will, therefore, not prejudice BPR.

It is extremely important that the legal document is drafted in terms of options to buy and options to sell.

It is clearly extremely important that the document is drafted in terms of options to buy and options to sell, a cross-option agreement, and that expert legal advice is taken in the drafting.

In the event of A dying the money from his or her policy will be held on trust for B and C. There will be no IHT implications here since the trust already owns the sum assured and B and C are beneficiaries. The only gift for IHT purposes has been the premiums which will almost certainly be allowed as gifts under normal expenditure (see IHT in Chapter 7). Either A's dependants or B and C can exercise the option to bring about the transfer of the money in return for the shares. Clearly time limits will have to be set in the agreement for exercising these options.

In the case of the critical illness situation it can be decided that only the partner suffering the critical illness should exercise the option. This would then be a single option agreement which can be written within the main document. Since

An expert professional valuer will be appointed.

this director is a member of the list of potential beneficiaries, the sum assured, or part of it, could revert to him or her. Some partnerships make provision for this depending on a time limit of a number of months to return to work. Clearly if the partner intends to return to work and remains reasonably capable he or she would not want to have sold his or her share of the partnership. Some partnerships provide, in this case, for the money to be used for the benefit of the business.

The cross-option agreement will also appoint an expert professional valuer who will value the relevant share of the partnership in the event of a death or critical illness if the dependants and remaining shareholders fail to reach an agreement on this in a given time.

An exact match between the policy proceeds and the value of the deceased partner's share will be unlikely. If at the time of death the deceased's policy does not produce enough money for the other partners to buy his or her share of the partnership from his or her beneficiaries, the legal document will usually stipulate that remaining payments should take place in instalments over a specified period of time with appropriate interest being paid.

If there is more money than needed then the question arises of what to do with the surplus. This decision must be made at outset by the partners and included in the legal document.

They may decide that the remaining partners will keep the surplus, perhaps to inject money into the business at a time when it may be needed. They may decide that it should go into the deceased partner's estate or, in the case of critical illness, revert to the partner himself or herself who, you will remember, is listed among the beneficiaries in the trust. In this case the documents must provide that the remaining partners covenant to do this.

In the event of the change of a beneficiary the amount of money concerned would be a capital transfer but it would not fall foul of the reservation of benefit rules. However, there would have been an appointment away from certain individuals and they would have to live for seven years thereafter to be totally free of IHT liability.

You may think that setting a fixed price in advance could avoid all this. However, there are reasons why this would not be a good idea:

1 If the price paid for the deceased partner's share is more or less than its open market value this could imply, for IHT purposes, a gift of the difference, and hence a liability to IHT.
2 Some years after the fixing of the price the true value of the share could be considerably different which means that the fixed price would have to be reviewed frequently.

If the partners do not hold equal shares in the partnership then in the event of a death or critical illness they may decide that the remaining partners will buy different proportions of the deceased partner's share. This will have to be reflected in the trust documents and also in the cross-option agreement.

After the exercise of an option the policies on the lives of the remaining partners will still be in force. There are three courses of action:

1 The policies can be appointed back to the remaining partners. The trust falls away and the partners take over the policies and can, if they wish, declare a new trust, for example, making children the new beneficiaries.
2 The beneficiaries can be changed in order to set up a new partnership agreement for the remaining partners and also to include, if necessary, any new partners. It is the power of appointment facility which enables this to be done.
3 The partners may decide that the interest of the deceased partner in the remaining policies should benefit his or her heirs. If so, provision for this should be made in the legal document.

In the event of a death all potential capital gains tax on the increase in the value of the partner's share is wiped out but there could be complications in the case of an option exercised following a critical illness. However, business retirement relief, dealt with earlier in this chapter, may be available to those 50 and over or who can satisfy the Inland Revenue that they are retiring 'on grounds of ill health'. Again independent expert advice should be taken on this matter.

The situation in Scotland

There are two points of difference in Scottish law but these should make no fundamental difference to the preceding discussion.

1 In Scotland a partnership is a legal entity existing in its own right apart from the partners, rather like a private limited company. In England a partnership has no separate existence apart from the partners.

2 An additional trustee must be appointed and sent a copy policy to comply with the Scottish requirement of delivery. The trust will then be governed by English law in the usual way.

Using life assurance written under pension legislation

Partners may wish to use term life assurance written under personal pension scheme legislation. Such life assurance can be written under a flexible trust without an interest in possession but the 10 year payment rules for discretionary trusts will not apply (Section 58(1)(d) and Section 151, Inheritance Tax Act (IHTA) 1984). This means the settlor can be named as a potential beneficiary without falling foul of the 'gift with reservation' rules (Inland Revenue Press Release, 19 July 1986).

It is still possible, however, to use the power of appointment to change the beneficiaries without triggering a charge to inheritance tax provided this does not occur more than two years after the settlor's death. This also makes it very easy to deal with left over policies since the benefits can be appointed back to the settlor or to a different configuration of partners.

THE SHARE PROTECTION PLAN

This scheme follows exactly the same structure as the partnership protection plan. There are, however, two differences which need discussion:

1 The proportion of shares held does not necessarily represent the same proportion of the value of the limited company. We have discussed this fully earlier in the chapter. It remains only to say that the sum assured for each shareholder must represent the true value of his or her shareholding.

2 In the plans we have described each shareholder will settle his or her own policy and therefore pay the premiums. In the case of the limited company, which you will remember is a separate entity, it would pay for the whole scheme by reimbursing the premiums to each director by way of a salary increase. If this is to be a complete reimbursement then the relevant tax and NIC will have to be catered for.

> The proportion of shares held does not necessarily represent the same proportion of the value of the limited company.

This latter point leads to the question, could the company pay directly for the premiums? The only way this could be done would be for the company to own the policies on a life of another basis. In which case on the death or critical illness of a director the sum assured would be paid to the company.

Since 1981 it has been possible for a company to buy its own shares, so the scheme would be something like the following.

The company owns policies, on a life of another basis, on each of the directors to the value of his or her shares. If a director dies or suffers a critical illness the sum assured is paid to the company. A cross-option agreement exists between the directors and the company and possibly a single option in the case of critical illness. When the option is exercised the company buys the shares. This leaves the remaining directors owning the company and the deceased director's dependants or himself or herself, in the case of critical illness, with the cash value of his or her shares. This has the effect of reducing the number of shares and changing the proportion held by the remaining directors.

> **Since 1981 it has been possible for a company to buy its own shares.**

■ Example 5.35

Mary Jones, Peter Rainworth and David Dixon own respectively 35%, 40% and 25% of the shares of Xenon Press Ltd. Their share protection scheme provides for the purchase of shares by the company. When Peter dies 40% of the shares are bought back by the company. If there were originally 1000 shares there are now only 600, of which Mary owns 350 and David 250.

Mary therefore owns $350/600 \times 100\% = 58.3\%$ of the shares and David 41.7%.

However, before such a purchase can be made there are strict company law conditions to meet if the purchase is to be allowed and strict tax conditions to satisfy if the payment is to be treated as a capital payment and not treated as a dividend subject to income tax.

The company law conditions are there to protect creditors of the company and minority shareholders. The tax conditions prevent the scheme being used as a tax avoidance scheme, a way of beneficially switching income tax into capital gains tax.

Company law conditions

It should be noted that these are not necessarily the same for quoted companies:

1 The articles of association must allow a purchase.
2 The shares purchased by the company must be cancelled.
3 If the shares are purchased from 'distributable profits', the nominal value must be transferred to a capital redemption reserve.
4 Where the purchase is to be paid out of capital, the directors have to make a statutory declaration that the company will be able to pay all its debts in the following year.
5 At least 75 per cent of the votes in respect of the shares in the company (excluding those being bought out) have to approve the purchase.
6 Where the purchase is to be paid from capital, publicity must be given to the proposed purchase.

Failure to meet any of these six conditions means it would be unlawful for the company to purchase any of the shares, i.e. impossible.

Tax conditions

1 The company must be a trading company.
2 The purchase must be for the benefit of the company's trade.
3 Tax avoidance must not be a main purpose of the purchase.
4 The vendor must be resident and ordinarily resident in the UK.
5 The vendor must have owned the shares for five years prior to the purchase (three years if the purchase takes place on or after death).
6 The percentage of the shares held by the individual after the purchase must be at least 25 per cent less than the percentage he or she held before the purchase.
7 After the purchase the shareholder must not have more than a 30 per cent interest in the company. The shares of both husband and wife are taken into account for testing the shareholder's percentage holding.

Failure to satisfy these rules would mean the payment being treated as a dividend and taxed to income tax.

It can be seen that this route is fraught with potential problems.

■ Example 5.36

Harold Proctor, Irene Proctor and Nancy Vilette own respectively 29%, 24% and 47% of the shares of Complete Fashions Ltd, valued at £500,000. They have a share protection scheme depending on the company purchasing its own shares of which there are 1000. Harold dies and the plan is brought into action. His 290 shares are bought for £75,000 by the company reducing the total shares to 710. Irene now owns 240 shares of a total 710, i.e.

$$\frac{240}{710} \times 100\% = 33.8\%$$

Unfortunately the shares of both husband and wife are taken into account in testing whether the 'less than 30% retained' condition has been met. Clearly with Irene owning 33.8% it has not. The payment of £75,000 is treated as a dividend and faces a tax liability of £30,000 as Harold was a higher rate tax payer.

This is just one example to illustrate the difficulty of ensuring that all the conditions imposed by this route will be met. It is clear that it is not a method to be entered into lightly.

Comparison of methods

■ Own life in trust

Each director has policies written in trust for the other directors. On death or critical illness the sum assured is paid to the other directors to be used for the purchase of shares from the dependants (see Fig. 5.9).

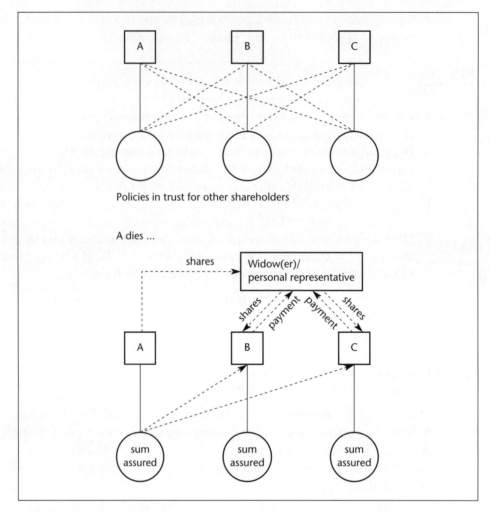

Fig. 5.9 Own life in trust

Advantages

1 Simple to set up and document.
2 Easily copes with large numbers.
3 Easy to modify with changes in shareholders.
4 Company can increase salaries to pay for premiums.
5 No fear of conditions disrupting the scheme at point of enactment.
6 Over provision can be dealt with easily.
7 Increases in sums assured easy to handle.

Disadvantages

1 More expensive for company.
2 Under provision could be a problem.

■ Life of another by individuals

Each director owns policies on the lives of the other directors set up on a life of another basis. On the death or critical illness of a director, the other directors own policies on him or her. These policies pay out to the director owning them (see Fig. 5.10).

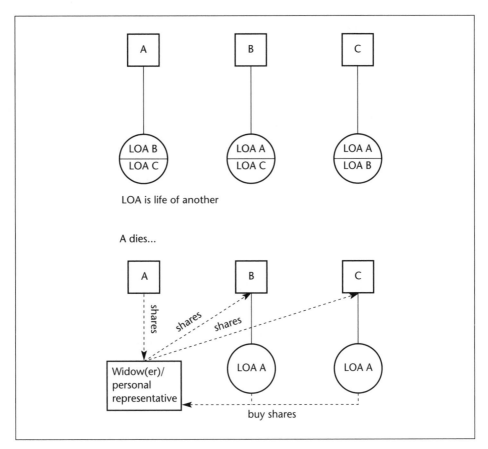

Fig. 5.10 Life of another by individuals

Advantages

1 Simple to set up for up to three shareholders.
2 Each director can pay an equitable amount based on what he or she stands to gain.
3 Company can increase salary to pay for premiums.
4 No fear of conditions disrupting the scheme at point of enactment.

Disadvantages

1 Unwieldy with more than three directors, e.g. if there are four lives assured, twenty policies are needed, both at outset and for any increases.
2 More expensive for the company.
3 Under provision is a problem.

■ Life of another by company

The company takes out policies on each of the shareholding directors written on life of another basis. On the death or critical illness of a director the policy pays out to the company which uses the money to purchase the shares from the dependants (see Fig. 5.11).

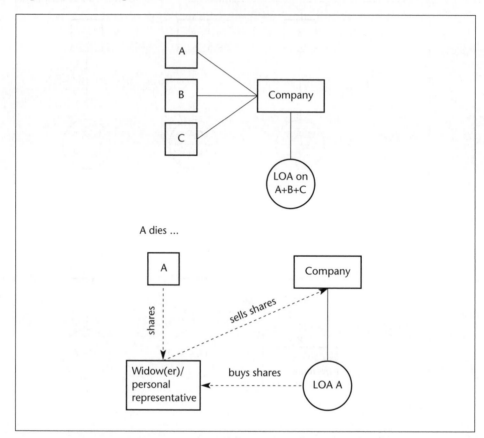

Fig. 5.11 Life of another by company

Advantages

1 Not as expensive for the company, no NIC to pay and tax limited to 31 per cent.
2 May be the only way in post mortem situations, where no funding was arranged prior to the death.

Disadvantages

1 A host of company law and tax conditions to be met. It is very easy to fall foul of these and negate the whole scheme.
2 Any overfunding will be sitting in the company and if it is decided that this should help the dependants it will be difficult to get it to them without tax implications.

3 There is considerable uncertainty about whether or not the Revenue will treat the purchase of the shares as a capital payment rather than a dividend. This is because, although it is possible to obtain clearance in advance, this is only possible where the proposed purchase is to be made at a known time, which, of course, is impossible in the case of death or critical illness.

4 There is no flexibility about the apportionment of the shares after an event, since the reduction of the total number dictates the resulting proportions. This may give rise to an undesirable situation.

5 Enormous amount of paperwork on setting up the scheme and at the point of an event.

6 At the death of a shareholder the remaining shareholders simply keep their original shares; there is no rebasing for the purposes of CGT. With the other two methods the surviving shareholders receive additional shares which have been rebased for CGT.

7 The cross-option agreement is much more complex than our earlier description.

THE APPROVED COMPANY PENSION SCHEME

Maximum pension

For those who joined a company scheme in the fiscal year 1997/98 the maximum allowable pension was 1/30th of final remuneration for every year of service with the company, with an overall maximum of 2/3rd of final remuneration. This maximum pension can be obtained after 20 years with the same company. It is also allowed to be indexed at 5 per cent per annum.

∎ Definitions of final remuneration

1 Remuneration on which Schedule E income tax liability, i.e. PAYE, has been assessed as final and conclusive, for any one of the five years preceding retirement. Remuneration includes basic salary, P11D benefits, discussed in Chapter 2, and the average of fluctuating payments such as bonus and commission averaged over a period of at least three consecutive years ending in the year in question.

2 The annual average of total earnings, as described in 1, over a period of at least three consecutive years, ending not earlier than 10 years before retirement.

In the case of a controlling director only definition 2 is acceptable.

∎ Example 5.37

Bernard Flucton, a controlling director, retired in July 1997. His earnings for the last 13 years ending at retirement are as shown in Table 5.5.

Table 5.5 Typical earnings of a controlling director for 13 years up to retirement

Year to July	Total remuneration	RPI July
1986	65,000	97.5
1987	65,000	101.8
1988	65,000	108.7
1989	71,000	115.5
1990	72,000	126.8
1991	73,000	133.8
1992	73,000	138.8
1993	73,000	140.7
1994	74,000	144.0
1995	76,000	149.1
1996	78,000	152.4
1997	80,000	157.5

Clearly the best three consecutive years are the last three which gives a final remuneration of:

$$\frac{76,000 + 78,000 + 80,000}{3} = £78,000$$

and a maximum annual pension of $2/3\text{rd} \times 78,000 = £52,000$.

■ Dynamised or indexed final remuneration

Final remuneration may be recalculated as a notional figure known as dynamised or indexed final remuneration by increasing the actual remuneration in a given year by the increase in the RPI between the end of the year in question and retirement date. The best three consecutive years can then be taken from these notional figures. The result is to produce a pension which is related to the remuneration which would have been received if salaries had kept pace with inflation. Adjusting Table 5.5 we end up with figures as shown in Table 5.6.

Final remuneration can be increased by the Retail Prices Index (RPI).

From Table 5.6 clearly the best three dynamised years are 1987, 1988 and 1989, giving a final dynamised remuneration of,

$$\frac{100,564 + 94,181 + 96,818}{3} = £97,188$$

and a maximum pension of $2/3\text{rd} \times 97,188 = £64,792$ per annum, an increase of £12,792 per annum.

Table 5.6 Controlling director's earnings after indexing

Year to July	Dynamised remuneration	
1986	$56{,}000 \times \dfrac{157.5}{97.5}$	= 90,461
1987	$65{,}000 \times \dfrac{157.5}{101.8}$	= 100,564
1988	$65{,}000 \times \dfrac{157.5}{108.7}$	= 94,181
1989	$71{,}000 \times \dfrac{157.5}{115.5}$	= 96,818
1990	$72{,}000 \times \dfrac{157.5}{126.8}$	= 89,432
1991	$73{,}000 \times \dfrac{157.5}{133.8}$	= 85,930
1992	$73{,}000 \times \dfrac{157.5}{138.8}$	= 82,835
1993	$73{,}000 \times \dfrac{157.5}{140.7}$	= 81,716
1994	$74{,}000 \times \dfrac{157.5}{144.0}$	= 80,938
1995	$76{,}000 \times \dfrac{157.5}{149.1}$	= 80,282
1996	$78{,}000 \times \dfrac{157.5}{152.4}$	= 80,610
1997		= 80,000

With this information a shareholding director within 13 years of retirement will be able to manipulate remuneration to give the best possible maximum pension. In the good years remuneration can be lifted relying on dynamisation to substantially increase these good figures. In the later years remuneration could be reduced in order to put as much into the pension as possible to lift the fund to the level that will produce the pension possible to take out at retirement.

Controlling director

In very simple terms a controlling director is someone who 'owns' or controls through relatives or trusts 20 per cent or more of the ordinary shares of the com-

pany providing the occupational pension scheme. In this sense 'controlling director' is not to be confused with a director who controls the company as discussed earlier, but is someone who will probably be taking part in the day-to-day decisions of the company. It can be seen that if such a person were eligible for the first definition of final salary then it would be possible for him

> **Anyone who owns or controls 20 per cent or more of the ordinary shares of a company is a 'controlling director'.**

or her to lift his or her salary to a level considerably higher than usual for only one year to accommodate the possibility of receiving a much higher pension.

The maximum amounts which could be put into a company pension were traditionally calculated on an emerging benefits basis. Thus assuming a maximum pension of two-thirds of final remuneration the first requirement was to calculate that final remuneration by indexing its current value over the period to retirement. Then, taking two-thirds of that figure and, using Revenue-approved annuities, the fund required to produce that pension could be calculated. Finally, using an approved rate of investment growth the premium required could be estimated and this would give the maximum funding level.

Prior to September 1994 the income could be indexed at 9 per cent per annum, the pension investment growth at 9 per cent per annum. The annuity then used was indexed at 8.5 per cent per annum.

Those calculations gave rise to maximum premiums which were assumed to stay level unless an excessive income increase took place when new calculations were necessary.

These criteria resulted in Table 5.7, which shows typical maximum contributions, assuming 20 years' service. Remember pensionable remuneration was capped at £84,000 per annum in the fiscal year 1997/98.

Table 5.6 shows the maximum regular contributions as a percentage of earnings for pensions escalating at 8.5 per cent per annum for those joining pension schemes after 1 June 1989. The relevant earnings cap would have been in place.

As insurance companies can use their own charge structure when calculating these figures, tables will vary very slightly from company to company.

In March 1994 the Inland Revenue announced, through the Association of British Insurers (ABI), a revised method of calculating maximum contributions to take effect from 10 September 1994 for insured schemes and from 1 June 1996 for small self-administered schemes (SSAS), to be treated later in this chapter.

Income was now to be limited to an increase of 6.9 per cent per annum thus reducing limits; pension investment was to be assumed to grow at no more than $8\frac{1}{2}$ per cent per annum, thus reducing limits and the Revenue-approved annuity was limited to an increase of 5% per annum, thus reducing limits.

In addition pension premiums were to be assumed to increase in line with earnings, i.e. at 6.9% per annum This introduced an element of age related limits since

Table 5.7 Maximum contribution levels as a percentage of earnings, for those joining schemes after 1 June 1989

Age	Males		Females		Age	Males		Females	
	NRD 60	NRD 65	NRD 60	NRD 65		NRD 60	NRD 65	NRD 60	NRD 65
20	81	68	95	82	42	107	83	125	99
21	82	69	96	82	43	110	85	129	101
22	83	69	97	82	44	113	86	133	103
23	83	69	97	83	45	117	88	137	105
24	84	70	98	83	46	122	90	142	108
25	84	70	99	84	47	127	92	128	110
26	85	71	99	84	48	133	95	156	113
27	86	71	100	85	49	140	98	164	117
28	86	72	101	86	50	151	101	176	121
29	87	72	102	86	51	163	105	191	125
30	88	73	103	87	52	179	109	210	131
31	89	73	104	88	53	199	115	233	137
32	90	74	105	88	54	226	121	265	145
33	91	74	107	89	55	261	130	306	155
34	92	75	108	90	56	314	141	367	168
35	94	76	109	91	57	401	154	469	184
36	95	77	111	92	58		172		205
37	96	78	113	93	59		195		233
38	98	78	115	94	60		225		269
39	100	79	117	95	61		271		323
40	102	81	119	96	62		346		413
41	104	82	122	98					

clearly for longer-term contributors the indexing factor will result in the same fund being produced for very much lower initial contributions than would be needed for level contributions.

These changes resulted in Table 5.8, which shows typical maximum contribution limits. The higher contribution levels for women result from their greater longevity resulting in dearer annuities.

This table shows the maximum regular contribution levels as a percentage of earnings, restricted to £84,000 per annum in the 1997/98 tax year, under new plans set up to provide maximum benefits assuming the member has 20 years' or more service at NRD (normal retirement date) and no other pension plans.

A further element was introduced at the same time which resulted in a further reduction in limits in some cases. This was the indexing of the earnings cap at 5.3 per cent per annum.

Thus an income indexed at 6.9 per cent and initially below the earnings cap could hit the earnings cap, indexed at 5.3 per cent per annum, before retirement.

Table 5.8 Company pension scheme revenue limits for maximum contributions

Age	Males		Females		Age	Males		Females	
	NRD 60	NRD 65	NRD 60	NRD 65		NRD 60	NRD 65	NRD 60	NRD 65
20	18	13	21	16	42	48	31	56	37
21	19	14	22	16	43	51	33	60	39
22	19	14	23	17	44	55	35	64	41
23	20	15	23	17	45	59	37	69	43
24	21	15	24	18	46	63	39	74	46
25	22	16	25	18	47	69	41	81	49
26	22	16	26	19	48	75	44	88	52
27	23	17	27	20	49	83	47	97	56
28	24	17	28	20	50	92	51	108	60
29	25	18	29	21	51	103	55	120	65
30	26	19	31	22	52	116	60	136	70
31	27	19	32	23	53	134	65	157	77
32	28	20	33	24	54	157	71	185	85
33	30	21	35	25	55	190	79	223	94
34	31	22	37	26	56	240	89	281	105
35	33	23	38	27	57	322	100	378	119
36	34	24	40	28	58		116		137
37	36	25	42	29	59		136		161
38	38	26	45	30	60		164		195
39	40	27	47	32	61		207		245
40	42	28	50	33	62		278		329
41	45	30	53	35					

■ Example 5.38

David Marchant, at 30, is earning £62,000 p.a. He proposes to retire at age 60. Final salary, using indexation of 6.9 per cent p.a. would be £458,905 p.a. The earnings cap of £84,000 indexed at 5.3% in 30 years' time would be £395,485 p.a. Hence this director's final annual salary would be capped at £395,485, considerably reducing the level of pension funding he could do. The breakpoint comes after approximately 24 years when both income and earnings cap would be approximately £251,723 p.a. (see Fig. 5.12).

In the case of those directors who have any sort of pension from previous employment these limits would be reduced accordingly.

The pension can also be funded to provide a pension in retirement for the widow or widower of two-thirds of the member's pension.

Table 5.9 gives an indication of the maximum additional contribution to provide a projected widow(er)'s pension on death after retirement of ⅔rds of the member's pension, as a percentage of the basic investment contribution.

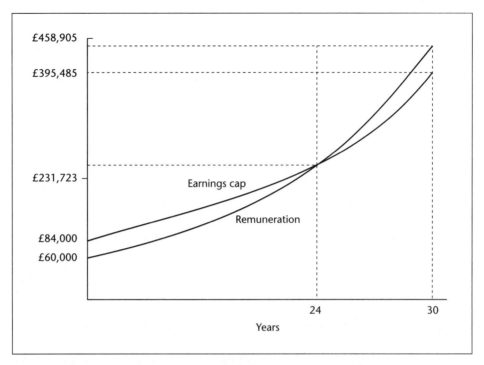

Fig. 5.12 Salary capped before retirement

Table 5.9 Funding for widow's or widower's pension on death in retirement as a percentage of the basic investment contribution sum benefit

| Male minus female | NRA : 60 | | NRA : 65 | |
| | Widow's | Widower's | Widow's | Widower's |
Age	pension	pension	pension	pension
−3	17.5	9.5	19.5	11.5
−2	18.5	9.0	20.5	10.5
−1	19.5	8.5	22.0	10.0
0	21.0	8.0	23.5	9.0
1	22.0	7.0	25.0	8.5
2	23.5	6.5	26.5	7.5
3	24.5	6.0	28.0	7.0
4	26.0	5.5	30.0	6.5
5	27.0	5.0	31.5	6.0
6	28.5	5.0	33.0	5.5
7	29.5	4.5	35.0	5.0

∎ **Example 5.39**

Graham Turner is a controlling director earning £40,000 p.a. He is 35 and his wife, Jennifer, is 32. He wants to retire at 60. Maximum contributions the company can make to an occupational pension scheme are, using Table 5.2 (p. 297),

$$= 33\% \text{ of } £40,000 = \frac{33}{100} \times 40,000 = £13,200 \text{ p.a.}$$

plus using Table 5.8,

$$\text{a further } 24.5\% \text{ of } £40,000 = \frac{24.5}{100} \times 40,000 = £9800 \text{ p.a.}$$

to fund for a widow's pension.

Total contribution = £13,200 + 9800 = £23,000 p.a. = £1917 per month.

In addition to these funding levels the pension can include life assurance cover the premiums for which are not included in the limits. This would come into effect if the member died in service and is therefore called 'death in service' (DIS). In addition to the four times salary cash sum mentioned in Chapter 2, life assurance can be provided specifically to be used to purchase a death in service pension for the widow or widower.

Table 5.10 shows the maximum life assurance allowed to fund a widow's or widower's death in service pension indexed at 5 per cent per annum. These amounts of life assurance will be calculated on allowing spouse a maximum DIS pension of $\frac{4}{9}$th of member's salary at death using annuity rates applicable to the age band.

Table 5.10 shows the maximum multiple of salary that can be provided at outset as a lump sum for a widow(er)'s death-in-service pension in addition to the four times salary life assurance benefit

Table 5.10 Maximum life assurance as a multiple of total remuneration for a DIS pension

Age of wife	Multiple of salary	Age of husband	Multiple of salary
24	13	23	13
25 to 34	12	24 to 32	12
35 to 42	11	33 to 39	11
43 to 48	10	40 to 45	10
49 to 54	9	46 to 51	9
55 to 60	8	52 to 56	8
61 to 65	7	57 to 62	7
66 to 69	6	63 to 67	6
		68 to 69	5

As spouse gets older annuities get cheaper and hence multiples of salary go down.

The figures in all of these tables assume the member can complete 20 years' service to retirement. They are reduced proportionately for shorter periods.

■ Example 5.40

Christine O'Driscoll, 39, on a salary of £35,000, James Turnbull, 25, on a salary of £28,000 and David Jones, 43, salary £42,000 p.a., own and run Benedict Management Consultants Ltd. They are all married and decide to start a company pension plan for themselves funded to the maximum.

They started the company four years ago, and by the time they are each 60 they will have all completed 20 years' service with the company.

Using Tables 5.9 and 5.10,

	Pension contribution £ p.a.	Man's age minus woman's age	Additional contribution for spouse £ p.a.	Total maximum possible contribution £ p.a.
Christine	28% of 35,000 = 9800	−3	9.5% of 35,000 = 3325	13,125
James	22% of 28,000 = 6160	3	24.5% of 28,000 = 6860	13,020
David	51% of 42,000 = 21,420	4	26% of 42,000 = 10,920	32,240

A shareholding director may have the chance to achieve a maximum pension of two-thirds of final remuneration even if he has left its funding very late.

It is interesting to see that although David has left his pension planning to a very late stage he can still end up with a pension of two-thirds of his 'final remuneration' indexed at 5% p.a. and should he die in retirement two-thirds of this, also indexed at 5% p.a., can continue for his widow.

Once again we see the enormous advantages at the later ages that those who own their own private limited companies have.

In addition to all this the three directors can also cater for life assurance of four times salary and an additional amount of life insurance to provide for a spouse's death in service pension of four-ninths times remuneration. Using Table 5.10 we see the total amounts of life assurance would be,

	Multiple of salary	Sum assured	Premium £ p.a.
Christine	4 + 11 = 15	455,000	906
James	4 + 13 = 17	476,000	691
David	4 + 11 = 15	630,000	2760

Approximate premiums are calculated using Table 3.8.

The whole package will cost the company £64,842. However, it can all be set off against corporation tax. And so a good measure of financial planning for these directors can be done totally tax free. And do remember this is in addition to their incomes, not out of their incomes as in the case of the self-employed.

It is important to note that all these extra benefits can be funded over and above the maximum pension for the shareholding director. The funding levels for the PPS must include all of these if desired. The difference between the two is now seen to be enormous. For example, a 50 year old controlling director with 20 years' service at retirement can fund for a maximum pension of two-thirds of final salary, pension indexed at 5 per cent per annum. A 50 year old sole trader just starting his or her pension can come nowhere near this. But, over and above all this the director can fund for a widow's or widower's pension of two-thirds of his or her own plus a pension of ⁴⁄₉th of remuneration if he or she dies in service plus four times remuneration lump sum death benefit.

Pensions in force before 17 September 1994 and being funded at levels higher than the new maximums will be allowed to continue for five years after that date and then will be brought into line. Any increase which takes place before that will immediately make them subject to the new limits.

The de minimus rule

There is a level of funding below which the contribution does not have to be checked against the new basis. This is called the de minimus contribution limit. This applies where total contributions, excluding contributions for death in service benefits, do not exceed the higher of,

- 15 per cent of remuneration (subject to the earnings cap)
- 6 per cent of the earnings cap rounded up to the nearest £1000, subject to the proviso that the contribution has not been reduced from a previous higher level. Contributions must not exceed 100 per cent of income.

Thus in the fiscal year 1997/98 this was a contribution level of,

$$6\% \text{ of } £84,000 = \frac{6}{100} \times 84,000 = £5040$$

which rounded up to the nearest £1000 is £6000 per annum.

> The de minimus rule can be of enormous advantage for spouse's pensions.

You will remember the discussion on company pensions for spouses earlier in the chapter. In these situations the de minimus rule will be particularly valuable.

In Examples 5.39 and 5.40 the premiums could be increased to £3000 per annum, thus providing even better benefits.

The tax-free lump sum

Part of the pension can, of course, be commuted for a tax-free lump sum using the criteria described in Chapter 2. The maximum lump sum available is 1½ times final salary calculated on the basis of ³⁄₈₀th of final salary for every year of service with the company up to retirement.

All of these maximums will be governed by the earnings cap, i.e. the amount of salary allowed to be pensioned. This was £84,000 in the fiscal year 1997/98 and will be increased in line with the Retail Prices Index (RPI). Thus someone who retired after 40 years' service on 3 June 1997 on a salary of £100,000 was able to take maximum tax-free cash of $1\frac{1}{2}$ × £84,000 = £126,000.

The maximum lump sum available is $1\frac{1}{2}$ times final remuneration.

Under these criteria the whole of the fund could be taken as tax-free cash. Let us say that the person in this example had built up a fund of £100,000 in his or her pension, thus, because he or she would be allowed to take up to £126,000 in tax-free cash he or she could take the whole £100,000 in this way.

Of course it is extremely unlikely today that anyone would ever complete 40 years with the same firm, but there is a way of achieving maximum tax-free cash of $1\frac{1}{2}$ × final salary after only 20 years' service. This is calculated on different criteria and is 2.25 times the pension which could have been taken had the whole of the fund been thus used. Unlike the retirement annuity contract (RAC) described in Chapter 2, this time it is 2.25 times a pension based on the type of actual pension taken. Thus if tax-free cash is taken together with a pension indexed at 5 per cent per annum it is by applying that type of pension to the whole fund that the tax-free cash is calculated. It will be remembered that in the case of the RAC whatever actual pension is taken the calculation is based on the maximum pension which could have been taken, i.e. single life, level, no guarantee, paid annually in arrears. It can be seen that if the pension is funded at the maximum possible then two-thirds of final remuneration can be taken as a pension and also indexed at 5 per cent per annum. We know that 2.25 times this can be commuted for a lump sum, i.e. $2.25 \times \frac{2}{3}$ of final salary,

$$\frac{9}{4} \times \frac{2}{3} \times \text{final salary} = 1\frac{1}{2} \times \text{final salary}$$

Company pension schemes are governed by the provisions of Finance Act 1989 and the 1991 Practice Notes. Limits were changed, as described earlier on 1 September 1994 and 1 June 1996. The Pensions Act of 1995 was largely concerned with administration in the aftermath of the Maxwell affair but did make mandatory an annual increase in pensions in payment (see later).

A company can set up however many company pension schemes it wishes.

A company can set up however many company pension schemes it wishes with different insurers, but maximum funding limits would apply to total premiums. It is often not clear that more than one company pension can be run by a limited company. It is possible to be a member of as many company pension schemes as wished.

Maximum funding limits before Finance Act 1989 and after Finance (No.2) Act 1987

Both of these acts are now consolidated in Part 14 of the Income and Corporation Taxes Act (ICTA) 1988.

The two acts govern limits for pension schemes established before 14 March 1989 for members who joined on or after 17 March 1987 and before 1 June 1989. The differences are:

1 For the maximum pension permitted there is no cap on earnings.
2 For the maximum tax-free cash pensionable income is restricted to £100,000 per annum, although this may be increased by treasury order. Thus for someone earning £200,000 on retirement his or her maximum pension could be $\frac{2}{3}$rd × £200,000 = £133,333 per annum but the maximum tax-free cash would be only $1\frac{1}{2}$ × £100,000 = £150,000.

Before Finance Act 1989 there was no cap on earnings to limit maximum permitted pension.

The tax-free cash is based on three eighteiths of final remuneration for every year of service up to retirement age with a maximum of $1\frac{1}{2}$ times final remuneration capped at £100,000, thus taking 40 years' service to attain. This time the accelerated rate using 2.25 times pension is not available. There is, however, an accelerated scale based on a three step formula:

$$\text{Step 1} \quad \frac{\text{Actual pension – basic pension (60th scale)}}{\text{Maximum pension (30ths scale) – basic pension (60th scale)}} \times 100 = \%$$

Step 2 (Maximum tax-free cash – basic tax-free cash × % in Step 1

Step 3 Add result of Step 2 to basic tax-free cash = Total tax-free cash permitted

The sixtieths scale pension is discussed later.

■ Example 5.41

Karen Jones retires on a final salary of £40,000 after 16 years of service with her company. The actual annual pension she receives is £18,000.

Using the $\frac{3}{80}$th scale she could commute some of this for tax-free cash of 16 × $\frac{3}{80}$ × 40,000 = £24,000. Using the formula,

Service 16 years
Final salary £40,000
Actual annual pension provided £18,000

Actual pension		= £18,000 p.a.
Basic pension ($\frac{1}{60}$)	= $\frac{16}{60}$ × 40,000	= £10,667 p.a.
Maximum pension ($\frac{1}{30}$)	= $\frac{16}{30}$ × 40,000	= £21,333 p.a.

Basic cash ($^3/_{80}$) $\qquad = \; ^{48}/_{80} \times 40,000 \quad = £24,000$

Maximum cash (see Table 5.12) $\; = \; ^{81}/_{80} \times 40,000 \quad = £40,500$

Step 1 $\dfrac{18,000 - 10,667}{21,333 - 10,667} \times 100 = \dfrac{7333}{10,666} \times 100 \quad = 68.75\%$

Step 2 $(40,500 - 24,000) \times \dfrac{68.75}{100} = 11,344$

Step 3 $11,344 + 24,000 = £35,344$

Hence the maximum tax-free cash could be £35,344.

■ Example 5.42

Service 23 years

Final salary £150,000

Actual annual pension provided £95,000

Actual pension $\qquad\qquad\qquad\qquad\qquad\qquad = \quad$ £95,000 p.a.

Basic pension ($^1/_{60}$) $\qquad\quad = \; ^{23}/_{60} \times 150,000 \; = \quad$ £57,500 p.a.

Maximum pension ($^1/_{30}$) $\qquad = \; ^2/_3 \times 150,000 \quad = £100,000$ p.a.

Basic cash ($^3/_{80}$) $\qquad\qquad = \; ^{69}/_{80} \times 100,000 \; = \quad$ £86,250

Maximum cash (see Table 5.12) $\; = \; 1^1/_2 \times 100,000 \quad = £150,000$

NB: For cash purposes remuneration is capped at £100,000.

Step 1 $\dfrac{95,000 - 57,500}{100,000 - 57,500} \times 100 = \dfrac{37,500}{42,500} \times 100 = 88.26\%$

Step 2 $(150,000 - 86,250) \times \dfrac{88.26}{100} = 56,266$

Step 3 $56,266 + 86,250 = £142,516$

Hence the maximum tax-free cash could be £142,516.

Maximum funding limits before Finance (No.2) Act 1987

This act brought about massive changes in limits since for schemes established before 17 March 1987 for members who joined before that date, the uplifted six-tieths scale was in effect.

The uplifted sixtieths scale

Table 5.11 shows how pension entitlement could be accelerated achieving a full two-thirds of final salary after only 10 years of service to retirement.

Table 5.11 The uplifted sixtieths scale

Years of service to normal retirement age	Maximum pension as a fraction of final salary
1–5	1/60th for each year
6	8/60
7	16/60
8	24/60
9	32/60
10 or more	40/60

In the same way the tax-free cash limits are governed by an uplifted eightieths scale (see Table 5.12).

Table 5.12 The uplifted eightieths scale

Years of service to normal retirement age	Maximum pension as a fraction of final salary
1–8	3/80ths for each year
9	30/80
10	36/80
11	42/80
12	48/80
13	54/80
14	63/80
15	72/80
16	81/80
17	90/80
18	99/80
19	108/80
20 or more	120/80

Clearly the benefits of the company pension have decreased over the years, those relating to pensions starting now being less favourable than those in operation before March 1989, which in turn were very much less favourable than those set up before 17 March 1987. However, it still compares extremely favourably at later ages with the personal pension scheme, its only disadvantage being the lack of a waiver of contribution option, making a pension guarantee policy desirable at a considerably greater cost.

> **Before Finance (No.2) Act 1987 a maximum pension could be achieved with only 10 years of service in the company.**

Continuity of service and continued or preserved rights

There are some interesting situations where 'continuity of service' and 'continued or preserved rights' are allowed. These would occur in such situations as management buy outs when the new management was substantially the same as before the buy out. Let us say the original company was running a pension scheme which had commenced pre-17 March 1987 and therefore carried the most favourable pension rights. However, the new company, for various reasons, decided to start a new company scheme shortly after the management buy out in June 1987. Those employees joining this scheme who had been members of the previous scheme before 17 March 1987 could claim continuity of service, which means the years of service used to calculate the pension would start from the time they joined the previous company. In the same way they could claim the benefit structure applicable to the pre-1987 pension. This would still apply even if there were a gap of a number of years between the termination of the original scheme and joining the new scheme. It is rather like any new or even additional company scheme being anchored to the original scheme from the point of view of years of service and benefit structure.

Other situations to which this would apply would be a member moving from one subsidiary to another of the same holding company running a different pension scheme. It would usually also apply to a new company with the same management and business arising from the ashes of a liquidated company, but this would be at the discretion of the Inland Revenue. Similarly a pre-1987 pension scheme which a company had cancelled some years ago could be restarted and continue to enjoy pre-1987 benefits. Even if the company for some reason decided to start a totally new scheme this new scheme anchored to the orginal would also enjoy pre-1987 benefits.

> A pre-Finance (No.2) Act 1987 company pension could be gold dust in your hand.

In all these scenarios it is important to confirm with the Pension Schemes Office (PSO) that this will be the case. If this is not done at the time of the change, problems could ensue.

Any shareholding director who is eligible to benefit from the above situations truly has gold dust in his or her hand.

Retirement ages

For schemes approved on or after 29 November 1991 normal retirement ages for men and women are between 60 and 75. For schemes approved before 29 November 1991, post-1989 members are restricted to the age range 60 to 75. The permitted ages for pre-1987 and 1987 to 1989 members are 60 to 70 for men and 55 to 70 for women, although for a controlling director or husband or wife of a controlling director, it is 60 to 70. Where it can be demonstrated that a member is likely to continue working beyond age 70, it is possible to obtain approval of a later normal retirement age.

Retained benefits

In general, when calculating maximum benefits possible from a current employer's pension scheme, previous pension benefits which are retained by the member have to be deducted.

Thus if a member's maximum possible pension from his or her current scheme were £20,000 per annum and a previous pension scheme would produce £3000 per annum then the maximum he or she would receive from his or her current scheme would be £17,000 per annum. These retained previous benefits have to be taken into account when calculating maximum premiums for a new company scheme to avoid any possibility of overfunding.

> **Retained benefits have to be taken into account when calculating maximum pension contributions.**

Retained benefits include:

1 Deferred pensions and pensions in payment in respect of previous employment.
2 The annuity equivalent of lump sums received or receivable from previous pension schemes.
3 Pensions and the annuity equivalent of lump sums arising from personal pension schemes or retirement annuity contracts relating to service with the same or a former employer, or to previous self-employment. (In the case of a post-1989 pensioned controlling director only those pensions relating to the same employer are taken into account.)
4 Benefits arising from transfer payments received by the current employer from a scheme of a different employer.

Where any of these benefits relate to a wholly concurrent employment or occupation they will not reduce the maximum benefits of the scheme being considered.

The sixtieths or straight sixtieths scale

If the member's maximum benefits are calculated on the straight sixtieths scale then retained benefits are not taken into account.

The exception to this rule is the controlling director in which case the value of personal pension schemes and retirement annuity contracts is taken into account if they relate to earnings from the same employer. This scale allows a pension of one-sixtieth of final remuneration for every year of service up to a maximum of two-thirds after 40 years, pension indexed at 5 per cent per annum.

> **The straight sixtieths scale can be enormously valuable in certain situations.**

Retained lump sum benefits are treated in exactly the same way under the same rules, the equivalent of the straight sixtieths scale for pensions being the three-eightieths scale for lump sums up to a maximum of $1\frac{1}{2}$ times final remuneration.

This scale can be enormously valuable in certain situations.

■ Example 5.43

Richard Porter has been head hunted at the age of 45. He can pretty well dictate his package. In his previous job his years of service entitled him to a full two-thirds of final salary indexed at 5% p.a. plus $^2/_3$ for his wife on death in retirement. He left that company on an annual salary of £120,000. This salary will be dynamised with respect to his pension but will be limited by the earnings cap. Hence it would appear that his new company is unable to offer him a pension because of his retained pension benefit. However, the straight sixtieths does not have to take retained benefits into consideration. This means a pension with the new company can be funded on the straight sixtieths scale to give Richard an additional pension of $^{15}/_{60}$th final salary, limited, of course, by the earnings cap.

Richard is in the very enviable position of receiving at retirement a pension from his previous company of two-thirds of final salary plus a further one quarter of final salary from his new company. In other words $(^2/_3 + ^1/_4)$ times final salary = eleven twelfths of final salary, but limited by the earnings cap.

The same situation will often be true of those retired from the armed forces in their mid-forties already in receipt of a pension. These retained benefits would often preclude pension contributions being made by their new employer. However, once again the straight sixtieths scheme can be used to great account.

In all these cases the individual would be eligible to invest in a personal pension scheme instead. Calculations would have to be done to determine the relevant merit of the two possibilities.

Pension increases

As a result of the Pensions Act 1995 schemes are required to increase pensions, derived from premiums paid after 6 April 1997, in payment by at least the lower of 5 per cent per annum or the increase in the RPI. Thus a final fund could be in two parts, one from premiums paid before 6 April 1997 and one after. The pension from the latter part must be indexed as indicated but that from the former could, if so wished, be level.

The company pension loanback

A loan to the sponsoring company can be taken directly from a small self-administered pension scheme (SSAS), and is known as a loanback (see later in this chapter). Most money purchase company schemes offered by insurance companies have what is called a loanback facility, which is not actually a loan from the funds of the scheme but a loan from the insurance company which takes the pension scheme as collateral. It is governed by exactly the same rules as the loan from the SSAS. In other words the loan cannot be more than 50 per cent of the value of the pension fund and in the first two years of the pension scheme only 25 per cent excluding any transfer values. Interest on the loan, which must be at a commercial rate, usually bank base rate + 3 per cent, is paid by the company to the insurance company. The company receives tax relief on the interest payments which, to all intents and purposes, end up gross in the pension fund. The insurance company usually has a special fixed interest fund into which this money goes. The company running the pension scheme switches a proportion of its funds equal to the amount of the loan into this fund, which is therefore growing, free of all UK taxes, at the same rate that the company is being charged. This is, therefore, equivalent to the company paying the interest on the loan into its own pension scheme which is what in fact happens in the case of the SSAS (see Fig. 5.13).

> **The company can borrow up to 50 per cent of the value of the pension fund against the pension.**

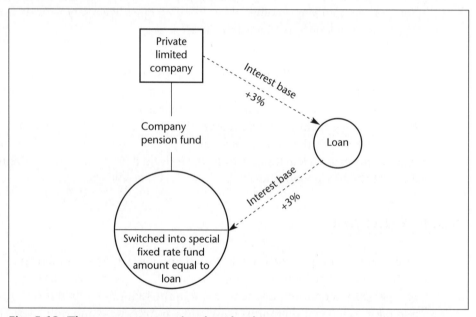

Fig. 5.13 The company pension loanback

The guidelines servicing the loanback are contained in Pension Schemes Office (PSO) Memorandum 58, February 1979. The loan has to be for bona fide commercial reasons and cannot, for example, be used to furnish the shareholding directors with a yacht. Each loan depends on its own individual circumstances. However, as a broad guide the following reasons would normally be acceptable:

1 To purchase commercial property such as offices, factory, warehouse.
2 To extend or modernise such an existing property.
3 To purchase capital items for use in the sponsoring company's business, such as:
   – plant and machinery
   – vehicles in a transport company

- aircraft for an aircraft leasing or taxiing company
- computer installation
- to provide new tools, moulds, dies, for an engineering company
- to finance additional research and development.

These are simply examples, the list is not extensive and it does not imply that any of the constituents would be automatically granted.

A regular pattern of borrowing will not be allowed and at least two years must elapse before the next loan. The PSO will occasionally check the company's accounts to follow through the use of the money.

The reoccurrence of any occasion similar to the Mirror Group situation is now totally protected by the Inland Revenue Practice Notes, July 1997 which state that only loanbacks against the pension funds of controlling directors (definition earlier in the chapter) will be allowed.

Although loanbacks can usually be repaid in part or in total at any time, payment must be completed not later than one year before retirement. Failure to do this would result in the funds of the pension scheme being reduced by the amount owed.

■ Use of the loanback

In a year when a company is faced with problems the loanback facility can be an extremely efficient instrument of solution.

■ Example 5.44

Three controlling directors running Delicious Biscuits Ltd are faced with considerable cashflow problems since the profits they can retain this year are only £79,000 when ideally they need around £180,000 for the purchase of new plant. Pension contribution for these directors is £50,000 p.a. each.

	Pension contribution paid £
Before tax profits	250,000
Pension contribution	150,000
Taxable profits	100,000
Corporation tax at 21%	21,000
Retained profits	79,000
Cash available for company	79,000

However, they have considerable funds in their company pension scheme which has been running for several years. They therefore decide to take a loanback of £101,000 which brings them up to the cashflow level they need. (The interest payable on the loan attracts tax relief and to all intents and purposes goes into the pension gross.) They had considered suspending their pension premiums for the year which would have produced the following figures.

	No pension £
Before tax profits	250,000
Pension contribution	Nil
Taxable profits	250,000
Corporation tax at 21%	52,500
Retained profits	197,500
Loanback	Nil
Cash available for company	197,500

This would have given them sufficient cashflow but at the expense of £150,000 less going into their pension. Pension contribution plus loanback results in,

	Pension contribution paid plus loanback £
Before tax profits	250,000
Pension contribution	150,000
Taxable profits	100,000
Corporation tax at 21%	21,000
Retained profits	79,000
Loanback	101,000
Cash available for company	180,000

Had the profit been £450,000, putting the company into the marginal tax rate of 33.5%, the effect of retaining the pension investment of £150,000 would have been even more dramatic, since it would have saved the company tax of £50,250.

THE SMALL SELF-ADMINISTERED PENSION SCHEME (SSAS)

This sort of company pension enables its members to exert a considerable degree of control over its investments since they are responsible either directly or indirectly for managing the scheme's administration and investment choice. These two aspects constitute a fundamental difference from the insured scheme where the insurance company will be responsible for them.

In all other aspects, such as funding limits and emerging benefits, the SSAS is exactly the same as the insured scheme. Even the loanback facility differs only from that of the insured scheme in that it is, in fact, a direct loan from the pension funds.

The range of investments that the directors, who will normally also be trustees of the scheme, can make is limited by Memorandum 58 issued by the Inland Revenue in February 1979. This prohibits investments in such 'pride of possession' assets as gold bullion, yachts, classic cars, antiques, works of art, jewellery etc. However, the range of possible investments is wide, including:

> **The small self-administered pension scheme cannot invest in such things as yachts and classic cars.**

- pension funds of any insurance company
- bank deposits
- loans to the company (the loanback)
- property
- UK and overseas equities
- pooled funds such as unit trusts and the investment funds of OEICs
- building society accounts
- national savings bonds
- investment accounts
- UK government stocks
- local authority bonds
- debentures of quoted UK companies
- financial futures
- traded options
- commodities
- the shares of the sponsoring company.

The members of the SSAS, the shareholding directors of a private limited company (not more than twelve), will probably see the two main attractions as the facility for the pension to buy commercial property and even to raise loans for that purpose and the possibility of the SSAS buying the shares of the sponsor's company. Very few directors of such companies will normally have either the expertise or time to benefit in any way from the facility to choose investments.

In addition to this and in contrast to the insured scheme, is a common trust fund which means there are no individual funds held for individual directors. The assets are held for the benefit of all the members as a whole. This could be an advantage in that if there is a surplus in a member's notional share it can be allocated across the other members, otherwise it would have to be returned to the company and taxed at 40 per cent. The disadvantage could be that in the event of a claim on the fund perhaps because of a death of a member the beneficiary would be entitled to the benefits of the proportion due to the member, for example, one-quarter. One-quarter of the fund would have to be realised. Suppose the

> **It is extremely important for the members of a SSAS to agree a common approach to investment.**

deceased member had insisted on investing what he or she saw as his or her share in investments which turned out to perform badly in comparison to the other investments. Although what he or she considered to be his or her investments would not actually equal one-quarter of the total value of the fund, the beneficiary would still be entitled to that full quarter of the value. Earmarked funds would have had the opposite effect. Clearly the members of the scheme would have to agree a common approach to investment which may not be easy.

The purchase of shares or property already owned by the company by the SSAS could be seen as a means of injecting money into the company, but it has to be remembered that this could raise a potential liability to capital gains tax and, in the case of a property, bring about the problem of double taxation, discussed earlier in this chapter.

■ The purchase of property

For property purchase the SSAS is allowed to borrow up to three times total annual contributions plus 45 per cent of the value of the existing fund.

The purchase of a property from which to run the company could be seen as desirable. The pension is allowed to borrow up to three times the amount of total annual contributions to the scheme, excluding any additional voluntary contributions, plus 45 per cent of the market value of the existing scheme investments. Normally a deposit will be needed so sufficient funds must already be in the pension.

Advantages

1 Company contributions to the scheme enabling the purchase of the property and paying off of the loan will attract tax relief.
2 Rental income can be offset as an expense for the purposes of corporation tax.
3 Rental income accumulates tax free in the SSAS.
4 When the property is sold no CGT is paid.

Disadvantages

■ If the property constitutes a large proportion of the total investment in the SSAS there would be considerable problems should funds be needed to provide benefits on death or transfer to another scheme. The property may have to be sold when the market is low.

Residential property may be considered if it is to house a caretaker or some such person or if it is occupied by the proprietor of a shop who rents the whole premises.

■ The purchase of sponsoring company shares

The Revenue is likely to allow up to 25 per cent approximately of the total pension fund to be invested in the shares of the sponsoring company and this should not exceed 30 per cent of the company's issued share capital.

This sort of investment could produce problems since the Revenue will want to be satisfied that it represents a reasonable investment. To do this substantial dividends would have to be declared and the directors may not wish to do this. In addition, when the shares need to be realised this may not be easy since close companies tend to be difficult to sell.

■ Life assurance

Life assurance can be included in the same way as with the insured scheme and this would simply be purchased through a life office.

■ The costs

These will include dealing with documentation and Revenue negotiation, actuarial reports initially and thereafter every three years which would include property valuation, a professional trustee called the pensioneer trustee, accounting and financial management and possibly the services of a stockbroker or at least dealing costs for the investments. In general a large scheme will cost less than its equivalent insured scheme.

The deferred annuity

The Pension Schemes Office (PSO) announced in May 1994 through Memorandum 119 that the purchase of an annuity may be deferred until the member reaches the age of 75 and the member's pension be paid directly from the scheme assets. The pension has to be within 10 per cent of the pension he or she would have received if an annuity had been taken. Tax-free cash can be taken at this time. Should the member die before his or her 75th birthday this whole arrangement passes to the spouse who must take an annuity before he or she reaches 75 or his or her husband or wife would have done so. If he or she dies before this the pension fund is returned to the trustees who, if there are still remaining dependants, can arrange pensions, within the usual limits, until they are 18 or finish normal full-time education. Any surplus funds can be reapportioned to other members of the SSAS. If this is not possible they are paid back to the company and taxed at 40 per cent. The director has to have been a member of the SSAS for at least five years before being able to take the deferred annuity. For any director joining the scheme after 1989 he or she would have to retire from the company at this point although he or she would still be able to continue as a consultant to it. Pre-1989 this was not a requirement.

> A director has to have been a member of a SSAS for at least five years before being able to take the deferred annuity.

■ The SSAS loanback

The SSAS has a true loanback situation where the pension fund actually lends to the sponsoring company. The rules for this are exactly the same as those for the insured scheme but this time the loan actually comes from the fund and the interest is paid directly into the fund.

COMPARISON OF THE THREE WAYS OF PURCHASING A COMPANY PROPERTY

Property purchased by the SSAS

The sale of a property inside a SSAS attracts no capital gains tax

---

The pension purchases the property either outright from existing funds or by raising a loan. The property is owned by the pension and rented to the sponsoring company, at a market rent. Rental payments attract corporation tax relief. The pension pays no tax on them since it is free of all UK taxes as follows.

1 When the property is sold there is no CGT liability.
2 By use of the deferred annuity and younger directors joining the pension fund there is no need to sell the property if there are sufficient other funds to eventually provide annuities. This is because the scheme is a common trust fund.
3 Rental paid attracts corporation tax relief.
4 The property is free from creditors, but this is true whatever investment is in; either a SSAS or an insured scheme.
5 Ownership of the property by the SSAS does not increase the tax-free cash available which is a maximum of $1\frac{1}{2}$ times income.
6 Prudent investors look for a spread of investments to ensure that the assets are not too dependent on one particular sector and there is obviously a considerable risk where a SSAS invests a very substantial part of its funds in a single property.
7 The property does not appear on the balance sheets of the company and cannot represent the collateral for future loans for expansion purposes, etc.
8 There are several possibilities, such as death of a director or him or her moving companies, which would cause the forced sale of the property, taking the choice out of the directors' hands and resulting in the full value not being realised.
9 There is little flexibility for the pension premiums since they must be at least one-third of the loan unless substantial funds were in the pension at the time of the purchase. They must also cover the repayment of both the capital and interest of the loan. Directors' salaries must be sufficient to allow the required premiums.
10 As the SSAS is subject to triennial actuarial reviews the property has to be valued every three years.

11 The SSAS does not receive tax relief on the loan interest payments as it does not pay tax.
12 As discussed earlier, Memorandum 58 limits the types of investment permitted to the SSAS. The purchase of property is allowed, provided it represents 'a reasonable part of the fund', which is normally considered to be no more than 50 per cent of the fund assets.
13 A considerable amount of time needs to be spent deciding on other investments in the SSAS. Most directors are fully occupied running their own companies and cannot afford to devote the time needed to make informed investment decisions.
14 A SSAS cannot be seen to trade which might inhibit future sale and purchase of properties.
15 The SSAS is a common trust fund so individual directors lose their individual investment choice.
16 There are restrictions on the borrowing by the SSAS. They are usually short-term loans, three to five years, making capital repayments high. They are restricted to three times pension premiums plus 45 per cent of existing funds.
17 Rental payments are likely to increase over the years.
18 There is no asset owned by an estate to pass on to children.

Property purchased by the company – pension need not be a SSAS

If the company does not have the funds for a deposit this could be borrowed from the company pension if there are sufficient funds in it. The company owns the property and would get tax relief on any interest paid on the loan or loans.

1 The indexing of capital gains, annual allowance and business retirement relief could substantially reduce CGT when the company is sold and therefore the property.
2 Clearly the property must be sold when the company is sold.
3 Interest paid attracts corporation tax relief.

The property bought by the company appears on the balance sheet and can represent the collateral for future loans.

4 Property not free from creditors.
5 Tax-free cash is available from the pension as well as the cash value of the property.
6 The property appears on the balance sheet of the company and can represent the collateral for future loans for expansion purposes, etc.
7 There is total flexibility of pension payments which can be increased, decreased, stopped and started, always, of course, within the limits of maximum allowed funding.
8 Interest payments are fully tax relievable.
9 Individual funds in an insured company pension scheme are earmarked for individual directors entirely at their personal choice.
10 The method of purchase is the simplest.

11 Capital could be paid off in a good year thus reducing interest payments.

12 There is a possible double liability to capital gains tax, discussed earlier in this chapter.

13 Problems could be caused to the director(s) when leaving an estate to dependants, e.g. a son works in the company which owns the property, but two daughters and their husbands do not. How is the director to leave the shares of the company? (This emphasises the need for long-term financial planning.)

14 Currently shares can be transferred to dependants or put in trust for them with no liability to inheritance tax. Part of the value of the shares will be represented by the property.

15 The balance sheet of the company would be strengthened by the inclusion of an increasingly valuable property which could be important in seeking a flotation in the future.

16 The intention to sell a company property to the SSAS could potentially cause loans secured by the property to be called in, apart from triggering a CGT liability.

17 It is likely that life assurance would be needed as collateral security and if not it would nevertheless be a wise outlay.

18 The company will probably be unable to negotiate a long-term loan on an interest only basis which will make the repayments heavy.

Property purchased by director(s) using the insured company pension as the vehicle for repaying the loan

They rent it to their company. Rental income can be set off against the interest payments with respect to income tax. They could repay the capital element of the loan from the tax-free cash available from the pension at retirement.

1 The property does not need to be sold on sale of the business and represents an income-producing asset. On death CGT is wiped out and the value of the property is rebased for CGT purposes. If it is sold before that indexing relief and annual relief apply as could business retirement relief. However the property need never be sold.

2 Rental paid attracts corporation tax relief.

3 Property not free from creditors.

4 Tax-free cash is available from the pension as well as the cash value of the property.

5 Pension premiums are constrained by needing to be sufficient to produce enough tax-free cash to pay off the loan.

6 Rental income can be set off against interest payments on the loan for income tax purposes.

7 Individual funds are earmarked for individual directors entirely at their personal choice.

8 The method of purchase is relatively simple and some of the cash could be

raised by capital raising against one's home which considerably reduces the rate of interest on that part of the loan.

9 Rental payments are likely to increase over the years.

10 Could assist inheritance planning since if a son or daughter is working in the company and he or she expects to inherit the company, the property could be left to other children.

11 The capital repayment of the loan is deferred into the future which means that inflation works for the director(s) and the loan is eventually repaid by discounted pounds from the pension fund. We have already seen in Chapter 3 that a pension-related loan is the most tax efficient method possible.

12 The growth in the value of the property together with the value of the company pension plan enables the director(s) to accumulate substantial wealth outside the company without having to take speculative risks (the tenant is guaranteed) and without diverting a considerable amount of time supervising the other investments in the SSAS. This allows the director(s) to achieve flexibility with regard to personal financial planning. Their future financial independence is now in three separate areas rather than two. The property and the director or directors' shareholdings can be disposed of entirely separately.

> **A company property owned by one or more shareholding directors could assist inheritance planning**

13 At retirement or sale of the company the property does not have to be sold. It will generate income additional to the pension.

14 Can be used as collateral security for a wide range of personal needs including financing new business ventures.

15 Maximum loan possible is usually a multiple of income, including rental. This could limit the sort of property possible.

16 Personal ownership protects the property against company creditors in the event of a failure. Unless, of course, personal guarantees have been given.

17 Business retirement relief (see later in this chapter) on the property is reduced or even wiped out if rental is charged. However, indexation relief is available.

18 If rental is replaced by increased salary then business retirement relief becomes available and increased pension contributions could be made.

19 It is likely that life assurance would be needed as collateral security and, if not, it would nevertheless be a wise outlay.

20 Fifty per cent of business property relief on IHT is available on death or transfer of the property (see Chapter 6).

INSURANCE-BASED HYBRID SMALL SELF-ADMINISTERED SCHEME

A market need became apparent for directors who wanted to put a company property into their pension scheme but have only a limited involvement with the administration and choice of other investments in the scheme. To cater for this need insurance companies have produced a hybrid scheme in which the ordinary insured scheme is included in a fully fledged SSAS. The insurance company then carries out limited administration of the scheme or provides a full service.

> **The hybrid SSAS offers perceived advantages but can limit involvement with investment or management decisions.**

In this way directors can avail themselves of the advantages they perceive in a SSAS while limiting the need to be over involved in investment or management decisions.

THE FUNDED UNAPPROVED RETIREMENT BENEFITS SCHEME (FURBS)

We have seen earlier how, since 1987, the level of benefits from the approved company pension scheme have been reduced. Perhaps the earnings cap represents the greatest limitation of all, especially as it is indexed in line with the Retail Prices Index (RPI) and not the Average Earnings Index (AEI). In Chapter 2 it was clear how quickly these two diverge (see Fig. 5.14). Therefore, those joining pension schemes after 1989 face ever reducing benefits as the earnings cap in real terms reduces these in relation to increasing salaries. This will be particularly so for the higher earner. This could affect badly the recruitment of high flyers since, although they will want to improve their career, they may not want to leave a company where their pension benefits relate to an earlier more favourable structure.

> **The earnings cap on pensions could affect adversely the recruitment of high flyers.**

For those not facing this difficult choice but with increasing responsibility and correspondingly increasing salaries a pension of two-thirds of a final capped remuneration may be very small in relation to actual final salary.

The funded unapproved retirement benefits scheme (FURBS) could be the answer. It has none of the limitations of the approved scheme apart from the need for its benefits to be commensurate with the duties and remuneration of the employee. Thus it could be funded to produce, together with a director's approved scheme, a pension of two-thirds of *actual* salary.

For employees or directors who cannot achieve even two-thirds of capped salary because of shortage of years they can spend with their new company it can be funded to achieve this. It was the Finance Act 1989, which, while putting more limitation on company pension benefits, at the same time allowed employers to establish FURBS.

The guidance notes from the Revenue suggest three situations where these schemes may be of particular value:

1 where an employer wants to offer some employees a pension greater than two-thirds of final salary

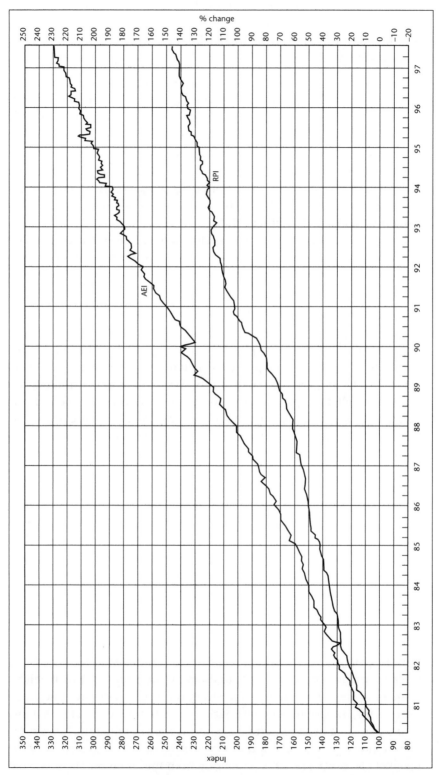

Fig. 5.14 Comparison of National Average Earnings Index (AEI) with Retail Prices Index (RPI)
Source: Micropal

2 where the employee has not completed the full 20 years' service to qualify for a full two-thirds pension

3 where the employee wants to pension earnings over the earnings cap which stands at £84,000.

Because of the future increasing gap between the earnings cap and the actual remuneration of higher earners, these people will see the company pension become a smaller and smaller percentage of their actual earnings. This will make FURBS particularly relevant. We saw in Chapter 2 the same sort of reduction that both the basic state pension and SERPS bore, in real terms, to actual earnings.

The scheme is written under trust and, once paid, the money cannot be reclaimed as a result of the employer being taken over or going into liquidation, or the employee leaving that particular company when he or she could, in fact, request its transfer to another FURBS.

The contributions can purchase a wide range of investments such as property, unit trusts, the funds of OEICs, shares and commercial loans to the employer. Life assurance and critical illness cover can also be included.

Tax

The contributions by the employer will usually be treated as a business expense and therefore qualify for corporation tax relief. Care would have to be taken with contributions for proprietorial directors as an over large contribution could prejudice tax relief. A proprietorial director is a director, with or without a shareholding, of a close company or an employee of that company who is so closely involved in the activities of the company that he or she is effectively involved in its control. An employee who is the spouse of a director will be within this definition.

Employee contributions would not receive tax relief but worse still they could trigger the gift with reservation rules and cause an IHT liability on any benefits paid to dependants. In addition they could involve the settlements provision under the Income and Corporation Taxes Act (ICTA) 1988 and the Taxation of Chargeable Gains Act (TCGA) 1992, possibly resulting in an additional tax charge on the fund. For this reason most insurance companies do not allow contributions to be made by employees. As far as the fund is concerned it is taxed on arising income and on chargeable capital gains at basic rate income tax which, in the fiscal year 1997/98,was 23 per cent.

At maturity the fund is encashed to pay benefits and any tax due at this point must be paid, e.g. CGT on capital growth in unit trusts. The benefit can be paid as a pension produced from a compulsory pension annuity which will be taxed as earned income, or as a lump sum which is free of tax because the employee has paid tax on the employer's contributions. It is therefore unlikely that any scheme would pay out a pension since if a pension were required the lump sum could be used to buy a purchased annuity which is favourably taxed (see chapter 6). The member can receive benefits on retiring from the company at any age between 50 and 75. Inheritance tax is not usually paid on death benefits since the trustees will have discretion with respect to whom the benefit is paid.

In the event of a critical illness the sum assured would be paid to the trustees of the FURBS. If the incapacity were such as to prevent the member's return to work the sum assured would be paid directly to him or her. If this were not the case it would be paid into his or her fund. A retirement age is not usually selected for the FURBS but is normally considered to be the same as his or her approved company pension or, indeed, personal pension scheme.

The contributions of the employer will be treated as a benefit in kind for the employee and reported on the annual P11D form. Income tax but no NIC will therefore have to be paid by the employee. The employer is allowed, except in the case of shareholding directors, to gross up the salary to cover this tax. However, in this case the grossing up amount not only attracts tax but also NIC. In this case the contributions will not appear on the P11D form.

THE HANCOCK ANNUITY

Another possibility for rectifying the situation of pensions which are less than maximum is the Hancock Annuity.

Employer's contributions to FURBS are treated as benefits in kind.

This is an annuity or deferred annuity purchased by an employer for an employee either on or after his or her retirement or for the dependant of a deceased employee.

The name derives from the case of *Hancock* v *Reversionary and Investment Company Ltd* (1918) which established that such a payment is an allowable expense for the employer in the year in which it is paid and is not regarded as additional remuneration to the employee.

This is now the only method of providing a pension for an employee who has attained age 75. It has not been possible to accumulate funds within an approved pension scheme and provide benefits after age 75 since the Finance Act 1989. The Income and Corporation Taxes Act (ICTA) 1988 makes the same stipulation for personal pension schemes and retirement annuity contracts.

NON-RESIDENCE IN THE UK

An individual will always be treated as resident in the UK for a tax year if the following applies.

The six month rule
The individual is present in the UK for 183 days or more during the tax year.

The three month average rule

The individual is present in the UK for an average of 91 days or more per annum over a period of four tax years.

It is important to note that days of arrival and departure are normally left out of account.

Non-residence will therefore apply in the case of an individual retiring abroad if he or she stays abroad for three tax years and 183 days since he or she could not then be caught by either of the above tests. During those three years he or she could, of course, return to the UK for an average of 60 days since his or her average over the total four years would be below 91.

Different rules apply if he or she goes abroad to work full time under a contract of employment and,

1 All the duties of the employment are performed abroad, or any duties he or she performs in the UK are incidental to his or her duties abroad.
2 The employment and his or her time abroad extend over a period covering a complete tax year.
3 Any interim visits to the UK during the period abroad do not total:
   – 182 days or more in any one tax year; or
   – an average of 90 days or more per tax year.

He will normally be regarded as not resident and not ordinarily resident in the UK on the day following the date of his or her departure until the day preceding the date of his or her return.

The tax advantage of particular value for a non-resident is that of not being liable for capital gains arising in the UK. If the individual is living in a country where there is no CGT such as the Isle of Man this can be of considerable benefit to him.

> **The non-UK resident is not liable for CGT on capital gains arising in the UK.**

As far as income arising in the UK is concerned there is often a 'double taxation agreement' or 'double taxation treaty' existing between the new country of residence of the individual and the UK. These agreements may provide tax exemption for certain income arising in the UK, for example,

1 Pensions paid by a UK company, or pension scheme.
2 Interest, which will usually be paid gross. In cases where tax has been withheld at source this may usually be reclaimed.
3 Dividends from UK companies.
4 Royalties.

Clearly, if the individual is resident in a country with a lower income tax regime, such as the Isle of Man at 20 per cent, this can be a considerable advantage.

PENSIONS AND INHERITANCE TAX

The occupational or company pension scheme is written under trust as mentioned earlier. The type of trust used is such that there is no 'interest in possession' which means there is no nominated beneficiary. It is the trustees who exercise absolute discretion to pay out the lump sum death benefit of up to four times salary, plus any personal contributions the member may have made, to a wide range of potential beneficiaries, which includes:

1 the member's spouse, children, and other issue
2 his or her dependants
3 the individuals entitled under his or her will to any interest in his or her estate
4 any individuals whose name the member has notified to the trustees in writing as being persons whom he or she wishes to be considered as possible recipients of any benefit payable on his or her death
5 his or her personal representatives.

The lump sum death benefit from an approved company pension is totally free of inheritance tax.

Because of this absolute discretion the benefit can form no part of the member's freely disposable estate for inheritance tax purposes and cannot, therefore, attract this tax. However, the trust is not a discretionary trust, which would be subject to 10 year payments, because it comes within the Inheritance Taxes Act (IHTA) 1984.

The director will normally express his or her wishes concerning beneficiaries to the trustees, although this will not bind them. As the trustees will usually be fellow directors he or she can feel reasonably certain that his or her wishes will be followed.

In the case of pensions on the death of a director, these can only be paid to spouse and children. They will not be subject to IHT but will incur income tax.

For someone who has a say in the running of his or her company and who can make his or her own decisions about the company pension scheme it might be valuable also to look at this from the IHT point of view. If four times remuneration death benefit has already been arranged, the capital sum passed free of IHT could be increased by increasing personal contributions. Although these are paid into the pension gross, unlike the company contributions, they are not free of NIC liabilities, so although there is an IHT advantage there is an NIC disadvantage.

■ Example 5.45

Priscilla Fisher, running her own limited company on a salary of £50,000 p.a. and company pension contribution of £9000 p.a. paid by the company, decides to pay the maximum possible of this personally in order to increase the amount of cash which would be paid to her dependants were she to die before retirement. This is,

$$15\% \text{ of } £50,000 = \frac{15}{100} \times 50,000 = £7500 \text{ p.a.}$$

Were she to die in 10 years' time the additional amount of fund paid out free of IHT would be £131,000, making the usual assumption of a growth of 12% p.a.

However, the company would have paid 10% of £12,000 = £1200 additional NIC each year, a total of £12,000.

Personal contributions paid out on death are defined by the Revenue as contributions plus a reasonable amount of growth. Certainly, in the past, a growth of 12% p.a. has not been seen as unreasonable.

In the case of a retired director running a pension guaranteed for five years and dying within that five years, the pension payments remaining within the guaranteed period can be paid to the trustees who can then, at their discretion, pay them to one or more persons from the range of potential beneficiaries described earlier. This payment would also be free of IHT.

> **Personal contributions to an approved company pension plus a reasonable degree of growth can be paid to dependants on death free of any IHT.**

Free-standing additional voluntary contributions (FSAVC), as we said earlier, would be written under trust with the particular insurance company as trustee. The same situation as just discussed would apply to these. It is worth a reminder at this point that if, for example, no life assurance were written under the pension at all, up to four times remuneration would first be paid as a lump sum on death in service from the investment fund and any remaining fund would provide pensions.

The personal pension scheme (PPS) and the retirement annuity contract (RAC) are not automatically governed by a trust, and so, on death, according to the rules of the particular insurance company, up to the whole fund would be paid into the deceased's estate, where it would, of course, potentially become liable to IHT. However, if these pensions are written in trust, on death of the settlor of the trust, the fund and the sum assured of any life assurance would be paid free of IHT.

The form of trust should be the same as that described for using life assurance written under pension legislation in the section on the partnership protection plan. In other words, it is a trust without interest in possession but does not pay the 10 year charge usual to discretionary trusts (Section 58 (1)(d) and Section 151 Inheritance Tax Act (IHTA) 1984). Also the settlor can be named as a potential beneficiary without triggering the gifts with reservation rules (Inland Revenue press release 19th July 1986) and so, as the trust carries a power of appointment, the benefits can be appointed back to the settlor without prejudicing IHT relief. Clearly this is crucial since the main point of a pension scheme is to provide a pension for the policy holder.

Regular premiums to these pension schemes in trust are ignored for IHT purposes because they are paid primarily to provide the scheme holder with a personal benefit, his or her pension, and the death benefit which has been gifted to the trust is incidental.

Regular contributions to provide a sum assured from a life assurance policy within the pension contract are not so ignored since they are paid to provide the in trust death benefit. But it would be unusual for them not to be regarded as 'normal expenditure', (see IHT in Chapter 6), and so exempt from transfer tax.

Personal pension schemes used for contracting out of SERPS and called 'protected rights' schemes can be put into trust in the same way with the same results with respect to IHT.

Paying relatively larger single contributions to a retirement annuity contract (RAC) or personal pension scheme (PPS) in trust or putting an existing scheme into trust, is also in principle a gift for IHT purposes.

> **It is clear that it is extremely important to ensure that all RACs and PPSs are written in trust.**

Such transfers are likely to be treated as negligible except where the policy holder dies from natural causes within two years when IHT at death rates would become payable on the relevant contribution or the market value of the policy at the time of putting it into trust. It is clear that it is extremely important to ensure that all RACs and PPSs are written in trust.

All of this shows how the pension scheme from all points of view avoids the payment of IHT. We have also seen how it can be actively manipulated to increase this benefit by changing company payments into personal payments.

There is another way in which it can be used to pass money free of IHT and this is to first employ your children in your company, perhaps while they are deciding on their eventual career, and then put in an approved company pension for them. This money passes into the pension with the benefit of corporation tax relief; it grows inside the pension free of all UK taxes and eventually produces a fund, part of which can be taken as tax-free cash, the rest as a pension taxed as earned income. The point being that money passes gross for the benefit of the children free of all IHT consideration, grows and years later produces benefits for them. The *de minimus* rules allow a pension investment of £6000 per annum against an annual income of £6000.

■ Example 5.46

Colin Barker, age 18, works in his or her father's company for two years on a remuneration of £6000 p.a. The company invests £6000 p.a. into an approved company pension scheme for him using the de minimus rules. When he becomes 60, based on a fund performance of 12% p.a. his or her pension fund, using Table 2.15 (p. 93), will be approximately £8,556,000.

CHOOSING THE BEST METHOD OF RUNNING A BUSINESS

Although there are considerable similarities in the structure of financial planning for a business by whatever method it is run, sole tradership, partnership or private limited company, we have seen there are many important differences. The question therefore arises, 'Which way is most beneficial?' It is an important question to consider before actually starting the business but just as important a matter to review regularly. Let us try to list the advantages and disadvantages of the different forms a business may take.

The sole trader

Advantages

- Easy to start up. No formalities needed.
- Able to make all decisions personally.
- Full control of all business activities.
- Decides own working hours.
- Shares profits with no-one else.
- Able to dictate one's own financial future.
- Pays NIC at a low level – Classes 2 and 4.
- Accounts not recorded publicly – privacy.

> **The sole trader has full control of all business activities.**

Disadvantages

- Not eligible for SERPS.
- Older people stand no chance of a pension of two-thirds of final salary indexed at 5 per cent per annum.
- No business partner to share responsibilities.
- Difficult to take a holiday or deal with illness – no cover.
- Total responsibility – can overwork.
- Unlimited liability. Personal assets cannot be separated from the business. Vulnerable to bankruptcy.
- Can quickly need to acquire new skills, e.g. may be good at making engine parts but have no idea of bookkeeping, business management, marketing etc.
- The sole trader is literally the business. If he or she is seriously ill or dies, there is no business.

The partnership

Advantages

- Easy to start up. No formalities needed.
- Decision making can be shared.
- Problems can be shared or passed to a partner with greater expertise in that particular area.
- Cover by other partners for holidays and sickness.
- Own boss. No employer as such.
- Synergy of working with others as a team. One plus one is more than two.
- Accounts not recorded publicly – privacy.
- Pay lower NIC contributions, Classes 2 and 4.

> **Partnership accounts are not recorded publicly thus there is total privacy.**

Disadvantages

- Not eligible for SERPS.
- Older people stand no chance of a pension of two-thirds of final salary indexed at 5 per cent per annum.
- Unlimited liability. Personal assets cannot be separated from business. Vulnerable to bankruptcy.
- Jointly and severally responsible. Responsible for other partners' mistakes in the business.
- Dependent on good relationships with other partners.
- Business property is owned by the partners. A change in the composition of the partnership may require changes in the title deeds.
- Disagreement leading to stalemate could arise with its concomitant disastrous consequences for the business.
- Finding the money to buy out a retiring partner.

The private limited company

Advantages

- The company is a separate entity. Its liabilities are those of the company and not the shareholders.
- The company's liability is limited.
- This limited liability is seen as an advantage to investors in the company.
- Enormously more favourable conditions for late starters to achieve maximum pension benefits and also provide for dependants on death both before retirement or after.
- Company property belongs to the company, so title deeds do not need changing when shareholders change.
- NIC contributions can be avoided by paying dividends.

> **The company is a separate entity. Its liabilities are those of the company, and not of the shareholders.**

- Has available the use of the pension loanback.
- The shareholding director is an employee and can, therefore, participate in group critical illness and medical insurance policies which cost the company less than they would an individual.
- On balance the business may look a more serious endeavour if incorporated.
- Has a wider range of possibilities for raising cash. Apart from loans, venture capital and business angels are available. Also flotation.
- SERPS is available.
- Easier to sell or pass on in part or total.
- The fact that corporation tax is lower than higher rate tax could be an advantage in certain circumstances.

Disadvantages

- More formalities needed to set up a private limited company.
- Less privacy – company accounts and information on shareholders, directors and salaries must be lodged annually in Companies House and are open to public inspection.
- Much higher NIC contributions paid by the shareholding directors and the company also pays NIC.
- There is always the possibility of double taxation on capital gain.
- Company accounts must be officially audited.

MOVING FROM ONE FORM OF BUSINESS TO ANOTHER

The sole trader

The sole trader is totally in charge of his or her business and has total responsibility. There is no distinction between him or her and the business. If he or she owns a commercial property from which the business operates, the business owns it. For BRR relief it will automatically form part of the business. There is unlimited liability.

The partnership

If the sole trader should decide to go into partnership, the partners are jointly and severally responsible and we have seen the importance of a partnership agreement or deed. This agreement is not mandatory and if not instigated the partnership will be automatically governed by the Partnership Act 1890 which in many ways could be a disadvantage. A partnership protection plan is extremely important. In this situation a business property could be owned by one or more partners and used by the partnership. Once again there is no distinction between the partners and the business. They are the business. There is unlimited liability.

The private limited company

Should either of the two previous firms decide to incorporate you will remember there is an automatic liability to stamp duty and CGT. The CGT, however, is deferred by hold-over relief so, in fact, makes no financial difference to the situation. Limited liability is immediately achieved and much thought needs to be given to any request for personal guarantees, usually from a lender, to be given as this immediately delimits that liability.

> **Incorporating a business triggers a CGT and stamp duty liability.**

A company commercial property may be owned by one or more shareholding directors of the business and used by the business. Any rent paid will affect the situation with respect to BRR.

THE SALE OF A BUSINESS

The sale of a business is more difficult for the sole trader. In the case of a partnership buying into it, or in other words buying a part of it which is more usual, especially in the professions such as law, medicine, accountancy etc., it is easier. The limited company is the easiest to sell, although still difficult as there is no ready market such as that which exists for the sale of the shares of a quoted company on the stock market or AIM.

A private limited company will usually be sold including a measure of retained profits sitting in the company to fund its running. The price of the business will be lifted by this cash, probably sitting on deposit, and therefore potential CGT will be increased.

Reducing potential CGT before sale

■ Paying a dividend

CGT can be reduced by paying a dividend.

Paying a dividend before the sale will reduce the CGT.

■ Example 5.47

Yasmin Silvester, at age 45, has been offered £2 million for her private limited company. Before tax profits in the company are £300,000. Tax to be paid will be 21% of 300,000,

$$\frac{21}{100} \times 300,000 = £63,000$$

leaving retained profit of £237,000.

The purchaser does not need retained profit in the company and would prefer to pay £2 million – 0.237 million = £1.763 million, with no retained profit. This will actually reduce CGT for Yasmin from 40% of £2 million = £800,000, to 40% of £1.763 million = £705,000.

If the company pays a dividend of £240,000 it will pay advanced corporation tax of £60,000, actually less than the corporation tax it would have paid, leaving no retained profit in the company.

Yasmin will receive a tax credit of £60,000 on her dividend and be liable for further tax of 20% on the grossed up amount of £300,000,

$$\frac{20}{100} \times 300,000 = £60,000$$

Hence total tax paid = £60,000 income tax + £705,200 CGT = £765,200, which is £33,800 less than the £800,000 CGT liable if no dividend is paid.

■ Pension contributions

If there is scope for paying additional single pension contributions to any member of the family this could significantly reduce the CGT.

Yasmin discovers she could pay £50,000 into her pension and £10,000 each into the pensions of her two children who work in the company.

Retained profits are reduced by £70,000 with no tax liability. Hence capital gain reduced by £70,000. Hence CGT reduced by £28,000. Apart from anything else this is an extremely efficient way of passing money to children free of inheritance tax.

Tax implications of selling a private limited company

> **Everyone owning all or part of the business he or she is working in, at age 50, is eligible for part or total BRR.**

A straightforward sale of a private limited company by a UK resident will, of course, attract CGT. All the allowances described earlier may be available. In the same way they are likely to be available also to spouse so gifting shares to him or her, if he or she has worked in the business, could reduce CGT liability considerably. Of course, BRR will only be available to him or her if he or she is 50 years of age or over and this will only reach maximum value if he or she has worked in the company for at least 10 years.

■ Example 5.48

Amy Fenwick, at 55, is about to sell her company for £500,000, which will all be liable for CGT. She has been running the company for 12 years with her husband, Benedict, who is 60. The tax situation will be,

Capital gains	£500,000
Less annual allowance of £6500	£493,500
Tax on first £250,000 gain	Nil
Tax on remaining £243,500 gain	
at 20%	£48,700
Total tax	£48,700

She decides to gift half the shares to Benedict, hold-over relief prevents any tax being paid at that point.

The new tax situation will be,

Amy: Capital gain £250,000, no tax under BRR. Annual allowance could be used for bed and breakfasting.

Benedict: Capital gain £250,000, no tax under BRR. Annual allowance could be used for bed and breakfasting.

The result is that a tax of £48,700 has been wiped out and their annual allowances are left free to use for bed and breakfasting.

Referring back to non-residence in the UK, we see that a non-resident is not liable for CGT on gains arising in the UK. This could be extremely useful for someone in this situation contemplating selling his or her UK business. It does however need to be considered carefully. It entails living and working abroad for a period greater than one full tax year, obviously in a country which has no CGT. Thus a period stretching from 5 April 1996 to 6 April 1997 gives non-resident status for the tax year 1996/97. Hence if a UK business is sold during that tax year there is no CGT liability. However, a word of warning. Let us say that for some reason there was a delay in selling the business until 2 June 1997 and return to the UK was on 22 June 1997. Although non-resident status existed at the time of the sale, because UK residence happened during the tax year in which the business was sold, i.e. 1997/98 there could still be a liability for CGT. Clearly expert professional advice is needed.

> **Timing of the sale of a UK business while non-UK resident is crucial.**

If no work permit were in force while living offshore then the period of non-residence would have to include three full tax years and the company be sold during that time.

INVOICE DISCOUNTING

Invoice discounting firms will offer to pay a client company up to about 80 per cent of a debt at the point of invoicing. The percentage will depend on the debt collecting record of the company. If for example the debts are well spread between a number of clients and no more than 90 days old then 80 per cent would usually be the figure. In the case of longer existing debts, called aged debts, the percentage would be less. Also if there were one very large debt among the debtors this would decrease the percentage. Interest would be charged the client company for what is in effect a loan from the point of providing the loan until the collection of the debt and a charge for administrating this service would be made. The client company would retain the responsibility for collecting the debt but would have the use of the money early to aid its cashflow.

FACTORING

Factoring gives exactly the same facility as invoice discounting with the added service that the factoring company would use its particular expertise to collect the debts for the client company leaving it to spend the time saved doing the things it does best. This extra service would, of course, carry extra charges.

VENTURE CAPITAL

Professional venture capital companies will provide funds for injection into a company in return for shares in the company. They will investigate thoroughly the proposition and make a decision about its feasibility and the possible potential future profit to be gained. For this purpose a very thorough business plan and cashflow projection will have to be professionally prepared by the applicant company. The venture capitalist will often see the procedure as leading to a flotation on the alternative investment market (AIM) or perhaps even the stock market, within a five year period or so. At that point, of course, a market is created for the sale of the shares which will enable a profit to be easily realised. The initial decision to become involved with the client company will depend on the venture capitalist's perception of the potential profit to be made. Some years ago minimum amounts of money before consideration of a project used to be injections of no less than £500,000. There are now firms who will go as low as £100,000, although they will not usually be looking, initially, at a flotation but at a long-term association with the client company and a continual flow of income, from profits, to the venture capitalist.

> Venture capital can be the gateway for expansion.

Business angels

A business angel is an individual with capital who wants involvement with a potentially profitable company merely as an investor who will hold shares in the company or as someone who will, in addition, want an involvement with the running of the company. He or she is often a person who has already been successful in business and who has money to invest. He or she might already have sold a successful company and be looking to repeat the process of leading a company to success. Of course the consideration of roll-over relief could also be an incentive.

> A business angel combined with the enterprise investment scheme could be the answer.

An added incentive, of course, would be engendered if all the tax advantages of an enterprise investment scheme (EIS) could be written into the process. The problem is the lack of any organised way in which a company can find a business angel and, therefore, this sort of specialised investment. However, firms are springing up whose main activity is to match a company to a business angel.

■ Case Study 5.1

Hubert Dene and Virginia Farnsworth have been running their private limited company very successfully for 11 years, each owning 50% of the shares. Hubert is 51 and Virginia 40. They have just produced the prototype of a new product and have successfully negotiated with Barbara Middleton, a business angel, the injection of money into their business in exchange for shares and an involvement in its running. Barbara is 51 and, having sold a similar company five years ago, wants to become active in the business again. The company was professionally valued at £1 million and Barbara has bought a 30% shareholding for £200,000, leaving Hubert and Virginia with 35% each.

Barbara immediately raises the question of a share protection plan. They all agree that this is important and they should each be insured for death and critical illness. As the company has recently been valued at £1 million, but they think that with the cash injection and the new product it will double in value in three years, they decide to insure for that value now. This is because if they insure for the lower value now and during the next three years one of them becomes uninsurable they will have big problems, and if they are overinsured for a short time the extra cash would be very valuable to have in the company during a crucial period of expansion. In the event of a shareholding director dying or suffering a critical illness the surplus sum assured would be kept by the remaining directors and loaned to the company.

Hence working on a company value of £2 million they take out life assurance and critical illness for sums assured of,

Hubert Dene	25% of £2 million	= £500,000
Virginia Farnsworth	25% of £2 million	= £500,000
Barbara Middleton	20% of £2 million	= £400,000

These policies are written in trust for the other directors on a fifty-fifty basis so that, for example, if Hubert dies Virginia will end up with 35% + 17$\frac{1}{2}$% = 52$\frac{1}{2}$% of the shares and Barbara 30% + 17$\frac{1}{2}$% = 47$\frac{1}{2}$% of the shares. They do it this way because they agree that the original director should retain day-to-day running control of the company.

They decide on key person policies on each director of a further £200,000 as they believe that this will be the amount needed if the company loses the particular expertise of either one.

Hubert and Virginia had been paying themselves £10,000 p.a. in salary and £40,000 in dividends to cut down the NIC contribution. They now propose this should be £10,000 salary and £30,000 dividend for all three. Barbara expresses concern at having no pension provision and discovers that the others have been so busy building up the company they have nothing either. They decide to get one started immediately. Virginia and Hubert will complete at least 20 years in the company, and will therefore be able to fund for a full two-thirds of final salary, but Barbara with only 9 years before she is 60 can only get 9 × $\frac{1}{30}$th = $\frac{9}{30}$th or $\frac{3}{10}$th of final salary. In today's terms this would be a pension of,

Hubert	$\frac{2}{3} \times 10,000$	= £6667 p.a.
Virginia	$\frac{2}{3} \times 10,000$	= £6667 p.a.
Barbara	$\frac{3}{10} \times 10,000$	= £3000 p.a.

because although dividends save NIC, they are not pensionable. They decide to compromise and lift salaries to £20,000 and reduce dividends to £20,000 p.a.

Looking at Table 5.9 (p. 345) they discover they can fund these pensions at,

Hubert	£20,000 p.a.
Virginia	£10,000 p.a.
Barbara	£12,667 p.a.

Because Virginia is only projecting 3/10ths of final salary as a pension, they decide to at least fund a FURBS for her at $12,667 \times \frac{7}{3} = £29,556$ p.a. giving her at least the funding to nominally achieve a full two-thirds final salary, apart from the fact that because the fund in FURBS is taxed this will not actually fully succeed.

They are now funding at a total of £72,223. As they are not quite in the marginal rate of tax this means they are saving corporation tax,

$$21\% \text{ of } 72,223 = \frac{21}{100} \times 72,223 = £15,169$$

However, they are now paying additional personal and company NIC of,

Personal = 10% of 30,000 = £3000
Company = 7% of 3 × 920 + 10% of 3 × 9080 = 7/100 × 3 × 920 + 10/100 × 3 × 9080 = 193.20 + 2724 = 2917
Total = 5917

So overall they are better off, saving 15,169 – 5917 = £9252 and have planned for considerably better pensions. They decide to increase this further once they have lifted their profits.

One year later they are achieving their goals and decide they need better premises. Hubert and Barbara want to continue renting, Virginia wants to buy. They decide Virginia will buy the property herself and it will be used by the company. She purchases something at £200,000 with an interest only loan of £140,000 over 20 years fixed at 11% p.a., which means annual payments of £15,400.

She decides to pay the loan back out of her pension knowing that she can take tax-free cash of 1½ times at age 60. She also knows that remuneration will increase enormously as the company grows and, even though pension contributions will be limited by the earnings cap, at a rate of inflation of even 5% p.a., using Table 2.15 (p. 93), this will be £84,000 × 2.65 = £222,600, fully catering for a loan of £140,000.

She asks for a market rent of £15,400 p.a. which is agreed and she is able to set this off against the interest payments and therefore pay no additional income tax. She thus has what she hopes will be an appreciating asset for a net outgoing of zero. As it will be repaid from the pension by premiums which will wash through the pension tax free on which if she took them in salary would eventually be costing her 40% in tax as her salary goes up. The £140,000 will only cost her net payments of 60% of £140,000 = $60/100 \times 140,000 = £102,000$.

Hence even if the property value grows only in line with an inflation rate of 5% p.a. it will be worth $£200,000 \times 2.65 = £530,000$, a return of 520% on her outlay over 20 years, which is a cumulative growth of 36.84% p.a. She feels quite happy about this and wonders where else this would be possible.

She will not be eligible for BRR on this capital gain because she is being paid a full market rent but as she plans not to sell the property when she sells her share of the company this will make no difference. At 60, when the loan is paid off, the rental which will hopefully at least have kept pace with inflation, will be an additional source of income.

A year later at their next annual company financial planning review they feel they can draw breath and take careful stock of the situation. Hubert says he has been very worried recently because one of the staff has told him about his or her brother who had become incapacitated and after six months' pay from his or her company now has to live entirely on the little the state provides.

They decide to provide a company PHI plan on a net salary basis ensuring that any staff suffering an incapacity could receive from the state and the company combined an income equal to 90% of net pay.

They also offer £50 per month into a pension for any member of staff who would like to match that and also offer to do this through salary sacrifice, thus considerably enhancing the employee's contribution. Hubert, who is still concerned about the effect of incapacity on a member of staff, suggests that the shareholders should fund waiver of contribution costs on the total pension for each employee and this meets with approval. They decide to do this through a group personal pension scheme because of the flexibility and ease of administration.

Barbara raises the question of converting to a SSAS because she feels it will give them more choice of investment. However, Hubert points out that she is already working a total of 10 hours per day and asks her when she is going to find the time to study investment. She sees the wisdom of this argument and they plump for status quo on the pension.

At this point we leave them but will meet them again in Chapter 6.

SUMMARY

In this age we have worked through the following:

1 The implications of a more responsible career position and higher income, including such things as planning an investment portfolio and inheritance tax.

2 Running a business as a sole trader, partner or shareholding director. This has involved considering such things as:
   ■ partnership protection
   ■ share protection
   ■ valuing a business
   ■ capital gains tax
   ■ the approved company pension in detail
   ■ pension loanback
   ■ the small self-administered pension scheme (SSAS)
   ■ comparison of the three ways of purchasing a company property
   ■ the funded unapproved retirement benefits scheme (FURBS)
   ■ the Hancock Annuity
   ■ non-residence in the UK.

3 Finally we have looked at choosing the best form for running a business, moving from one form of business to another and the sale of a business.

ANSWERS

■ Exercise 5.2

The business can contribute to an occupational pension scheme for Janet an amount equal to 45% of her remuneration. This will be,

$$\frac{45}{100} \times 3000 = £1350 \text{ p.a. or } £112.50 \text{ per month}$$

Using Table 2.15 (p. 93) and taking 20 years, the nearest to Janet's time to age 60 of 22 years, we see that £100 per month produces a fund of £73,400.

Hence £112.50 per month will produce 112.50/100 × 73,400 = £82,575.

From Table 2.16 (p. 94) the annuity described has a yield of 8.17%. Hence pension produced is 8.17/100 × 82,575 = £6746 p.a.

Using Table 2.17 (p. 95), inflation of 5% p.a. over 22 years gives a factor of 2.93. Hence the personal allowance when Janet is 60 will be 2.93 × 4045 = £11,852 p.a. So Janet's pension will be totally free of all UK taxes in her hands since it will be below the projected personal allowance.

Hence in this case the family's net spendable income has reduced by £21,598 – £21,280 = £318 p.a. but they have in exchange for this a pension contribution of £1350 p.a. (See the income tax and NIC analysis forms on pp. 386–7.)

■ Exercise 5.4

Greg's maximum contributions are:

17½% of £84,000 for 16 years to age 36 =

$$\frac{17.5}{100} \times 84,000 \times 16 = \quad £235,200$$

20% of £84,000 for 10 years to age 46 =

$$\frac{20}{100} \times 84,000 \times 10 = \quad £168,000$$

25% of £84,000 for 5 years to age 51 =

$$\frac{25}{100} \times 84,000 \times 5 = \quad £105,000$$

30% of £84,000 for 5 years to age 56 =

$$\frac{30}{100} \times 84,000 \times 5 = \quad £126,000$$

35% of £84,000 for 4 years to age 60 =

$$\frac{35}{100} \times 84,000 \times 4 = \quad £117,600$$

Total   £751,800

Ralph's maximum contributions are:

18% of £84,000 for 40 years to age 60 =

$$\frac{18}{100} \times 84,000 \times 40 = \quad £604,800$$

This time the PPS gives the better deal.

Exercise 5.2 (continued)

■ INCOME TAX AND NIC ANALYSIS

INCOME TAX			
Name Duncan Graham		*Year* Before	
	£	*Remaining income £*	*Tax £*
Gross income	28,000		
Gross contribution to pension paid personally*			
Personal allowance	4045	23,955	Nil
Income taxed at 20%	4100	19,855	820.00
Income taxed at basic rate 23%	19,855	Nil	4566.65
Income taxed at higher rate 40%			
Total	28,000		5386.65
Less married couple's allowance 15% of £1830			274.50
Total tax payable			5112.15

* Some pension contributions paid personally are net of basic rate tax. For the purposes of this form this would need to be grossed up.

NATIONAL INSURANCE CONTRIBUTION (NIC) (Employed)			
	£	*Remaining income £*	*NIC £*
Gross income			
Income up to LEL £3224 p.a. NIC at 2%			
Income up to UEL £24,180 p.a. minus £3224 p.a., the LEL NIC at 10%			
Total			

NATIONAL INSURANCE CONTRIBUTION (NIC) (Self-employed)	
Flat rate paid if income over £3480 p.a. £6.15 p.w.	319.80
On profits between £7010 and £24,180 p.a. 6.0% $(24{,}180 - 7010) \times \dfrac{6}{100}$	1030.20
Total	1350.00
Income after tax and NIC deductions $28{,}000 - 5112.15 - 1350 = £21{,}537.85$	
Net spendable income	£21,538

Exercise 5.2 (continued)

■ **INCOME TAX AND NIC ANALYSIS**

<table>
<tr><td colspan="4">INCOME TAX</td></tr>
<tr><td>Name   Duncan Graham</td><td colspan="2">Year   After</td><td></td></tr>
<tr><td></td><td>£</td><td>Remaining income £</td><td>Tax £</td></tr>
<tr><td>Gross income</td><td>28,000 – 3000 – 1350
= 23,650</td><td></td><td></td></tr>
<tr><td>Gross contribution to
pension paid personally*</td><td>Nil</td><td>23,650</td><td></td></tr>
<tr><td>Personal allowance</td><td>4045</td><td>19,605</td><td>Nil</td></tr>
<tr><td>Income taxed at 20%
Income taxed at basic rate 23%
Income taxed at higher rate 40%</td><td>4100
15,505</td><td>15,505
Nil</td><td>820.00
3566.15</td></tr>
<tr><td>Total</td><td>28,000</td><td></td><td>4386.15</td></tr>
<tr><td colspan="3">Less married couple's allowance 15% of £1830</td><td>274.50</td></tr>
<tr><td colspan="3">Total tax payable</td><td>4111.65</td></tr>
<tr><td colspan="4">* Some pension contributions paid personally are net of basic rate tax. For the purposes of this form this would need to be grossed up.</td></tr>
<tr><td colspan="4">NATIONAL INSURANCE CONTRIBUTION (NIC) (Employed)</td></tr>
<tr><td></td><td>£</td><td>Remaining income £</td><td>NIC £</td></tr>
<tr><td>Gross income</td><td></td><td></td><td></td></tr>
<tr><td>Income up to LEL
£3224 p.a.
NIC at 2%</td><td></td><td></td><td></td></tr>
<tr><td>Income up to UEL
£24,180 p.a. minus £3224 p.a.,
the LEL NIC at 10%</td><td></td><td></td><td></td></tr>
<tr><td>Total</td><td></td><td></td><td></td></tr>
<tr><td colspan="4">NATIONAL INSURANCE CONTRIBUTION (NIC) (Self-employed)</td></tr>
<tr><td colspan="3">Flat rate paid if income over £3480 p.a. £6.15 p.w.</td><td>319.80</td></tr>
<tr><td colspan="3">On profits between £7010 and £24,180 p.a. 6.0%

$(23,650 - 7010) \times \dfrac{6}{100}$</td><td>998.40</td></tr>
<tr><td colspan="3">Total</td><td>1318.20</td></tr>
<tr><td>Income after tax and NIC deductions</td><td colspan="3">23,650 – 4111.65 – 1318.20 = £18,220.15</td></tr>
<tr><td>Net spendable income</td><td colspan="3">£18,220 + 3000 = £21,220</td></tr>
</table>

■ Exercise 5.5

Between July 1987 and July 1997 the RPI increases by,

$$\frac{157.5}{101.8} \times 100\% = 54.7\%$$

The rebased value of shares Tina bought is,

$$10{,}000 + \frac{54.7}{100} \times 10{,}000 = £15{,}470$$

These make a real gain of 25,000 − 15,470 = £9530.

Increase in the RPI from July 1989 to July 1990 is,

$$\frac{126.8}{115.5} \times 100\% = 9.8\%$$

Hence real value of gifted shares in July 1990 is,

$$10{,}000 + 10{,}000 \times \frac{9.8}{100} = £10{,}980$$

Increase in the RPI from July 1990 to July 1997 is,

$$\frac{157.5}{126.8} \times 100\% = 24.2\%$$

Real value of gifted shares in July 1997 is,

$$10{,}980 + 10{,}980 \times \frac{24.2}{100} = 10{,}980 + 2657.16 = £13{,}637.16$$

Hence the capital gain on these shares is,

$$18{,}900 - 13{,}637.16 = £5262.84$$

So Tina makes a total real capital gain of,

$$9{,}530 + 5262.84 = £14{,}792.84$$

She first deducts her annual allowance of £6500 reducing the gain to £8292.84.

She then sets off her earlier losses against this finally reducing the gain to £4792.84.

Using Form 2.1 we see that all of this falls in the basic rate tax band and is taxed at 23%. Her capital gains tax, due on 31 January 1999 is £1102.35.

Exercise 5.5 (continued)

INCOME TAX AND NIC ANALYSIS

INCOME TAX			
Name Tina Bramwell		Year 1997	
	£	Remaining income £	Tax £
Gross income	25,000		
Gross contribution to pension paid personally*			
Personal allowance	4045	20,955.00	Nil
Income taxed at 20%	4100.00	16,955.00	820.00
Income taxed at	16,955.00	Nil	3876.65
basic rate 23%	4792.84 Add	4792.84	1102.35
Income taxed at higher rate 40%			
Total			
Less married couple's allowance			
Total tax payable			

* Some pension contributions paid personally are net of basic rate tax. For the purposes of this form this would need to be grossed up.

■ Exercise 5.6

Nominal gain = £400,000.

Increase in RPI between July 1986 and July 1997 is,

$$\frac{157.5}{97.5} \times 100\% = 61.5\%$$

Indexed purchase price is,

$$100,000 + \frac{61.5}{100} \times 100,000 = £161,500$$

Real capital gain = 500,000 – 161,500	= £338,500
Less annual allowance of £6500	= £332,000
Less losses of £50,000	= £282,000
Tax on first £250,000	Nil
Tax on remaining £32,000 at 20% =	
$\dfrac{20}{100} \times 32,000 =$	£6400
Total tax	£6400

CHAPTER 6

THE AGE OF
RETIREMENT

Birth and education	Work	Marriage	Parenthood	Career development	Retirement	Old age

FINANCIAL PLANNING AT A GLANCE –
THE AGE OF RETIREMENT

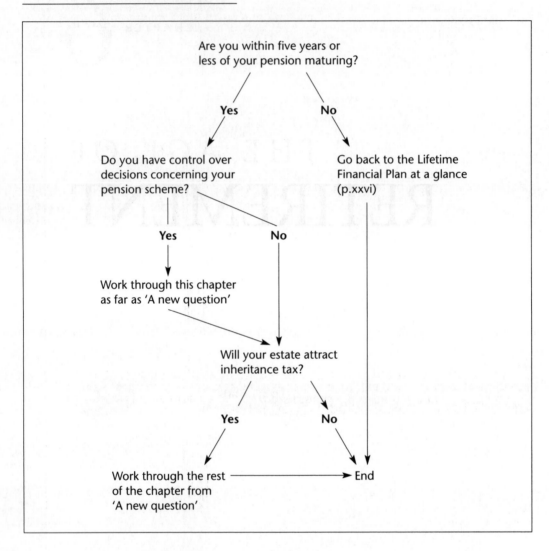

Are you within five years or less of your pension maturing?

Yes

No

Do you have control over decisions concerning your pension scheme?

Go back to the Lifetime Financial Plan at a glance (p.xxvi)

Yes

No

Work through this chapter as far as 'A new question'

Will your estate attract inheritance tax?

Yes

No

Work through the rest of the chapter from 'A new question'

End

CONTENTS

In this age the following is discussed:

- switching to a SSAS
- protecting the pension fund against fluctuations in the stock market
- using the tax-free cash wisely
- choosing remuneration levels carefully at three years before pension maturity
- the choice of annuity
- phased retirement
- deferring the annuity
- the deferred annuity facility of the SSAS
- the income withdrawal facility
- comparison of the two methods
- to defer or not to defer
- passing on as much as possible
- the final question on pension benefits
- a new question – and inheritance tax (IHT)
- the will trust
- the dead settlor rule
- the use of life assurance to solve the problem of IHT
- the will trust using a home
- inheritance tax (IHT)
- those subject to inheritance tax
- domicile
- what is chargeable to IHT?
- the value of a transfer
- deed of variation
- transfers which are exempt from IHT
- potentially exempt transfers (PET)
- reservation of benefit
- the seven year rule
- business property relief (BPR)
- business property relief for agricultural property
- woodlands
- quick succession relief
- the legitim rules in Scotland

INTRODUCTION

Five years, four years and three years before pension maturity are extremely important dates.

In this age you are in the age of retirement. This age starts five years before the maturity of your pension. The reason for this is that there is at least one decision which has to be made at that point, another approximately one year later and yet another one year after that.

SWITCHING TO A SSAS

Some people may consider it of value to retire from a small self-administered scheme (SSAS) in order to use the deferred annuity facility described in Chapter 5.

For someone with control over his or her company pension scheme which happens to be the usual money purchase type, it is possible to switch this into an SSAS since most insurance companies will usually run the hybrid scheme into which the usual scheme can be subsumed. However, it will be remembered that the member cannot use the deferred annuity facility until he or she has been in the SSAS for five years or more. Thus the crucial importance of reviewing the situation at the point five years before pension maturity. However, since the Finance Act 1995 there has been an alternative method for deferring the taking of an annuity. This is usually called the income withdrawal facility or income withdrawal account, and, in fact, is a good deal more flexible than deferring the taking of an annuity from a SSAS. This method involves the transfer of funds to a personal pension scheme offering this facility which could, if wished, be a SIPP. There will usually be an upfront charge and an annual management charge. However, the point is that it can be done, if wished, just after the maturity of the approved company pension scheme or indeed the straightforward personal pension scheme (PPS) or retirement annuity contract (RAC). In the case of early retirement from age 50 on the same comments would apply.

PROTECTING THE PENSION FUND AGAINST FLUCTUATIONS IN THE STOCK MARKET

For those who have decided the annuity route is the one for them at retirement date it would be extremely important to consider the particular current investment funds being used in the pension. If these funds contain any element of equity investment it would be wise to consider again the figure we saw in Chapter 1 which showed the short-term potential volatility of these investments (see Fig. 6.1).

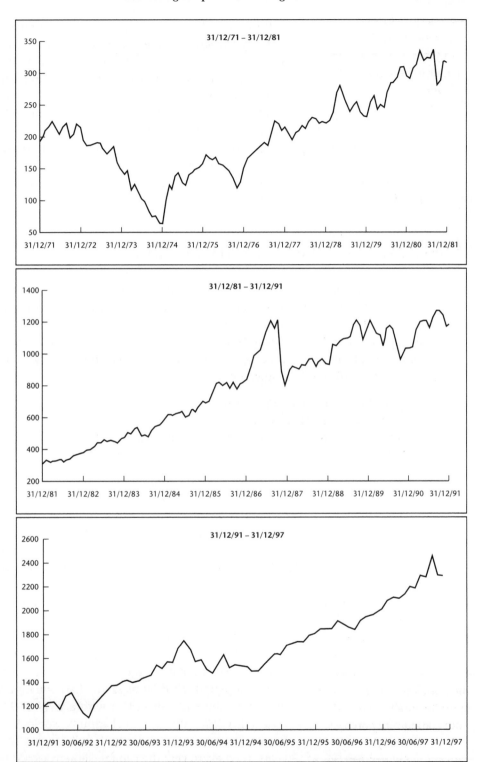

Fig. 6.1 The FT Actuaries All-Share Index – performance 1971–97
Source: Micropal

> **It would be bad news if shortly before purchasing an annuity the stock market were to drop badly.**

It would be bad news if shortly before purchasing the annuity the stock market were to suffer a large drop in value. Hence four years before pension maturity it would be wise to address this question and consider switching funds into fixed interest. Of course it is unlikely the same kind of growth will be achieved in the fixed interest fund but neither will there be a sudden loss.

For those employees with no control over their company pension these decisions will not be possible. However, most of these will be in a defined benefit scheme with a guaranteed level of benefit whatever happens to the investment climate.

USING THE TAX-FREE CASH WISELY

There is the choice for most people whether or not to commute a part of the pension at maturity for tax-free cash. If cash is required at that point for a special reason such as refurbishing a house for retirement, buying a new car or taking a very special holiday then the decision is easy. If there is no such motivation then it would be wise to consider the question carefully. If only income is required then the choices open are,

1 Use all the fund to buy a pension.
2 Take tax-free cash and use the remaining fund to buy a pension. Then:
   - invest the tax-free cash to build up an investment portfolio;
   - or buy what is known as a purchased life annuity (PLA).

The annuity the pension fund buys is called a compulsory purchase annuity (CPA). There is a considerable difference between these two types of annuity. The CPA is taxed as earned income. Part of the income from the PLA, however, is deemed to be return of the capital paid for the annuity and is untaxed. This is very similar to the 5 per cent per annum of income that the investment bond holder can receive tax-free in his or her hands over a period of 20 years because this is deemed to be return of capital, i.e. 20×5 per cent = 100 per cent, the whole of the capital.

The interesting question here then is, 'Over what period of time is part of the payment from the PLA deemed to be return of the capital paid for the annuity?' It is in fact the remaining life expectancy of the purchaser. Thus a man aged 60, having reached this age, has, statistically, a further life expectancy of 21.47 years.

> **The purchased life annuity is more favourably taxed than the compulsory purchase annuity.**

His return of capital would be deemed to be paid out over that period. Thus let us say he had bought a single life, level, non-guaranteed PLA with a yield of 9.05 per cent. With £100,000 his annual annuity would be £9050. If part of this is capital deemed to be repaid in 21.47 years, then every year the capital element would be,

$$\frac{100,000}{21.47} = £4658$$

In other words, of his total annuity of £9050 per annum £4658 would be deemed to be return of capital and therefore untaxed. This would go on for however long the annuity was paid, even after the 21.47 years. Assuming he is paying tax at 23 per cent then the tax paid would be 23 per cent of (£9050 – £4658) =

$$\frac{23}{100} \times 4392 = £1010.16$$

Hence the net amount he would receive from his PLA would be £9050 – £1010.16 = £8039.84 per annum.

Had the annuity been a CPA it would all have been taxed. He would have paid tax of 23 per cent of £9050 =

$$\frac{23}{100} \times 9050 = £2081.50$$

and therefore would have received net £9050 – £2081.50 = £6968.50 per annum which is £1071.34 per annum less.

The moral of this story is never use the whole pension fund to buy the CPA, instead buy a PLA with the tax-free cash and a CPA with the remaining fund.

This is not quite the whole story since there is a small difference in the price of the PLA and the CPA. The PLA is slightly more expensive, because everyone who has a pension has to buy a CPA, so we get a wide range of lives including those who are not 100 per cent fit and will not live so long. The insurance company selling the annuity makes money out of these because the amount paid out will be less than the cost of the annuity. The position is reversed for those who live longer. Now in general it will be the fitter among us who will purchase the PLA, those who are not so fit will not want to risk their tax-free cash but will want to keep it and pass it on or spend it. This slightly biases the situation and produces statistics showing that those buying the PLA on average live longer than those who receive the CPA. Thus the insurance companies charge more for the PLA. A typical difference between the cost for a woman age 60 for a single life, level, non-guaranteed annuity makes the PLA 1.2 per cent dearer than the CPA. This is not likely to outweigh the considerable tax advantage.

> Moral: never use the whole pension fund to buy a compulsory purchase annuity.

■ Example 6.1

Muriel Hunter, at age 60, referring to Table 2.16 (p. 94), sees that a typical yield for a single life, level, non-guaranteed CPA is 8.17%. Thus £100,000, the value of his or her PPS fund, would buy his or her an annual income of £8170. As she is a higher rate taxpayer she will pay tax on this at 40%, i.e.

$$\frac{40}{100} \times 8170 = £3268$$

Hence his or her net annual income will be £8170 – £3268 = £4902.

However, using his or her allowed £25,000 for a PLA giving a yield of 8.07%, she gets £2017.50 p.a. Statistically his or her life expectancy is a further 24.81 years so his or her capital is deemed to be repaid over that period. In other words,

$$\frac{25,000}{24.81} = £1007.66 \text{ p.a.}$$

is deemed to be return of capital and untaxed.

Hence the taxable amount is £2017.50 – £1007.66 = £1009.84 and the tax paid is,

$$\frac{40}{100} \times 1009.84 = £403.94$$

giving a net annual pension of £2017.50 – £403.94 = £1613.56.

Had the £25,000 bought a CPA the yield would have been 8.17% giving £2042.50 p.a. and the tax would have been,

$$\frac{40}{100} \times 2042.50 = £817$$

Hence his or her net pension would have been £2042.50 – £817 = £1225.50. She is better off by £1613.56 – £1225.50 = £388.06 p.a.

CHOOSING REMUNERATION LEVELS CAREFULLY AT THREE YEARS BEFORE PENSION MATURITY

For those who have total control over their approved company pension, funding will have been governed only by Revenue limits and what could be afforded. In this age it would be very important to remember that final pensions and tax-free cash will depend on final remuneration and remembering how this is defined in Chapter 5, these last few years to pension maturity are crucial from the point of view of remuneration received. It will be a careful balance between the projected fund value at maturity and final salary, and if it is a matter of a certain amount of profit to be divided between remuneration and pension payments then in this run up to pension maturity careful calculations will need to be done.

■ Example 6.2

Sebastian Price will have completed 20 years' service with the limited company he owns by the time he reaches 60 in three years time. He sees that over recent years his remuneration has not grown as expected but that his pension investment has done extremely well. In fact the result of careful calculations shows that if pension contributions continue at their present level thus limiting his remuneration, then at 60 his pension fund will be considerably larger than that needed to produce the benefits his salary will allow. This is the time to make careful decisions. He decides to stop his pension funding and in the last three years at work to throw everything he can into his remuneration thus raising the pension benefits allowable and making full use of his pension fund. You may want to refer back to the definition of final salary for controlling directors in Chapter 5.

The three years before pension maturity can be very important.

It is clear that these three years before pension maturity are extremely important for careful financial planning.

■ Example 6.3

Regina Broomhill has been running his or her own company for 20 years and is three years from retirement at 60. Her pension fund is currently £445,793. Her annual salary is £25,000 and pension contribution is £20,000. She needs to keep the total of salary plus pension contributions the same until retirement because of cashflow considerations.

She decides to have a good look at this situation and do some good financial planning.

If we assume his or her pension will grow by 12% p.a. for the next three years, assuming no further contributions, the fund will be,

At end of year 1 $\quad 445,793 + 445,793 \times \dfrac{12}{100} = £499,288$

At end of year 2 $\quad 499,288 + 499,288 \times \dfrac{12}{100} = £559,203$

At end of year 3 $\quad 559,203 + 559,203 \times \dfrac{12}{100} = £626,307$

Referring to Table 2.16, and choosing an annuity indexed at 5% p.a., single life, guaranteed for five years, we see the annual yield is 4.79%. Thus the pension produced will be,

$$626,307 \times \dfrac{4.79}{100} = £30,000 \text{ p.a.}$$

As she is entitled to a maximum pension of two-thirds of final salary indexed at 5% p.a. she sees that currently this would be,

$\quad \frac{2}{3} \times 25,000 = £16,667$ p.a.

Obviously his or her pension is vastly overfunded if she does nothing. She switches her annual pension contribution of £20,000 into salary, increasing this to £45,000. Now she can take a pension of $\frac{2}{3} \times 45,000 = £30,000$ p.a. which is what her pension fund can provide.

THE CHOICE OF ANNUITY

We have already seen that an annuity can be compulsory purchase (CPA) or purchased life (PLA) and that the latter, while being slightly more expensive, is considerably more favourably taxed.

There is also the unit-linked annuity. This will be available to those with unit-linked funds. Depending on the annuity required, single life, joint life etc., a certain proportion of the units in the fund is normally set aside. The pension then paid by the insurance company will be the value of that portion of the fund at the time of payment. Clearly if the fund goes up in value, so does that portion of the fund and so, therefore, does the pension. The opposite will be true if the fund goes down. The hope is that the fund will go up and eventually the pension will be bigger than that from a corresponding straightforward annuity.

This special annuity can be linked to the fund of choice, managed, UK equity, property etc. It will usually start at a lower level than the others but the hope is it will increase and overtake.

Whatever annuity is chosen there will be relevant questions to answer:

1 Am I in good health? In which case, and especially if there is a history of longevity in the family, the choice will probably be an annuity starting lower but indexed, or perhaps the unit-linked annuity. This should help to keep the payments at least in line with inflation.

   However, if the opposite is true and it is a matter of poor health and possibly shortened life expectancy then it would probably be best to take as much as possible now and opt for a level annuity. There are some insurers who provide 'impaired life' annuities which start at a higher level.

2 If the choice is unit linked and it falls in value are there other sources of income to fall back on?

3 Will wife or husband have a separate income? This will bear on the question of single life or joint and whether the annuity should be guaranteed or not.

4 Cost of the various annuities? If, for example, the difference in cost between guaranteed and non-guaranteed is small this may tip the balance in favour of guaranteed.

We see from Table 2.16 that the yield for a single life, male, indexed at 5 per cent per annum, non-guaranteed, is 5.78 per cent while guaranteeing it reduces the yield to 5.74 per cent.

Thus from £100,000 non-guaranteed comes an income of,

$$\frac{5.78}{100} \times 100,000 = £5780 \text{ per annum}$$

while guaranteeing the income for five years gives,

$$\frac{5.74}{100} \times 100,000 = £5740 \text{ per annum}$$

a difference of only £40 per annum or £3.33 per month.

5 Is my spouse in good health? If he or she is then his or her life expectancy is likely to be good which will dictate a joint life annuity, especially in the case of a man, as women's life expectancies are greater than men's. If he or she is not, it might be better to have single life which will be higher and give a better lifestyle for both over a few years.

Once again from Table 2.16 we see the different yields from £100,000 for a man including his wife at 50 per cent,

Single life $\dfrac{5.78}{100} \times 100{,}000 = £5780$ per annum

Joint life $\dfrac{4.83}{100} \times 100{,}000 = £4830$ per annum

A woman including her husband gives a much smaller difference:

Single life $\dfrac{4.81}{100} \times 100{,}000 = £4810$ per annum

Joint life $\dfrac{4.62}{100} \times 100{,}000 = £4620$ per annum

which of course, reflects the greater life expectancy of the woman. Hence to include husband would cost little to cater for the smaller likelihood that he would outlive her.

PHASED RETIREMENT

Because pension policies today are usually divided into 100 or more separate contracts 'phased retirement' is possible. In other words, at maturity, a certain number of contracts can be used to produce a pension sufficient for any needs at that point, perhaps coinciding with working less and receiving less remuneration. A little later more contracts can be used in this way and so on until the whole pension fund has been used. While doing this investment can continue to be made into the scheme.

This is, of course, applicable only to the personal pension scheme since any benefits taken from an approved company pension scheme dictate retirement from the company and benefits cannot be phased in this way.

Another version of this is to use the tax-free cash as income. Thus the income required in the first year would be tax-free cash with an annuity bought from the remainder of that part of the fund used. In the second year a smaller amount of tax-free cash is needed because there is already a pension in existence. The remaining part of the fund used for the second year produces a further annuity to be added to the income.

■ Example 6.4

Claude Beamish, at 60, has built up a fund of £100,000 in his personal pension scheme. He proposes to use a phased encashment of the fund using the tax-free cash as income to produce a net pension starting at £4000 p.a. indexed at 5% and paid monthly in arrears with no guarantee.

Consulting Table 2.16, we see that this type of annuity would produce an annual yield of 5.78%. As Claude is a basic rate tax payer this would produce a net annual figure of 4.45%.

At 75 he would have to use whatever fund is left to purchase an annuity or an annuity plus tax-free cash.

Assuming annuity yields vary only with age, we can produce an illustration of what might happen over the years and compare this with the result had he purchased a similar annuity outright with the £100,000. This is just for comparison because clearly he would have used £25,000 of this fund to purchase a PLA.

Assuming a growth in the fund of 12% p.a., the result appears in Table 6.1.

Table 6.1 Phased pension vs immediate pension (net figures)

At the end of year	Tax-free cash £	Phased net pension £	Total net income £	Fund remaining £	Immediate pension £
1	3550	465	4015	95,100	4450
2	3098	1100	4198	91,600	4673
3	2733	1710	4443	89,400	4906
4	2350	2285	4635	88,700	5151
5	2038	2829	4867	89,400	5409
6	1758	3362	5120	91,300	5679
7	1532	3876	5408	94,500	5963
8	1287	4367	5654	99,000	6261
9	1085	4852	5937	105,000	6575
10	949	5327	6276	112,000	6903
11	772	5792	6564	121,000	7249
12	622	6252	6874	131,000	7611
13	518	6706	7224	143,000	7992
14	478	7175	7653	156,000	8391
15	318	7635	7953	172,000	8811

Clearly the figures cannot be exact because of the number of variables but the above gives a typical example of the sort of thing an insurance company can produce for illustration purposes. Annuities will undoubtedly vary from those assumed but the general principle is shown. At age 75 the remaining fund must be used for an annuity or cash plus an annuity.

As we said before, it is possible to continue investment into the pension contracts which have not been encashed. Also, this system or the simpler one described earlier could be used in conjunction with the income withdrawal facility.

DEFERRING THE ANNUITY

It is possible to defer taking an annuity and simply take an income from the pension funds even for as long as up to the 75th birthday.

Clearly decisions have to be taken here and the factors involved will need to be carefully considered. 'To defer or not to defer', that is the question.

Let us first look at the two available methods for deferring.

■ The deferred annuity facility of the SSAS (DFA)

A full description of this method of deferment will be found in Chapter 5.

■ The income withdrawal facility (IWA)

Without warning, the government white paper, 'Security, Equality, Choice; the Future for Pensions', proposed changes to personal pensions bringing about very much greater flexibility. These changes were confirmed in the Finance Act 1995, allowing holders of personal pension schemes to take tax-free cash equal to 25 per cent of the fund from age 50 and defer the purchase of an annuity up to the age of 75. While the annuity is being deferred an income must be taken from the remaining fund, which continues to take part in all investment growth. This income must be within Revenue limits which means it cannot be more than the notional annuity that the policy holder could obtain using rates published by the Government Actuary, which depend on the yield of 15 year gilts, but could be as little as 35 per cent of it. This maximum figure is subject to readjustment every three years.

> The income withdrawal facility makes possible an income between 35 and 100 per cent of the actual annuity possible.

Once this facility starts it is not possible to switch providers so very careful consideration has to be given at outset. It is, however, possible to combine the income withdrawal facility, income drawdown scheme, pension fund withdrawal scheme, income withdrawal scheme or income withdrawal account with a self-invested personal pension which at least allows the providers of the investment funds to be switched if so desired. If the policy holder dies while withdrawing income from the fund, spouse may continue that facility up until the policy holder would have reached the age of 75 when an annuity has to be purchased. Spouse may, of course, decide to purchase an annuity before that. If spouse should die before that time the fund can pass to the children or any others nominated in a trust, subject to a tax charge of 35 per cent. If this fund goes directly into the estate it could also be subject to a charge to inheritance tax. Clearly it is extremely important to put the personal pension scheme into trust.

> The income withdrawal facility can be part of a SIPP.

After all this good news there is yet something more. Because most of these pensions are divided into 100 or more contracts the income withdrawal facility could be in operation on a proportion of these contracts allowing the continuation of payment of premiums into the remaining portion.

Comparison of the two methods

1 DFA – must retire from company.
IWA – not necessary.

2 DFA – no transfer so no upfront charge.
IWA – transfer and thus an upfront charge.

3 DFA – SSAS charges continue.
IWA – new management charges.

4 DFA – tax-free cash governed by approved company pension rates.
IWA – in the case of a transfer from an approved company pension, the tax-free cash will be the lesser of 25 per cent of the fund and whatever it could have been if taken directly from the company scheme. This could reduce the tax-free cash and should therefore be considered carefully.

5 DFA – pension taken must be within 10 per cent of what could have been taken in an annuity. However, once the type of annuity has been decided upon it is this annuity which is being deferred. It will be this annuity which will eventually be taken. There is not the possibility of changing it. On death, if spouse continues to defer taking the annuity it would be his or her part of it which is being deferred, i.e. if the original choice had been 50 per cent passing to spouse that would be what the spouse would defer.
IWA – pension taken can be between 35 and 100 per cent of what it could have been. This is totally flexible, can be changed and on taking the annuity could be changed again. On death before this the whole arrangement can pass to spouse.

6 DFA – on death of both partners before taking the annuity pensions can only be provided for dependants while in full-time education. The fund then either returns to the SSAS or to the company where it is taxed at 40 per cent.
IWA – on death of both partners the fund can pass to any beneficiary nominated in the trust after it has been taxed at 35 per cent.

7 DFA – must be applied to whole fund.
IWA – allows application to part of the fund at a time. It can thus be phased.

There are, therefore, two questions:

1 To defer or not to defer?
2 If the choice is to defer should it be the DFA or IWA?

The second question can be answered by matching personal situations to the comparison just carried out.

To defer or not to defer

Taking an annuity is an irrevocable decision – once taken it cannot be changed. An annuity is a promise, not a guarantee, to pay an income for life and perhaps for part or all of that income to continue for spouse. There is no longer a fund,

Taking an annuity is an irrevocable decision.

that has been given to the insurer in return for the promise. What if, after taking the annuity, the situation changes and a different choice would have been advantageous? It is too late to change.

Deferring is delaying. It is a wait and see what happens approach. Perhaps the situation will change, perhaps it will become clearer, making a decision easier. Perhaps annuity rates will improve enabling a bigger pension to be purchased. Perhaps the fund will grow exceptionally enabling a bigger pension to be purchased. We will see later a method which might be considered to give some insight into these considerations and help the decision process.

■ Example 6.5

Morris Hunter retires at 60 using his pension fund of £200,000 to purchase a joint life annuity indexed at 5% p.a., non-guaranteed and 50% to continue at his death for his wife Veronica who is 57. The annuity yield is 4.82%. Hence pension starts at £9640 p.a. Two years later his wife dies. A single life annuity, non-guaranteed, indexed at 5% would have given a yield of 5.78% p.a. with an annual pension commencing at £11,360. The decision is clear: if spouse is in ill health, with only a few years at most to live, defer the annuity.

Similarly, if the pension member is in ill health with only a few years to live. The decision is clear, defer the annuity so that the whole arrangement can pass intact to spouse. Of course, if a pension is not needed then the choice might be just to delay taking any income whatsoever. Unfortunately in the case of the approved company pension scheme this would preclude retirement since at retirement

At retirement from a company at selected retirement age the benefits of the approved company pension scheme have to be taken.

from a company the benefits have to be taken. In the case of the shareholding director he or she could continue to take a small salary and not retire. His or her spouse would then get the best deal possible with a tax-free lump sum equal to four times final salary which would be the average of any three consecutive years occuring in the period just under thirteen years from retirement and dynamised. The rest of the fund would

be used to purchase a pension for him or her. This could, of course, only be four-ninths of final salary. There could be surplus funds which would then be paid back to the company and taxed at 40 per cent. If this looked like the case then a switch into the income withdrawal facility taking tax-free cash at the same time, would be preferable, or indeed a straight switch into a PPS, written in trust, when the whole fund would pass to the beneficiaries on death. It would only be free from IHT if seven years had passed since the setting up of the trust, unless it was left to spouse where there would be no IHT as there is none between spouses. Another side benefit of switching to the PPS is that he or she does not have to go on working in the business if he or she so wishes. Clearly expert advice is needed in order to make a satisfactory decision.

Ill health then, of either member or spouse, could dictate a choice.

What if both are in good health?

Passing on as much as possible

What if those contemplating these decisions are concerned to pass as much to their children, or even grandchildren, as possible? Taking an annuity immediately uses the pension fund. There is no longer anything to pass on. If this considera-tion is really important then the choice must be the income withdrawal facility. If member and spouse should then die before the member would have reached his or her seventy-fifth birthday the remaining fund would pass to the children after tax at 35 per cent. It would be crucial to put into trust the PPS running the IWA so that that fund would not also be subject to IHT.

If income is not needed, then the fund could simply be transferred to a PPS put in trust. In which case the whole fund would eventually pass untaxed to the beneficiaries.

All of these considerations give some reasonably strong indications which will influence the choice.

What if none of these considerations apply?

The final question on pension benefits

Then we are finally faced with the questions, 'What is the best buy? Will I do better to take an annuity now or might I do better in the future?'

An annuity will be based on the yield of long-term gilts, 15 to 20 years. These yields will go up and down as we saw in Chapter 2. When gilts are cheap to buy then the yield will be higher. Just as a reminder, when a gilt is issued it will have a stated yield, e.g. a 15 year gilt yields say 6 per cent. Hence investing £1000 will produce an annual income of £60. Suppose the price of the gilt on the market drops so that £900 now buys £1000 worth of these gilts. The annual income is still £60 but now the yield is,

$$\frac{60}{900} \times 100\% = 6.67\%$$

The converse is, of course, true; when gilts go up in price the yield will be lower. Now there is a tenuous connection between equities and gilts in that when the stock market is high in value, the yield will be low, gilts will become more attrac-tive, pushing their price up and therefore reducing their yield. So stock market value high, gilt yield low.

Annuities are linked to the yield from 15 to 20 year gilts, because this period of time is an estimate for life expectancy. The insurance company will put a bonus factor on top based on that life expectancy. When the annuitant dies before this time the insurance company makes a profit and vice versa. Taking all these factors into account the annuity yield is set to make the insurance company a profit, while making it higher than that to be expected from the corresponding gilt.

> **In general a stock market high in value means low yields from gilts.**

When the stock market increases in value so does the pension fund, but so does the value of gilts leading to a decrease in yield, leading to a decrease in annuity yield or, in other words, making the same yield more expensive to buy.

This increased value in pension fund gives more money for purchase of an annuity which is now more expensive, the one cancelling out the other. There are, however, the occasions when the market goes up very quickly, leaving the gilt market dragging behind on low values and higher yields, making the annuity purchase cheaper. This time both variables are working together just as the sun and the moon working in tandem give rise to a higher tide. Clearly it is times like this which are truly advantageous for the purchase of an annuity.

How can these arguments and this history help? Suppose we go back 20 years and track the FTSE All-Share Index (see Fig. 6.1, p. 395).

Then we track the yields on annuities back over those 20 years.

Table 6.2 Typical annuities for single life, male, level, non-guaranteed, paid monthly in arrears at age 60

August	1988	11.14%	August	1993	9.16%
	1989	10.96%		1994	10.24%
	1990	12.41%		1995	9.88%
	1991	10.96%		1996	9.70%
	1992	10.84%		1997	9.16%

Now if we combine the information in Figure 6.1 with the pattern of information shown in Table 6.2 we get the graph shown in Figure 6.2.

Clearly at any peak the value of the pension fund has been high and the annuity yield has also been high. This would have been an excellent time to purchase the annuity. Now if we smooth out the graph cancelling the peaks against the troughs we get a straight line (see Fig. 6.3).

When the graph coincides with this line it is a neutral time, neither a good nor bad time to purchase an annuity. Above the line it is 'yes', it is a good time, below the line it is 'no', a bad time. Feed in a bit of caution and say 'Well above the line is yes, well below the line is no'.

We get two lines, the 'yes' line and the 'no' line (see Fig. 6.4).

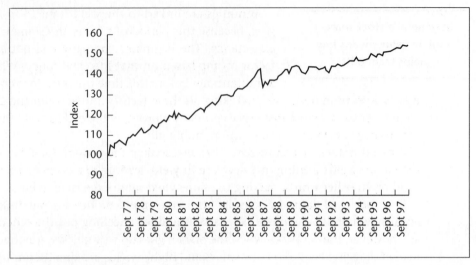

Fig. 6.2 The Annuity Price Index (I)
Source: Datastream

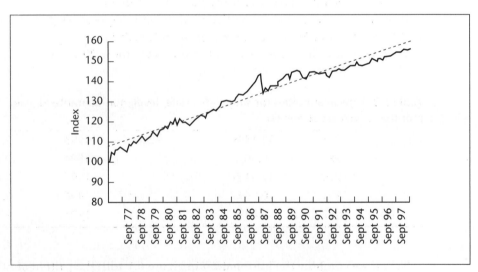

Fig. 6.3 The Annuity Price Index (II)
Source: Datastream

Above the yes line is a good time, below the no line is a bad time, between the lines is anybody's guess. Now we project forward, making the assumption that similar patterns will happen in the future. We say if today the graph is above the yes line then this is a good time to buy. There may be better times in the future but this is a good time. This is a reasonable assumption to make but it could always be wrong. Similarly we say if the graph is between the lines today it could be a good time, or a bad time, to purchase an annuity. If the graph is below the no line, this is definitely not the time to purchase. Again an assumption.

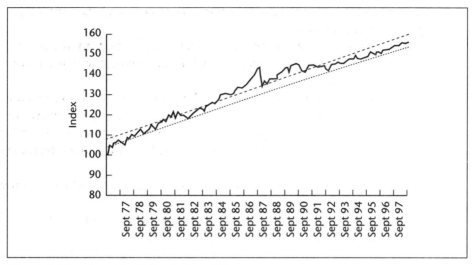

Fig. 6.4 The Annuity Price Index (III)
Source: Datastream

Many insurance companies and firms of actuaries will produce these sorts of forecasts but clearly the most important thing to say is that it is complex and expert professional advice is a must.

> **To defer or not to defer is a complex question needing expert advice.**

It is not enough to look at some published graph and make a decision. Especially since in the case, for example, we have just considered it relates to a fund invested in UK equities. If a particular fund is invested quite differently then factors relating specifically to that fund must be considued.

A NEW QUESTION – WHAT HAPPENS TO OUR ESTATE WHEN WE DIE?

In this age financial independence has been achieved. Your lifetime financial plan has brought you safely to this point. Throughout the earlier ages three questions have been predominant:

- What happens if I become medically unable to work before financial independence has been achieved?
- What happens if I die too soon before financial independence has been achieved, leaving dependants unprovided for?
- What happens if I live too long when work days are over, there is no earned income and financial independence has not been achieved?

In Chapter 5, the questions were also asked about staff, partners or your fellow shareholding directors.

The answer we have always sought has been, 'I and my dependants will be totally financially independent and will be able to deal with whatever financial contingencies might arise.'

In this age, all three questions have been substantially answered and are now largely redundant. The question we have so far attempted to answer in this age has been, 'How do I best apply my pension fund?' In other words we have tried to fine tune that financial independence. We have tried to do the same exercise for our dependants.

Now a new question arises, 'What happens to our estate when I and my spouse die?'

The reason this question arises is because a tax barrier blocks the passing on of the estate. That tax barrier is inheritance tax (IHT).

This tax lies in the forefront of this age. It has cropped up before in Chapter 5, and aptly so since acquaintance with it is wise from the age of at least 40. Now, however, the question really does need to be answered.

Inheritance tax is a voluntary tax, since steps can be taken to deal with it. It is a combined gift tax and death duty. It applies to gifts and deemed gifts during life and to the whole estate on death. The lifetime rate is 20 per cent. The death duty rate is 40 per cent. There is no IHT between spouses. In the fiscal year 1997/98 the first £215,000 of chargeable transfers for each person was free of IHT. This is called the 'nil rate band'. This band has increased over the years and it is to be hoped that this process will continue.

Inheritance tax is a voluntary tax.

■ Example 6.6

Oswald Frampton leaves his estate of £450,000 to his wife Prunella. There is no IHT, since there is none between spouses. When Prunella dies eight years later her estate amounts to £650,000 which she leaves to her four children.

Total estate	£650,000	
Less nil rate band	£215,000	
Taxable estate	£435,000	
Tax at 40%		£174,000
Estate left to children	£476,000	
Each receives	£119,000	
The taxman gets	£174,000	

The taxman gets the biggest share. What a pity Oswald and Prunella had done no IHT planning.

■ **Exercise 6.1**

Robin and Valerie Price have done nothing about IHT. They have the sort of will which is very usual. If one dies everything goes to the other, thereafter to the three children. If the total estate is £430,000 calculate how much each child will receive.

■ **Exercise 6.2**

Why not do this for your own situation?

Let us have a look at some of the comments which have been made about inheritance tax in the past. In 1974 Denis Healey, the then Chancellor of the Exchequer, said of the new capital transfer tax,

> A tax which will make the rich hurt until the pips squeak.

In May 1980, in a speech to the Institute of Chartered Accountants, Sir Geoffrey Howe commented that,

> We must accept that some form of capital taxation is here to stay. After all, the estate duties have been with us for more than 80 years, other capital taxes for much longer.

Lord James Avon Clyde (1863–1944) the then Lord Justice-General of Scotland, stated circa 1935,

> No man in this country is under the smallest obligation, moral or other, so to arrange his legal relations to his business or his property as to enable the Inland Revenue to put the largest possible shovel into his stores.

Andrew Dilnot, director of the influential Conservative think tank, the Institute of Fiscal Studies, commented that,

> It [IHT] has become a tax on people who can't get proper tax advice or who die unexpectedly.

Roy Jenkins (budget debate, House of Commons), 19 March 1986,

> It [IHT] is, broadly speaking, a voluntary levy paid by those who distrust their heirs more than they dislike the Inland Revenue.

Kenneth Clarke, 26 November 1996,

> It [IHT] is largely paid by people of modest means who either cannot or simply do not make careful plans to avoid it.

Returning to the Framptons in Example 6.6, their situation is pictured in Fig. 6.5.

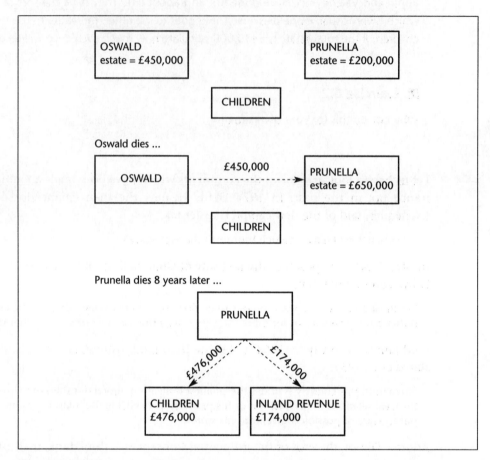

Fig. 6.5 The Framptons' situation

If the Framptons had just remembered that each person can pass up to £215,000 tax-free their situation would have been as that pictured in Fig. 6.6.

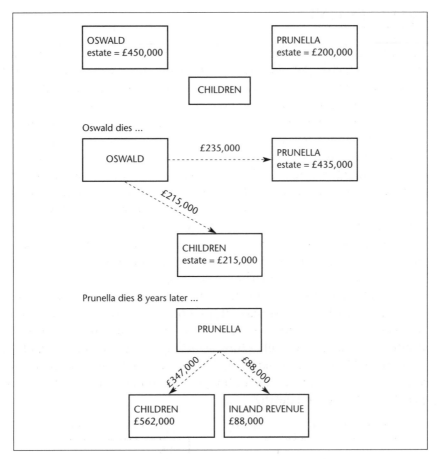

Fig. 6.6 The Framptons do some financial planning

Now they have reduced the IHT paid by £86,000 to £88,000. In other words they have saved tax of £86,000 and passed £86,000 more to their children simply by changing their will. Cost? Probably about £150 to have the will changed.

Prunella's will would work in exactly the same way so that if she died first, £200,000, her total estate, would pass directly to the children, thus saving £80,000 tax. It is clear they are not quite making the most of this £215,000 which can pass tax free. The answer here is for Oswald to transfer £15,000 to Prunella, which attracts no transfer tax, enabling £215,000 to be passed directly to the children from her and this saves tax of £86,000.

There is, of course, a potential problem in this scenario. On the first death, the income from an investment of £215,000 would be lost to the surviving spouse, say 5 per cent per annum, which is £10,750. This would, in some cases, cause hardship and so the figures all have to be carefully calculated and the best compromise made. Remember, 'the practice of financial planning is the art of compromise'.

However, this is perhaps the one time when compromise is not inevitable.

THE WILL TRUST

The will trust will allow the proverbial cake to be had and eaten at the same time. It is a trust which is put into effect on death and this is written into the will. What goes into the trust? Something we have met several times before – the investment bond. This is because it produces no income which has to be paid out to the beneficiaries. So the method will only be available to those who have liquid assets which can be invested in a bond or who already own such an investment and that is why it was recommended in Chapter 5 that this present section should be worked through before final decisions were made on an investment portfolio.

If we again take the example of the Framptons, each spouse invests up to £215,000 in one or more investment bonds. Oswald has passed £15,000 to Prunella for this purpose. They have to be owned individually but be written on both lives, in other words they are joint life second death policies. So, for example, Oswald Frampton would invest £215,000 into an investment bond. He would own it and his would be the first life assured, Prunella the second.

You will remember that death triggers a chargeable event and the bond is immediately cashed in and taxed. If this bond were written only on Oswald's life it would be cashed in and any gain in the value liable to tax as income on his death. Depending on his other income during that tax year there could be a further tax of 17 per cent. Chargeable events and the taxation of bonds was dealt with in Chapter 1. In the case of the joint life bond no chargeable event is triggered until the second death.

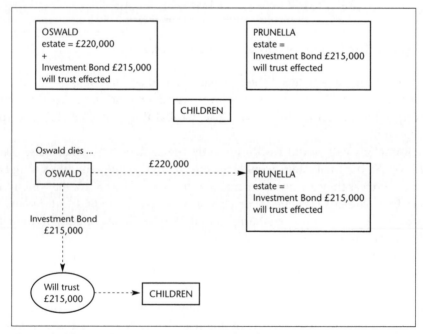

Fig. 6.7 The position when Oswald dies having done effective financial planning

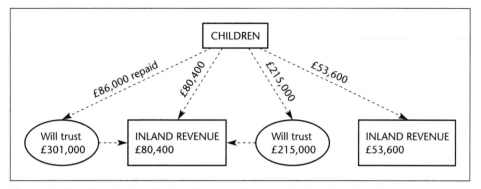

Fig. 6.8 The final episode in effective financial planning for the Framptons

The dead settlor rule

The fact that the bond is now in trust has a very beneficial effect since when the bond is eventually cashed in, triggering a chargeable event, it is the settlor of the trust who is liable for any tax which may be due. If the bond is cashed in after the tax year in which the settlor died there can be no tax, since the settlor is no longer paying income tax. Hence the total growth in the bond is totally tax free. This is the dead settlor rule. It is the trust which makes this very advantageous difference since a bond not in trust simply passing to a dependant would be taxed in the normal way on the second death.

So, at this point we have one bond owned by Oswald written on both lives and one owned by Prunella written on both lives. Their wills have been changed to include a will trust each. Remember that they can both draw an income from their bonds of 5 per cent per annum tax free in their hands and they can continue to do this for 20 years.

The trust to be set up will be a flexible trust, naming the children, or even the grandchildren, as the current beneficiaries with spouse as one of the reserve beneficiaries. The situation is shown in Figure 6.7.

Oswald's bond has gone into the trust. There has been no IHT to pay because the £215,000 represents his nil rate band. There has been no IHT to pay on the £220,000 left to Prunella because there is no IHT between spouses.

Eight years later Prunella dies. Fig. 6.8 shows the situation.

Prunella has been drawing her 5 per cent per annum from her bond but, in addition, the trustees have been encashing 5 per cent per annum from the bond in the trust and lending it to Prunella over the last eight years. This is allowed because she is a beneficiary. She has therefore borrowed a total of,

$$8 \times \frac{5}{100} \times £215,000 = £86,000$$

The first point to make here is that she has not lost the income from that £215,000 in trust for the children as she would have done without the will trust. She therefore has an annual income from both bonds totalling £21,500 but with no further tax to pay on it.

First the £86,000 Prunella has borrowed from the trust is paid back making the total investments in the trust £301,000.

Prunella's remaining estate:		
Bond	£215,000	
which now suffers a chargeable event but is unlikely to pay any income tax since her existing taxable income is zero		
Rest of estate £220,000 – £86,000 =	£134,000	
Total	£349,000	
Nil rate band	£215,000	
Taxable estate	£134,000	
Tax at 40%		£53,600
Estate passed to children	£295,400	

Therefore, this time, a total of £215,000 + £86,000 + £295,400 = £596,400 is available for the children. The taxman has got only £53,600 out of this.

In order to illustrate the principle simply, a growth of 5 per cent per annum has been assumed in the bonds and none in the remainder of the estate, which would probably have been their house.

THE USE OF LIFE ASSURANCE TO SOLVE THE PROBLEM OF IHT

As we said earlier the will trust can only be used if there are liquid assets to invest in the bonds. If not we need to think of other ways of solving the problem. Life assurance is the good old standby for dealing with IHT. It is simple, straightforward and inexpensive. A joint life second death, whole of life policy is used. Second death means that it pays out on the death of the second partner. This would be at the point when the total estate finally passes to the children. It is whole of life because it literally goes on until both partners have died or it is cashed in, perhaps because the situation has changed, e.g. a divorce and a second marriage. There is usually an investment aspect to these policies and on cancelling there would be a cash value. If one of the partners had died before cashing in then this cash value would usually be greater, and more so if it was the wife who had died. These aspects are governed by mortality statistics. We have had a preview of these figures in Chapter 5.

How does it work?

The policy is written on both lives and put in trust for the children. Thus the proceeds would be paid to them free of tax and totally bypass the parents' estate for the purposes of probate. If the sum assured or death benefit is equal to the potential IHT then this can be paid off leaving the estate totally free of tax.

It would be wise to make sure that the policy is indexed so that the sum assured will go up each year and hopefully keep pace with increasing estate value and, therefore, increasing potential IHT. Although the nil rate band, hopefully, will be indexed, in normal circumstances an estate will make a growth over and above this. It might even be worth insuring for more than the potential IHT to ensure the cover keeps pace with inflation. If the sum assured turns out to be more than the potential IHT, it is still all paid to the children tax free and will increase their inheritance. This is also a good idea since at this age the premiums will be considerably less expensive than later. It might also be worth looking at possible inheritances to be received in the future and covering these with the sum assured.

■ Example 6.7

Vivian Spooner (61) and Trudy Spooner (58) are surprised to find their house is worth £260,000 and to have confirmation that their antique furniture is valued at £120,000. They are both smokers. They are living on Vivian's pension and have a few thousand in a building society. They decide to tot up the value of their estate on Form 6.1.

Referring to Table 5.1 (p. 266), the nearest age to Vivian is 60 and Trudy is three years younger. They can therefore get an approximate cost for solving their problem using life assurance.

■ Form 6.1 INHERITANCE TAX PLANNING – VALUE OF ESTATE

Names Vivian and Trudy Spooner		
	£	
House	260,000	
Contents	20,000	
Jewellery	5000	
Car(s)	16,000	
Investments		
Building society	5000	
Antique furniture	120,000	
Probable inheritances	50,000	
Total	476,000	
Nil rate band	215,000	(They can't afford to rearrange wills to make better use of the individual's nil
Taxable estate	261,000	rate band and have no liquid assets)
Tax at 40%		£104,400
Estate available to pass on	371,600	

$$\text{Premium} = \frac{104,400}{100,000} \times 102.88 = £107.41 \text{ per month}$$

$$\text{Addition for smoker rate} = 107.41 \times \frac{31}{100} = £33.30 \text{ per month}$$

$$\text{Total cost} = 107.41 + 33.30 = £140.71 \text{ per month}$$

This will cost them £1688.52 p.a. which is,

$$\frac{1688.52}{104,400} \times 100\% = 1.62\% \text{ of the potential tax.}$$

They would have paid the whole of the tax in premiums if they lived a further 100/1.62 years = 61.7 years, which at their ages is unlikely.

So this looks like a reasonably sound method to use.

■ Exercise 6.3

Hedley and Jessica Willmot decide to do some IHT planning. Hedley is 57 and Jessica 54. Their house is worth £250,000, contents £20,000, Jessica's jewellery £4000, their car £5000. They have £60,000 in a building society. They are both non-smokers. They expect to inherit £100,000. Assuming they leave a contingency fund in the building society of £5000, do some IHT planning for them. Calculate potential tax. Use £55,000 for a will trust. Recalculate the potential tax and cost a second death whole of life policy to cover this using Form 6.2.

■ Form 6.2 INHERITANCE TAX PLANNING – VALUE OF ESTATE

Names	
	£
House	
Contents	
Jewellery	
Car(s)	
Investments	
Probable inheritances	
Total	
Nil rate band	215,000
Taxable estate	
Tax at 40%	
Estate available to pass on	

■ **Exercise 6.4**

You may like to use Form 6.3 to calculate the value of your own estate and the potential IHT and hence the cost of solving the problem using life assurance.

■ **Form 6.3 INHERITANCE TAX PLANNING – VALUE OF ESTATE**

Names	
	£
House	
Contents	
Jewellery	
Car(s)	
Investments	
Probable inheritances	
Total	
Nil rate band	215,000
Taxable estate	
Tax at 40%	
Estate available to pass on	

THE WILL TRUST USING A HOUSE

In fact there is another solution Vivian and Trudy could have used. This will be the same will trust with exactly the same structure, but putting their house into it. Like most people they own their home jointly, i.e. joint ownership. In such a situation, if one dies the house goes automatically to the other. They cannot leave their notional half to someone else since the whole is owned by each of them. Hence in this form it could not be used. They first have to change the form of ownership to tenants in common owning simply half the house each. Then Vivian can put his half into a will trust, beneficiaries the children, and Trudy can do the same.

Let us suppose Vivian dies, his share of their home goes immediately into the will trust. Hence he has transferred an asset worth £130,000 to a trust for the children. There is no IHT at this point because it is well within the nil rate band. He leaves the rest of his estate to Trudy and once again there is no IHT because there is none between spouses.

Trudy's estate is now worth,

£476,000 – £130,000 =	£346,000	
Nil rate band	£215,000	
Taxable estate	£131,000	
Tax at 40%		£52,400
Estate available to pass on	£293,600	
Already passed on	£130,000	
Total	£423,500	

They could now finish the job by taking the equivalent policy as before but for a sum assured of £52,400 and a premium of 52,400/100,000 × 135.31 = £70.62 a month.

With no will trust used in this method and leaving half the house directly to the children it is possible that considerable problems could arise. Suppose son-in-law was suddenly in great need of cash, he could approach the courts for permission to sell the house to realise the value of his share. This could result in the surviving spouse being evicted. The trust should protect this situation to some extent since the surviving spouse will be a trustee, but clearly expert professional advice should be taken.

MORE ABOUT INHERITANCE TAX (IHT)

Those subject to inheritance tax

Anyone domiciled in the UK is subject to IHT on property owned anywhere in the world.

■ Domicile

Domicile is a concept of general living and is not to do with being resident or ordinarily resident. The basic concept is that a person is domiciled in the country which he or she regards as his or her real home. An individual normally acquires his or her father's domicile at birth, which is called his or her 'domicile of origin'.

As far as IHT is concerned an individual is deemed to be domiciled in the UK for a tax year if he or she has been resident in the UK for 17 out of 20 tax years which end with the current year (Section 267 Inheritance Tax Act (IHTA) 1984).

What is chargeable to IHT?

1 Lifetime transfers of value.
2 One's estate on death.

Lifetime transfers of value will, of course, include all gifts but need not necessarily be a gift. For example where a person deliberately sells an asset at less than its market value a transfer of value has been made. In the same way the beneficiary of a flexible trust who dies, although he or she does not own the assets of the trust, is deemed to have made a transfer. You will remember our extensive discussion of this relating to the partnership protection plan treated in Chapter 5.

The value of a transfer

It is usually very easy to see the value of what has been transferred and therefore assess the IHT to be levied but the fact that the value is assessed on the donor's reduction in wealth can give rise to some interesting situations.

> **The value of a transfer is assessed on the donor's reduction in wealth.**

You will remember that in Chapter 5 the value of certain proportions of shares in a company was discussed. For example 51 per cent of the shares could be worth about 55 per cent of the value of the company, whereas 49 per cent could be worth about 35 per cent.

■ Example 6.8

Leonard Kendrick owns 51% of the 1000 issued shares in his own company which is valued at £1 million. He wants his son, Jasper, to be truly part of the company and gives him 20 shares which represents $20/1000 \times 100 = 2\%$ of the total shares of the company, i.e. practically no value at all. However, the value of Leonard's share in the company has decreased from about $55/100 \times 1$ million = £550,000 to about $35/100 \times 1$ million = £350,000 reducing Leonard's wealth by £200,000. It would be this amount which would be taxed under IHT.

This is just an illustrative example, as we shall see later in the chapter that, in the fiscal year 1997/98, there was no transfer tax on the shares of a private limited company.

Deed of variation

> **A will can be varied without attracting IHT.**

A will can be varied, redirecting property without attracting IHT. The revised disposition is treated as having taken place on the deceased person's death.

■ Example 6.9

Barbara Steel dies leaving her estate to her husband Felix who redirects £215,000 of the inheritance to their son, Dennis. He does this to make use, rather belatedly, of Barbara's nil rate band. In this case it is not treated as a transfer from Felix to Dennis.
Certain conditions must be satisfied,

1 It must be executed within two years of death and an election must be filed within six months of the deed being executed.
2 The deed must be in writing and must specifically refer to the provisions of the will which are to be varied.
3 It must be signed by the person who would otherwise have benefited.

4 Only one deed of variation in respect of a particular piece of property can be effective for IHT purposes.

5 No payment or other consideration must pass in respect of the deed of variation, except that inheritances can be exchanged with a cash adjustment.

Transfers which are exempt from IHT

1 Gifts between spouses.
2 Normal expenditure.

These will be gifts:

which come out of income
of a regular nature
such as to leave the donor sufficient income to maintain his or her normal standard of living.

A typical example would be the premium for a policy written under trust.

3 £250 small gifts exemption. This covers any number of individual small gifts up to a value of £250 in any one tax year.

4 Annual £3000 exemption. Each individual is exempt up to £3000 of any gift in any tax year. Any part of this not used can be carried forward to the next tax year if the exemption for that year is fully used.

5 Wedding gifts:
   – Each parent   up to £5000
   – Each grandparent or great-grandparent   up to £2500
   – Bride or groom   £2500
   – Any other person   £1000

Parents may gift to both participants in the marriage. Thus the parents of the bride could gift up to £5000 each to the groom. Gifts should be conditional on the marriage taking place.

6 Gifts to charities.
7 Gifts for national purposes.
8 Gifts for public benefit.
9 Gifts to political parties.
10 Certain transfers to employee trusts.

■ Potentially exempt transfers (PET)

An irrevocable gift made with no reservation of any benefit is a potentially exempt transfer. It is potential because the donor has to live seven years after the gift to make it actually exempt.

■ Reservation of benefit

Any benefit which is reserved by the donor will turn the PET into a gift with reservation (GWR) and it will be treated as a chargeable transfer.

An example of this would be the gift of a house with the donor reserving the benefit of using one of the rooms, even if the donee could, in law, require the donor to vacate the property at any time. We saw in Chapter 5, when discussing the share protection plan, that if the settlor of a trust were included in the list of potential beneficiaries this would cause the gifts to the trust to be considered as gifts with reservation. It will be clear now why it was so important to get these aspects correct in the case of the share protection plan.

> **Reserving a benefit when making a gift will bring about a tax charge.**

The seven year rule

A PET becomes actually exempt if the donor lives for seven years after the gift. If however, he or she dies within three years it is added back into his or her estate for the purposes of IHT.

In years four to seven there is a sliding scale. After three years, the transfer is taxed at 80 per cent of its value; after four years it is taxed at 60 per cent; after five years 40 per cent; and six years 20 per cent.

Tax on a PET which becomes a chargeable transfer because of the transferrer's death is payable by the recipient of the gift.

Business property relief (BPR)

This relief is given on transfer of business property where,

1 The property has been owned during the previous two years or if it is inherited from a spouse, then the combination of the time it has been owned by the individual plus the period of ownership of the spouse exceeds the two years.
2 It must not be subject to a binding contract for sale. You will remember this was a very important element of the cross-option agreement discussed in Chapter 5.

> **Passing shares in an unquoted company attracts no IHT.**

For sole traderships, a partner's share of a partnership and shares in an unquoted trading company, the relief is 100 per cent. Shares on the alternative investment market (AIM) are treated as unquoted.

Relief is available on quoted shares only if the person making the transfer had voting control of the company before that. In the case of transferring an asset owned by a partner and used in his or her partnership, or an asset owned by a controlling shareholder and used by his or her trading company, 50 per cent relief will apply.

In the case of someone making a PET sometime before death but within the seven years then business property relief will apply only if these conditions are satisfied at the time of the gift and of the death.

■ Example 6.10

Duncan McDougal gives his daughter 23% of the shares in his private limited company. Two years later the company is sold and the daughter receives cash for her shares. Two years later Duncan dies. Business property relief will not normally be available as the necessary conditions are not satisfied at the time of death.

If daughter had reinvested the proceeds in another private company, business property relief might have been allowed.

Assuming the same criteria as above, but this time daughter retains the shares and they are still unquoted at death: the shares attract 100% relief which is not prejudiced if they are sold later.

Using the same criteria again with daughter retaining the shares but this time the business is floated and the shares become quoted: at death no business property relief is available since the shares are quoted and the daughter does not control the company.

■ Business property relief for agricultural property

Farmland in the UK, Channel Islands and the Isle of Man will attract 100 per cent relief where the transferrer has occupied it for two years prior to the date of transfer. This relief is also available for land owned by an individual but occupied by a business of which he or she is a partner or by a company of which he or she is the controling shareholder.

Fifty per cent relief is given for farmland which is let to a tenant before 1 September 1995. For a tenancy granted after 1 September 1995 the relief is 100 per cent. The land must normally have been owned for seven years.

■ Woodlands

BPR is normally available on woodlands after two years of ownership.

Quick succession relief

A person dying where tax has already been paid on property he or she has recently inherited could give rise to a heavy burden if the same property again becomes liable to IHT. The same property could have been taxed twice in a short period of time.

Quick succession relief alleviates this by giving credit for a proportion of the tax already charged on the first occasion, against the tax liable on the second death, as follows,

Both deaths happen within	Proportion
1 year	100%
2 years	80%
3 years	60%
4 years	40%
5 years	20%

The relief is not affected if the property has been sold or given away before the second death.

■ Example 6.11

Beverley Masters inherited property worth £75,000 in March 1994. Inheritance tax was paid on the estate at an average of 25% so the grossed up amount was £100,000, i.e. tax paid,

$$\frac{25}{100} \times 100{,}000 = £25{,}000 \text{ leaving property worth £75,000.}$$

Hence the tax was £25,000.

Beverley died in June 1997. The maximum amount on which quick succession relief can be claimed is,

$$\frac{75{,}000}{100{,}000} \times 25{,}000 = £18{,}750$$

Since three full years have passed the proportion of relief which can be claimed is 60% of £18,750,

$$\frac{60}{100} \times 18{,}750 = £11{,}250$$

The legitim rules in Scotland

You will remember from the section on intestacy in Chapter 4 that under the legitim rules of Scottish law a person must leave part of his or her estate to his or her children. A will not taking account of this can be set aside. However, legislation provides that children can renounce this right and if done within two years of the death no chargeable transfer is deemed to have been made and the property is treated as having passed to the widow in accordance with the will. The deed renouncing the right must satisfy the rules for deeds of variation.

Children under 18 can renounce their right within two years of becoming 18.

For children under 18 the executors can make the choice. If, when the child reaches the age of 18 this choice has been found to be wrong it can be nulified. The tax situation will also have to be so rectified. If the executors went for renunciation and the child decided against, then the tax which would have been paid is recalculated and interest paid in addition. If the reverse is the case then the tax paid by the child is refunded by the Revenue with the requisite interest.

■ Case Study 6.1

Ronald Smithers suddenly realises that his company pension will be maturing in a few months' time. He has been enormously busy running his company and sadly has not taken time for this stage of his financial planning, although Ruth, his wife, has often mentioned it to him. He will be selling his company at age 60 when Ruth will be 57. He has wisely spread the shares between himself and Ruth so the £400,000 they will receive will be entirely free of capital gains tax because of business retirement relief (see Chapter 5). Ronald and Ruth sit down together to plan their retirement.

Using Form 6.4 they see that their potential IHT is £206,800 and decide something must be done about that as they want to pass as much on to the children as possible.

■ Form 6.4 INHERITANCE TAX PLANNING – VALUE OF ESTATE

Names Ronald and Ruth Smithers		
	£	
House	200,000	
Contents	22,000	
Jewellery	4000	
Car(s)	12,000	
Investments		
PEPs	24,000	
Building society	10,000	
Sale of company	400,000	
Probable inheritances	60,000	
Total	732,000	
Nil rate band	215,000	
Taxable estate	517,000	
Tax at 40%		206,800
Estate available to pass on	525,200	

Because of this they decide that Ronald will transfer his pension fund of £200,000 to a personal pension scheme to make use of the income withdrawal facility, putting the whole arrangement into trust. Their thinking here is that they do not need to take the whole of the pension yet because of the £400,000 they have to invest and if they should die before Ronald is 75 the remaining fund after 35% tax would pass to their children. The tax-free cash available from the company scheme would have been £35,000 so this will be the amount they will be able to take from the income withdrawal facility because it is less than 25% of the fund, which is £200,000.

So now they have total cash of,

Proceeds of company	£400,000
Tax-free cash from pension	£35,000
Building society	£10,000
Total	£445,000

They decide to set up a will trust investing £215,000 each into investment bonds from which they can take 5% p.a. with no further tax to pay because they plan to be basic rate taxpayers, i.e. £26,100 p.a. after allowances in the tax year 1997/98. They, therefore, feel that the minimum joint life pension, indexed at 5% p.a. with 50% continuing for Ruth will be the thing to go for. Referring to Table 2.16 (p. 94), and assuming for the purposes of illustration these rates are those published by the government actuary, we can see this would produce an annuity yielding 4.83%,

$$\frac{4.83}{100} \times 165,000 = £7970 \text{ p.a.}$$

As they feel they will have enough income without this they reduce it to the minimum of 35%,

$$\frac{35}{100} \times 7970 = £2790 \text{ p.a.}$$

This will be paid to Ronald.

They have £15,000 over which they leave in the building society as a contingency fund. It produces 6% gross,

$$\frac{6}{100} \times 15,000 = £900 \text{ p.a.}$$

We can see that they will pay no income tax on their income whatsoever.

By using the will trust they have saved 40% of £215,000 tax = $40/100 \times 215,000 =$ £86,000.

In fact this will eventually be more depending on the years between the first one to die and the last one when the survivor will be borrowing money from the first trust.

So their potential tax bill will now be 206,800 − 86,000 = £120,800.

They decide on a whole of life second death policy to cover this. They are both non-smokers. Ronald is 60 and Ruth 57 and we can get the cost from Table 5.1 (p. 266).

$$\text{Premium} = \frac{128,000}{100,000} \times 102.88 = £124.28 \text{ per month}$$

They both feel happy that they have addressed their financial planning in this age successfully.

SUMMARY

In this age we have worked through the following:

1 Beginning to plan how the pension will be taken five years before its maturity in order to maximise it.

2 The different types of annuity, phased retirement and deferring the annuity.

3 A method for helping to decide to defer or not to defer.

4 Inheritance tax (IHT) and what can be done about it.

ANSWERS

■ Exercise 6.1

Total estate	£430,000	
Less nil rate band	£215,000	
Taxable estate	£215,000	
Tax at 40%		£86,000
Estate left to children	£344,000	
They each receive	£114,667	

INHERITANCE TAX PLANNING – VALUE OF ESTATE

Names Hedley and Jessica Wilmot		
	£	
House	250,000	
Contents	20,000	
Jewellery	4000	
Car(s)	5000	
Investments		
Building society	60,000	
Probable inheritances	100,000	
Total	439,000	
Nil rate band	215,000	
Taxable estate	224,000	
Tax at 40%		89,600
Estate available to pass on	349,400	

Set up a will trust of £27,500 each.

we have saved tax on £27,500 at 40% = £11,000.

so now tax is £78,600 and estate passed £360,400.

we need a second death whole of life policy, sum assured £78,600.

the nearest age to Hedley is 55.

$$\text{Cost of premium} = \frac{78,600}{100,000} \times 70.18 = £55.16 \text{ per month}$$

This will cost them £661.92 p.a. which is,

$$\frac{661.92}{78,600} \times 100\% = 0.84 \text{ of } 1\% \text{ of the potential tax bill}$$

They would have to live a further 100/0.84 = 119 years to make this uneconomical.

CHAPTER 7

THE AGE OF
OLD AGE

Birth and education	Work	Marriage	Parenthood	Career development	Retirement	Old age

FINANCIAL PLANNING AT A GLANCE – THE AGE OF OLD AGE

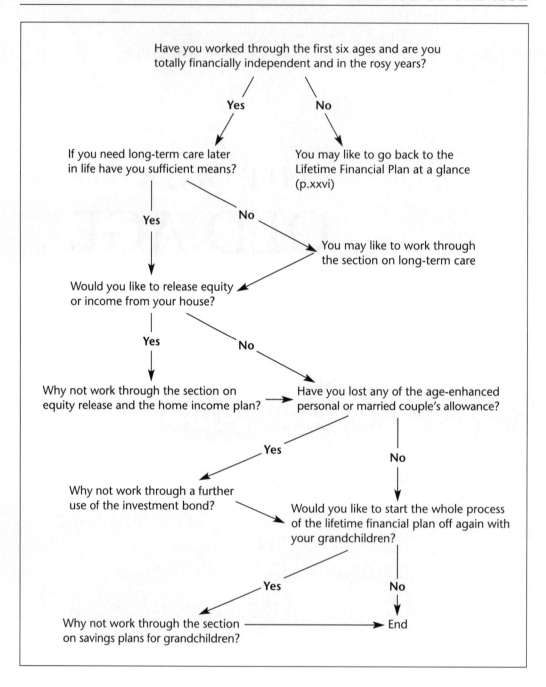

Have you worked through the first six ages and are you totally financially independent and in the rosy years?

Yes → If you need long-term care later in life have you sufficient means?

No → You may like to go back to the Lifetime Financial Plan at a glance (p.xxvi)

If you need long-term care later in life have you sufficient means?

Yes → Would you like to release equity or income from your house?

No → You may like to work through the section on long-term care

Would you like to release equity or income from your house?

Yes → Why not work through the section on equity release and the home income plan?

No → Have you lost any of the age-enhanced personal or married couple's allowance?

Why not work through the section on equity release and the home income plan? → Have you lost any of the age-enhanced personal or married couple's allowance?

Have you lost any of the age-enhanced personal or married couple's allowance?

Yes → Why not work through a further use of the investment bond?

No → Would you like to start the whole process of the lifetime financial plan off again with your grandchildren?

Why not work through a further use of the investment bond? → Would you like to start the whole process of the lifetime financial plan off again with your grandchildren?

Would you like to start the whole process of the lifetime financial plan off again with your grandchildren?

Yes → Why not work through the section on savings plans for grandchildren?

No → End

Why not work through the section on savings plans for grandchildren? → End

CONTENTS

In this age the following is discussed:

INTRODUCTION

In this age, if you have been working through the first six ages of financial health and you have regularly attended to your lifetime financial plan, you and your dependants will be totally financially independent. Now you can do all the things you have dreamed of doing but perhaps not had the time. I well remember the seventy year old happily commencing his mathematics degree.

These are the rosy years.

However, all through the book the theme has been, 'We never know what lies around the corner, what life may throw at us.' And so we have one last question to answer, 'What happens if I need long-term care in later life?'

LONG-TERM CARE

We discussed in the Introduction to this book the problem of what is an ageing population 'which will need long-term care for the duration of a much longer lifetime expectancy'. We saw how the proportion of pensioners to working people in the year 2030 will be three times what it was in the 1940s.[1]

The fact that increasing need for long-term care relates directly to an ageing population is illustrated by the growth in the number of residential care homes which on 1 April 1970 offered a total of 172,500 places, growing to 302,000 on 1 April 1996, an increase of 75.1 per cent in 26 years. The number of places in private nursing homes grew from 20,300 on 1 April 1970 to 217,800 on 1 April 1996, an increase of 1073 per cent in 25 years. Amalgamating figures we get an increase in care home places of 270 per cent in 26 years.[2]

One in four men and one in three women will need such care.[3]

Clearly this is an extremely important question and needs investigation. Further questions need to be asked:

■ What are the costs?
■ What will the state provide?

What are the costs?

There are three distinct types of long-term care.

■ Care in one's own home

This could be simple and straightforward, for example cleaning, shopping, washing etc., but could extend to full-time nursing care. The cost for this could range from £5 to £20 an hour. From two hours a day at £5 an hour, a cost of £3650 per annum, to 22 hours a day at £20 an hour, a cost of £175,200 per annum. Clearly only a millionaire could afford the latter and most of us in these circumstances would opt for a nursing home.

■ Care in a residential home for the elderly

This would apply to someone not needing nursing care but who is frail and can no longer cope in his or her own home. Residential care home costs can vary from an average of £228 per week in the North West to a top cost of £425 per week in Greater London.

■ Care in a nursing home

This would mean that nursing care is available if needed 24 hours of the day. The cost for this, although nowhere near what 24 hour nursing care in the home could be, ranges from an average of £311 per week in the East Midlands to a top cost of £500+ per week. In Greater London 24 per cent of nursing homes have a maximum cost of over £500 per week. For the North the figure is 23 per cent; for the South it is 15 per cent.

Table 7.1 from Laing and Buisson provides some interesting data.[4]

Table 7.1 Regional variations in fees to private homes for the elderly, February 1997

A Nursing homes	£ per week	B Residential homes	£ per week
North	314	North	235
Yorkshire/Humberside	317	Yorkshire/Humberside	230
North West	317	North West	228
West Midlands	329	West Midlands	249
East Midlands	311	East Midlands	234
East Anglia	350	East Anglia	245
Northern Home Counties	412	Northern Home Counties	292
London	423	London	325
Southern Home Counties	373	Southern Home Counties	255
South West	328	South West	240
Wales	314	Wales	229
Scotland	334	Scotland	257
Northern Ireland	314	Northern Ireland	228
[Averages are weighted.]			

Source: Laing and Buisson

What will the state provide?

The Community Care Act became law in April 1993. As a result of this the local authority is responsible for all long-term care in the community. The state, through the National Health Service, is responsible for the provision of,

- district nursing
- chiropody and physiotherapy
- supplies for people who are incontinent.

The local authority is obliged to use private care organisations as much as possible. In the past an increasing proportion of residential care costs were met by government. This expenditure grew from an annual £10 million in December 1979 to £2575 million in February 1993, since when it has been decreasing.[5]

Since the 1993 Act whether or not the local authority will bear part or all of the cost of care in the home is entirely at its own discretion.

In the case of the individual needing long-term residential or nursing home care there is now a means test. Those with more than £16,000 in savings and investments are unlikely to get any help from the local authority.

Certain investments are not usually counted,

- The house if spouse, child under 16, or relative who is either 60 or more, or ill, or disabled, still lives there.
- Neither is the house counted for those living in a rest home temporarily or those selling the house in order to buy more suitable accommodation.
- The cash-in value of any life assurance or annuity policy.
- The value of any personal possessions, unless they were bought in order to reduce savings for the purpose of obtaining benefit.
- If savings and investments are below £16,000 then the local authority may provide all or part of the cost of a care home.

The amount is calculated in two stages.

1 The type of care needed is first decided, e.g. residential home or nursing home. Then reference is made to a table published every April to find the weekly limit guidelines (see Table 7.2).

The figures in Table 7.2 are guidelines meant to set the maximum that local authorities will pay towards care, some authorities exceed these.

The authority then assumes a need for an additional £14.10 weekly to pay for such things as toiletries, trips out and personal shopping.

Table 7.2 Local authority care limits

Residential care home		Nursing home	
London	Rest of UK	London	Rest of UK
£249	£208	£357	£311

[Social security benefit rates from April 1997 published by the Department of Social Security, November 1996.]

2 The next stage is to take into account the income of the individual. For those with investments between £10,000 and £16,000 an additional notional income is added, called 'tariff income'. In other words investments are converted into a notional income which is £1 per week for every £250 or part of £250 above £10,000.

■ Example 7.1

Pauline Drew has a net weekly income of £200 and investments totalling £12,900. The number of £250s above £10,000 is 11.6, so her ' tariff income' will be calculated at £12 per week.

Therefore her total weekly income will be considered to be £200 + £12 = £212.

She is entering a nursing home in London whose weekly fees are £370. The local authority will pay £357 + £14.10 − £212 = £159.10 per week towards this. She will have to find £370 − £159.10 = £210.90 per week.

If Pauline's house were not exempt because her husband is living in it, it too would be taken into account after 26 weeks if not sold and a 'charge' placed upon it. This would mean money that had been paid by the local authority would be reclaimed and as investments would now clearly be greater than £16,000, no help would be received until total investments were below £16,000 again. It can be seen that the fees would soon begin to erode the estate, diminishing what would eventually be passed on.

■ Exercise 7.1

Sara Newstone has a net income of £100 per week and investments of £13,350. She is entering a residential home in Sussex where the weekly fees are £208. Calculate how much she will have to pay towards this.

■ Example 7.2

Kenneth Vince is a 65 year old widower. His annual income consisting of state pensions and a small additional pension is £8000 gross. His house is worth £150,000 and he has £6000 in a building society, his contingency fund. He has to go into a nursing home with weekly fees of £400. Clearly he gets no help from the local authority and has to sell his house. He invests the money and receives an annual income of 5% gross, which is,

$$\frac{5}{100} \times 150,000 = £7500 \text{ p.a.}$$

He is also getting 5% p.a. from his building society investment which is,

$$\frac{5}{100} \times 6000 = £300$$

Hence total gross income is 8000 + 7500 + 300 = £15,800 p.a.

Using Form 7.1 we see that his net annual income is £13,490.

His fees are £20,800 p.a. Hence his shortfall in the first year is £7310. By the end of his first year his capital has reduced to £156,000 − £7310 = £148,690. So his income in year two has reduced by,

$$\frac{5}{100} \times 7310 = £366 \text{ p.a. gross, £281 net}$$

■ Form 7.1 INCOME TAX AND NIC ANALYSIS

INCOME TAX			
Name Kenneth Vince		*Year* 1997	
	£	*Remaining income £*	*Tax £*
Gross income	15,800		
Gross contribution to pension paid personally*			
Personal allowance	5220	10,580	
Income taxed at 20%	4100	6480	820.00
Income taxed at basic rate 23%	6480	Nil	1490.40
Income taxed at higher rate 40%			
Total	15,800		2310.40
Less married couple's allowance			
Total tax payable			

* Some pension contributions paid personally are net of basic rate tax. For the purposes of this form this would need to be grossed up.

NATIONAL INSURANCE CONTRIBUTION (NIC) (Employed)			
	£	*Remaining income £*	*NIC £*
Gross income			
Income up to LEL £3224 p.a. NIC at 2%			
Income up to UEL £24,180 p.a. minus £3224 p.a., the LEL NIC at 10%			
Total			

NATIONAL INSURANCE CONTRIBUTION (NIC) (Self-employed)			
Flat rate paid if income over £3480 p.a. £6.15 p.w.			
On profits between £7010 and £24,180 p.a. 6.0%			
Total			
Income after tax and NIC deductions	15,800 − 2310.40 = 13,490		
Net spendable income	£13,490		

Hence his shortfall in year two is £7310 + £281 = £7591 and his capital reduces by this amount by the end of year two to £148,690 – £7591 = £141,099. We can see that his capital is eroded by an increasing amount each year.

Continuing the same calculations we see that at the end of year five his capital has reduced from £156,000 to £116,529. At the end of year ten his capital would stand at £62,898.

We have assumed for ease of calculation that fees remain constant and yield from investments also. It is likely they will both keep pace with inflation, so cancelling one another out.

The situation will depend on how long Kenneth lives and any changes in the level to which investments have to reduce before aid is given.

Clearly his estate is eroded by an increasing amount each year and he may have wished to pass as much to his children as possible.

C. Hammett estimates that between 32,000 and 40,000 houses are sold each year to pay for care. At the lower figure he estimates that this would represent in cash terms £2.6 billion.[6]

It should not be assumed, of course, that £2.6 billion is lost to inheritance, that the collective beneficiaries have lost £2.6 billion, because, although the houses are sold not all their value will necessarily be used in care house fees before the residual amount is passed on. For example, if Kenneth Vince had lived to 75 he would still have passed £116,529 to his children from an original £156,000.

However, there is clearly a potentially serious problem here for which early planning would be wise.

Another interesting statistic from 1995 is,

■ £1.2 billion was paid in inheritance tax from 23,000 estates.
■ £3.5 billion was paid in long-term care bills by 500,000 people.[7]

This makes the paying for long-term care a bigger problem than that of inheritance tax whether or not it comes from capital or income.

Potential erosion of capital is not the only problem. Reduction in income for a spouse not in care is another. A third is that lack of adequate funds could severely limit the choice of care house, be it residential or nursing and which, like anything else, will vary in quality.

Luckily like all the other potential problems we have encountered there is a solution. This is the long-term care policy. For a single or monthly premium this policy will pay out a monthly benefit to pay for long-term care if the policy holder qualifies. Qualification is usually based on the inability to perform two or more of a list of daily activities or by the onset of mental impairment. Benefit can then be paid, tax free, either to the policy holder or to the carer which will be in the form of residential or nursing house or care in one's own house. There is usually an additional benefit available which is the provision of assistive devices to make possible the performance of some of these daily activities. These policies are described in detail later in the chapter.

THE EQUITY RELEASE PLAN

There will be cases where there is a desire to provide for long-term care by a policy but no liquid assets to pay the premium. The equity release plan could be a possible answer to this dilemma. It literally releases equity from one's house which can be used for any purpose, in this case the long-term care policy.

A certain percentage of the value of the house is sold to an insurance company or bank which does not take up ownership until the owner or owners of the house die. They are allowed to live in the house until then, when the house will be sold and the insurance company or bank will take the share they have paid for some years previously, which may have made a growth in value.

The point to be very clear about is that the house owners will not receive the full value of the percentage they have sold. This will be considerably discounted according to age and therefore life expectancy of the house owners and the nominal interest that might have been paid on an equivalent loan, albeit paid upfront.

Typical figures for a male house owner aged 70 would result in 46 per cent of the equity sold being paid to the house owner.

■ Example 7.3

Howard French, age 70, decides to release equity from his house in order to purchase a long-term care policy. He discovers that if he sells £50,000, representing 50% of the equity of his house, he will actually receive 46% of this,

$$\frac{46}{100} \times 50,000 = £23,900$$

cash in hand and when the house is eventually sold, 50% of its value at that time will go to the insurance company.

A typical figure for a woman age 70 would be 40 per cent, relating to a longer life expectancy and hence longer payment of notional interest.

For a couple both aged 70 a typical figure would be nearer to 38 per cent, representing a combined longer life expectancy.

THE HOME INCOME PLAN

Perhaps a more favoured use for these sorts of schemes where the equity in one's house is used is what is usually called a home income plan. As the name suggests such plans are used to produce an income. This can be done in two ways. The first is simply to purchase an annuity with the equity released from the property. The insurance company will usually arrange the whole thing internally so that the house owner releases equity and receives an income from the insurance company which comes from an annuity produced by it. These are sometimes called reversion schemes.

The alternative is to borrow money from the insurance company against the house. This purchases an annuity which produces an income. These schemes can be very useful in cases where financial independence has not been achieved but a house is owned. Again the insurance company arranges the whole thing internally with the result of additional income for the house owner.

These annuities will be purchased life annuities (PLA) and it will be remembered that part of the payment is deemed to be return of capital and thus untaxed, the rest is taxed at whatever rate the recipient will be paying. There are two pieces of good news with this method. One is that there will be MIRAS on up to £30,000 of the loan and the other that most providers offer a fixed rate of interest.

A typical example for a woman age 70 would be,

Advance	£30,000	
Gross annuity	£2960	per annum
Interest at 8.25% net of MIRAS	£2103.75	per annum
Annuity paid net of interest	£856.25	per annum
Taxable amount of annuity	£1168.40	
Tax at 20%		£253.68
Net annuity	£622.57	
Tax at 23%		£268.73
Net annuity	£587.52	
Tax at 40%		£467.36
Net annuity	£380.89	

Two further points need to be considered here:

1 Any amount borrowed over £30,000 will not attract MIRAS.
2 Referring to Table 7.3 in we see that the personal allowance increases with age.

Table 7.3 Tax rates and allowances (fiscal year 1997/98)

Income tax rates

£0 – £4100	20%	
£4101 – £26,100	23%	
Over £26,100	40%	

Personal allowance (basic)	£4045
Personal allowance (age 65–74)	£5220
Personal allowance (age 75 and over)	£5400

Allowances restricted to 15%

Married couple's allowance (basic)	£1830
Married couple's allowance (age 65–74) (only has to apply to one spouse)	£3185
Married couple's allowance (age 75 and over) (only has to apply to one spouse)	£3225

Table 7.3 (continued)

Notes

1 The higher personal allowance for those over 65 is only applicable, in total, to incomes of £15,600 a year or below. Any income over this reduces the 'age allowance' by an amount equal to 50% of the excess. Thus someone in receipt of income, for example, of £16,100 is £500 over and hence the allowance of, say, £5220 would be reduced by $^1/_2 \times 500 = £250$ to £4970.

2 A husband whose legally married wife is living with him can claim the married couple's allowance. A wife can claim 50% of it. Husband and wife together can elect for the whole allowance to apply to wife's income. If neither has income to use his or her share of it the unused part can be transferred to the other.

3 Only husband's income affects the age-related married couple's allowance and once he has lost the additional age-related personal allowance with an income of £17,950 p.a. any income above this affects the married couple's allowance in the same way.

Thus for our 70 year old the personal allowance, in the tax year 1997/98, was £5220.

This means her annual income will have to be 5220 + 4100 = £9320 before she moves into basic rate tax at 23 per cent.

Another difference to note between the reversion scheme and the mortgage method is that if the annuitant has to move into a care home and sell the house, in the case of the mortgage scheme the interest payment stops which increases the income. In our example the gross income would immediately jump to £2960 per annum. In the case of the reversion scheme the interest has already been paid upfront based on life expectancy.

These schemes do, of course, carry additional charges, among which can be an arrangement fee of something like 1 per cent plus VAT of the property value, survey fee and a notional rental of £12 per annum.

SAVINGS PLANS FOR GRANDCHILDREN

Now you have planned for all normal financial contingencies. There is nothing more to do but enjoy the rosy years. Part of that enjoyment might be starting the grandchildren off with their lifetime financial plan, putting in a savings plan for them.

The policy will be owned by the donor and written under a life of another arrangement. The insurable interest will be that the policy is being taken out with the current intention of benefiting the life assured. The policy itself will be completed with the child's details and signed by the parent or guardian if the child is under a certain age, usually 18, and otherwise by the child himself or herself.

Finally the policy is put in trust for the child, preferably using a flexible trust just in case new grandchildren arrive and they need to be added as beneficiaries.

Having completed the whole process of financial planning you now see it starting once again with the first age of financial health.

A FURTHER USE OF THE INVESTMENT BOND

We saw in Chapter 2 how the enhanced age allowance can be lost if income is over a certain limit and that this income would be taxed at a marginal rate of 34.5 per cent.

The investment bond, in some cases, could help this situation.

■ Example 7.4

Rosalind Melwood is 67. She has a pension producing a gross annual income of £15,000 and £50,000 in a building society producing a gross equivalent income of £3000 p.a. She therefore has an annual income £2400 in excess of £15,600 and has lost £1200 of her age allowance. This excess £2400 is therefore being taxed at a rate of 34.5%.

By switching £40,000 of her deposit to an investment bond she reduces her gross income by £2400 getting back her full personal allowance of £5220. Thus she has saved tax of 34.5% on £2400. She can now draw 5% p.a., i.e, £2000, from her bond free of tax.

DETAILED INFORMATION AND ANALYSIS

THE LONG-TERM CARE POLICY

A monthly or single premium will obtain a monthly benefit for long-term care on qualification to receive it. The policy will usually also provide up to three times the monthly benefit for assistive devices to assist in performing certain daily tasks.

The usual daily tasks which determine the payment are,

- **Mobility** – The ability to move from room to room in the normal place of residence.
- **Washing** – The ability to wash by any means resulting in a reasonable level of personal cleanliness.
- **Dressing** – The ability to put on, remove, fasten and unfasten all necessary clothing and, if necessary, any surgical appliances or artificial limbs.
- **Feeding** – The ability to feed oneself with food made available.
- **Toiletry** – The ability to get on and off the toilet or commode.
- **Continence** – The ability to manage bladder or bowel function, using protective undergarments or surgical appliances if necessary, resulting in a reasonable level of personal hygiene.

The test of qualification for benefit is the failure to perform these activities without the help of special equipment, devices or modified clothing and as a result the help of another person is needed every time.

There are usually various levels of policy offered, the more expensive paying out when there is failure to perform two of these activities and the cheaper based on the inability to perform three. An intermediate type policy would pay out half benefit when two cannot be performed and full benefit for three.

When the policy holder qualifies assistive devices will be provided to make possible the performing of the failed activities. These will range from simple levers to help with the turning of taps to wheelchairs and stairlifts.

The next stage comes when the policy holder cannot perform two or more of these activities even with the assistive devices. It is then that the long-term care benefit latches in.

The other qualifying condition is mental impairment. This usually means organic brain disease which results in progressive deterioration of mental faculties affecting memory, intellect, judgement, personality and emotional control and is irreversible.

There is usually a deferment period after qualification for benefit until payment commences, the most usual time being three months. Long-term care will either be supplied in the home, including daily domestic tasks such as cooking, household cleaning, ironing, washing clothes, shopping and nursing, enabling the performance of the activities of daily living. They can, of course, also be supplied in a residential or nursing home.

The benefit is paid tax free either directly to the policy holder or the carer and will continue as long as the policy holder qualifies. The benefits do not prejudice other benefits such as attendance allowance or disability living allowance. They would, however, affect any payment towards fees the local authority might make since they would be considered to be income.

Most policies include automatic indexing in line with the increase in the Retail Prices Index (RPI), others will make this dependent on an extra payment. Some will allow an increase every three years with no further medical evidence being required. They can, of course, be increased whenever wished, but in this case medical evidence will be required. Costs of increases will be those relevant to age and medical condition at the time.

A medical examination of non-rigorous level is usually required. This can be carried out in the policy holder's home and will include such things as height, weight, pulse rate and blood pressure measurements, medical history and simple cognitive tests. Policies are usually available to ages between 20 and 85 and premiums are set at a level that the insurance company confidently expects will enable it to provide the benefits specified.

However, there could be significant changes in risk so reviews are usually written in at, for example, ten years and every five years, thereafter. If experience is positive, cover could automatically increase and in the reverse situation the policy holder could be asked for an additional premium or to accept a lower level of benefit. Once benefits are being paid there are not usually any further reviews.

Often insurance companies give discounts for couples, living together, who take out policies at the same time.

Should the cost of the care be less than the specified benefit the balance would usually be paid to the policy holder. There is normally no cash benefit with these policies on death or if cashed in.

Most insurance companies will supply additional support facilities which will be accessible by telephone. These will give guidance on such things as how to make a claim, clarification of a policy condition, changes in state provisions, counselling, confidential advice, form filling, dealing with social services, help in choosing a care supplier, residential or nursing home and arranging regular reviews of the care being provided. Typical premiums are shown in Table 7.4.

Table 7.4 Typical single premiums for long-term care benefit policies

	One off lump sum premiums for a benefit of £1200 monthly					
	1st level		2nd level		3rd level	
	Man	Woman	Man	Woman	Man	Woman
Age	£	£	£	£	£	£
50	17,244	28,170	14,138	23,234	10,875	18,064
55	17,172	28,447	14,182	23,685	11,014	18,784
60	17,018	28,748	14,109	24,038	11,055	19,389
65	16,776	29,022	13,956	24,359	11,082	19,747
70	16,448	29,261	13,807	24,802	11,104	20,051
75	16,078	29,481	13,737	25,400	11,131	20,514
80	15,702	29,693	13,718	26,197	11,172	21,209

[There is often a discount of approximately 5% if both members of a couple take out plans at the same time.]

■ Example 7.5

Mark Beemish is 68, his net annual income is £10,000. His house is worth £140,000. He wants to make sure he will be able to pay for long-term care if he needs it. He knows the weekly fees of his local nursing home are £380 (£1647 per month). He calculates his shortfall to be 1647 − 833 = £814 per month. Using Table 7.4 the nearest age to him is 70. Hence his approximate cost is,

$$\text{1st level} \quad \frac{814}{1200} \times 16{,}448 = £11{,}157$$

$$\text{2nd level} \quad \frac{814}{1200} \times 13{,}807 = £9366$$

$$\text{3rd level} \quad \frac{814}{1200} \times 11{,}104 = £7532$$

These costs would be recouped in about 14 months at £814 per month of benefit at the 1st level, in about 12 months at the 2nd level, and in just over 9 months at the 3rd level.

He hopes the indexation on his policy will take care of increases in fees and that he will be able to leave his house, unencumbered, to his children and be able to live in the house of his choice.

■ Exercise 7.2

Rex and Veronica Chalmers decide they will plan for the possible need for long-term care. They want to make sure they have choice and that their estate is not unduly eroded.

They have a house worth £300,000, investments of £100,000 and net income of £20,000 p.a.

They have done their inheritance tax planning and feel it would be a dreadful shame if long-term care fees eroded the inheritance they wish to pass to their children, or indeed if one were left running the house with a reduced income because of care home fees. They would both probably choose the top nursing home in their area with fees currently at £329 per week. Rex is 79 and Veronica 67.

They decide to each cover all the fees with a long-term care policy. Calculate the three levels of premiums for each of them. Assume a 5% discount as they will both be buying at the same time.

■ Exercise 7.3

Why not calculate your own situation using whatever forms we have already encountered that you feel might help?

So now you have worked through the seven ages of financial health. I sincerely hope you have enjoyed creating your lifetime financial plan.

Jack Oliver

SUMMARY

In this age we have worked through the following:

1 Long term care.

2 The equity release plan.

3 The home income plan.

4 Savings plans for grandchildren.

References

1 Peter Lilley, Department of Social Security, 5 March 1997.

2 Market Survey 1997, Laing and Buisson.

3 Swiss Reinsurance Company Ltd, September 1997.

4 Market Survey 1997, Laing and Buisson.

5 Department of Social Security, in later years from Quarterly Enquiries: Residential Care and Nursing Home Reports.

6 Inheritance in Britain, an independent survey commissioned by PPP Lifetime Plc 1992, updated 1996 by C. Hammett.

7 1995 Estimates, Inland Revenue 1996.

ANSWERS

■ Exercise 7.1

The number of £250s above £10000 is 13.4, so her tariff income will be calculated at £14 per week. Hence total income is £114 per week. Maximum the local authority would pay is £208 + £14.10 = £222.10 per week. Actual amount the local authority will pay is £222.10 – 114 = £108.10 per week. She will have to find £114 per week.

■ Exercise 7.2

Fees needed for each of them would be £1426.

The nearest age for Rex is 80. Hence the cost is,

$$\text{1st level} \quad \frac{1426}{1200} \times 15{,}702 = £18{,}659$$

$$\text{2nd level} \quad \frac{1426}{1200} \times 13{,}718 = £16{,}302$$

$$\text{3rd level} \quad \frac{1426}{1200} \times 11{,}172 = £13{,}276$$

The nearest age for Veronica is 65. Hence the cost is:

$$\text{1st level} \quad \frac{1426}{1200} \times 29{,}022 = £34{,}488$$

$$\text{2nd level} \quad \frac{1426}{1200} \times 24{,}359 = £28{,}947$$

$$\text{3rd level} \quad \frac{1426}{1200} \times 19{,}747 = £23{,}466$$

CHAPTER 8

SOME LIFETIME FINANCIAL PLANS IN ACTION

Birth and education	Work	Marriage	Parenthood	Career development	Retirement	Old age

■ The age of birth and education

At almost the same time, on the same day, Peter Thorpe and Sally Brown were born.

A few days later Sally's happy grandparents set up a savings scheme for her. They did this carefully, writing it in trust to make sure there were no adverse tax implications. They had in their minds that the money could serve to pay for a wedding, a special 21st birthday gift, school fees or perhaps a special holiday for Sally at some point in the future. They were able to do this because they had carried out careful financial planning throughout their lives and could therefore afford to give this money for the benefit of Sally, their first grandchild. They knew all about it because earlier in their lives they had used such a scheme to save for a cruise around the world they had dreamed of.

Peter's grandparents could not follow this example as they had attempted very little financial planning, were retired and living on their old age pension and a very small amount from the state earnings-related pension scheme (SERPS).

Peter and Sally, living in the same locality, went to the same school. Sally later paid her way through university with a grant, a student loan, holiday work, very careful planning and, of course, the very welcome sum of money that came to her because of the forethought of her grandparents.

■ The age of work

Peter could not afford to go to university so left school at 16 and entered the local estate agents.

On graduation Sally joined one of the big multinational companies. She was somewhat surprised to find that her contract included a good pension scheme and protection in the event of her becoming medically unable to work. In other words she was safeguarded to the age of 60 and an adequate indexed income was guaranteed to her. She was told that her pension was a defined benefit scheme and therefore if she was with her company for 40 years she would retire on a pension equal to two-thirds of her salary. No-one had talked to Sally before about financial planning, all of this was brand new to her and she was very excited about it. The very next time she met Peter she described it all to him in great detail.

Peter had been busily and successfully selling houses and had given no thought to the future apart from climbing the ladder of success in the estate agency business and, maybe, at some point, starting on his own. Nobody at work had mentioned financial planning to him and the company had made no such provision for him.

As he walked home that evening he felt a certain degree of shock and later found that it was difficult to sleep. His mind continually ran on the disaster it would be if he were medically unable to work and had no income. He knew his parents were too poor to support him. He realised that he could only afford to eat, drink, run his car, have holidays and pay for his accommodation with his parents if he were earning. The picture before his eyes left him sweating.

In the morning he remembered reading articles in the newspaper which suggested that the welfare state could no longer be afforded and such things as state pensions were being cut. He wondered what state provision might be available in the event of his becoming medically unable to work. That morning in a spare moment, he rang the Department of Social Security and was shocked to discover how little provision there was. He knew then he must protect his income in the event of his becoming medically unable to work.

Six months earlier one of Peter's colleagues had been made redundant and had been unable to find new work. It was clear that this colleague was already in an extremely difficult financial situation. Suddenly Peter thought, 'What if this happened to me?' Once again he began to break out in a cold sweat and decided to pop out for a cup of coffee.

Sitting in the sunlit cafe he remembered one of his school friends, Bill Thompson, who had joined a big insurance company, and decided to give him a ring immediately. He hurried back to his office and picked up the telephone. Bill was friendly, telling Peter he should look at a number of things such as permanent health insurance, critical illness, redundancy cover and building a contingency fund. All of this sounded double Dutch to Peter but he arranged to meet Bill that evening to discuss this in detail.

Bill was a very competent and imaginative financial planning consultant and Peter had soon set up the protection that he and Bill decided he needed, namely permanent health insurance and redundancy cover.

However, he was not feeling entirely secure as Bill had put another little seed of thought into his mind which over the next month or two worried away at him. Bill had asked Peter when he felt he wanted to be financially independent, whether Peter was working or not. 'When do you want the time to come, Peter', he had said, 'when you wake up in the morning and you can decide to go to work or not? You don't need the money produced by work any longer. You are totally financially independent, you can work or not, it's your choice.' Peter had now decided he would talk to Bill again about this particular worry.

They had another very productive meeting. This time Peter came away feeling totally secure as they had worked out together exactly the pension that Peter needed to make him financially independent at the age that he had decided. The figures that Bill had produced had also convinced him to contract out of the state earnings-related pension scheme.

Peter and Sally met occasionally at the parties and weddings of mutual friends and Peter always expressed his thanks to Sally for making him aware of financial planning. They both become aware that many of their friends had made no provision whatsoever.

■ The age of marriage

A few years later when they were both 25 Peter received an invitation to Sally's wedding and telephoning to congratulate her found she was marrying Edward Townsend, a young man two years her senior, who was working in the same company. Edward had a similar package to Sally and so they thought there were no changes to be made in their financial planning as they were not financially dependent on each other. However, they decided to start their married life in their own home and started thinking about buying a house.

At this stage Peter was able to repay his debt to Sally as the happy couple approached him for his advice. Clearly they did not have enough money to purchase the house outright and Peter spoke to them of the need for a mortgage. They had both been saving in a contingency fund and found they had an adequate deposit to put down.

Peter told them how the mortgage would be related to their incomes and they could choose from a number of products currently on the market, such as fixed interest, discounts etc. With Peter's help they soon found a lovely house which they could afford. A fixed rate mortgage was negotiated. As it was not demanded by the lender they took no life assurance or critical illness cover with it to protect each other and soon their friends were enjoying the house warming party of the year.

Almost immediately Sally and Edward started to save in their contingency funds once again, something Sally had learnt from careful budgeting while at university.

Two years went by and Peter had made very good progress in his job and had received several promotions. He was now head hunted by another firm of estate agents and discovered that this time there was a company pension scheme.

Peter had built up a great trust in Bill, his financial planning adviser and, on hearing that he now had a company pension scheme, immediately turned to Bill for advice. He was told that the company scheme and his own personal scheme came under different legislation and he could not run both of them at the same time. Although he was obliged to make a contribution to his company scheme the major part of the funding was from the company. Bill told him the scheme was unit-linked money purchase and explained this. He was absolutely adamant that Peter must not refuse this offer of a company pension and told him that if he wished he could run his personal pension now on top of his company scheme in the form of a free-standing additional voluntary contribution scheme.

Bill then went on to point out that the excellent guarantee in the event of medical inability Peter had enjoyed with his personal pension scheme, in the form of waiver of contribution, must drop away as this was not available with either his company pension or his free-standing additional voluntary contribution scheme. This worried Peter as he had remained very conscious of the effects of being medically unable to work. He was relieved that he could retain his permanent health insurance which would support him adequately till age 60 but asked Bill, 'What happens then?'

'You are absolutely right,' answered Bill, 'these are early days and you have very little, so far, in your fund. The answer is a "pension guarantee policy"!' He explained that this was a critical illness policy which would pay Peter a lump sum of money, tax free, should he suffer one of a long list of serious illnesses. This money could be invested and one would expect an income of 4 to 5 per cent a year rising at least in line with inflation if it were invested on the stock market by way of a pooled investment. If this policy were indexed, so that whenever a critical illness might occur, it remained in line with inflation, it would solve the problem of an inadequate pension at age 60. Once again Peter felt secure and bought Bill his favourite malt on the strength of it.

■ The age of parenthood

At Peter's 27th birthday party he was told the good news that Sally and Edward were expecting their first baby. At this point they did not confide in Peter that they had had long, difficult and detailed discussions on how their life would change when the baby arrived.

Sally was in the better job. She was earning more than Edward. Her career potential was greater. They therefore came to the decision that Edward would become a househusband. He would give up his position with the company and stay at home to look after the house and baby. He would do the cooking, the washing and all the other jobs needed to provide a happy home for the family.

They knew they would lose one of their incomes. They knew they would lose the protection Edward had in the event of his becoming medically unable to work. They knew his company pension would be suspended. Knowing how Peter trusted Bill they turned to him for financial advice.

After a thorough analysis of their current and potential financial situation Bill began to ask questions. 'What would happen if Sally were to die?' he asked.

'Well,' Sally replied, 'Edward would receive the death benefit from my pension of four times salary, also a widower's pension.' This they quickly calculated.

'How much would you need to live on, Edward, and bring up the child?' asked Bill.

They calculated that and found that there was a discrepancy between what was needed and what would be available.

'What would you do about this?' continued Bill.

'Well, I could take up my job again,' Edward replied.

'Your child would have lost its mother,' said Bill, 'would you want it to almost completely lose its father also, and see very little of him?'

They decided they would not like this and gradually came to the conclusion that Sally would need more life assurance.

Bill then asked, 'What would happen if Sally became medically unable to work?'

Once again they did the calculations to see if Sally's income from the company permanent health insurance would be sufficient. Finding that it would not they decided they needed to take out critical illness insurance on Sally.

Breathing a sigh of relief they thought they had solved all their potential problems.

However, Bill continued, 'What happens if Edward dies? What happens if Edward becomes medically unable to function?' This time they saw very quickly they would need life assurance on Edward's life, and also critical illness cover. This would enable Sally to continue earning the income she and the child, or the three of them, would need and make it possible for them to employ a nanny or possibly a nurse/nanny.

But Bill had not finished. 'Would you like still having to pay for the mortgage if any of these situations arose?' he continued. They turned to the mortgage again and discussed it fully, deciding to switch it into interest-only linked to PEPs, since with only one pension they did not want to decrease this by using the tax-free cash to pay off the loan. They saw before Bill could mention it that additional life and critical illness cover would be desirable to remove what would be a millstone around the neck if something happened to either of them.

Edward started for the drinks cupboard but Bill chuckled quietly, 'There's more to come. Let's do a proper job while we're at it.'

He then pointed out that in the event that Sally became medically unable to work, the company permanent health policy would pay her an income but would make no contributions to her pension and she would hardly be able to make them herself although her cover was a 'net pay' scheme. Clearly a pension guarantee policy was needed.

Bill finished by discussing private education and school fees schemes but when Sally and Edward saw the cost of a private education this confirmed them in their decision to go for state education.

At last Edward got the drinks, and both he and Sally expressed their heartfelt gratitude to Bill, because, although they had only just that evening become aware of all these potential problems they knew they were now solved and the family was secure.

As Bill got up to leave he mentioned the fact that it would be wise for them to make a will. 'I know your estate is not large at the moment but we must at least appoint guardians for the child in the event of you both dying. And, of course, if one of you were to die the house would then become unencumbered and therefore of some considerable value. Without a will the intestacy rules would apply and this could be a severe problem. When the child comes we must write the life assurance policies in trust just in case it so happened you were both killed in a car accident, meaning that the life assurance would funnel into the estate with a potential inheritance tax liability for the child, and at least a delay while probate is granted.'

■ The age of career development

Sally and Edward had a fine boy whom they called Michael. They bought a dog and after quite a few minor mishaps in the kitchen and the nursery Edward settled very happily into his new occupation. Sally got another promotion. Her parents took out a savings plan for Michael which they put in trust for him and life seemed good.

At Michael's third birthday party Peter quietly told them he had decided to start his own estate agency business. He had been doing extremely well at the new company, had increased his contingency fund considerably and felt he was ready and could now afford to be his own boss operating as a sole trader.

'I expect this will be another long session with Bill in addition to your annual review,' said Edward, and he was right.

'Well,' said Bill, 'now you are entirely and solely responsible for your own financial well being. You have your income protection, which you've kept going through the years; we must keep a careful eye on your profit over the next few months as you will probably take a drop in income and we must make sure that you are not over insured and adjust the level of your income protection to coincide with your income. As that income will probably drop for a while you might want to supplement your income protection with some critical illness cover.

'Clearly your company pension scheme will become suspended; we might look at transferring that at some point into your own personal scheme, but a careful analysis of the advantages and disadvantages will have to be done. We will need to switch your free-standing additional voluntary contribution scheme back into a personal pension and adjust that to coincide with the level of your profit. As your outlay on starting the new business has been considerable you clearly need to start growing your contingency fund once again. Once you have been going a couple of years you would become liable for redundancy payments if the business failed because of your death or medical inability to work, so we should look at that when the time comes.

'And you may wish to put in some financial planning for your two new employees. You could have a very tough moral dilemma in the future if one or both became medically unable to work. You probably couldn't afford to continue paying them after a few months, but how very difficult it would be for you to know they had very little money once their salary stopped.

'I suggest you put in income protection for both of them, paid for by the company with the company owning the policies. You might also like to consider running a small pension for them both.' Bill then showed Peter the advantages to his staff if they decided to invest in this pension by way of salary sacrifice and suggested that, anyway, the pension should be dependent on the staff making a contribution.

Sally and Edward decided to have a garden party to celebrate their tenth wedding anniversary. Sally had had another promotion and they now had two more children, Anne and Lynne. Edward had started painting with oils in the few moments he could snatch from the demands of the children and his domestic responsibilities. Peter was now living in his own house, still working hard, very successful, but at the age of 35 feeling a little lonely. At the party Sally introduced him to Penelope, a friend of hers, three years her junior and a high-powered personal secretary. Their mutual attraction was immediate and within the year Anne and Lynne were bridesmaids and Michael was pageboy at their wedding.

Shortly afterwards Peter, Penelope and Bill got together to discuss the new situation in the light of financial planning. Peter and Penelope were both financially independent in their own right as long as they continued to work. They told Bill they had decided to sell their individual houses and buy a much bigger property for both of them as they planned to have children. Peter would arrange this and also negotiate the mortgage. As previously single people their existing mortgages were unprotected by life assurance. They decided the new mortgage would be pension linked and this time, because they were both involved, that it would be covered by life assurance written on both their lives so that if one of them died the mortgage would immediately be paid off.

Bill suggested they cover the mortgage with a critical illness policy as well. Apart from this change Peter's existing arrangements were all still totally valid.

They discovered that Penelope had started a personal pension some time ago but rather haphazardly without doing the careful calculations needed to achieve the degree of financial independence she would want. Also she had no cover in the event that she became medically unable to work. They decided that she would rectify these omissions straight away.

However, Penelope also had her own medical insurance and was very keen on private medicine. They decided they would turn this into a family policy that included Peter. They also decided a will was now necessary.

A year later Peter and Penelope had their first baby, a lovely girl whom they decided to call Margaret. Penelope decided to leave her job but to help Peter part time working from home, spending a few hours each day, as looking after their house and baby would not be enough for her.

Peter had by now firmly established the habit of consulting Bill whenever a change in his life occurred. Once again they sat down together and Peter described his new situation. He had now become almost a financial planner himself and started the conversation by saying, 'If I were to die Penelope would go back to work, she misses it badly anyway. She is very marketable and can earn a very good salary.'

'Do you mean full-time work?' asked Bill.

'Oh yes,' came the answer, 'why?'

'Well,' continued Bill, 'Margaret would have lost you. Are you happy with her also seeing very little of her mother?'

'No. I hadn't thought of that.' Peter answered strongly, and continued, 'so we ought to calculate Penelope's financial position in this event. Well, she would have the house and it would be unencumbered because we made sure the mortgage was covered by life assurance. She might sell that and move to something smaller, investing for income the capital which would be released. She would have the business but without me there it would sell for only a small amount. And that would be that. How short sighted of me. Of course I badly need life assurance.

'I suspect,' continued Peter, 'that I also need to review my level of critical illness cover, since if I am unable to work and Penelope is not working, although the mortgage would be paid off and I would have my permanent health insurance, my cover would have to look after three people!'

'What about if Penelope dies or becomes medically unable to function?' asked Bill.

'I know,' answered Peter, 'I couldn't look after everything at home and also run my business.'

The clear conclusion from this discussion was to put in place life assurance on both Peter's and Penelope's lives and also to make sure their level of critical illness cover was adequate for all eventualities. Bill pointed out that reducing term cover would be adequate for Penelope since once Margaret was 16 or so a nanny would not be necessary.

'Well,' said Bill, 'do you really need to talk to me any longer? You seem to be able to do this yourself.'

'I'm sure,' said Peter, 'you will suggest something that I hadn't thought of.'

'Well,' said Bill, 'Penelope's going to spend a few hours every day helping you in the business; you should obviously pay her a salary. I suggest this is below the level at which she would pay tax and below the level at which she and you would pay national insurance contributions. At the moment this would be about £3000 per annum.'

'Too small, I suppose, for her to do any sort of pension or to be on the company group personal pension plan,' asked Peter.

'You can,' answered Bill, 'put in an occupational pension scheme for her which, using the de minimus rules, could be as much as 100 per cent of the salary you are paying her as this is below £6000 a year. This would be in addition to her salary, in other words it would not come out of her salary. This way you are making use of her tax-free personal allowance and building up a pension for her so that in retirement she will have an income at least at the level of her tax-free personal allowance at that time, assuming the sort of indexations which have been taking place over the past years.'

'That sounds marvellous,' said Peter, 'but I thought we could only put in 17.5 per cent of her income.'

'Ah,' said Bill, 'you're thinking of the personal pension levels. The occupational pension levels are calculated in a totally different way and are different from those of the personal pension.'

'Excellent!' said Peter, 'I told you I would always need you as my financial planning consultant.'

A few months later the Thorpes and the Townsends were having dinner together and the conversation turned to Sally's parents. Mr and Mrs Brown had recently been discussing with Sally their will and the steps they had taken to avoid inheritance tax.

'Well,' said Peter, 'I remember when you were a little girl of six, Sally, telling me of the savings plan your grandparents had taken out for you and giving me a garbled account of the way they had put it into trust, so I know very well your parents have always considered financial planning important and I am sure they will have everything in apple pie order.'

'Yes,' answered Sally, with a small element of doubt in her voice. 'They've always had excellent advice. I wonder, however, at this stage whether they should take a second opinion, just for an overview of the situation. Would it be alright with you, Peter, if I suggested they talk to Bill?'

'Of course,' said Peter. 'I'm sure Bill would be delighted.'

A week later an appointment was made and Bill did his usual careful, detailed financial analysis with the Browns. They were indeed excellently financially planned and had set up a joint life, second death life assurance policy in their mid-fifties to deal with inheritance tax. This was indexed and had kept up with the growth in their estate to a certain extent.

However, they had not made use of the will trust and as they had liquid assets this was eminently suitable for them. They were very excited about this and saw that by using it their potential inheritance tax problem would be totally solved. Bill also suggested that since Sally and Edward were reasonably affluent the Browns might want to consider skipping a generation and leaving part of their estate to the three grandchildren, but obviously they would want to discuss this aspect of their planning with Sally and Edward.

Bill Thompson had now reached a high position in his company and dealt mostly with corporate financial planning. So Sally was grateful that he had taken the time to help her parents and once again felt her financial affairs were in good order.

After the party that Peter and Penelope gave for their third wedding anniversary the Townsends stayed on after everyone had gone for a last drink and a more intimate talk. Sally had now reached a very responsible position in her company, was working longer and longer hours and depended very much on Edward and the warm, comfortable surroundings he had created in their home. He was spending a little more time on his painting, as the children were older, and had begun to sell a few here and there and to earn a small income. He had, of course, consulted Bill about this and Bill had given him his usual advice for a sole trader starting up, i.e. consider income protection and personal pension. They had also looked at the pension which Edward had had in his former employment and done careful calculations to see whether this should be transferred or not.

Peter had been extremely successful and now had three branches in three different towns in their locality.

Penelope had found she was very frustrated as a housewife and wanted very much to get back to work so she and Peter had decided she would now work full time in one of the branches and they would employ a nanny/housekeeper. Some of her married friends were very happy looking after their children and the home but she felt she had discovered this was just not for her and she thought she would therefore go back to work.

Peter now began to tell them of his imminent plans to go into partnership. He was ambitious, good at his business and very energetic. He loved what he was doing but wanted to expand much faster than was happening at the moment. He had been having long talks with an estate agent in the adjoining area who also ran a property management business and was very good at the lower end of the market whereas Peter had become expert in more expensive properties. They felt very much that they would complement each other, that the synergy they would create by working together would expand the business rapidly. Peter's next sentence was of course anticipated by all of them.

'I've made an appointment for a discussion with Bill and shall ask him to recommend a good solicitor and to review the financial planning details.'

After a detailed analysis of the financial affairs of Peter's prospective partner Bill turned to them both and said, 'Well, of course, you know you will now be jointly and severally responsible for the business. Both partners are responsible for any expenditure either partner makes on behalf of the business. They are both also responsible for any debt either partner incurs.

'We need to answer the question, "What happens if one of you dies?" We need to answer the question, "What happens if one of you becomes medically unable to work?" We need to look at partnership agreements and a partnership protection plan.

'It might also be a good idea to examine the provisions you have for staff in the way of income protection and pension, and you might also consider medical insurance for them.'

When the business discussion was finished Bill turned to Peter. 'I just wanted to mention that with Penelope back at work you might consider lifting her company pension and putting some permanent health insurance in for her. I think you should retain the reducing term protection you already have as if anything happened to her this would pay for a nanny.'

The next few years were particularly busy for everyone. Peter and Penelope decided on private education and started funding PEPs to the maximum. At 13, and with Edward giving him special coaching at home, Michael won a scholarship to one of the famous public schools.

The four of them next met properly four years later at the christening of Peter and Penelope's new daughter, Ruth. They all regretted the passing of time without proper contact and that evening sat down together at dinner looking forward to a long discussion.

First Peter and Penelope told the Townsends that Penelope had really missed not being with Margaret, after all, and was shocked to realise she was already five. She had decided to leave work for good. This did not really seem to surprise anyone.

A little while later Sally astounded the Thorpes by giving them her news. The international company where she was so successful had decided to hive off the section in which she worked. 'This would probably have meant the loss of my job,' she said, 'so two of the other executives and myself have approached a venture capitalist and we are going to buy the company. Edward and I have agreed to use our contingency fund and we have remortgaged the house for as much as we could get. The venture capitalist will have 51 per cent, I shall have 20 per cent and the other two directors 29 per cent between them.'

'Funny that Bill said nothing to me,' replied Peter, 'because I'm sure you've consulted him.'

It turned out Bill had advised a share protection plan to make sure that none of the 49 per cent of shares would go out of the hands of the three shareholding directors. He had also advised a full funding programme for their pensions as they were all members of the previous company's pension scheme before 17 March 1987 and could claim continuity of service and continuation of benefits which meant they would all be able to achieve a pension of a full two-thirds of final salary, whatever that might be at retirement, with no capping on it whatsoever.

The venture capitalist would be taking income by way of dividends and would want to move gently to a full flotation on the stock market in 10 years. Bill had done an analysis for the Townsends and felt that it was a very desirable programme.

Peter and Penelope's only financial planning changes would be, of course, the suspension of Penelope's pension and the dropping of her permanent health policy.

Three years later Peter's partnership had the chance to buy a small chain of estate agents in the next county which they jumped at. This chain owned all the office property, but Peter's partner was against buying this. They decided that Peter would buy it and allow the partnership to use it. He considered switching his personal pension scheme to a self-invested personal pension and arranging for the pension to buy the property but decided he wanted to keep it separate because with two daughters one might come into the business and one not, so he would need some assets outside to make estate planning more flexible.

He, of course, consulted Bill who agreed with his reasoning. Bill also apologised for not discussing inheritance tax with Peter before, but he had been extremely busy. He soon repaired the damage and before long the Thorpes had put in place a whole of life, second death life assurance to cover what they calculated their tax liability would be. They were surprised to learn they could leave the business out of the calculation because of business property relief. 'But surely if both Penelope and I were killed in a car accident,' said Peter, 'the children would receive cash from the partnership protection plan which would then be liable for inheritance tax.'

'No,' smiled Bill, 'they would be left the business free of inheritance tax and capital gains would be wiped out. They would then sell it to your partner in return for cash. No tax implications whatsoever.'

'My goodness,' said Peter, 'that's really magic, Bill.'

Bill immediately contacted the Townsends and suggested they deal with the problem of inheritance tax, which they decided to do.

Things went on smoothly for some years, Edward had a successful exhibition of his paintings and commissions began to come in.

At Michael's graduation party Sally told the Thorpes she had just been successful in head hunting a real high flyer who was going to help her company enormously and enable them to reach the requirements for flotation in four years' time. She told them it almost had not come off because he was very loath to leave the pension scheme he had with his previous company. This was because it was not capped and if he moved it could become retained benefits and mean that a pension scheme with the new company could provide only very inadequate benefits. 'However,' laughed Sally, 'you know who solved it for us I'm sure.

He suggested what he calls a straight sixtieths scheme plus a funded unapproved retirement benefit scheme and that seems to have made our high flyer perfectly happy.'

Just before flotation Bill was called in. They valued the company using expert professional advice and Bill went through the capital gains tax implications on sale of shares any time after the flotation. It was clear there was going to be a massive capital gain and thus a potential massive capital gains tax. Sally would not, of course, be eligible for business retirement relief, because the company would be quoted by the time shares were sold. However, that done, the company was floated and on her fifty-second birthday Sally and Edward held a big celebration party.

Bill was guest of honour and clearly got very embarrassed when he was mentioned in every speech.

Two years later Lynne Townsend's marriage was announced. Sally and Edward wanted to give the young couple something towards a house but wondered if there were any tax implications. Bill explained to them about potentially exempt transfers but told them there were exemptions from inheritance tax for wedding presents and they could give the couple up to £20,000 with no tax implications whatsoever. They decided on £10,000. Peter found them a lovely little house and negotiated a suitable mortgage for them. Their first baby arrived a year later and the Townsends started on the savings plans in trust for grandchildren route.

■ The age of retirement

Bill announced that both Sally and Peter were five years out from pension maturity and it would be wise to look at this in detail each year from now on. There was nothing for Peter to do at this point since his was a personal pension scheme. However, Bill discussed the small self-administered scheme with Sally in case she wanted to make use of the deferred annuity because, if she did she would need to switch into the small self-administered scheme now. Sally felt that she did not want to make this decision five years out, that she would probably go for a straight annuity because both Edward and she were in extremely good health. 'Anyway,' she said, 'now you have also explained the income withdrawal facility, I could always fall back on that.' However, she did want to discuss inheritance tax again and with the increased value of the Townsends' company shares saw that inheritance tax planning was now sadly out of step and something had to be done.

They discussed a will trust but had very small liquid assets and selling their company shares to produce liquidity would involve a large capital gain. All they could do here would be to sell a few every year to take up their personal allowances. They decided to increase their second death inheritance tax policy very considerably.

Bill thought he ought to check on Peter's inheritance tax situation as well. He and Penelope had ploughed almost all the profit back into the business and thus had no liquid assets. They decided on Bill's advice to use their house for the will trust. Currently their ownership was joint so they first had to change this into tenants in common. Bill suggested a good solicitor and this was soon done with all the necessary precautions written in.

One year later Bill talked to them again about their pension funds and raised the question of whether they wanted to switch into the deposit fund. None of them went for that idea, saying there was always the income withdrawal facility to fall back on if the market suddenly dropped. They felt this would give them the chance to wait for it to come back up again.

Margaret Thorpe, after finishing school, announced her wish to join Peter's business. He felt very pleased he had kept the company property separate from the business because it now looked as if he would leave his share of the partnership to Margaret while Ruth, who seemed unlikely to join the business, wanting to go on the stage, could be left the property.

Three years out from pension maturity Sally and Bill had another detailed discussion resulting in adjustments to remuneration and pension contributions in order to maximise the final pay out.

Michael, who was now a successful lawyer, benefiting from Bill's financial planning advice, announced his marriage and Lynne produced another baby. Penelope was now very involved in a local charity and was about to become chair of the county section. Edward spent most of his time painting, which he thoroughly enjoyed.

The two families met in their entirety to celebrate the sixtieth birthdays of Sally and Peter. Neither had retired nor looked like doing so yet. They all told and listened to all the news. Anne's news was outstanding. At 31 she had just been made the youngest registrar ever in the local hospital. Michael and his wife had produced a son and Ruth Thorpe had a place at the Royal Academy of Dramatic Art.

However, there was a small shadow. Sally, at 60, had looked extremely tired and older than her years. Her older daughter had continually glanced at her with a worried frown and at last asked if she had remembered to have her annual check up. On being told no she pressed her mother to do it soon. 'It's just that you look very tired Mum and probably need a holiday,' smiled Anne.

A month later Peter received a telephone call from Edward to say Sally was not at all well and had been advised to take it very easy. 'You know Sally though, Peter,' he said, 'she wouldn't rest till she had asked Bill over for a long discussion. However, she now feels all her affairs are in order and can rest with an easy mind.'

It had, in fact, been a difficult meeting as Sally had been very shocked to find she was not 100 per cent fit as she had always been. The doctors had said there was no reason why, if she took things easily, she could not look forward to many years yet.

She raised the question of her pension and now had doubts about an annuity, although the investment climate pointed to that. She and Edward were in the very lucky financial position of not needing the pension and she wondered if there were some way of passing the fund to the children. After long discussion with Bill she decided to move the fund to a personal pension scheme with an income withdrawal facility but just leave it there to grow, for the moment.

The next step was to put it into trust actually for the grandchildren, thus skipping a generation. That way, she felt, if she did die the whole fund would pass to them and if she lived for seven years it would pass tax free. Bill thought there would be no problem with the Inland Revenue as it was not as if she had been told she was going to die in the next two years. Sally retired from the business and she and Edward went on a round the world cruise.

Margaret married and produced a daughter. She and her husband decided they would both work and employ a nanny. Lynne now had three children who kept her very busy.

At 62, Peter decided to retire and consulted Bill about his pension. They consulted the various graphs produced by Bill's company which gave an indication of whether to take an annuity or go for income withdrawal. These all suggested the time was right for the annuity. However, Bill, always cautious and thorough, took Peter to a firm of specialist actuaries who confirmed that the annuity was currently the answer. Peter passed his share of the partnership to Margaret and the business property to Ruth. The first was exempt from inheritance tax under the rules of business property relief and the second 50 per cent exempt under the same rules. However, as it was a potentially exempt transfer, if Peter lived seven years it would become actually exempt.

■ The age of old age

Three years later Sally had to go into a nursing home for long-term care.

Apart from their concern Peter and Penelope were aghast at the cost and asked Bill if there was anything they could do to protect against these fees. They were shown the details of long-term care policies and both decided to invest in these as their estate bore no comparison to the Townsends' and such fees would make a nasty dent in it.

Edward's children gave a dinner for his seventieth birthday and although they were all very sad that Sally had died two years before, it was a warm occasion for people who had known each other so long. Bill, of course, was there and was asked to say briefly whether Sally's pension fund got to the grandchildren untaxed. Apparently it was six years after putting it into trust when Sally died. This meant that only 20 per cent of the full inheritance tax liability had to be paid. The money was still in the flexible trust in case other grandchildren arrived and also Edward felt the present grandchildren should not receive the money until they were considerably older. He gave a little speech in which he talked a lot about Sally, but was very comforted by their children, grandchildren and his dog. He talked of the seven ages of financial health starting all over again with his grandchildren and how life goes on. He hoped they would find someone like Bill who was now, of course, retired, and said how grateful he was for the long friendship of the Thorpes. As they all left the party in the twilight they felt life had been good and would continue to be. They were thankful they had had excellent lifetime financial plans to sustain them.

APPENDIX

The environment in which financial planning takes place is always changing and often very quickly. This appendix covers those changes which have occurred since the writing of *The Lifetime Financial Plan* began.

■ **Gilt Edged Securities**

From 6 April 1998 interest from gilts can be received gross if so wished.

■ **The Individual Savings Account (ISA)**

The ISA will start on 6 April 1999 and be guaranteed to run for at least 10 years with a review after seven years to decide on any changes after this 10 year period.

The ISA will be free of all UK taxes. In the case of dividends from UK equities this will be achieved by the payment of a 10 per cent tax credit for the first five years.

Withdrawals will be allowed at any time without loss of tax benefits.

The ISA will be able to include all bank, building society and supermarket accounts; stocks and shares currently qualifying for PEPs; taxable National Savings products; and life assurance.

The annual subscription per person will be £5000, of which up to £1000 can be in cash and £1000 in life assurance. In the first year the subscription can be £7000 of which up to £3000 can be in cash and £1000 in life assurance.

The rules will be more relaxed and simplified than those currently governing investment in PEPs.

Those eligible to invest in the ISA will be over 18 years old and resident and ordinarily resident in the UK for tax purposes.

■ **Personal Equity Plans**

Contributions to PEPs can be made until 5 April 1999.

All PEPs held at 5 April 1999 can continue to be so held with tax advantages exactly the same as the ISA.

The value of any PEP holdings will not affect eligibility to invest in ISAs.

■ **TESSAs**

TESSAs can be opened until 5 April 1999. Payments can continue under existing rules for the full five year lifetime.

The capital from maturing TESSAs can be transferred into the cash component of the ISA.

Neither annual subscriptions to TESSAs nor the investment of maturing capital in an ISA will limit subscriptions to that ISA.

■ Enterprise Investment Schemes (EIS)

From 6 April 1998 the amount an individual can invest increased from £100,000 to £150,000 and the maximum amount of investment which can be carried back to a previous tax year increased from £15,000 to £25,000.

■ Venture Capital Trusts (VCT)

At least 10 per cent of the total investment in any company must be held in ordinary non-preferential shares.

■ Friendly Societies

The payment of a 10 per cent tax credit described under ISA to be extended to the policies of Friendly Societies.

■ Pensions

The payment of tax credits to pension funds was abolished from 2 July 1997.

It will be remembered that pension funds are free of all UK taxes. In the case of dividends from UK shares this was achieved by the fund reclaiming the tax which had already been paid. In other words they were paid the tax credit.

This means that pension funds are still free of UK capital gains tax but pay 20 per cent tax on income from UK shares.

It is important to note that those funds containing no UK equities whatsoever are totally unaffected. Thus the tax treatment of a fund invested 25 per cent Europe, 25 per cent North America, 25 per cent Far East, 25 per cent Gilt Edged Securities, is totally unchanged.

Any fund with UK equities will be affected. Most investors will be in either a with-profits fund or a unit-linked mixed fund. These will contain 50 to 60 per cent and at most 70 per cent UK equities. The average income from a spread of UK equities will be four per cent per annum.

Let us examine, then, a fund of which 55 per cent is invested in UK equities. Let us say the total fund is £1000 and its overall growth is 12 per cent per annum, which is the top figure assumed in illustrations. Then the growth in one year is £120. Of the total growth we are getting four per cent on £550 in the form of UK dividends = 4/100 x 550 = £22.

Now if this is taxed at 20 per cent it pays 20/100 x 22 = £4.40 tax, which means the growth net of tax is now £115.60.

Hence, instead of making a growth of 12 per cent per annum on the fund, a growth of 11.56 per cent per annum is made due to taxation on the income from UK shares.

At the end of one year, had there been no tax, a fund of £1000 would have become 1000 + 12/100 x 1000 = £1120. With tax it becomes 1000 + 11.56/100 x 1000 = £1115.60.

Continuing this exercise, if we assume an investment of £1000 per annum for 30 years, we get,

Fund with no tax =   £241,332
Fund with UK dividends taxed at 20% =   £221,651

This is a difference of £19,681, which represents a reduction of,

$$\frac{19,681}{241,332} \times 100\% = 8.5\% \text{ in the final fund.}$$

To simplify the calculation, charges have been ignored. In any case these will vary from company to company.

Hence to make this up we need to invest another

$$\frac{8.2}{100} \times 1000 = £82 \text{ per annum.}$$

Over 20 years the reduction is five per cent. In order to make this up we need to invest £50 per annum more, and over a 10 year period the reduction is 2.1 per cent, so an additional £21 per annum is needed. This sort of information should make possible good financial planning in spite of a small reduction in the benefits of the pension scheme.

It is important to note that from 6 April 1999 the tax credits reduce to 10 per cent so that it will then be only 10 per cent tax on UK dividends that pension funds will be unable to claim. Using exactly the same earlier arguments, but with this lesser level of tax, we see that the effect over 30 years will be to reduce the final fund by 4.2 per cent, over 20 years by 2.5 per cent, and over 10 years by 1.1 per cent.

The earnings cap on pensions for the tax year 1998/99 is £87,600.

■ de Minimus

With effect from the 31 March 1998 the benefits of the de Minimus pension funding have been withdrawn.

■ National Insurance Contributions (NIC)

From 6 April 1999 National Insurance is to be paid only on earnings above the starting point. This is to be aligned with the personal allowance for income tax.

The employer's NIC is to be replaced with a single rate of 12.2 per cent.

■ Private medical insurance

Tax relief on premiums for private medical insurance has been abolished.

Contracts negotiated and premiums commenced before 1 August 1997 will continue to receive tax relief. However, since these contracts are for one year only, tax relief finally comes to an end for all policies on 31 July 1998.

■ Stamp duty

The half per cent duty on transfers of shares is unaffected. However, on transfers of property the duty has increasesd to two per cent for properties of value over

£250,000, and three per cent for those over £500,000. These changes do not affect transfers made pursuant to contracts established on or before 17 March 1998.

■ The offshore portfolio bond

In the case of those bonds holding 'personalised investments', such as quoted stocks and shares or shares in one's own private limited company, an annual tax on gains deemed to be 15 per cent of the investment will be paid.

This tax will be at the marginal rate of the investor, i.e. the rate of tax he is paying at the time. The deemed capital gain will be cumulative.

■ Example A1

James McPherson invests £10,000 in one of these bonds. He is a 40% tax payer.

At the end of year one he will pay 40% of £1500,

$$\frac{40}{100} \times 1500 = £600$$

At the end of year two the policy will be taxed on 15% of £11,500,

$$\frac{15}{100} \times 11,500 = £1725$$

As James is now a basic rate taxpayer the tax will be 23% of £1725,

$$\frac{23}{100} \times 1725 = £258.75$$

Where a chargeable event occurs the deemed capital gain will be subtracted from the actual capital gain before taxation.

This commences for policy years ending on or after April 1999.

This is not the case for those bonds holding only pooled investments such as unit trusts.

■ Corporation tax

For the tax year 1999/2000 the main rate reduces to 30 per cent, with a small companies rate of 20 per cent and a marginal rate of 32.5 per cent.

■ Tax on dividends

Tax credits continue to be set off against tax liability.

It will be remembered that dividends are currently received having already been taxed at 20 per cent. Thus a gross dividend of £100 would be paid to the investor, less 20 per cent tax, and he or she would receive £80. If the investor were a higher rate tax payer he or she would pay a further 20 per cent tax on the £100, i.e. £20, and so the total tax on the dividend would amount to 40 per cent. A concession at the moment is that a lower- to basic-rate taxpayer has no further tax to pay and has, in the case of the basic rate taxpayer, paid 20 per cent tax rather than 23 per cent. A non-taxpayer has been able to reclaim the tax.

From 6 April 1999 the tax-credit rate falls to 10 per cent and the non-taxpayer is no longer able to reclaim the tax.

Lower or basic rate taxpayers will have no further tax to pay.

A higher rate taxpayer will pay an additional 22.5 per cent on the grossed up dividend. Thus on £100 of gross dividend it will be paid net of a tax of 10 per cent, the investor receiving £90. He or she will pay an additional 22.5 per cent on the grossed up amount, i.e. £22.50. Hence tax will be paid on dividends at a rate of 32.5 per cent.

■ Advanced corporation tax

This is abolished from 6 April 1999.

■ Capital Gains Tax (CGT)

For the tax year 1998/99 the annual exemption is increased to £6,800.

From 17 March 1998 any gain or loss made on shares sold and repurchased within 30 days is deemed not to have been made. This now prevents the practice of bed and breakfasting used for the amelioration of capital gains tax.

For periods after 6 April 1998 indexation allowance is removed. It is replaced by a tapering reduction in tax liability. Thus for any gain made after 6 April 1998 tax liability will reduce over a ten year period, from 100 per cent to 60 per cent, and, in the case of business assets, from 100 per cent to 25 per cent.

■ Example A2

Pauline Thompson starts a business on 6 April 1998 and sells it eight years later. Her gain is £100,000. Her gain for tax purposes is reduced by,

$$\frac{8}{10} \times 75\% = 60\%$$

Hence she pays tax on 40% of £100,000,

$$\frac{40}{100} \times 100,000 = £40,000$$

Assets which were acquired before 17 March 1998 qualify for an addition of one year of taper relief to the period for which they are treated as held after 5 April 1998.

■ Example A3

Basil Price bought £10,000 of shares on 3 March 1998. He sold on 8 April 1999. He can claim indexation relief till 5 April 1998 and two years taper relief, one full year after 5 April 1998, plus the additional year.

■ Business retirement relief

This is to be phased out from 6 April 1999 by a gradual reduction in relief thresholds. The relief will cease to be available from 6 April 2003. Hence the £250,000 untaxed will reduce by £50,000 each year till it disappears, and the £750,000 taxed at 20% will reduce by £150,000 each year until it disappears.

■ Non-residence in the United Kingdom

New rules prevent avoidance of CGT by selling assets while temporarily non-resident.

■ Inheritance Tax (IHT)

From 6 April 1998 each person is allowed to pass £223,000 free of IHT.

■ The Dead Settlor Rule

This tax advantage changed from 6 April 1998. Before this date a beneficiary receiving the proceeds from a cashed-in investment bond in trust, in a tax year after that in which the settlor died, would pay no tax. This is not now the case. After 6 April 1998 in such an event tax applies with an overall rate of 34 per cent regardless of the tax rate of the beneficiary. Thus in the case of an offshore investment bond the beneficiary pays the full 34 per cent and in the case of an onshore investment bond a tax of the marginal rate is paid, i.e. 34 per cent, minus basic rate tax. Hence in the tax year 1998/99 this would be 34 per cent – 23 per cent = 11 per cent.

■ Income tax rates 1998/99

Bands of taxable income £	Rate %	Tax on band £
0–4,300	20	860
4,300–27,100	23	5,244
Over 27,100	40	–

■ Personal allowances

Personal and married couple's allowances

The allowances which apply for 1998/99 (figures for 1997/98 in italics) are:

Age	Personal Allowance £		Married Couple's Allowance £	
Under 65	4,195	*4,045*	1,900	*1,830*
65 to 74	5,410	*5,220*	3,305	*3,185*
75 and over	5,600	*5,400*	3,345	*3,225*

Note: Married Couple's allowances – relief is restricted to 15% in 1998/99 (restricted to 10% in 1999/00).
The income limit for persons aged 65 and over is £16,200 (*£15,600*).
Where the taxpayer's total income exceeds this limit, the age related allowances are reduced by £1 for every £2 of income over the limit. The allowances are not reduced below the level of the basic personal or married couple's allowances.

■ Company cars

Fuel benefit

The amounts which apply for 1998/99 are:

Cars with a recognised cylinder capacity	Cash equivalent £
Petrol cars	
1400cc or less	1,010
1401cc–2000cc	1,280
More than 2000cc	1,890
Diesel cars	
2000cc or less	1,280
More than 2000cc	1,890

Note: There are no special rules linking taxation of fuel benefit to the amount of business mileage.
The cash equivalent is based on engine size only; no account is taken of the car's age and cost.

■ National Insurance Contributions 1998/99

Contracted-in

Employer contributions		Employee contributions		
Earnings £pw	% on remainder	Earnings £pw	% on first £64	% on remainder
0–63.99	0	0–63.99	0	0
64–109.99	3	64–485	2	10
110–154.99	5	Over 485	2	10% up to £485
155–209.99	7			
210–4385	10			
Over 485	10			

Contracted-out

	Employer contributions				Employee contributions		
Earnings £pw	% on first £64	(a)% on remainder	(b)% on remainder		Earnings £pw	% on first £64	% on remainder
0–63.99	0	0	0		0–63.99	0	0
64–109.99	3	0	1.5		64–485	2	8.4
110–154.99	5	2	3.5		Over 485	2	8.4% up to £485
155–209.99	7	4	5.5				
210–4385	10	7	8.5				
Over 485	10	7/10*	8.5/10				

*7% of earnings between £64 per week and £485 per week 10% on excess.
(a) Contracted-out Salary Related
(b) Contracted-out Money Purchase

Self-employed contributions

Class 2 Contributions: where earnings are over £3,590. Flat weekly rate increased from £6.15 per week to £6.35 per week.

Class 4 Contributions: 6% on earnings between £7,310 and £25,220 per annum.

■ State benefits 1998/99

Statutory sick pay	
For those earning £3328 p.a. or more	£3000.40 p.a.
Incapacity benefit	
Short term lower rate	£2537.60 p.a.
Short term higher rate	£3000.40 p.a.
Long term	£3364.40 p.a.
Additional payments	
Adult dependant allowance (first 52 weeks)	£1570.40 p.a.
53rd week on	£2012.40 p.a.
Child dependant allowance	
First child	£514.80 p.a.
Each subsequent child	£587.60 p.a.
Age allowance	
Under 35	£707.20 p.a.
35 to 44	£353.60 p.a.
Over 44	Nil

Note: Those changes above which were announced in the budget of 17 March 1998 are still to be ratified in the relevant finance act.

INDEX